THE GREEK
HISTORIANS

The Viking Portable Library

Each Portable Library volume is made up of
representative works of a favorite modern or
classic author, or is a comprehensive anthology
on a special subject. The format is designed
for compactness and for pleasurable reading.
The books average about 700 pages in length.
Each is intended to fill a need not hitherto
met by any single book. Each is edited by
an authority distinguished in his field, who
adds a thoroughgoing introductory essay and
other helpful material. Most "Portables" are
available both in durable cloth and
in stiff paper covers.

THE VIKING PORTABLE LIBRARY

THE GREEK HISTORIANS

The Essence of

HERODOTUS
THUCYDIDES
XENOPHON
POLYBIUS

Selected and Edited by

M. I. FINLEY

Fellow of Jesus College, Cambridge

THE VIKING PRESS · NEW YORK

Copyright © 1959 by The Viking Press, Inc.

First published in 1959 by The Viking Press, Inc.
Fourteenth printing December 1972

VIKING PORTABLE LIBRARY EDITION
Issued in 1960 by The Viking Press, Inc.
625 Madison Avenue, New York 22, N. Y.

Distributed in Canada by
The Macmillan Company of Canada Limited

SBN 670-35244-6 (hardbound)
SBN 670-01065-0 (paperbound)
Library of Congress catalog card number: 59-8353
Printed in the U.S.A. by The Murray Printing Company

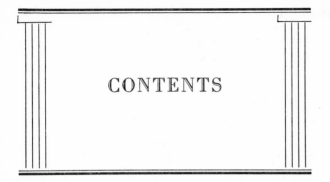

CONTENTS

INTRODUCTION	1
A BRIEF READING LIST	22
MAP	24-25

HERODOTUS — 27

From BOOK I
Lydia — 29

From BOOK II
The Antiquity of Egypt — 63
The Nile Flood — 65
Manners and Customs — 68
Origins of the Greek Gods — 71
The Truth about the Trojan War — 74
The Building of the Pyramids — 79

From BOOK VII
The Persian War after Marathon — 81

From BOOK VIII
The Persian War after Marathon (*Continued*) — 157

THUCYDIDES — 217

From BOOK I
The Beginnings — 218

From BOOK II
The Funeral Oration of Pericles — 265
The Plague in Athens — 273

From BOOK III
  The Mitylenian Debate 278
  Sedition in Corcyra 290
From BOOK VI
  The War in Sicily 298
From BOOK VII
  The Sicilian Disaster 347

XENOPHON: *The Anabasis* 381

From BOOK I 383
From BOOK II 390
From BOOK III 417
From BOOK IV 424

POLYBIUS 441

From BOOK I
  Introduction 442
From BOOK II
  Aratus of Sicyon and the Achaean League 447
From BOOK VI
  The Roman Constitution 473

THE GREEK
HISTORIANS

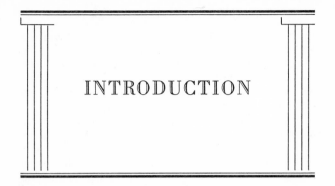

INTRODUCTION

History in its root sense means *inquiry*. For a considerable time before it took on the specific, narrower meaning the word now has, and even long thereafter—we still say "natural history"—the stress was on the inquiry as such, regardless of subject matter, on the search for explanation and understanding. Man is a rational being: if he asks rational questions, he can, by the unaided efforts of his intellect, discover rational answers. But first he must discover that about himself. The Greeks did, in the seventh century B.C. (insofar as so abstract a notion can be dated at all), and thereby they established the greatest of their claims to immortality. Significantly, the inquiry was first directed to the most universal matters, the nature of being and the cosmos. Only later was if extended to man himself, his social relations and his past.

It was no accident that this profound intellectual revolution took place in the region the Greeks called Ionia (the west coast of Turkey). There they were in closest touch with the older cultures of the ancient Near East. Greek-speaking peoples first migrated into the lower Balkans by 2000 or 1900 B.C. and eventually spread eastward across the Aegean Sea (and later west to Sicily and southern Italy). Like all invaders, they adopted and adapted a variety of ideas and institutions from their new neighbours. How much they borrowed we are only beginning to appreciate, as one after another the lost languages of the area are recovered, most recently Mycenaean Greek itself. In the course of centuries religious ideas, gods, myths and rituals, scientific and technological information found their way from Babylonians, Hittites, Hurrites, and other peoples of the Near East and were embodied in Greek ways of life and thought on a scale undreamed of by historians fifty or a hundred years ago.

Paradoxically, the more we learn about this process of diffusion and adaptation, the more astonishing is the originality of the Greeks. One need only read their earliest poetry or look at their archaic statues and vases to catch some of the genius. Then one turns to the Ionian intellectual revolution for another side of it, the spirit of rational inquiry. Without Babylonian mathematics and astronomy and metallurgy there could have been no Thales or Anaximander. But it was the Ionian Greeks, not their Babylonian forerunners, who first asked the *critical* questions about the earth and the stars and metals and matter. And so, too, with man himself and his past. The older civilizations had their records and their chronicles, but the essential element of inquiry, of history, was lacking. The writers of these accounts, the late R. G. Collingwood pointed out, were "not writing history," they were "writing religion"; they were not inquiring, they were recording "known facts for the information of persons to whom they are not known, but who, as worshippers of the god in question, ought to know the deeds whereby he has made himself manifest." [1] It was the Ionians, again, who first thought to ask questions in a systematic way about the supposedly known facts, in particular about their meaning in rational, human terms.

The magnitude and boldness of this innovation must not be underestimated. Today we too easily assume, without giving it much thought, that a concern with history is a natural human activity. All men have memories and "live in the past" to a greater or less extent. Is it not natural that they should be interested in their ancestors and the past of their community, people, nation? Yes, but such an interest is not necessarily the same thing as history. It can be satisfied

[1] *The Idea of History* (Oxford: Clarendon Press, 1946), pp. 12-15.

entirely by myth, and, in fact, that is how most of mankind has customarily dealt with the past (and, in a very real sense, still does). Myth serves admirably to provide the necessary continuity of life, not only with the past but with nature and the gods as well. It is rich and vivid, it is concrete and yet full of symbolic meanings and associations, it explains institutions and rites and feelings, it is instructive—above all, it is real and true and immediately comprehensible. It served the early Greeks perfectly.

When myth was finally challenged, by the Ionian enlightenment, the attack was directed not to the events and the stories, such as the details of the Trojan War, but to the mythic view of life and the cosmos, to its theogony and divine interventions. "Homer and Hesiod have attributed to the gods everything that is disgraceful and blameworthy among men: theft, adultery, and deceit." So runs the famous protest by Xenophanes of Colophon, who was born about 570 B.C. Such criticism helped bring about a new cosmology and a new ethics; it did not, of itself, lead to the study of history. The skeptics stripped the traditional accounts of irrational elements and contradictions, but they neither doubted the remaining hard core nor tried to extend it by research of their own. They historicized myth, they did not write history. A remarkable example will be found in the first fifteen chapters of Thucydides. Here is a rapid review of the evolution of Greek society in which not a single trace of the mythic conception survives: the gods have disappeared completely, and with them fate and fortune and every other extra-human agency. In their place Thucydides put common-sense human causes and impulses, and the result looks so much like history that many people today, even historians who should know better, praise it as a great piece of historical writing. In fact what Thucydides did was to take the common Greek traditions, divest them of what he considered to be their false trappings, and reformulate them in a brilliantly coherent picture by thinking hard about them, using as his sole tools what he knew about the world of his own day, its institutions and its psychology.

It takes more than skepticism about old traditions to produce historical investigation. A positive stimulus is needed, and again Ionia provided the starting point. That part of the Greek world was not only in closest contact with other peoples, eventually it was also subjected to them, first to the Lydians and then to the Persians. The Greeks thought it was important to know something about their overlords, and so they investigated the subject and wrote books putting together the geography, antiquities, customs, and bits of history of the nations with whom they were concerned. Significantly, this had never been done before: the prevailing view, as any reader of the Old Testament must realize, was totally ethnocentric. Nations other than one's own had no intrinsic interest. Significantly, too, the Greek innovation was for a long time a restricted one: they were not attracted to ethnography as such, or history as such, but to the manners and institutions of the two nations with whom their lives were now closely bound. The Greeks had no myths to account for the past of the Lydians and Persians. That is why their first steps toward historical writing—for these works were not histories in any proper sense—were about foreign nations, not about themselves.

None of this writing survives apart from scattered quotations. Its general character, however, is clear enough from the first half of Herodotus' book. Herodotus, born early in the fifth century B.C. in the city of Halicarnassus in Asia Minor, planned a *periodos* on an unprecedented scale. Stimulated no doubt by the Persian Wars, which demonstrated that thinking Greeks must widen their horizons, Herodotus decided to extend the inquiry to more peoples and places. He proposed to investigate as much as he could personally, to confront and cross-question a variety of expert witnesses, and to report faithfully and accurately what he learned, distinguishing for his audience between first- and second-hand information, between probable and improbable (or impossible) accounts, between what he believed to be true and what he disbelieved but repeated because it had significance nonetheless. Every reader can judge for himself how successfully Herodotus carried out his program. But, had he done no more, it is unlikely that we should now have this opportunity: in the end, his writings would have disappeared like those of Hecataeus and the others, and Herodotus would be just another name today, the author of a few surviving fragments of books called *Lydiaca, Aegyptiaca, Scythica,* and so on.

We know virtually nothing about the life of Herodotus, and therefore we can only infer when and why he made a radical shift in his program. It seems most likely that this happened in Athens, toward the middle of the century. There Herodotus began a new inquiry, one utterly unlike any which had been attempted before. He determined to reconstruct, by personal investigation, the generation of the Persian Wars. In the process, he assembled much material about still earlier generations of Greek history, and he tied his account to the mythical tradition, which he rationalized and historicized as well as he could. The final product is an amalgam, for Herodotus did not abandon his earlier work. The *Aegyptiaca* and *Scythica* appear as long digressions; the Lydians and Persians have their story woven in with Greek affairs, but they are also given space for customs and manners; and the Greeks themselves appear in semi-mythical form at times (with unmistakable influences from epic and tragedy). Yet the work as a whole is surely a history.

No twentieth-century reader can really visualize Herodotus at work, under conditions which make both his effort and the final result a miracle of human enterprise. Written records did not exist, for all practical purposes, and few men who had any direct knowledge of the Persian Wars (let alone the still earlier years) could have been alive when he began this part of his study. Everything—the politics and the battles and the ravaging of cities and the intrigues—had to be rescued from oral tradition, as it was preserved and transmitted among the great families of Athens or the priests of Delphi or the kings of Sparta. These traditions were fragmentary, unreliable, self-serving, and often contradictory. That he nevertheless undertook so difficult and unprecedented a task implies some overpowering impulse, and I have little doubt that it was a political one, in the broadest sense of that term. Democratic Athens, under Pericles, was asserting itself with more and more pressure in the Greek world, offering leadership and military security, but at the same time demanding, and if necessary compelling, tribute and a measure of dependence. Difficult problems were raised— political problems which were, as always, at heart moral questions. Discussion was lively and often heated; out of it the sophists, and later Socrates, created the new discipline of ethics and, as a subdivision, political theory. Herodotus was no philosopher, he was not even a systematic thinker; but he was no less sensitive than the sophists and the tragedians to the great moral issues, and he made a unique contribution to the discussion. He found a moral justification for Athenian dominance in the role she had played in the Persian Wars, and he sought to capture that story and fix it before its memory was lost.

Herodotus had a most subtle mind, and the story he told was complex, full of shadings and paradoxes and qualifications. In traditional religion, for example, he stood somewhere between outright skepticism and the murky piety of Aeschylus. His political vision was Athenian and democratic, but it lacked any trace of chauvinism. He was committed, but not for one moment did that release him from the high obligation of understanding. His great discovery was that one could uncover moral problems and moral truths in history, in the concrete data of experience, in a discourse which was neither freely imaginative like that of the poets nor abstract like that of the philosophers. That is what history meant to Herodotus; nothing could be more wrongheaded than the persistent and seemingly indestructible legend of Herodotus the charmingly naïve storyteller.

It did not follow as a self-evident and automatic consequence that the new discovery was at once welcomed or that histories and historians arose on all sides to advance the new discipline. The Athenians appreciated Herodotus, obviously, and yet a full generation was to elapse before anyone thought it a good idea to write a complete history of Athens, and even then the step was taken by a foreigner, Hellanicus of Lesbos, and he was an annalist, a chronicler, not a historian, and he continued to repeat the traditional myths alongside more recent, verifiable history. Other Greeks naturally resented the phil-Athenianism of Herodotus and his version of their role in the Persian Wars, but they did not rush to reply by writing their own histories. They objected and they challenged a detail here and there, and they eventually pinned the label "Father of Lies" to him, a late echo of which can still be read in Plutarch's essay *On the Malice of Herodotus*. The new discipline, in short, remained highly problematic. In all honesty men could doubt whether it was possible to know the past, and whether the effort to find out was worth the trouble.

One man who read Herodotus carefully and fully appreciated his achievement (and the inherent difficulties) was Thucydides. He was probably in his late twenties when the second decisive struggle in Greek history broke out in 431 B.C., the war between Athens and Sparta, and he decided immediately that he would be its historian. Apart from the acute prognostic sense which Thucydides revealed thereby, his decision was a critical one for the future of Greek historical writing in general. There could be no more complete turning of one's back on the past than this, the idea of writing a history of an event which lay in the future. The war lasted twenty-seven years and Thucydides survived it, possibly by five years. All through it he worked away at his book with a remarkable singleness of purpose, collecting evidence, sifting, checking and double-checking, writing and revising, and all the time thinking hard about the problems: about the war itself, its causes and issues, about Pericles, about the Athenian Empire, about politics and man's behaviour as a political animal.

The book was not finished: that is obvious at a glance, and the way it breaks off more than six years before the end of the war leaves us with something of a puzzle. Possibly Thucydides found himself in a bitter impasse, unable to resolve to his own satisfaction either the general problems of politics, which concerned him more and more as the war continued, or the more technical questions of how to present to the public what he thought and what he had learned. The book is filled with tension, not merely the external tensions inevitable in so long and difficult a war, but also the inner conflicts of the author, as he tried to fight through the mass of facts and the complex moral issues which became obsessive with him, to a basic understanding of politics and ethics. He certainly did not abandon his life work in the year in which the manuscript suddenly stops. There are things in the earliest portions which could not have been said until after the end of the war in 404 B.C. There are unmistakable evidences of rethinking and rewriting. Very probably the Funeral Oration and Pericles' last speech were among the latest sections Thucydides wrote, and they (together with the so-called Melian Dialogue at the end of the fifth book) sum up the whole generation as Thucydides saw it at the end of his life.

From the standpoint of the history of historical writing, Thucydides' political ideas are perhaps not so interesting as his technique. To begin with, he set out consciously to overcome certain weaknesses in Herodotus: hence the insistence on careful checking of eyewitness testimony, on precise chronology, on the total elimination of "romance" from his work, on a rational analysis which has no patience with oracles and supernatural interventions and divine punishments. His account of the great plague in Athens, for example, is a model of reporting; Thucydides even equipped himself with the most advanced medical knowledge, and his technical language and accuracy on this subject are unparalleled among lay writers in the whole of antiquity. All this is so impressive and has such an aura of earnestness and sincerity that, even though we have no independent evidence for virtually anything Thucydides tells us, we believe him without hesitation. The same cannot be said of any other historian in the ancient world.

It is no underestimation of these remarkable qualities in Thucydides to say that none of this—whatever its worth *sub specie aeternitatis*—locates him in the development of Greek historiography. Our admiration, however warranted, tends to divert attention from the crucial fact that his subject was contemporary, that he was writing about things which were happening under his eyes, or in sight of others whom he could cross-examine, not about events of the literally dead past. Therefore in his very explicit statement of his working methods and principles there is not one word about research into documents or traditions; there are only the rules to be followed in eliciting accurate information from eyewitnesses. When Thucydides did make a brief excursion into earlier times, as in the first fifteen chapters or in the sketch of developments from the point at which Herodotus' history breaks off to the beginning of the account of the Peloponnesian War, his motives were either to justify his own work or to provide certain necessary background materials, nothing more. They were not history, either in Thucydides' sense or in ours; they were introductory to his proper subject. Only contemporary history could be really known and grasped; if one worked hard enough and with sufficient intelligence and honesty, one could know and write the history of one's own age: that, we may say, was Thucydides' answer to the doubters, to the men who challenged Herodotus and the validity of his enterprise.

But what about the past? If one is interested in it, then what? In a famous and unique digression, Thucydides set out at some length to prove that, contrary to the common and official view, Harmodius and Aristogeiton, who had assassinated Hipparchus near the end of the previous century, were not the liberators of Athens from tyranny, because it was Hippias who was the elder son of Pisistratus, and therefore he (and not his brother Hipparchus) was the reigning tyrant at that time. There has been much speculation about Thucydides' reasons for this digression, which adds nothing to his story, and the most likely explanation is that he inserted it, at a late date, in reply to something—perhaps the publication of Hellanicus' chronicle of Athens—which annoyed him. His proof, which is perfectly sound, rested on two dedicatory inscriptions. This is an astonishing performance precisely because of its irrelevance, for it is one of the very few instances in which he quoted a document of any kind. Nothing else in the work shows so decisively what a great historian of the past Thucydides could have been. Here, he seems to be saying in contemptuous anger, is the way to go about writing the history of the past, if you think it is worth the bother.

Thucydides himself emphatically did not think it was. He shared the firm conviction, general among Greek thinkers, that mere knowledge of facts for their own sake was pointless (and sometimes harmful). Curiosity, a desire to know, had to lead to understanding, virtue, action. Of course, it is impossible to guess just what the young Thucydides had in mind when he decided, in 431 B.C., to become the war's historian. Perhaps he had no clear idea himself. But the time came—and I believe very quickly—when he set himself the goal of uncovering, through the story of his own generation, the essentials of man's behaviour, his political behaviour. That would be the "possession for all time" he would give to the world. And that, I suggest, is why Thucydides abandoned the past for the present. Human nature and human behaviour were for him essentially fixed qualities, the same in one century as in another. The good and the bad, the rational and the passionate and irrational, the moral and the immoral, the attractions and excesses of power—these were always present and operative, in various combinations. Therefore they could best be brought to light, where they could be studied and known, in the contemporary world rather than in the bygone generations which one could never really know. For Thucydides the choice was made even simpler and more obvious by the Peloponnesian War, which, he took pains to demonstrate in his introduction, was the greatest power struggle in Greek history.

By moving from history, in its narrower sense of a narrative of the war, to the basic political questions, Thucydides set himself an unattainable goal. It was difficult enough for him to reach the depth of understanding he desired. There remained the equally difficult problem of finding ways to communicate to his readers what he had learned. Merely to write the history of the Peloponnesian War, no matter how accurately and completely, would not do: that would add up to nothing more than a succession of concrete events, and how could the general ideas emerge from this mass of facts, each a particular and unique datum? To be sure, there is no explicit statement by Thucydides to say that he thought in those terms; nevertheless, the book he wrote seems to me to suffer no other explanation.

To begin with, there is the question of his selection of materials. All historical writing, like any form of rational discourse, must choose the relevant and discard the rest, must group and organize data, establish connections and patterns. But very often Thucydides' exclusions transcend the limits of the permissible by any definition of history that the modern world would recognize. For example, he wrote a long analysis of the civil disturbance (*stasis*) in Corcyra and thereafter he ignored this major factor of fifth-century Greek history almost completely, to the extent of not mentioning a number of other occurrences at all, not even those which had a demonstrably important bearing on the war. The balance is equally lopsided with the men in the war: instead of the expected proportions, according to Thucydides' judgement of the significance of the various generals and politicians, the method tends to be all or nothing. Of the popular leaders in Athens after the death of Pericles, only Cleon is given a role; the others receive no attention and are sometimes not even named. This cannot be dismissed as carelessness. Thucydides was too intelligent and serious a writer; we must assume that a principle of selection was at work, and I find it in his search for general ideas. Having demonstrated the nature and meaning of *stasis,* or the character and function of the demagogue, he saw no necessity to report other instances of the same general phenomenon. One good example was sufficient for his purposes; the rest would be useless repetition.

It is to be noticed, further, how the ideal demagogue is

portrayed, in the shape of Cleon. Although Cleon was the decisive personality in Athens for at least five years, among the most crucial in the war, he is allowed but three full-dress appearances, much like the character in a play. Thucydides required no more in order to fix the image of Cleon completely, and he left everything else out. We are not told anything about Cleon's rise to power, or about his financial measures, or about his program in any proper sense. And characteristically, one of the three appearances is in the Mitylene debate, in which Cleon was outvoted in the assembly. Speeches, often in antithetical pairs, were Thucydides' favorite device, and his most problematical one. Despite his explicit statement about his method with respect to speeches, they have preplexed and upset commentators from antiquity to our own day. It is simply undeniable that all the speeches are in the same style, Thucydides' own, and that some of the remarks could not have been made by the speakers in question. Worse still, in the Mitylene debate, whether Cleon and Diodotus are accurately reported in substance or not, the whole tone is false. From what Thucydides himself said in introducing the two speeches, his choice of these two out of the many which were actually delivered that day in the assembly distorted the actual issues, and distorted them badly. Thucydides was surely not unaware of the effect he was creating—that would be too stupid—and therefore we have still another instance of how his interest in general ideas prevailed over mere reporting, and, in that sense, over historical accuracy. When it comes, finally, to the Melian Dialogue (which I have not included among the selections), history goes by the boards altogether. For whatever reason, Thucydides chose that point in his story to write a little sophistical piece, thinly disguised as a secret discussion between two groups of unnamed negotiators, in which he played with abstract ideas of justice and empire, right and might, freedom and slavery.

In the end we are confronted with two different, and almost unrelated, kinds of writing brought together under one cover as Thucydides' "history" of the Peloponnesian War.

On the one hand there is the painstaking, precise, almost impersonal reporting, filled with minor details arranged in strict chronology. And on the other hand there are the many attempts, varied in form and tone, to get beneath and behind the facts, to uncover and bring into clear focus the realities of politics, the psychology of political behaviour, the rights and wrongs of power. These are, by and large, much the more interesting and enduring sections of the work, and the most personal (though rarely in the naïve dress of outright editorializing). They are the most dramatic, in form more than in content; they are the freest, in their portrayal of a few men and events and their exclusion of many others, in their accent, and even, I may say, in their preaching. They represent the Thucydides who restricted Cleon to three appearances; the other is the historian who solemnly put down the names and patronymics of endless obscure commanders and ship captains.

None of this is said in criticism of Thucydides. Few historians have goaded and whipped themselves so mercilessly for the better part of a lifetime to achieve complete accuracy and at the same time to discover and communicate those truths which would give value to, which would justify, their effort. I do not believe Thucydides ever came to the point of being satisfied that he had found the answers, either to the great questions of political life or to the more philosophical one of moving from the concrete and particular event to the general truth. Increasingly, however, he seemed to feel himself impelled away from narrow historical presentation. The paradox is that to give meaning to history he tended to abandon history. If the historian, by definition, concentrates on the concrete event, then Thucydides, for all his advance over his predecessor in techniques of investigation and checking, was a poorer historian, or at least less a historian, than Herodotus. It is plain that he could have been a greater one—I do not speak of charm and elegance of style —but he chose otherwise. And his reasons, which I have indicated, were beyond reproach.

No Greek again undertook a task so difficult and unrewarding. The surviving histories after Thucydides number less than a dozen, but we know the names of nearly a thousand writers of history, of one sort or another, and all the evidence leaves no doubt that not one of them approached Thucydides in intellectual rigour or insight. At least five men in the middle or second half of the fourth century wrote continuations of Thucydides' history. One work survives, Xenophon's *Hellenica,* and it is very unreliable, tendentious, dishonest, dreary to read, and rarely illuminating on broader issues. Such talents as Xenophon had lay elsewhere, and that is why in this volume he is represented not by the *Hellenica* but by the *Anabasis,* the long story of the expedition of some ten thousand Greek mercenaries into the interior of the Persian Empire in support of an unsuccessful palace revolt, and of their difficult and exciting retreat. Xenophon was an officer on this march, and his account is superb. That kind of contemporary history he could master, but not the broader canvas.

Probably some, and perhaps all four, of the continuators of Thucydides were better historians than Xenophon. That is to say, they were more accurate, more penetrating in their analysis of events, and more skilful in combining and relating movements in various parts of the Greek world. But no more. We have no reason to believe that they appreciated the real problems of historiography which Thucydides saw, or that they really understood what troubled Thucydides and drove him to re-examine his ideas and his methods over and over again. Nor did the so-called Atthidographers, the six men more or less contemporary with them who wrote—compiled, rather—lengthy chronicles of Athens, year by year, in which the mythological age received the same attention, on the same level and in the same tone, as the historical era proper. Thucydides saw in the study of contemporary history a road to understanding. Those who came after generally lowered their sights to far lesser goals: local patriotism, object lessons for politicians, elementary moralizing, and, above all, entertainment, high or low. The quality of their

work, even at its best, was no better than their purposes
deserved.

From Xenophon in the middle of the fourth century B.C.
to Polybius two hundred years later, nothing survives. Our
knowledge of these two centuries has suffered much as a
result, but it is hardly conceivable that the art (or science)
of history has lost anything of value. It is perhaps curious
that the career of Alexander the Great failed to stimulate
anything better than it did, memoirs written by several men
closely associated with him and a large and constantly growing body of legend.[2] But then, neither did Napoleon; his
campaigns produced great novels, not great histories. After
the fifth century Greek politics lacked the epic element which
nourished Herodotus and Thucydides, and it was Rome
which in the end provided the stimulus for the only Greek
historian who was in any sense a worthy successor. Polybius
also obeyed an impulse which was political, in his case stated
much more explicitly. How did Rome succeed in conquering
and dominating the world in so short a time? To answer that
he produced a huge work, nothing less than a history of the
"world," that is to say, of both Greek and Roman affairs,
from the middle of the third century on.

Polybius was a good historian in many ways. If he was
not of the calibre of Thucydides, I attribute that as much to
his time as to his personal capacities. His expressed intentions and methods of work were sound, but his performance
is often slovenly and inaccurate, his political analysis is very
shallow, he is flagrantly partisan, and he repeatedly descends
to the rhetorical tricks and sensationalism which he does not
hesitate to censure severely in his predecessors. Nevertheless, he belongs to the great tradition of Greek historians
because he, too, insisted that history must be instructive and
that politics is its proper and serious subject, with the stress
on the contemporary (it is noteworthy that his excuse for

[2] These works are reasonably well known, at reliable second hand,
from the *Anabasis* of Arrian, who wrote about the middle of the
second century of our era.

going back several generations is essentially aesthetic: every story must have a beginning, a middle, and an end); and because, within his limitations, he felt the danger of submerging the central problems and issues in the mass of concrete events. He editorialized all the time, so that no reader could possibly miss his points, and he digressed at length in one pivotal book, the sixth, in which he described the Roman constitution, explained and exemplified the theory of the cycle of governmental forms, and, with understandable caution, suggested that Rome would not escape this inevitable movement. Once again history failed a Greek historian. In order to demonstrate the cycles, which, if they are anything, are a historical phenomenon, Polybius made not the slightest attempt to write history. Instead, he gave a purely speculative account, of a kind long familiar to Greek philosophers from whom he borrowed it, into which he worked a number of comparative illustrations, inadequate, inconsistent, and all floating in the air, without historical context or concreteness.

Historians continued to write in Greek for centuries after Polybius. A few of them are not without interest—Diodorus, who used scissors and paste to compose a universal history; Dionysius of Halicarnassus, who, at the end of the first century B.C., wrote a voluminous *Roman Antiquities;* Arrian; and Dio Cassius—but they belong essentially to Roman history, and, for all their effort and their knowledge of the past, they did not advance the art of history one bit. Nothing new will be learned from them about this subject. Only Plutarch was genuinely creative and original, and his kind of biographical writing brushes history very lightly. His interests were ethical and psychological. His selection of events, his organization of the material he chose, and his assessments—in short, his portraits—often came out of history (but often, too, from myth). They are live, real, profound, moral; but they remain abstractions from the past, not the history of a period or a career, not even biographies, in the historian's sense. There is a simple test: one need only try to re-create either fourth-century Athenian politics or Demosthenes' role in it from Plutarch's life of Demosthenes.[3]

The second half of the fifth century B.C. has been called the Greek age of enlightenment. The parallel is tempting, not least in the view of history: there are the same dissatisfaction with the prevailing mythical accounts of the past, the same insistence on a strictly rational explanation of events, the same feeling that a proper study of history could be illuminating. But the eighteenth-century enlightenment was followed, at once, by the emergence of modern historiography, with its technical refinements, its demand for absolute accuracy, its unflagging search for more and more evidence, its vast scale of investigation and interests. History became a discipline and its study a profession. Not so in ancient Greece. In biology, mathematics, and astronomy, in grammar and rhetoric, great work of systematic investigation and classification still lay ahead of the Greeks when the fifth century came to an end. Herodotus and Thucydides, however, led nowhere. What came after them was less systematic, less accurate, less serious, less professional. The fathers of history produced a stunted, sickly stock, weaker in each successive generation apart from a rare sport like Polybius.

It is not easy to explain the different outcomes of the two enlightenments; it is altogether impossible until we rid ourselves of the assumption that the study of history is a natural, inherent, inevitable kind of human activity. That few Greeks, if any, took this for granted is immediately apparent from the regularity with which most historians opened their works by justifying themselves, their efforts, and the particular subjects they chose. Utility or pleasure: that was how they customarily posed the alternative. Those who aimed at the latter were defeated before they began. Poetry was too deeply entrenched in Greek life, and, when the highest forms were epic and tragedy, both "historical," there was no chance for history unless it could demonstrate its value in other

[3] It is only fair to add that some of his Roman biographies, such as the lives of the Gracchi, are much more "historical" than the Greek. But that is a mere difference in degree.

than aesthetic terms. How could Xenophon or Ephorus or Phylarchus compete with Homer, from whom every literate Greek learned his ABCs? Many tried, by rhetoric and sensationalism, by writing "tragic history" as Polybius contemptuously called it, and they failed on all scores: they still gave less pleasure than the poets and in the process their history became pseudo-history.

As for utility, somehow the essential intellectual and social conditions were lacking, at least in sufficient strength. One obstacle was the Greek passion for general principles. History, Aristotle said in a famous passage dismissing the subject, tells us only "what Alcibiades did and what he suffered." [4] And any Greek who was serious enough to inquire about such matters wanted to know not what happened, but why, and by what fixed principles, in human affairs as in the phenomena of nature. Not even Thucydides could find the solution in his historical work, and surely none of his successors, all lesser men. Poetry and philosophy gave the answers, and they valued the immutable and universal qualities far more than the individual and transient. There was no idea of progress—here the parallel with the modern enlightenment and its aftermath breaks down completely—and therefore there was no reason to look to the past for a process of continuing growth. What one found instead was either a cyclical movement, an endless coming-to-be and passing-away; or a decline from a golden age. Either way the objective was to discover the great absolute truths and then to seek their realization in life, through education and legislation. History, as the nineteenth century with its geneticism and its fact-mindedness understood the study, was obviously not the answer to the needs which the Greeks felt for themselves.

The presence or absence of the idea of progress (on a significant scale) is not just an intellectual phenomenon. It is not merely a matter of someone's having thought the idea up, and then of its being widely accepted (or not) simply because it appealed to aesthetic sensibilities or emotions or

[4] *Poetics*, Chapter 9.

logic. In the nineteenth century such an idea seemed self-evident: material progress was visible everywhere. In ancient Greece, after the emergence of the classical civilization of the fifth century, it was not visible at all. Everyone knew, of course, that there had been an earlier stage in Greek society and that non-Greeks, barbarians, lived quite differently, some of them (such as the Thracians or Scythians) being what we would call more "primitive." This rudimentary conception fell short of the modern idea of progress in at least two respects, each fundamental and critical. In the first place, whatever advances were conceded were chiefly moral and institutional rather than material. Second, the Greeks of the fifth and fourth centuries B.C. were unanimous (insofar as any people can ever be) in thinking that the city-state was the only correct political structure, in rejecting territorial expansion and growth in the size of the political organism as a road to social and moral improvement, and in ignoring completely the possibility of further technological and material progress (or the notion that this could have anything to do with the good life or a better life).

The differences which were observed were explained partly by differences in the quality of the men—as between Greeks and barbarians above all; and partly by differences in institutions. The former obviously invites no significant historical investigation. The latter might, but to them it rarely did, thanks to their *idée fixe* that current political institutions could be explained sufficiently by the genius of an original "lawgiver" and the subsequent moral behaviour of the community. That is why so much writing about Sparta gravitated around the largely legendary Lycurgus; or of Athens around Solon, who was a real person to be sure, but who by the middle of the fifth century B.C. had been mythicized beyond recognition. This kind of writing may, at its best as in Plutarch, have the air of history, but in fact it is not much more historical than the *Iliad* or the *Odyssey* or Sophocles' *Oedipus Rex*. And at its worst, it became a wild farrago about divine ancestors, their feuds, philanderings, and settlements. The great national rivalries of the nineteenth century stimulated serious historical study; the sharp Greek inter-city competition led to little more than a continual re-his-toricizing of myth to meet the shifting requirements of prestige and power. The one sought to explain and justify current politics by historical development, the other by a foundation myth and ethical claims.

In the end, its intense political orientation, which was the great force behind the histories of Herodotus and Thu-cydides, was the fatal flaw in Greek historical writing. Poli-ticians have always created the history they needed, and Greek politicians were no exception. Those Greek thinkers who were able to raise themselves above the immediate needs of their particular cities turned to philosophy for wisdom. And after Alexander the Great, Greek politics became too parochial and paltry to stimulate serious political thought of any kind. Then men turned entirely to nonpolitical questions, or they turned to Rome and Roman political problems, or they remained within the small compass that was left in the Greek city-state, its cult and legends and ancient glories. Of all the lines of inquiry which the Greek initiated, history was the most abortive. The wonder is not so much that it was, as that, in its short and fruitless life, its two best exponents still stand with the greatest the world has seen.

A Note on the Selections and Translations

The principles of selection have been, first, to offer at least one long, continuous narrative from each of the four works; second, to choose other portions which would ex-emplify (always at some length) the various techniques, conceptions, and objectives of each of the historians; and third, to illustrate, insofar as is possible without going outside the major historians, Greek ideas and knowledge, both about themselves and about the world they knew. Because the emphasis is wholly Greek, by design, I have given some of Polybius' account of the wars in his homeland rather than the more famous story of the Hannibalic War, of course adding his chapters on the Roman constitution and the theory of cycles. Each section has been reproduced completely or nearly so. The deletions will be recognized from the conventional divisions of the works (dating from Hellenistic and even Renaissance times) into numbered books, chapters, and sections.

The translations were all made in the nineteenth century: Herodotus by George Rawlinson (1858-1860), Thucydides by Richard Crawley (1874), Xenophon by J. S. Watson (1854), and Polybius by Evelyn S. Shuckburgh (1889). I have checked them against the Greek original and I have made changes where I thought strict accuracy demanded it or when the translator followed an unacceptable convention, notably Rawlinson's regular transcription of the names of Greek gods into their Roman counterparts (such as Jupiter for Zeus). I have not sought consistency of style (not even of geographical terms) nor a scholarly apparatus. The few footnotes are all mine, as is the occasional explanatory insertion of a date or identification, placed in square brackets in the text itself.

A Brief Reading List

Bury, J. B. *The Ancient Greek Historians*. London: Macmillan, 1909.

Cochrane, C. N. *Thucydides and the Science of History*. Oxford University Press, 1929.

Cornford, F. M. *Thucydides Mythistoricus*. London: Arnold, 1907.

Finley, John H., Jr. *Thucydides*. Cambridge, Massachusetts: Harvard University Press, 1942.

Fritz, Kurt von. *The Theory of the Mixed Constitution in Antiquity: Critical Analysis of Polybius' Political Ideas*. New York: Columbia University Press, 1954.

Gomme, A. W. *The Greek Attitude to Poetry and History*. Berkeley and Los Angeles: University of California Press, 1954.

Grene, David. *Man in His Pride: A Study in the Political Philosophy of Thucydides and Plato*. Chicago: University of Chicago Press, 1950.

Grundy, G. B. *Thucydides and the History of His Age*. 2nd ed., 2 vols. Oxford: Basil Blackwell, 1948.

Lovejoy, A. O., and Boas, George. *Primitivism and Related Ideas in Antiquity*. Baltimore: Johns Hopkins Press, 1935.

Pearson, Lionel. *Early Ionian Historians*. Oxford: Clarendon Press, 1939.

Powell, J. E. *The History of Herodotus*. Cambridge, England: Cambridge University Press, 1939.

Myres, J. L. *Herodotus, Father of History*. Oxford: Clarendon Press, 1953.

Spiegelberg, W. *The Credibility of Herodotus' Account of Egypt,* translated by A. M. Blackman. Oxford: Basil Blackwell, 1927.

THE EASTERN

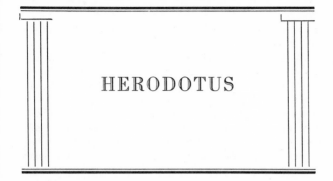

HERODOTUS

Halicarnassus in Asia Minor, where Herodotus was born and reared, was a Greek settlement ruled by a Carian dynasty under the higher suzerainty of the Persian king. Its population was much intermingled, and the name of one of Herodotus' kinsmen, the poet Panyassis, indicates that his family, too, though Greek in its culture and aristocratic in status, had a Carian strain. Herodotus' partiality for the Carian queen Artemisia is familiar to every reader of the *History*; she is presented as the most sensible and most effective of Xerxes' advisers in Greece.

Herodotus was born in the 480s B.C., too late to have any significant personal memories of the Persian Wars. When he was a young man his family was forced to leave Halicarnassus for political reasons and they settled on the island of Samos, which became his second home. By the time he was forty he had completed much of the research for the book he originally planned, a geographic and ethnographic survey of a large part of the "barbarian" world. Not only had he travelled fairly widely in Asia Minor and the Aegean islands, but he had visited Egypt, the coasts of Syria and Phoenicia, Thrace, the edge of the Scythian territory north of the Black Sea, and eastern regions as far as Babylon (but not Persia proper). He travelled for information, not to explore, and therefore he concentrated on main centers such as Memphis and Babylon, and he seems to have moved quickly. His stay in Egypt, for example, can be fixed at a

27

maximum of four months by his personal observations of the Nile flood.

By the mid-440s Herodotus had moved to the Greek mainland, where he gave public readings from his work. In Athens, at least (and no doubt in other cities), he was acclaimed officially, though whether by some purely honorific gesture or by a more material reward is unknown. There, too, where he became acquainted with the Periclean circle and made a friend of Sophocles, he was inspired to transform his book into a history of the Persian Wars. And again he began to travel in search of material, inspecting battle sites and routes, visiting Sparta, Thebes, Delphi, and other key Greek centers, and going as far north as Macedonia. How long he was occupied in this way is not known, nor is the date when (or the reason why) he migrated to Thurii on the Gulf of Tarentum in southern Italy, a Panhellenic settlement founded in 443 under the sponsorship of Pericles.

Presumably he spent the final years of his life in the west, writing his book and occasionally making short trips in Italy and Sicily and once to Cyrene in North Africa. The exact date of his death is also unknown, but it is demonstrable that, just as his life began in the final years of the Persian Wars, it closed early in the Peloponnesian War, which broke out in 431. There is no reference in the *History* to anything that occurred after 430 and there are things which he could hardly have said (or failed to say) after 424. The probability is that his death occurred nearer 430 than 424. His book was published in the 420s, soon after his death, most likely. All the details regarding the publication are unknown, and that is the final uncertainty in this short list of probabilities and possibilities which constitutes everything we know about the life of Herodotus.

—M. I. F.

From BOOK I

Lydia

These are the researches of Herodotus of Halicarnassus, which he publishes in the hope of thereby preserving from decay the remembrance of what men have done, and of preventing the great and wonderful actions of the Greeks and the barbarians from losing their due meed of glory; and withal to put on record what were their grounds of feud.

1. According to the Persians best informed in history, the Phoenicians began the quarrel. This people, who had formerly dwelt on the shores of the Erythraean Sea,[1] having migrated to the Mediterranean and settled in the parts which they now inhabit, began at once, they say, to adventure on long voyages, freighting their vessels with the wares of Egypt and Assyria. They landed at many places on the coast, and among the rest at Argos, which was then pre-eminent above all the states included now under the common name of Hellas. Here they exposed their merchandise, and traded with the natives for five or six days; at the end of which time, when almost everything was sold, there came down to the beach a number of women, and among them the daughter of the king, who was, they say, agreeing in this with the Greeks, Io, the child of Inachus. The women were standing by the stern of the ship intent upon their purchases, when the Phoenicians, with a general shout, rushed upon them. The greater part made their escape, but some were seized and carried off. Io herself was among the captives. The Phoenicians put the women on board their vessel, and set sail for Egypt.

2. Thus did Io pass into Egypt, according to the Persian

[1] The Persian Gulf and Indian Ocean.

story, which differs widely from the Greek: and thus commenced, according to their authors, the series of outrages. At a later period, certain Greeks, with whose name they [the Persian sources] are unacquainted, but who may have been Cretans, made a landing at Tyre, on the Phoenician coast, and bore off the king's daughter, Europa. In this they only retaliated; but afterwards the Greeks, they say, were guilty of a second violence. They manned a ship of war, and sailed to Aea, a city of Colchis, on the river Phasis; from whence, after despatching the rest of the business on which they had come,[2] they carried off Medea, the daughter of the king of the land. The monarch sent a herald into Greece to demand reparation of the wrong, and the restitution of his child; but the Greeks made answer that, having received no reparation of the wrong done them in the seizure of Io the Argive, they should give none in this instance.

3. In the next generation afterwards, according to the same authorities, Alexander[3] the son of Priam [king of Troy], bearing these events in mind, resolved to procure himself a wife out of Greece by violence, fully persuaded that, as the Greeks had not given satisfaction for their outrages, so neither would he be forced to make any for his. Accordingly he made prize of Helen; upon which the Greeks decided that, before resorting to other measures, they would send envoys to reclaim the princess and require reparation of the wrong. Their demands were met by a reference to the violence which had been offered to Medea, and they were asked with what face they could now require satisfaction, when they had formerly rejected all demands for either reparation or restitution addressed to them.

4. Hitherto the injuries on either side had been mere kidnappings; but in what followed the Persians consider that the Greeks were greatly to blame, since before any attack had been made on Europe, they led an army into Asia. Now as for the carrying off of women, it is the deed, they say, of a rogue; but to make a stir about such as are carried

---

[2] The winning of the Golden Fleece.
[3] More commonly known by his other name, Paris.

off, argues a man a fool. Men of sense care nothing for such women, since it is plain that without their own consent they would never be forced away. The Asiatics, when the Greeks ran off with their women, never troubled themselves about the matter; but the Greeks, for the sake of a single Lacedaemonian girl, collected a vast armament, invaded Asia, and destroyed the kingdom of Priam. Henceforth they ever looked upon the Greeks as their open enemies. For Asia, with all the various tribes of barbarians that inhabit it, is regarded by the Persians as their own; but Europe and the Greek race they look on as distinct and separate.

5. Such is the account which the Persians give of these matters. They trace to the attack upon Troy their ancient enmity towards the Greeks. The Phoenicians, however, as regards Io, vary from the Persian statements. They deny that they used any violence to remove her into Egypt; she herself, they say, having formed an intimacy with the captain, while his vessel lay at Argos, and perceiving herself to be with child, of her own freewill accompanied the Phoenicians on their leaving the shore, to escape the shame of detection and the reproaches of her parents. This is what the Persians and the Phoenicians say. Whether this account be true, or whether the matter happened otherwise, I shall not discuss further. I shall proceed at once to point out the person who first within my own knowledge inflicted injury on the Greeks, after which I shall go forward with my history, describing equally the greater and the lesser cities of men. For the cities which were formerly great have most of them become insignificant; and such as are at present powerful were weak in the olden time. I shall therefore discourse equally of both, convinced that human happiness never continues long in one stay.

6. Croesus, son of Alyattes, by birth a Lydian, was lord [c. 560-546 B.C.] of all the nations to the west of the river Halys. This stream, which separates Syria [i.e., Cappadocia] from Paphlagonia, runs with a course from south to north, and finally falls into the Black Sea. So far as our knowledge goes, he was the first of the barbarians who had dealings

with the Greeks, forcing some of them to become his tributaries, and entering into alliance with others. He conquered the Aeolians, Ionians, and Dorians of Asia, and made friends with the Lacedaemonians. Up to that time all Greeks had been free. For the Cimmerian attack upon Ionia, which was earlier than Croesus, was not a conquest of the cities, but only an inroad for plundering.

7. The sovereignty of Lydia, which had belonged to the Heraclids, passed into the family of Croesus, who were called the Mermnadae, in the manner which I will now relate. There was a certain king of Sardis, Candaules by name, whom the Greeks called Myrsilus. He was a descendant of Alcaeus, son of Hercules. The first king of this dynasty was Agron, son of Ninus, grandson of Belus, and great-grandson of Alcaeus; Candaules, son of Myrsus, was the last. The kings who reigned before Agron sprang from Lydus, son of Atys, from whom the people of the land, called previously Meonians, received the name of Lydians. The Heraclids, descended from Hercules and [Omphale,] the slave-girl of Iardanus, having been entrusted by the descendants of Lydus with the management of affairs, obtained the kingdom by an oracle. Their rule endured for two and twenty generations of men, a space of five hundred and five years; during the whole of which period, down to Candaules, the crown descended in the direct line from father to son.

8. Now it happened that this Candaules was in love with his own wife; and not only so, but thought her the fairest woman in the whole world. Full of this thought—among his bodyguard his favourite was Gyges, the son of Dascylus, to whom he entrusted all affairs of greatest moment—Candaules used to fill Gyges with excessive praise of his wife's beauty. After a brief period, Candaules, who was fated to end ill, addressed Gyges as follows: "I see you do not credit what I tell you of my lady's loveliness; but come now, since men's ears are less credulous than their eyes, contrive some means whereby you may behold her naked." At this the other loudly exclaimed, saying, "What most unwise speech is this, master, ordering me to behold my mistress when she

is naked? When she puts off her clothes, a woman also puts off her modesty. Long ago men learned the wise precepts by which one should be taught. There is an old saying, 'Let each look on his own.' I hold your wife for the fairest of all womankind. Only, I beseech you, ask me not to do wickedly."

9. Gyges thus endeavoured to decline the king's proposal, trembling lest some evil should befall him through it. But the king replied to him, "Courage, Gyges; suspect me not of the design to test you by this discourse; nor fear my wife, lest mischief befall you on her account. Be sure I will so manage that she shall not even know that you have looked upon her. I will place you behind the open door of the chamber in which we sleep. As soon as I have gone in, my wife will also enter to go to bed. There stands a chair close to the entrance, on which she will lay her clothes one by one as she takes them off. You will thus be able to look at her at your leisure. Then, when she is moving from the chair towards the bed, and her back is turned to you, take care that she does not see you as you pass through the doorway."

10. Gyges, unable to escape, could but declare his readiness. Then Candaules, when bedtime came, led Gyges into his chamber, and a moment after the queen followed. She entered, and laid her garments on the chair, and Gyges gazed on her. After a while she moved towards the bed, and her back being then turned, he glided stealthily from the apartment. As he was passing out, however, she saw him, and, instantly divining what had happened, she neither screamed, as her shame impelled her, nor even appeared to have noticed aught, purposing to take vengeance upon Candaules. For among the Lydians, and indeed among the barbarians generally, it is reckoned a deep disgrace, even to a man, to be seen naked.

11. No sound or sign of intelligence escaped her at the time. But in the morning, as soon as day broke, she hastened to choose from among her retinue such as she knew to be most faithful to her, and, preparing them for what was to ensue, summoned Gyges. Now it had often happened before that the queen had desired to confer with him, and he

was accustomed to come to her at her call. He therefore obeyed the summons, not suspecting that she knew aught of what had occurred. Then she addressed these words to him: "Take your choice, Gyges, of two courses which are open to you. Slay Candaules, and thereby become my lord, and obtain the Lydian throne, or die this moment, so that never again, obeying all behests of your master, shall you behold what is not lawful for you. It must needs be, that either he perish by whose counsel this thing was done, or you, who saw me naked, and so did break our usages." At these words Gyges stood awhile in mute astonishment; recovering after a time, he earnestly besought the queen that she would not compel him to so hard a choice. But finding he implored in vain, and that necessity was indeed laid on him to kill or to be killed, he made choice of life for himself, and replied by this inquiry: "If it must be so, and you compel me against my will to put my lord to death, come, let me hear how you will have me set on him." "Let him be attacked," she answered, "on that spot where I was by him shown naked to you, and let the assault be made when he is asleep."

12. All was then prepared for the attack, and when night fell, Gyges, seeing that he had no retreat or escape, but must absolutely either slay Candaules, or himself be slain, followed his mistress into the bedroom. She placed a dagger in his hand, and hid him carefully behind the self-same door. Then Gyges, when the king was fallen asleep, entered privily into the chamber and struck him dead. Thus did the wife and kingdom of Candaules pass into the possession of Gyges, of whom Archilochus the Parian, who lived about the same time, made mention in a poem written in iambic trimeter verse.

13. Gyges was afterwards confirmed in the possession of the throne by an answer of the Delphic oracle. Enraged at the murder of their king, the people flew to arms, but the partisans of Gyges came to terms with them, and it was agreed that if the Delphic oracle declared him king of the Lydians, he should reign; if otherwise, he should yield the throne to the Heraclids. As the oracle was given in his favor

he became king. The Pythoness, however, added that, in the fifth generation from Gyges, vengeance should come for the Heraclids; a prophecy of which neither the Lydians nor their princes took any account till it was fulfilled.

14. Such was the way in which the Mermnadae deposed the Heraclids, and themselves obtained the sovereignty. When Gyges was established on the throne, he sent no small presents to Delphi, as his many silver offerings at the Delphic shrine testify. Besides this silver he gave a vast number of vessels of gold, among which the most worthy of mention are the goblets, six in number, and weighing altogether thirty talents, which stand in the Corinthian treasury, dedicated by him. (I call it the Corinthian treasury, though in strictness of speech it is the treasury not of the whole Corinthian people, but of Cypselus, son of Eetion.) Excepting Midas, son of Gordias, king of Phrygia, Gyges was the first of the barbarians whom we know to have sent offerings to Delphi. Midas dedicated the royal throne whereon he was accustomed to sit and administer justice, an object well worth looking at. It lies in the same place as the goblets presented by Gyges. The Delphians call the whole of the silver and the gold which Gyges dedicated, after the name of the donor, Gygian.

As soon as Gyges was king he made an inroad on Miletus and Smyrna, and took the city of Colophon. Afterwards, however, though he reigned eight and thirty years, he did not perform a single great exploit. I shall therefore make no further mention of him, (15) but pass on to his son and successor in the kingdom, Ardys. He took Priene and made war upon Miletus. In his reign the Cimmerians, driven from their homes by the nomads of Scythia, entered Asia and captured Sardis, all but the citadel.

16. Ardys reigned forty-nine years, and was succeeded by his son, Sadyattes, who reigned twelve years. Then Alyattes mounted the throne. This prince waged war with the Medes under Cyaxares, the grandson of Deïoces, drove the Cimmerians out of Asia, conquered Smyrna, the Colophonian colony, and invaded Clazomenae. From this

last contest he did not come off as he could have wished, but met with a sore defeat.

17. In the course of his reign, Alyattes performed other actions very worthy of note, of which I will now proceed to give an account. Inheriting from his father a war with the Milesians, he pressed the siege against the city by attacking it in the following manner. When the harvest was ripe on the ground he marched his army into Milesia to the sound of pipes and harps, and flutes masculine and feminine. The buildings that were scattered over the country he neither pulled down nor burnt, nor did he even tear away the doors, but left them standing as they were. He cut down, however, and utterly destroyed all the trees and all the corn throughout the land, and then returned to his own dominions. It was idle for his army to sit down before the place, as the Milesians were masters of the sea. The reason that he did not demolish their buildings was that the inhabitants might be tempted to use them as homesteads from which to go forth to sow and till their lands; and so each time that he invaded the country he might find something to plunder.

18. In this way he carried on the war with the Milesians for eleven years, in the course of which he inflicted on them two terrible blows—one in their own country in the district of Limeneium, the other in the plain of the Maeander. During six of these eleven years, Sadyattes, the son of Ardys, who first lighted the flames of this war, was king of Lydia, and made the incursions.[4] Only the five following years belong to the reign of Alyattes, son of Sadyattes, who (as I said before) inheriting the war from his father, applied himself to it unremittingly. The Milesians throughout the contest received no help at all from any of the Ionians, excepting those of Chios, who lent them troops in requital of a like service rendered them in former times, the Milesians having fought on the side of the Chians during the whole of the war between them and the people of Erythrae.

[4] This sentence contradicts the preceding one; perhaps it is a tentative or marginal correction by Herodotus himself which somehow crept into the final text.

19. It was in the twelfth year of the war that the following mischance occurred from the firing of the harvest. Scarcely had the corn been set alight by the soldiers when a violent wind carried the flames against the temple of Athena Assesia, which caught fire and was burnt to the ground. At the time no one made any account of the circumstance; but afterwards, on the return of the army to Sardis, Alyattes fell sick. His illness continued, whereupon, either advised thereto by some friend, or perchance himself conceiving the idea, he sent messengers to Delphi to inquire of the god concerning his malady. On their arrival the Pythoness declared that no answer should be given them until they had rebuilt the temple of Athena, burnt by the Lydians at Assesus in Milesia.

20. Thus much I know from information given me by the Delphians; the remainder of the story the Milesians add.

The answer made by the oracle came to the ears of Periander, son of Cypselus, who was a very close friend to Thrasybulus, tyrant of Miletus at that period. He instantly despatched a messenger to report the oracle to him, in order that Thrasybulus, forewarned of its tenor, might the better adapt his measures to the posture of affairs. This is how it happened, say the Milesians.

21. Alyattes, the moment that the words of the oracle were reported to him, sent a herald to Miletus in hopes of concluding a truce with Thrasybulus and the Milesians for such a time as was needed to rebuild the temple. The herald went upon his way; but meantime Thrasybulus had been apprised of everything; and, conjecturing what Alyattes would do, he contrived this artifice. He had all the corn that was in the city, whether belonging to himself or to private persons, brought into the market-place, and issued an order that the Milesians should hold themselves in readiness, and, when he gave the signal, should, one and all, fall to drinking and revelry.

22. The purpose for which he gave these orders was the following. He hoped that the Sardian herald, seeing so great store of corn upon the ground, and all the city given up to festivity, would inform Alyattes of it, which fell out as he

anticipated. The herald observed the whole, and when he had delivered his message, went back to Sardis. This circumstance alone, as I gather, brought about the peace which ensued. Alyattes, who had hoped that there was now a great scarcity of corn in Miletus, and that the people were worn down to the last pitch of suffering, when he heard from the herald on his return from Miletus tidings so contrary to those he had expected, made a treaty with the enemy by which the two nations became friends and allies. He then built at Assesus two temples to Athena instead of one, and shortly after recovered from his malady. Such were the chief circumstances of the war which Alyattes waged with Thrasybulus and the Milesians.

23. This Periander, who apprised Thrasybulus of the oracle, was son of Cypselus, and tyrant of Corinth. In his time a very wonderful thing is said to have happened. The Corinthians and the Lesbians agree in their account of the matter. They relate that Arion of Methymna, who as a harper was second to no man living at that time, and who was, so far as we know, the first to compose dithyrambs, to give them that name, and to recite in them at Corinth, was carried to Taenarum on the back of a dolphin.

24. He had lived for many years at the court of Periander, when a longing came upon him to sail across to Italy and Sicily. Having gained great wealth in those parts, he wanted to recross the seas to Corinth. He therefore hired a vessel, the crew of which were Corinthians, thinking that there was no people in whom he could more safely confide; and, going on board, he set sail from Tarentum. The sailors, however, when they reached the open sea, formed a plot to throw him overboard and seize upon his riches. Discovering their design, he beseeched them to spare his life, making them welcome to his money. But they refused; and required him either to kill himself outright, if he wished for a grave on the dry land, or without loss of time to leap overboard into the sea. In this strait Arion begged them, since such was their pleasure, to allow him to mount upon the quarter-deck, dressed in his full costume, and there to play and sing, and

promising that, as soon as his song was ended, he would destroy himself. Delighted at the prospect of hearing the very best harper in the world, they consented, and withdrew from the stern to the middle of the vessel, while Arion dressed himself in the full costume of his calling, took his harp, and, standing on the quarter-deck, chanted the Orthian hymn. His strain ended, he flung himself, fully attired as he was, headlong into the sea. The Corinthians then sailed on to Corinth. As for Arion, a dolphin, they say, took him upon his back and carried him to Taenarum, where he went ashore, and thence proceeded to Corinth in his musician's dress, and told all that had happened to him. Periander, however, disbelieved the story, and put Arion in ward, to prevent his leaving Corinth, while he watched anxiously for the return of the mariners. On their arrival he summoned them before him and asked them if they could give him any tidings of Arion. They returned for answer that he was alive and in good health in Italy, and that they had left him at Tarentum, where he was doing well. Thereupon Arion appeared before them, just as he was when he jumped from the vessel: the men, astonished and detected in falsehood, could no longer deny their guilt. Such is the account which the Corinthians and Lesbians give; and there is to this day at Taenarum an offering of Arion's at the shrine, which is a small figure in bronze, representing a man seated upon a dolphin.

25. Having brought the war with the Milesians to a close, and reigned over the land of Lydia for fifty-seven years, Alyattes died. He was the second prince of his house who made offerings at Delphi. His gifts, which he sent on recovering from his sickness, were a great bowl of pure silver, with a salver in soldered iron, a work among all the offerings at Delphi the best worth looking at. Glaucus, the Chian, made it, the man who first invented the art of soldering iron.

26. On the death of Alyattes, Croesus, his son, who was thirty-five years old, succeeded to the throne. Of the Greek cities, Ephesus was the first that he attacked. The Ephesians, when he laid siege to the place, dedicated their city to Artemis by stretching a rope from the town wall to the temple of the

goddess, which was distant from the ancient city, then besieged by Croesus, a space of seven furlongs. They were, as
I said, the first Greeks whom he attacked. Afterwards, on
some pretext or other, he made war in turn upon every
Ionian and Aeolian state, bringing forward, where he could,
a substantial ground of complaint; where such failed him,
advancing some poor excuse.

27. In this way he made himself master of all the Greek
cities in Asia, and forced them to become his tributaries;
after which he began to think of building ships, and attacking the islanders. Everything had been got ready for this
purpose, when Bias of Priene (or, as some say, Pittacus the
Mytilenean) put a stop to the project. The king had made
inquiry of this person, who was lately arrived at Sardis, if
there were any news from Greece; to which he answered,
"Yes, sire, the islanders have purchased ten thousand horses,
designing an expedition against you and your capital."
Croesus, thinking he spoke seriously, broke out, "Ah, might
the gods put such a thought into their minds as to attack
the sons of the Lydians with cavalry!" "It seems, O King,"
rejoined the other, "that you earnestly desire to catch the
islanders on horseback upon the mainland—you know well
what would come of it. But what do you think the islanders
desire better, now that they hear you are about to build ships
and sail against them, than to catch the Lydians at sea, and
there revenge on them the wrongs of their brothers upon the
mainland, whom you hold in slavery?" Croesus was charmed
with the turn of the speech; and thinking there was reason in
what was said, gave up his shipbuilding and concluded a
league of amity with the Ionians of the isles.

28. Croesus afterwards brought under his sway almost
all the peoples to the west of the Halys. The Lycians and
Cilicians alone continued free; all the others he reduced and
held in subjection. They were the following: the Lydians,
Phrygians, Mysians, Mariandynians, Chalybians, Paphla-
gonians, Thynian and Bithynian Thracians, Carians, Ionians, Dorians, Aeolians, and Pamphylians.

29. When all these conquests had been added to the

Lydian empire, and the prosperity of Sardis was now at its height, there came thither, one after another, all the sages of Greece living at the time, and among them Solon, the Athenian. He was on his travels, having left Athens to be absent ten years, under the pretence of wishing to study, but really to avoid being forced to repeal any of the laws which he had introduced. Without his sanction the Athenians could not repeal them, as they had bound themselves by great oaths to be governed for ten years by the laws which Solon should lay down for them.

30. On this account, as well as to study, Solon set out upon his travels, in the course of which he went to Egypt to the court of Amasis, and also to Croesus at Sardis.[5] Croesus received him as his guest, and lodged him in the royal palace. On the third or fourth day after, he bade his servants conduct Solon over his treasuries, and show him all their greatness and magnificence. When he had seen them all, and, so far as time allowed, inspected them, Croesus addressed this question to him. "Stranger of Athens, we have heard much of your wisdom and of your travels through many lands, from love of knowledge and a wish to see the world. I am curious therefore to inquire of you, whom, of all the men that you have seen, you deem the most happy?" This he asked because he thought himself the happiest of mortals: but Solon answered him without flattery, according to his true sentiments, "Tellus of Athens, sire." Full of astonishment at what he heard, Croesus demanded sharply, "And wherefore do you deem Tellus happiest?" To which the other replied, "First, because his country was flourishing in his days, and he himself had sons both beautiful and good. and he lived to see children born to each of them, and these children all grew up; and further because, after a life spent in what our people look upon as comfort, his end was surpassingly glorious. In a battle between the Athenians and their neighbours near Eleusis, he came to the assistance of his countrymen, routed the foe, and died upon the field most

[5] In fact, neither Amasis nor Croesus was king during the ten years following Solon's legislative activity.

gallantly. The Athenians gave him a public funeral on the spot where he fell, and paid him the highest honours."

31. Thus did Solon admonish Croesus by the example of Tellus, enumerating the manifold particulars of his happiness. When he had ended, Croesus inquired a second time, who after Tellus seemed to him the happiest, expecting that at any rate, he would be given the second place. "Cleobis and Biton," Solon answered; "they were of Argive race; their fortune was enough for their wants, and they were besides endowed with so much bodily strength that they had both gained prizes at the games. Also this tale is told of them: There was a great festival in honour of the goddess Hera at Argos, to which their mother must needs be taken in a car. Now the oxen did not come home from the field in time, so the youths, fearful of being too late, put the yoke on their own necks, and themselves drew the car in which their mother rode. Five and forty furlongs did they draw her, and stopped before the temple. This deed of theirs was witnessed by the whole assembly of worshippers, and then their life closed in the best possible way. Herein, too, the god showed forth most evidently, how much better a thing for man death is than life. For the Argive men, who stood around the car, extolled the vast strength of the youths; and the Argive women extolled the mother who was blessed with such a pair of sons; and the mother herself, overjoyed at the deed and at the praises it had won, standing straight before the image, besought the goddess to bestow on Cleobis and Biton, the sons who had so mightily honoured her, the highest blessing to which mortals can attain. Her prayer ended, they offered sacrifice and partook of the banquet, after which the two youths fell asleep in the temple. They never woke more, but so passed from the earth. The Argives, looking on them as among the best of men, caused statues of them to be made, which they dedicated at Delphi."

32. When Solon had thus assigned these youths the second place, Croesus broke in angrily, "What, stranger of Athens, is our happiness, then, so utterly set at nought by

you, that you do not even put us on a level with private men?"

"O Croesus," replied the other, "you asked a question concerning the condition of man, of one who knows that the god is full of jealousy, and fond of troubling our lot. A long life gives one to witness much, and experience much oneself, that one would not choose. Seventy years I regard as the limit of the life of man. In these seventy years are contained, without reckoning intercalary months, twenty-five thousand and two hundred days. Add an intercalary month to every other year, that the seasons may come round at the right time, and there will be, in the seventy years, thirty-five such months, making an addition of one thousand and fifty days. The whole number of the days contained in the seventy years will thus be twenty-six thousand two hundred and fifty, whereof not one but will produce events unlike the rest. Hence man is wholly accident. For yourself, O Croesus, I see that you are wonderfully rich, and are king over many men; but with respect to that whereon you questioned me, I have no answer to give, until I hear that you have closed your life happily. For assuredly he who possesses great store of riches is no nearer happiness than he who has what suffices for his daily needs, unless it so hap that luck attend upon him, and so he continue in the enjoyment of all his good things to the end of life. For many of the wealthiest men have been unfavoured of fortune, and many whose means were moderate have had excellent luck. Men of the former class excel those of the latter but in two respects; these last excel the former in many. The wealthy man is better able to content his desires, and to bear up against a sudden buffet of calamity. The other has less ability to withstand these evils (from which, however, his good luck keeps him clear), but he enjoys all these following blessings: he is whole of limb, a stranger to disease, free from misfortune, happy in his children, and comely to look upon. If, in addition to all this, he end his life well, he is of a truth the man of whom you are in search, the man who may rightly be termed happy. Call him, however, until he die, not happy but for-tunate. Scarcely, indeed, can any man unite all these ad-vantages: as there is no country which contains within it all that it needs, but each, while it possesses some things, lacks others, and the best country is that which contains the most; so no single human being is complete in every respect—something is always lacking. He who unites the greatest num-ber of advantages, and, retaining them to the day of his death, then dies peaceably, that man alone, sire, is, in my judgment, entitled to bear the name of 'happy.' But in every matter it behoves us to mark well the end: for oftentimes the god gives men a gleam of happiness, and then plunges them into ruin."

33. Such was the speech which Solon addressed to Croesus, a speech which brought him neither largess nor honour. The king saw him depart with much indifference, since he thought that a man must be an arrant fool who made no account of present good, but bade men always wait and mark the end.

34. After Solon had gone away a dreadful vengeance, sent of the god, came upon Croesus, to punish him, it is likely, for deeming himself the happiest of men. First he had a dream in the night, which foreshowed him truly the evils that were about to befall him in the person of his son. For Croesus had two sons, one blasted by a natural defect, be-ing deaf and dumb; the other, distinguished far above all his co-mates in every pursuit. The name of the last was Atys. It was this son concerning whom he dreamt a dream, that he would die by the blow of an iron weapon. When he woke, he considered earnestly with himself, and greatly alarmed at the dream, instantly made his son take a wife, and whereas in former years the youth had been wont to command the Lydian forces in the field, he now would not suffer him to accompany them. All the spears and javelins, and weapons used in the wars, he removed out of the male apartments, and laid them in heaps in the storerooms, fear-ing lest perhaps one of the weapons that hung against the wall might fall and strike his son.

35. Now it chanced that while he was making arrangements for the wedding, there came to Sardis a man under a misfortune, who had upon him the stain of blood. He was by race a Phrygian, and belonged to the family of the king. Presenting himself at the palace of Croesus, he prayed to be admitted to purification according to the customs of the country. Now the Lydian method of purifying is very nearly the same as the Greek. Croesus granted the request, and went through all the customary rites, after which he asked the suppliant of his birth and country, addressing him as follows: "Who are you, stranger, and from what part of Phrygia did you flee to take refuge at my hearth? And whom, moreover, what man or what woman, did you slay?" "O King," replied the Phrygian, "I am the son of Gordias, son of Midas. I am named Adrastus. The man I unintentionally slew was my own brother. For this my father drove me from the land, and I lost all." "You are the offspring," Croesus rejoined, "of a house friendly to mine, and you have come to friends. You shall want for nothing so long as you remain with me. Bear your misfortune as easily as you can, so will it go best with you." Thenceforth Adrastus lived with the king.

36. It chanced that at this very same time there was in the Mysian Olympus a huge monster of a boar, which went forth often from this mountain country, and wasted the cornfields of the Mysians. Many a time had the Mysians collected to hunt the beast, but instead of doing him any hurt they came off always with some loss to themselves. At length they sent ambassadors to Croesus, who delivered their message to him in these words: "O King, a mighty monster of a boar has appeared in our parts, and destroys the labor of our hands. We do our best to take him, but in vain. Now therefore we beseech you to let your son accompany us back, with some chosen youths and hounds, that we may rid our country of the animal." Such was the tenor of their prayer.

But Croesus bethought him of his dream, and answered, "Say no more of my son going with you; that may not be in any wise. He is but just joined in wedlock, and is busy enough with that. I will grant you a picked band of Lydians, and all my huntsmen and hounds; and I will charge those whom I send to use all zeal in aiding you to rid your country of the brute."

37. With this reply the Mysians were content; but the king's son, hearing what the prayer of the Mysians was, came suddenly in, and, on the refusal of Croesus to let him go with them, thus addressed his father: "Formerly, my father, it was deemed the noblest and most suitable thing for me to frequent the wars and hunting parties, and win myself glory in them; but now you keep me away from both, although you have never beheld in me either cowardice or lack of spirit. What face meanwhile must I wear as I walk to the Agora or return from it? What must the citizens, what must my young bride think of me? What sort of man will she suppose her husband to be? Either, therefore, let me go to the chase of this boar, or give me a reason why it is best for me to do according to your wishes."

38. Then Croesus answered, "My son, it is not because I have seen either cowardice in you or aught else which has displeased me that I keep you back; but because a vision which came before me in a dream as I slept, warned me that you were doomed to die young, pierced by an iron weapon. It was this which first led me to hasten on your wedding, and now it hinders me from sending you upon this enterprise. Fain would I keep watch over you, if by any means I may cheat fate of you during my own lifetime. For you are the one and only son that I possess; the other, whose hearing is destroyed, I regard as if he were not."

39. "Ah, Father," returned the youth, "I do not blame you for keeping watch over me after such a dream; but if you are wrong, if you do not apprehend the dream aright, it is no blame for me to show you wherein you err. Now the dream, you yourself said, foretold that I should die stricken by an iron weapon. But what hands has a boar? What iron weapon does he wield? Had the dream said that I should die by a tooth, or by something similar, then you would have done well to keep me away; but it said a

weapon. Now here we do not combat men; therefore, let me go with them."

40. "There you have me, my son," said Croesus. "Your interpretation is better than mine. I yield to it, and change my mind, and consent to let you go."

41. Then the king sent for Adrastus, the Phrygian, and said to him, "Adrastus, when you were smitten with the rod of affliction—no reproach, my friend—I purified you, and have taken you to live with me, and have been at every charge. Now, therefore, it behooves you to requite the good offices which you have received at my hands by consenting to go with my son on this hunting party, and to watch over him, if perchance you should be attacked upon the road by some band of daring robbers. Even apart from this, it were right for you to go where you may make yourself famous by noble deeds. They are the heritage of your family, and you too are stalwart and strong."

42. Adrastus answered, "Except for your request, O King, I would rather have kept away from this hunt; for methinks it ill beseems a man under a misfortune such as mine to consort with his happier compeers; and besides, I have no heart to it. On many grounds I had stayed behind; but, as you urge it, and I am bound to pleasure you (for truly it does behoove me to requite your good offices), I am content to do as you wish. For your son, whom you give into my charge, be sure you shall receive him back safe and sound, so far as depends upon a guardian's carefulness."

43. Thus assured, Croesus let them depart, accompanied by a band of picked youths, and with dogs of chase. When then reached Olympus, they scattered in quest of the animal; he was soon found, and the hunters, drawing round him in a circle, hurled their weapons at him. Then the stranger, the man who had been purified of blood, whose name was Adrastus,[6] he also hurled his spear at the boar, but missed his aim and struck Atys. Thus was the son of Croesus slain by the point of an iron weapon, and the warning of the vision was fulfilled. Then one ran to Sardis to bear the tidings to

[6] The Greek word *adrastos* means "not running away (escaping)."

the king, and he came and informed him of the combat and of the fate that had befallen his son.

44. If it was a heavy blow to the father to learn that his child was dead, it yet more strongly affected him to think that the very man whom he himself once purified of a murder had done the deed. In the violence of his grief he called aloud on Zeus Catharsius to be a witness of what he had suffered at the stranger's hands. Afterwards he invoked the same god as Zeus Ephistius and Hetaereus—using the one term because he had unwittingly harboured in his house the man who had now slain his son, and the other because the stranger, who had been sent as his child's guardian, had turned out his most cruel enemy.

45. Presently the Lydians arrived, bearing the body, and behind them followed the homicide. He took his stand in front of the corpse, and, stretching forth his hands to Croesus, delivered himself into his power with earnest entreaties that he would sacrifice him upon the body of his son —that his former misfortune was burden enough; now that he had added to it a second, and had brought ruin on the man who purified him, he could not bear to live. Then Croesus, when he heard these words, was moved with pity towards Adrastus, notwithstanding the bitterness of his own calamity; and so he answered, "Enough, my friend; I have all the satisfaction that I require, since you give sentence of death against yourself. But it is not you who have injured me, except so far as you were unwittingly the instrument. Some god is the author of my misfortune, he who forewarned me of it a long time ago." Croesus after this buried the body of his son, with the customary rites. As for Adrastus, son of Gordias, son of Midas, the destroyer of his brother in time past, the destroyer now of his purifier, regarding himself as the most unfortunate wretch whom he had ever known, so soon as all was quiet about the place, he slew himself upon the tomb.

46. Croesus, bereft of his son, gave himself up to mourning for two full years. At the end of this time, he ceased from his mourning upon learning that Cyrus, the son of Cambyses,

had destroyed the [Median] empire of Astyages, the son of Cyaxares; and that the Persians were becoming daily more powerful. This led him to consider with himself whether it were possible to check the growing power of that people before it came to a head. With this design he resolved to make instant trial of the several oracles in Greece, and of the one in Libya. So he sent his messengers in different directions, some to Delphi, some to Abae in Phocis, and some to Dodona; others to the oracle of Amphiaraus; others to that of Trophonius; others, again, to the sanctuary of the Branchidae in Milesia. These were the Greek oracles which he consulted. To Libya he sent another embassy, to consult the oracle of Ammon. These messengers were sent to test the knowledge of the oracles, that, if they were found really to return true answers, he might send a second time, and inquire if he ought to attack the Persians.

47. The messengers who were despatched to make trial of the oracles were given the following instructions: they were to keep count of the days from the time of their leaving Sardis, and, reckoning from that date, on the hundredth day they were to consult the oracles, and to inquire of them what Croesus the son of Alyattes, king of Lydia, was doing at that moment. The answers given them were to be taken down in writing, and brought back to him. None of the replies remain on record except that of the oracle at Delphi. There, the moment that the Lydians entered the inner sanctuary, and before they put their questions, the Pythoness thus answered them in hexameter verse:

"I can count the sands, and I can measure the ocean;
   I have ears for the silent, and know what the dumb man meaneth;
   Lo! on my sense there striketh the smell of a shell-covered tortoise,
   Boiling now on a fire, with the flesh of a lamb, in a cauldron,—
   Bronze is the vessel below, and bronze the cover above it."

48. These words the Lydians wrote down at the mouth of the Pythoness as she prophesied, and then set off on their return to Sardis. When all the messengers had come back with the answers which they had received, Croesus undid the rolls and read what was written in each. Only one approved itself to him, that of the Delphic oracle. This he had no sooner heard than he instantly made an act of adoration, and accepted it as true, declaring that the Delphic was the only really oracular shrine, the only one that had discovered in what way he was in fact employed. For on the departure of his messengers he had set himself to think what was most impossible for anyone to conceive of his doing, and then, waiting till the day agreed on came, he acted as he had determined. He took a tortoise and a lamb, and cutting them in pieces with his own hands, boiled them both together in a brazen cauldron, covered over with a lid which was also of bronze.

49. Such then was the answer returned to Croesus from Delphi. What the answer was which the Lydians who went to the shrine of Amphiaraus and performed the customary rites obtained of the oracle there, I have it not in my power to mention, for there is no record of it. All that is known is that Croesus believed himself to have found there also an oracle which spoke the truth.

50. After this Croesus, having resolved to propitiate the Delphic god with a magnificent sacrifice, offered up three thousand of every kind of sacrificial beast, and besides made a huge pile, and placed upon it couches coated with silver and with gold, and golden goblets, and robes and vests of purple; all which he burnt in the hope of thereby making himself more secure of the favour of the god. Further he issued his orders to all the people of the land to offer a sacrifice according to their means. When the sacrifice was ended, the king melted down a vast quantity of gold, and ran it into ingots, making them six palms long, three palms broad, and one palm in thickness. The number of ingots was a hundred and seventeen, four being of refined gold, in weight two talents and a half each; the others of white gold, and in weight

two talents each. He also caused a statue of a lion to be made in refined gold, the weight of which was ten talents. At the time when the temple of Delphi was burnt to the ground [in 548 B.C.], this lion fell from the ingots on which it was placed; it now stands in the Corinthian treasury [in Delphi] and weighs only six talents and a half, having lost three talents and a half by the fire.

51. On the completion of these works Croesus sent them away to Delphi, and with them two bowls of an enormous size, one of gold, the other of silver, which used to stand, the latter upon the right, the former upon the left, as one entered the temple. They too were moved at the time of the fire; and now the golden one is in the Clazomenian treasury, and weighs eight talents and forty-two minae; the silver one stands in the corner of the ante-chapel, and holds six hundred amphorae. This is known, because the Delphians mix wine and water in it at the time of the Theophania. It is said by the Delphians to be a work of Theodore the Samian, and I think that they say true, for assuredly it is the work of no common artist. Croesus sent also four silver casks, which stand in the Corinthian treasury, and two lustral vases, a golden and a silver one. On the former is inscribed the name of the Lacedaemonians, and they claim it as a gift of theirs, but wrongly, since it was really given by Croesus. The inscription upon it was cut by a Delphian, who wished to pleasure the Lacedaemonians. His name is known to me, but I forbear to mention it. The boy through whose hand the water runs, is (I confess) a Lacedaemonian gift, but they did not give either of the lustral vases. Besides these various offerings, Croesus sent to Delphi many others of less account, among the rest a number of round silver basins. Also he dedicated a female figure in gold, three cubits high, which is said by the Delphians to be the statue of his baking woman;[7] and further, he dedicated the necklaces and the girdles of his wife.

[7] Plutarch (*On the Pythian Oracle,* 16) preserves the story that she had saved Croesus from his stepmother's plot to feed him poisoned bread.

52. These were the offerings sent by Croesus to Delphi. To the shrine of Amphiaraus, with whose valour and misfortune he was acquainted, he sent a shield entirely of gold, and a spear, also of solid gold, both head and shaft. They were still existing in my day at Thebes, laid up in the temple of Ismenian Apollo.

53. The messengers who had the charge of conveying these treasures to the shrines received instructions to ask the oracles whether Croesus should go to war with the Persians, and, if so, whether he should strengthen himself by the forces of an ally. Accordingly, when they had reached their destinations and dedicated the gifts, they proceeded to consult the oracles in the following terms: "Croesus, king of Lydia and other countries, believing that these are the only real oracles in all the world, has sent you such presents as your discoveries deserved, and now inquires of you whether he shall go to war with the Persians, and, if so, whether he shall strengthen himself by the forces of a confederate." Both the oracles agreed in the tenor of their reply, which was in each case a prophecy that if Croesus attacked the Persians he would destroy a mighty empire, and a recommendation to him to look and see who were the most powerful of the Greeks, and to make alliance with them.

54. At the receipt of these oracular replies Croesus was overjoyed, and, feeling sure now that he would destroy the empire of the Persians, he sent once more to Pytho, and presented to the Delphians, the number of whom he had ascertained, two gold staters apiece. In return for this the Delphians granted to Croesus and the Lydians the privilege of precedency in consulting the oracle, tax exemption, the most honourable seat at the festivals, and the perpetual right of becoming at pleasure citizens of their town.

55. After sending these presents to the Delphians, Croesus a third time consulted the oracle, for having once proved its truthfulness, he wished to make constant use of it. The question whereto he now desired an answer was whether his kingdom would be of long duration? The following was the reply of the Pythoness:

"Wait till the time shall come when a mule is monarch of
    Media;
Then, thou delicate Lydian, away to the pebbles of
    Hermus;
Haste, oh haste thee away, nor blush to behave like a
    coward."

56. Of all the answers that had reached him, this pleased
him far the best, for it seemed incredible that a mule should
ever come to be king of the Medes, and so he concluded that
the sovereignty would never depart from himself or his seed
after him. Afterwards he turned his thoughts to the alliance
which he had been recommended to contract, and sought to
ascertain by inquiry which was the most powerful of the
Grecian states. His inquiries pointed out to him two states as
pre-eminent above the rest. These were the Lacedaemonians and the Athenians, the former of Doric the latter of
Ionic race. . . .

59. On inquiring into the condition of these two nations,
Croesus found that one, the Athenian, was held down and
disunited under Pisistratus, the son of Hippocrates, who was
at that time tyrant of Athens. Hippocrates, when he was a
private citizen, is said to have gone once upon a time to
Olympia to see the games, when a wonderful prodigy happened to him. As he was employed in sacrificing, the cauldrons which stood near, full of water and of the flesh of the
victims, began to boil without the help of fire, so that the
water overflowed the pots. Chilon the Lacedaemonian, who
happened to be there and to witness the prodigy, advised
Hippocrates, if he were unmarried, never to take into his
house a wife who could bear him a child; if he already had
one, to send her back to her friends; if he had a son, to dis-
own him. Chilon's advice did not at all please Hippocrates,
who disregarded it, and some time after became the father of
Pisistratus. This Pisistratus, at a time when there was civil
contention in Attica between the party of the Coast headed
by Megacles the son of Alcmaeon, and that of the Plain
headed by Lycurgus, the son of Aristolaïdes, formed the

project of making himself tyrant, and with this view created a third faction. Gathering together a band of partisans, and giving himself out for the protector of the highlanders, he contrived the following stratagem. He wounded himself and his mules, and then drove his chariot into the Agora, professing to have just escaped an attack of his enemies, who had attempted his life as he was on his way into the country. He besought the people to assign him a guard to protect his person, reminding them of the glory which he had gained when he led the attack upon the Megarians, and took the town of Nisaea, at the same time performing many other exploits. The Athenians, deceived by his story, appointed him a band of citizens to serve as a guard, who were to carry clubs instead of spears, and to accompany him wherever he went. Thus strengthened, Pisistratus broke into revolt and seized the Acropolis. In this way he acquired the sovereignty of Athens, which he continued to hold without disturbing the previously existing offices or altering any of the laws. He administered the state according to the established usages, and his arrangements were wise and salutary.

60. However, after a little time, the partisans of Megacles and those of Lycurgus agreed to forget their differences, and united to drive him out. So Pisistratus, having by the means described first made himself master of Athens, lost his power again before it had time to take root. No sooner, however, was he departed than the factions which had driven him out quarrelled anew, and at last Megacles, wearied with the struggle, sent a herald to Pisistratus, with an offer to re-establish him as tyrant if he would marry his daughter. Pisistratus consented, and on these terms an agreement was concluded between the two, after which they proceeded to devise the mode of his restoration. And here the device on which they hit was the silliest that I find on record, more especially considering that the Greeks have been from very ancient times distinguished from the barbarians by superior sagacity and freedom from foolish simpleness, and remembering that the persons on whom this trick was played were not only Greeks but Athenians, who are said to sur-

pass all other Greeks in judgement. There was in the Paeanian district a woman named Phya, whose height fell short of four cubits by only three fingers' breadth, and who was altogether comely to look upon. This woman they clothed in complete armour, and, instructing her as to the carriage which she was to maintain in order to beseem her part, they placed her in a chariot and drove to the city. Heralds had been sent forward to precede her, and to make proclamation to this effect: "Citizens of Athens, receive again Pisistratus with friendly minds. Athena, who of all men honours him the most, herself conducts him back to her own citadel." This they proclaimed in all directions, and immediately the rumour spread throughout the country districts that Athena was bringing back Pisistratus. They of the city also, fully persuaded that the woman was the veritable goddess, offered prayers to her, and received Pisistratus back.

61. Pisistratus, having thus recovered the tyranny, married, according to agreement, the daughter of Megacles. As, however, he already had adolescent sons, and the Alcmaeonids were supposed to be under a curse, he determined that there should be no offspring of his new wife, and he had only unnatural intercourse with her. His wife at first kept this matter to herself, but after a time either her mother questioned her, or it may be that she told it of her own accord. At any rate, she informed her mother, who told her father. Megacles, indignant at this affront from Pisistratus, in his anger instantly made up his differences with the opposite faction, on which Pisistratus, aware of what was planning against him, took himself out of the country. Arrived at Eretria [on the island of Euboea], he held a council with his sons to decide what was to be done. The opinion of Hippias [the elder] prevailed, and it was agreed to aim at regaining the tyranny. The first step was to obtain gifts from such cities as were under obligation to them. By these means they collected large sums from several cities, especially from the Thebans, who gave them far more than any of the rest. To be brief, time passed, and all was at length got ready for their return. A band of Argive mercenaries arrived from the Pelo-

ponnesus, and a certain Naxian named Lygdamis, who volunteered his services, was particularly zealous in the cause,
supplying both men and money.

62. In the eleventh year of their exile the family of Pisistratus set sail from Eretria on their return home. They made
the coast of Attica, near Marathon, where they encamped,
and were joined by their partisans from the city and by numbers from the country districts, who loved tyranny better
than freedom. At Athens, while Pisistratus was obtaining
funds, and even after he landed at Marathon, no one paid
any attention to his proceedings. When, however, it became
known that he had left Marathon, and was marching upon
the city, preparations were made for resistance, the whole
force of the state was levied, and led against the returning
exiles. Meantime the army of Pisistratus, which had broken
up from Marathon, meeting their adversaries near the temple of the Pallenian Athena, pitched their camp opposite
them. Here a certain soothsayer, Amphilytus by name, an
Acarnanian, moved by a divine impulse, came into the
presence of Pisistratus, and approaching him uttered this
prophecy in the hexameter measure:

"Now has the cast been made, the net is out-spread in the
    water,
  Through the moonshiny night the tunnies will enter the
    meshes."

63. Such was the prophecy uttered under a divine inspira-
tion. Pisistratus, apprehending its meaning, declared that he
accepted the oracle, and instantly led on his army. The
Athenians from the city had just finished their midday meal,
after which they had betaken themselves, some to dice, others to sleep, when Pisistratus with his troops fell upon them
and put them to the rout. As soon as the flight began,
Pisistratus bethought himself of a most wise contrivance,
whereby the Athenians might be induced to disperse and
not unite in a body any more. He mounted his sons on horse-

back and sent them on in front to overtake the fugitives, and exhort them to be of good cheer, and return each man to his home.

64. The Athenians took the advice, and Pisistratus became for the third time master of Athens. Upon this he set himself to root his power more firmly, by the aid of a numerous body of mercenaries, and by keeping up a full exchequer, partly supplied from native sources, partly from the countries about the river Strymon [in Thrace]. He also demanded hostages from many of the Athenians who had stood firm and not fled at his approach; and these he sent to Naxos, which he had conquered by force of arms, and given over into the charge of Lygdamis. Further, he purified the island of Delos, according to the injunctions of an oracle, after the following fashion. All the dead bodies which had been interred within sight of the temple he dug up, and removed to another part of the isle. Thus was the tyranny of Pisistratus established at Athens, some of the Athenians having fallen in the battle, and others having fled the country together with the Alcmaeonids.

65. Such was the condition of the Athenians when Croesus made inquiry concerning them. Proceeding to seek information concerning the Lacedaemonians, he learnt that, after passing through a period of great reversals, they had been victorious in a war with the people of Tegea; for, during the joint reign of Leon and Agasicles, kings of Sparta, the Lacedaemonians, successful in all their other wars, suffered continual defeat at the hands of the Tegeans. At a still earlier period they had been the very worst governed people in Greece, as well in matters of internal management as in their relations towards foreigners, from whom they kept entirely aloof.

The circumstances which led to their being well governed were the following. Lycurgus, a man of distinction among the Spartans, had gone to Delphi to consult the oracle. Scarcely had he entered into the inner sanctuary, when the Pythoness said,

"Oh! thou great Lycurgus, that com'st to my beautiful
  dwelling,
Dear to Zeus, and to all who sit in the halls of Olympus,
Whether to hail thee a god I know not, or only a mortal,
But my hope is strong that a god thou wilt prove, Lycur-
  gus."

Some report, besides, that the Pythoness delivered to him
the entire system of laws which are still observed by the
Spartans. The Lacedaemonians, however, themselves assert
that Lycurgus, when he was guardian of his nephew,
Leobotas, king of Sparta, introduced them from Crete; for as
soon as he became regent, he altered the whole of the existing laws, substituting new ones, which he took care should
be observed by all. After this he arranged whatever apper-
tained to war, establishing the *enomotiae, triacades,* and *sys-
sitia,* besides which he instituted the council of elders and
the ephorate.

66. Such was the way in which the Lacedaemonians became a well-governed people. On the death of Lycurgus
they built him a temple, and ever since they have worshipped
him with the utmost reverence. Their soil being good and
the population numerous, they sprang up rapidly to power,
and became a flourishing people. In consequence they soon
ceased to be satisfied to stay quiet; and, regarding the Arcadians as very much their inferiors, they sent to consult the
oracle about conquering the whole of Arcadia. The Pythoness thus answered them:

"Cravest thou Arcady? Bold is thy craving. I shall not con-
  tent it.
Many the men that in Arcady dwell, whose food is the
  acorn—
They will never allow thee. It is not I that am niggard.
I will give thee to dance in Tegea, with noisy foot-fall,
And with the measuring line mete out the glorious
  champaign."

When the Lacedaemonians received this reply, leaving the rest of Arcadia untouched, they marched against the Tegeans, carrying with them fetters, so confident had this oracle (which was, in truth, but of base metal) made them that they would enslave the Tegeans. The battle, however, went against them, and many fell into the enemy's hands. Then these persons, wearing the fetters which they had themselves brought, measured out the Tegean plain as they executed their labours. The fetters in which they worked were still, in my day, preserved at Tegea where they hung round the walls of the temple of Athena Alea.

67. Throughout the whole of this early contest with the Tegeans, the Lacedaemonians met with nothing but defeats; but in the time of Croesus, under the kings Anaxandrides and Ariston, fortune had turned in their favour, in the manner which I will now relate. Having been worsted in every engagement by their enemy, they sent to Delphi, and inquired of the oracle what god they must propitiate to prevail in the war against the Tegeans. The answer of the Pythoness was that before they could prevail they must remove to Sparta the bones of Orestes, the son of Agamemnon. Unable to discover his burial place, they sent a second time, and asked the god where the body of the hero had been laid. The following was the answer they received:

"Level and smooth is the plain where Arcadian Tegea standeth;
　There two winds are ever, by strong necessity, blowing,
　Counter-stroke answers stroke, and evil lies upon evil.
　There all-teeming Earth doth harbour the son of Atrides;
　Bring thou him to thy city, and then be Tegea's master."

After this reply, the Lacedaemonians were no nearer discovering the burial place than before, though they continued to search for it diligently; until at last a man named Lichas, one of the Spartans called agathoërgi, found it. The agathoërgi are citizens who have just served their time among the knights. The five eldest of the knights go out every year, and are bound during the year after their discharge to go wherever the state sends them, and actively employ themselves in its service.

68. Lichas was one of this body when, partly by good luck, partly by his own wisdom, he discovered the burial place. Intercourse between the two states existing just at this time, he went to Tegea, and, happening to enter into the workshop of a smith, he saw him forging some iron. As he stood marvelling at what he beheld, he was observed by the smith who, leaving off his work, went up to him and said, "Certainly, then, you Spartan stranger, you would have been wonderfully surprised if you had seen what I have, since you make a marvel even of the working in iron. I wanted to make myself a well in this room, and began to dig it, when I came upon a coffin seven cubits long. I had never believed that men were taller in the olden times than they are now, so I opened the coffin. The body inside was of the same length. I measured it, and filled up the hole again."

Such was the man's account of what he had seen. The other, on turning the matter over in his mind, conjectured that this was the body of Orestes, of which the oracle had spoken. He guessed so, because he observed that the smithy had two bellows, which he understood to be the two winds, and the hammer and anvil would do for the stroke and the counter-stroke, and the iron that was being wrought for the evil lying upon evil. This he imagined might be so because iron had been discovered to the hurt of man. Full of these conjectures, he sped back to Sparta and laid the whole matter before his countrymen. Soon after, by a concerted plan, they brought a charge against him, and began a prosecution. Lichas betook himself to Tegea, and on his arrival acquainted the smith with his misfortune, and proposed to rent his room of him. The smith refused for some time; but at last Lichas persuaded him, and took up his abode in it. Then he opened the grave, and collecting the bones, returned with them to Sparta. From henceforth, whenever the Spartans and the Tegeans made trial of each other's skill in arms, the Spartans always had greatly the advantage; and by the time to which we are now come they were masters of most of the Peloponnesus.

69. Croesus, informed of all these circumstances, sent messengers to Sparta, with gifts in their hands, who were to ask the Spartans to enter into alliance with him. They received strict injunctions as to what they should say, and on their arrival at Sparta spoke as follows:

"Croesus, king of the Lydians and of other nations, has sent us to speak thus to you: 'O Lacedaemonians, the god has bidden me to make the Greek my friend; I therefore apply to you, in conformity with the oracle, knowing that you hold the first rank in Greece, and desire to become your friend and ally in all true faith and honesty.' "

Such was the message which Croesus sent by his heralds. The Lacedaemonians, who were aware beforehand of the reply given him by the oracle, were full of joy at the coming of the messengers, and at once took the oaths of friendship and alliance: this they did the more readily as they had previously contracted certain obligations towards him. They had sent to Sardis on one occasion to purchase some gold, intending to use it on a statue of Apollo—the statue, namely, which remains to this day at Thornax in Laconia, when Croesus, hearing of the matter, gave them as a gift the gold which they wanted.

70. This was one reason why the Lacedaemonians were so willing to make the alliance; another was that Croesus had chosen them for his friends in preference to all the other Greeks. They therefore held themselves in readiness to come at his summons, and they further had a huge vase made in bronze, covered with figures all round the outside of the rim, and large enough to contain three hundred amphorae, which they sent to Croesus as a return for his presents to them. The vase, however, never reached Sardis. Its miscarriage is accounted for in two quite different ways. The Lacedaemonian story is that when it reached Samos, on its way towards Sardis, the Samians, having knowledge of it, put to sea in their ships of war and made it their prize. But the Samians declare that the Lacedaemonians who had the

vase in charge, happening to arrive too late, and learning that Sardis had fallen [to the Persians] and that Croesus was a prisoner, sold it in their island, and the purchasers (who were, they say, private persons) made an offering of it at the shrine of Hera; the sellers were very likely on their return to Sparta to have said that they had been robbed of it by the Samians. Such, then, was the fate of the vase.

71. Meanwhile Croesus, taking the oracle in a wrong sense, led his forces into Cappadocia, fully expecting to defeat Cyrus and the Persian power. While he was still engaged in making preparations for his attack, a Lydian named Sandanis, who had always been looked upon as a wise man, but who after this obtained a very great name indeed among his countrymen, came forward and counselled the king in these words:

"You are about, O King, to make war against men who wear leather trousers, and have all their other garments of leather; who feed not on what they like, but on what they can get from a rocky soil; who do not indulge in wine, but drink water; who possess no figs nor anything else that is good to eat. If, then, you conquer them, what can you get from them, seeing that they have nothing at all? But if they conquer you, consider how much that is precious you will lose; if they once get a taste of our pleasant things, they will keep such hold on them that we shall never be able to make them loose their grasp. For my part, I am thankful to the gods that they have not put it into the hearts of the Persians to invade Lydia."

Croesus was not persuaded by this speech, though it was true enough; for before the conquest of Lydia the Persians possessed none of the luxuries or delights of life.

From BOOK II

The Antiquity of Egypt

· · · · · ·

2. Now the Egyptians, before the reign of their king Psammetichus, believed themselves to be the most ancient of mankind. Since Psammetichus, however, made an attempt to discover who were actually the primitive race, they have been of opinion that while they surpass all other nations, the Phrygians surpass them in antiquity. This king, finding it impossible to make out by dint of inquiry what men were the most ancient, contrived the following method of discovery: He took two newly born children, selected at random, and gave them over to a herdsman to bring up at his folds, strictly charging him to let no one utter a word in their presence, but to keep them in a sequestered cottage, and from time to time introduce goats to their apartment, see that they got their fill of milk, and in all other respects look after them. His object herein was to know, after the indistinct babblings of infancy were over, what word they would first articulate. It happened as he had anticipated. The herdsman obeyed his orders for two years, and at the end of that time, on his one day opening the door of their room and going in, the children both ran up to him with outstretched arms, and distinctly said, "Becos." When this first happened the herdsman took no notice; but afterwards when he observed, on coming often to see after them, that the word was constantly in their mouths, he informed his lord, and by his command brought the children into his presence. Psammetichus then himself heard them say the word, upon which he proceeded to make inquiry what people there was who called anything "becos," and hereupon he learnt that "becos" was

the Phrygian name for bread. In consideration of this circumstance the Egyptians yielded their claims, and admitted the greater antiquity of the Phrygians. That these were the real facts I learnt at Memphis from the priests of Hephaestus. The Greeks, among other foolish tales, relate that Psammetichus had the children brought up by women whose tongues he had previously cut out.

3. But the priests said their bringing up was such as I have stated above. I got much other information also from conversation with these priests while I was at Memphis, and I even went to Heliopolis and to Thebes, expressly to try whether the priests of those places would agree in their accounts with the priests at Memphis. The Heliopolitans have the reputation of being the wisest of all the Egyptians. What they told me concerning their religion it is not my intention to repeat, except the names of their deities, which I believe all men know equally. If I relate anything else concerning these matters, it will only be when compelled to do so by the course of my narrative.

4. Now with regard to mere human matters, the accounts which they gave, and in which all agreed, were the following. The Egyptians, they said, were the first to discover the solar year, and to portion out its course into twelve parts. They obtained this knowledge from the stars. (To my mind they contrive their year much more cleverly than the Greeks, for these last every other year intercalate a whole month, on account of the seasons, but the Egyptians, dividing the year into twelve months of thirty days each, add every year a space of five days besides, whereby the circuit of the seasons is made to return with uniformity.) The Egyptians, they went on to affirm, first brought into use the names of the twelve gods, which the Greeks adopted from them; and first erected altars, images, and temples to the gods; and also first engraved upon stone the figures of animals. In most of these cases they proved to me that what they said was true. And they told me that the first man who ruled over Egypt was Min, and that in his time all Egypt, except the Thebaic nome, was a marsh, none of the land below Lake Moeris

then showing itself above the surface of the water. This is a distance of seven days' sail from the sea up the river.

5. What they said of their country seemed to me very reasonable. For anyone who sees Egypt without having heard a word about it before must perceive, if he has only common powers of observation, that the Egypt to which the Greeks go in their ships is an acquired country, the gift of the river. . . .

The Nile Flood

19. Now the Nile, when it overflows, floods not only the Delta, but also areas of the countries on both sides, called Libya and Arabia, up to two days' journey from its banks, sometimes more, sometimes less.

Concerning the nature of the river, I was not able to gain any information either from the priests or from others. I was particularly anxious to learn from them why the Nile, at the commencement of the summer solstice, begins to rise, and continues to increase for a hundred days—and why, as soon as that number is past, it forthwith retires and contracts its stream, continuing low during the whole of the winter until the summer solstice comes round again. On none of these points could I obtain any explanation from the inhabitants, though I made every inquiry, wishing to know what was commonly reported—they could neither tell me what special virtue the Nile has which makes it so opposite in its nature to all other streams, nor why, unlike every other river, it gives forth no breezes from its surface.

20. Some of the Greeks, however, wishing to get a reputation for cleverness, have offered explanations of the phenomena of the river, for which they have accounted in three different ways. Two of these I do not think it worth while to speak of, further than simply to mention what they are. One pretends that the Etesian winds cause the rise of the river by preventing the Nile water from running off into the sea. But in the first place it has often happened, when the Etesian winds did not blow, that the Nile has risen ac-

cording to its usual wont; and further, if the Etesian winds produced the effect, the other rivers which flow in a direction opposite to those winds ought to present the same phenomena as the Nile, and the more so as they are all smaller streams, and have a weaker current. But these rivers, of which there are many both in Syria and Libya, are entirely unlike the Nile in this respect.

21. The second opinion is even more unscientific than the one just mentioned, and also, if I may so say, more marvellous. It is that the Nile acts so strangely because it flows from the ocean, and that the ocean flows all round the earth.

22. The third explanation, which is very much more plausible than either of the others, is positively the furthest from the truth; for there is really nothing in what it says either. It is that the inundation of the Nile is caused by the melting of snows. Now, as the Nile flows out of Libya, though Ethiopia, into Egypt, how is it possible that it can be formed of melted snow, running, as it does, from the hottest regions of the world into cooler countries? Many are the proofs whereby anyone capable of reasoning on the subject may be convinced that it is most unlikely this should be the case. The first and strongest argument is furnished by the winds, which always blow hot from these regions. The second is, that rain and frost are unknown there. Now whenever snow falls, it must of necessity rain within five days; so that, if there were snow, there must be rain also in those parts. Thirdly, it is certain that the natives of the country are black with the heat, that the kites and the swallows remain there the whole year, and that the cranes, when they fly from the rigours of a Scythian winter, flock thither to pass the cold season. If, then, in the country whence the Nile has its source, or in that through which it flows, there fell ever so little snow, it is absolutely impossible that any of these circumstances could take place.

23. As for the writer [Hecataeus] who attributes the phenomenon to the ocean, his account is involved in such obscurity that it is impossible to disprove it by argument. For my part I know of no river called Ocean, and I think

that Homer, or one of the earlier poets, invented the name, and introduced it into his poetry.

24. Perhaps, after censuring all the opinions that have been put forward on this obscure subject, one ought to propose some theory of one's own. I will therefore proceed to explain what I think to be the reason of the Nile's swelling in the summer time. During the winter, the sun is driven out of his usual course by the storms, and removes to the upper parts of Libya. This is the whole secret in the fewest possible words; for it stands to reason that the country to which the sun god approaches the nearest, and which he passes most directly over, will be scantest of water, and that there the streams which feed the rivers will shrink the most.

25. To explain, however, more at length, the case is this. The sun, in his passage across the upper parts of Libya, affects them in the following way. As the air in those regions is constantly clear, and the country warm through the absence of cold winds, the sun in his passage across them acts upon them exactly as he is wont to act elsewhere in summer, when his path is in the middle of heaven—that is, he attracts the water. After attracting it, he again repels it into the upper regions, where the winds lay hold of it, scatter it, and reduce it to a vapour, whence it naturally enough comes to pass that the winds which blow from this quarter—the south and southwest—are of all winds the most rainy. And my own opinion is that the sun does not get rid of all the water which he draws year by year from the Nile, but retains some about him. When the winter begins to soften, the sun goes back again to his old place in the middle of the heaven, and proceeds to attract water equally from all countries. Till then the other rivers run big, from the quantity of rain-water which they bring down from countries where so much moisture falls that all the land is cut into gullies; but in summer, when the showers fail, and the sun attracts their water, they become low. The Nile, on the contrary, not deriving any of its bulk from rains, and being in winter subject to the attraction of the sun, naturally runs at that season, unlike all other streams, with a less burden of water than in the sum-

mer time. For in summer it is exposed to attraction equally with all other rivers, but in winter it suffers alone. The sun, therefore, I regard as the sole cause of the phenomenon.

26. It is the sun also, in my opinion, which, by heating the space through which it passes, makes the air in Egypt so dry. There is thus perpetual summer in the upper parts of Libya. Were the position of the heavenly regions reversed, so that the place where now the north wind and the winter have their dwelling became the station of the south wind and of the noonday, while, on the other hand, the station of the south wind became that of the north, the consequence would be that the sun, driven from the mid-heaven by the winter and the northern gales, would betake himself to the upper parts of Europe, as he now does to those of Libya, and then I believe his passage across Europe would affect the Danube exactly as the Nile is affected at the present day.

27. And with respect to the fact that no breeze blows from the Nile, I am of opinion that no wind is likely to arise in very hot countries, for breezes love to blow from some cold quarter.

28. Let us leave these things, however, to their natural course, to continue as they are and have been from the beginning. . . .

Manners and Customs

35. Concerning Egypt itself I shall extend my remarks to a great length, because there is no country that possesses so many wonders, nor any that has such a number of works which defy description. Not only is the climate different from that of the rest of the world, and the river unlike any other rivers, but the people also, in most of their manners and customs, exactly reverse the common practice of mankind. The women attend the markets and trade, while the men sit at home at the loom; and here, while the rest of the world works the woof up the warp, the Egyptians work it down; the women likewise carry burdens upon their shoulders, while the men carry them upon their heads. The women urinate

standing, the men crouching. They eat their food out of doors, but retire for private purposes to their houses, giving as a reason that what is unseemly, but necessary, ought to be done in secret, but what has nothing unseemly about it, should be done openly. A woman cannot serve the priestly office, either for god or goddess, but men are priests to both. Sons need not support their parents unless they choose, but daughters must, whether they choose or no.

36. In other countries the priests have long hair, in Egypt their heads are shaven; elsewhere it is customary, in mourning, for near relations to cut their hair close: the Egyptians, who wear no hair at any other time, when they lose a relative, let their beards and the hair of their heads grow long. All other men pass their lives separate from animals, the Egyptians have animals living with them; others make barley and wheat their food; it is a disgrace to do so in Egypt, where the grain they live on is spelt, which some call *zea*. Dough they knead with their feet; but they mix mud, and even take up dirt, with their hands. They are the only people in the world—they at least, and such as have learnt the practice from them—who do not leave their genitals in their natural state but practise circumcision. Their men wear two garments apiece, their women but one. They put on the rings and fasten the ropes to sails inside; others put them outside. When they write or calculate, instead of going, like the Greeks, from left to right, they move their hand from right to left; and they insist, notwithstanding, that it is they who go to the right, and the Greeks who go to the left. They have two quite different kinds of writing, one of which is called sacred [hieroglyphics], the other common [demotic].

37. They are religious far beyond any other race of men, and observe the following rules: They drink out of brazen cups, which they scour every day; there is no exception to this practice. They wear linen garments, which they are specially careful to have always fresh washed. They practise circumcision for the sake of cleanliness, considering it better to be cleanly than comely.

The priests shave their whole body every other day, that

no lice or other impure thing may adhere to them when they are engaged in the service of the gods. Their dress is entirely of linen, and their shoes of the papyrus plant: it is not lawful for them to wear either dress or shoes of any other material. They bathe twice every day in cold water, and twice each night; besides which they observe, so to speak, thousands of ceremonies. They enjoy, however, not a few advantages. They consume none of their own property, and are at no expense for anything; but every day bread is baked for them of the sacred grain, and a plentiful supply of beef and of goose's flesh is assigned to each, and also a portion of wine made from the grape. Fish they are not allowed to eat, and beans—which none of the Egyptians ever sow, or eat, if they come up of their own accord, either raw or boiled—the priests will not even endure to look on, since they consider it an unclean kind of pulse. Instead of a single priest, each god has the attendance of a college, at the head of which is a chief priest; when one of these dies, his son is appointed in his stead.

38. Male kine are reckoned to belong to Epaphus, and are therefore tested in the following manner: One of the priests appointed for the purpose searches to see if there is a single black hair on the whole body, since in that case the beast is unclean. He examines him all over, standing on his legs, and again laid upon his back; after which he takes the tongue out of his mouth, to see if it be clean in respect of the prescribed marks (what they are I will mention elsewhere); he also inspects the hairs of the tail, to observe if they grow naturally. If the animal is pronounced clean in all these various points, the priest marks him by twisting a piece of papyrus round his horns, and attaching thereto some sealing-clay, which he then stamps with his own signet ring. After this the beast is led away; and it is forbidden, under the penalty of death, to sacrifice an animal which has not been marked in this way. . . .

Origins of the Greek Gods

43. The account which I received of this Hercules makes him one of the twelve gods. Of the other Hercules, with whom the Greeks are familiar, I could hear nothing in any part of Egypt. That the Greeks, however (those I mean who gave the son of Amphitryon that name), took the figure from the Egyptians, and not the Egyptians from the Greeks, is I think clearly proved, among other arguments, by the fact that both the parents of Hercules, Amphitryon as well as Alcmene, were of Egyptian origin. Again, the Egyptians disclaim all knowledge of Poseidon and the Dioscuri, and do not include them in the number of their gods; but had they adopted any god from the Greeks, these would have been the likeliest to obtain notice, since the Egyptians, as I am well convinced, practised navigation at that time, and the Greeks also were some of them mariners, so that they would have been more likely to know these gods than Hercules. But the Egyptian Hercules is one of their ancient gods. Seventeen thousand years before the reign of Amasis, the twelve gods were, they affirm, produced from the eight, and of these twelve, Hercules is one.

44. In the wish to get the best information that I could on these matters, I made a voyage to Tyre in Phoenicia, hearing there was a temple of Hercules at that place, very highly venerated. I visited the temple, and found it richly adorned with a number of offerings, among which were two pillars, one of pure gold, the other of emerald, shining with great brilliancy at night. In a conversation which I held with the priests I inquired how long their temple had been built, and found by their answer that they, too, differed from the Greeks. They said that the temple was built at the same time that the city was founded, and that the foundation of the city took place two thousand three hundred years ago. In Tyre I remarked another temple where the same god was worshipped as the Thasian Hercules. So I went on to Thasos, where I found a temple of Hercules which had been built by

the Phoenicians who colonized that island when they sailed in search of Europa. Even this was five generations earlier than the time when Hercules, son of Amphitryon, was born in Greece. These researches show plainly that there is an ancient god Hercules; and my own opinion is that those Greeks act most wisely who build and maintain two temples of Hercules, in the one of which the Hercules worshipped is known by the name of Olympian, and has sacrifice offered to him as an immortal, while in the other the honours paid are such as are due to a hero.

45. The Greeks tell many tales without due investigation, and among them the following silly fable respecting Hercules: "Hercules," they say, "went once to Egypt, and there the inhabitants took him, and, putting a chaplet on his head, led him out in solemn procession, intending to offer him a sacrifice to Zeus. For a while he submitted quietly; but when they led him up to the altar and began the ceremonies, he put forth his strength and slew them all." Now to me it seems that such a story proves the Greeks to be utterly ignorant of the character and customs of the people. The Egyptians do not think it allowable even to sacrifice cattle, excepting pigs, and the male kine and calves, provided they be pure, and also geese. How, then, can it be believed that they would sacrifice men? And again, how would it have been possible for Hercules alone, and, as they confess, a mere mortal, to destroy so many thousands? In saying thus much concerning these matters, may I incur no displeasure either of god or hero. . . .

48. To Dionysus, on the eve of his feast, every Egyptian sacrifices a hog before the door of his house, which is then given back to the swineherd by whom it was furnished, and by him carried away. In other respects the festival is celebrated almost exactly as Dionysiac festivals are in Greece, excepting that the Egyptians have no choral dances. They also use instead of phalli another invention, consisting of puppets about a cubit high, pulled by strings, with a phallus (not much smaller than the rest of the body) which moves. These the women carry round among the villages; a

flutist goes in front, and the women follow, singing hymns in honour of Dionysus. As to why these images have a disproportionately large phallus and why that part of the body alone moves, a sacred legend is told about it.

49. Melampus, the son of Amytheon, cannot (I think) have been ignorant of this ceremony—nay, he must, I should conceive, have been well acquainted with it. He it was who introduced into Greece the figure of Dionysus, the ceremonial of his worship, and the procession of the phallus. He did not, however, so completely apprehend the whole doctrine as to be able to communicate it entirely, but various sages since his time have carried out his teaching to greater perfection. Still it is certain that Melampus introduced the procession of the phallus, and that the Greeks learnt from him the ceremonies which they now practise. I therefore maintain that Melampus, who was a wise man, and had acquired the art of divination, having become acquainted with the worship of Dionysus through knowledge derived from Egypt, introduced it into Greece, with a few slight changes, at the same time that he brought in various other practices. For I can by no means allow that it is by mere coincidence that the Dionysiac ceremonies in Greece are so nearly the same as the Egyptian—they would then have been more Greek in their character, and less recent in their origin. Much less can I admit that the Egyptians borrowed these customs, or any other, from the Greeks. My belief is that Melampus got his knowledge of them from Cadmus the Tyrian, and the followers whom he brought from Phoenicia into the country which is now called Boeotia.

50. Almost all the divine figures came into Greece from Egypt. My inquiries prove that they were all derived from the barbarians, and my opinion is that Egypt furnished the greater number. For with the exception of Poseidon and the Dioscuri, whom I mentioned above, and Hera, Hestia, Themis, the Graces, and the Nereids, the other gods have been known from time immemorial in Egypt. This I assert on the authority of the Egyptians themselves. The gods with whom they profess themselves unacquainted, the Greeks re-

ceived, I believe, from the Pelasgi, except Poseidon. Of him they got their knowledge from the Libyans, by whom he has been always honoured, and who were anciently the only people that had such a god. The Egyptians differ from the Greeks also in paying no divine honours to heroes. . . .

53. Whence the gods severally sprang, whether or no they had all existed from eternity, what forms they bore—these are questions of which the Greeks knew nothing until the other day, so to speak. For Homer and Hesiod were the first to compose Theogonies, and give the gods their epithets, to allot them their several offices and occupations, and describe their forms; and they lived but four hundred years before my time, as I believe. As for the poets who are thought by some to be earlier than these, they are, in my judgement, decidedly later writers. In these matters I have the authority of the priestesses of Dodona [in Epirus] for the former portion of my statements; what I have said of Homer and Hesiod is my own opinion. . . .

The Truth about the Trojan War

113. The [Egyptian] priests, in answer to my inquiries on the subject of Helen, informed me of the following particulars. When Alexander [Paris] had carried off Helen from Sparta, he took ship and sailed homewards. On his way across the Aegean a gale arose, which drove him from his course and took him down to the sea of Egypt; hence, as the wind did not abate, he was carried on to the coast, when he went ashore, landing at the Salt Pans, in that mouth of the Nile which is now called the Canobic. At this place there stood upon the shore a temple, which still exists, dedicated to Hercules. If a slave runs away from his master, and taking sanctuary at this shrine gives himself up to the god, and receives certain sacred marks upon his person, whosoever his master may be, he cannot lay hand on him. This law still remained unchanged to my time. Hearing, therefore, of the custom of the place, the attendants of Alexander deserted him, and fled to the temple, where they sat as suppliants. While there,

wishing to damage their master, they accused him to the Egyptians, narrating all the circumstances of the rape of Helen and the wrong done to Menelaus. These charges they brought not only before the priests, but also before the warden of that mouth of the river, whose name was Thonis.

114. As soon as he received the intelligence, Thonis sent a message to Proteus, who was at Memphis, to this effect: "A stranger is arrived, by race a Teucrian, and has done a wicked deed in Greece. Having seduced the wife of the man whose guest he was, he carried her away with him, and much treasure also. Compelled by stress of weather, he has now put in here. Are we to let him depart as he came, or shall we seize what he has brought?" Proteus sent a man with this reply: "Seize the man, be he who he may, that has dealt thus wickedly with his host, and bring him before me, that I may hear what he will say for himself."

115. Thonis, on receiving these orders, seized Alexander, and stopped the departure of his ships; then, taking with him Alexander, Helen, the treasures, and also the suppliant slaves, he went up to Memphis. When all were arrived, Proteus asked Alexander who he was, and whence he had come. Alexander replied by giving his descent, the name of his country, and a true account of his late voyage. Then Proteus questioned him as to where he got possession of Helen. In his reply Alexander became confused, and diverged from the truth, whereon the slaves interposed, confuted his statements, and told the whole history of the crime. Finally, Proteus delivered judgement as follows: "Did I not regard it as a matter of the utmost consequence that no stranger driven to my country by adverse winds should ever be put to death, I would certainly have avenged the Greek by slaying you. Basest of men—after accepting hospitality, to do so wicked a deed! First, you seduced the wife of your own host—then, not content therewith, you must violently excite her mind, and steal her away from her husband. Nay, even so you were not satisfied, but on leaving, you must plunder the house in which you had been a guest. Now then, as I think it of the greatest importance to put no stranger to death,

I suffer you to depart; but the woman and the treasures I shall not permit to be carried away. Here they must stay, till your Greek host comes in person and takes them back with him. For yourself and your companions, I command you to begone from my land within the space of three days—and I warn you that otherwise at the end of that time you will be treated as enemies."

116. Such was the tale told me by the priests concerning the arrival of Helen at the court of Proteus. It seems to me that Homer was acquainted with this story, and, while discarding it, because he thought it less adapted for epic poetry than the version which he followed, showed that it was not unknown to him. This is evident from the travels which he assigns to Alexander in the *Iliad*—and let it be borne in mind that he has nowhere else contradicted himself—making him be carried out of his course on his return with Helen, and after divers wanderings come at last to Sidon in Phoenicia. The passage is in the Bravery of Diomedes,[1] and the words are as follows:

> "There were the robes, many-coloured, the work of
> Sidonian women:
> They from Sidon had come, what time god-shaped Alexander
> Over the broad sea brought, that way, the high-born
> Helen."

In the *Odyssey* also the same fact is alluded to, in these words: [2]

> "Such, so wisely prepared, were the drugs that her stores
> afforded,
> Excellent; gift which once Polydamna, partner of
> Thonis,
> Gave her in Egypt, where many the simples that grow in
> the meadows,
> Potent to cure in part, in part as potent to injure."

[1] *Iliad,* VI, 290-92.
[2] *Odyssey,* IV, 227-30.

Menelaus too, in the same poem, thus addresses Tele-machus:[3]

"Much did I long to return, but the Gods still kept me in
  Egypt—
  Angry because I had failed to pay them their hecatombs
  duly."

In these places Homer shows himself acquainted with the voyage of Alexander to Egypt, for Syria borders on Egypt, and the Phoenicians, to whom Sidon belongs, dwell in Syria.

117. From these various passages, and from that about Sidon especially, it is clear that Homer did not write the *Cypria*.[4] For there it is said that Alexander arrived at Ilion with Helen on the third day after he left Sparta, the wind having been favourable, and the sea smooth; whereas in the *Iliad,* the poet makes him wander before he brings her home. Enough, however, for the present of Homer and the *Cypria*.

118. I made inquiry of the priests, whether the story which the Greeks tell about Ilion is a fable or no. In reply they related the following particulars, of which they declared that Menelaus had himself informed them. After the rape of Helen, a vast army of Greeks, wishing to render help to Menelaus, set sail for the Teucrian territory; on their arrival they disembarked, and formed their camp, after which they sent ambassadors to Ilion, of whom Menelaus was one. The embassy was received within the walls, and demanded the restoration of Helen with the treasures which Alexander had carried off, and likewise required satisfaction for the wrong done. The Teucrians gave at once the answer in which they persisted ever afterwards, backing their assertions some-times even with oaths, to wit, that neither Helen nor the treasures claimed were in their possession; both the one and the other had remained, they said, in Egypt; and it was not just to come upon them for what Proteus, king of Egypt, was detaining. The Greeks, imagining that the Teucrians were merely laughing at them, laid siege to the town, and never

[3] *Ibid.*, IV, 351-52.
[4] A lost poem in the cycle of Trojan epics.

rested until they finally took it. As, however, no Helen was found, and they were still told the same story, they at length believed in its truth, and despatched Menelaus to the court of Proteus.

119. So Menelaus travelled to Egypt, and on his arrival sailed up the river as far as Memphis, and related all that had happened. He was given rich gifts of hospitality, received Helen back unharmed, and recovered all his treasures. After this friendly treatment Menelaus, they said, behaved most unjustly towards the Egyptians; for as it happened that at the time when he wanted to take his departure, he was detained by the wind being contrary, and as he found this obstruction continue, he had recourse to a most impious expedient. He seized two children of the people of the country, and offered them up in sacrifice. When this became known, the indignation of the people was stirred, and they went in pursuit of Menelaus, who, however, escaped with his ships to Libya, after which the Egyptians could not say whither he went. The rest they knew full well, partly by the inquiries which they had made, and partly from the circumstances having taken place in their own land, and therefore not admitting of doubt.

120. Such is the account given by the Egyptian priests, and I am myself inclined to regard as true all that they say of Helen from the following considerations: If Helen had been at Ilion, the inhabitants would, I think, have given her up to the Greeks, whether Alexander consented to it or no. For surely neither Priam nor his family could have been so infatuated as to endanger their own persons, their children, and their city, merely that Alexander might possess Helen. At any rate, if they determined to refuse at first, yet afterwards when so many of the Trojans fell on every encounter with the Greeks, and Priam too in each battle lost a son, or sometimes two, or three, or even more, if we may credit the epic poets, I believe that even if Priam himself had been living with her he would have delivered her up to the Achaeans, with the view of bringing the series of calamities to a close. Nor was it as if Alexander had been heir to the crown, in

which case he might have had the chief management of affairs, since Priam was already old. Hector, who was his elder brother, and a far braver man, stood before him, and was the heir to the kingdom on the death of their father Priam. And it could not be Hector's interest to uphold his brother in his wrong, when it brought such dire calamities upon himself and the other Trojans. But the fact was that they had no Helen to deliver, and so they told the Greeks, but the Greeks would not believe what they said—Divine Providence, as I think, so willing, that by their utter destruction it might be made evident to all men that when great wrongs are done, the gods will surely visit them with great punishments. Such, at least, is my view of the matter. . . .

The Building of the Pyramids

124. Till the death of Rhampsinitus, the priests said, Egypt was excellently governed, and flourished greatly; but after him Cheops succeeded to the throne, and plunged into all manner of wickedness. He closed the temples, and forbade the Egyptians to offer sacrifice, compelling them instead to labour, one and all, in his service. Some were required to drag blocks of stone down to the Nile from the quarries in the Arabian range of hills; others received the blocks after they had been conveyed in boats across the river, and drew them to the range of hills called the Libyan. A hundred thousand men laboured constantly, and were relieved every three months by a fresh lot. It took ten years' oppression of the people to make the causeway for the conveyance of the stones, a work not much inferior, in my judgement, to the pyramid itself. This causeway is five furlongs in length, ten fathoms wide, and in height, at the highest part, eight fathoms. It is built of polished stone, and is covered with carvings of animals. To make it took ten years, as I said—or rather to make the causeway, the works on the mound where the pyramid stands, and the underground chambers, which Cheops intended as vaults for his own sepulchre: these last were built on a sort of island, surrounded

by water introduced from the Nile by a canal. The pyramid itself was twenty years in building. It is a square, eight hundred feet each way, and the height the same, built entirely of polished stones, perfectly joined; no stone is less than thirty feet in length.

125. The pyramid was built in steps, battlement-wise, as it is called, or, according to others, altar-wise. After laying the stones for the base, they raised the remaining stones to their places by means of machines formed of short wooden planks. The first machine raised them from the ground to the top of the first step. On this there was another machine, which received the stone upon its arrival, and conveyed it to the second step, whence a third machine advanced it still higher. Either they had as many machines as there were steps in the pyramid, or possibly they had but a single machine, which, being easily moved, was transferred from tier to tier as the stone rose—both accounts are given, and therefore I mention both. The upper portion of the pyramid was finished first, then the middle, and finally the part which was lowest and nearest the ground. There is an inscription in Egyptian characters on the pyramid which records the quantity of radishes, onions, and garlic consumed by the labourers who constructed it; and I perfectly well remember that the interpreter who read the writing to me said that the money expended in this way was sixteen hundred talents of silver. If this then is a true record, what a vast sum must have been spent on the iron tools used in the work, and on the feeding and clothing of the labourers, considering the length of time the work lasted, which has already been stated, and the additional time—no small space, I imagine—which must have been occupied by the quarrying of the stones, their conveyance, and the cutting of the underground canal.

126. The wickedness of Cheops reached to such a pitch that, lacking funds, he placed his own daughter in a brothel, with orders to procure him a certain sum—how much I cannot say, for I was not told; she procured it, however, and at the same time, bent on leaving a monument which should perpetuate her own memory, she required each man to

make her a present of a stone. With these stones she built the pyramid which stands midmost of the three that are in front of the great pyramid, measuring along each side a hundred and fifty feet.

127. Cheops reigned, the Egyptians said, fifty years, and was succeeded at his demise by Chephren, his brother.

Chephren imitated the conduct of his predecessor, and, like him, built a pyramid, which did not, however, equal the dimensions of his brother's. Of this I am certain, for I measured them both myself. It has no subterraneous apartments, nor any canal from the Nile to supply it with water, as the other pyramid has. In that, the Nile water, introduced through an artificial duct, surrounds an island, where the body of Cheops is said to lie. Chephren built his pyramid close to the great pyramid of Cheops, but he lowered the height forty feet. For the foundation he employed the many-coloured stone of Ethiopia. These two pyramids stand both on the same hill, an elevation not far short of a hundred feet in height. The reign of Chephren lasted fifty-six years, they said.

128. Thus the affliction of Egypt endured for the space of one hundred and six years, during the whole of which time the temples were shut up and never opened. The Egyptians so detest the memory of these kings that they do not much like even to mention their names. Hence they commonly call the pyramids after Philitis, a shepherd who at that time fed his flocks about the place.

From BOOK VII

The Persian War after Marathon

1. Now when tidings of the battle that had been fought at Marathon [490 B.C.] reached the ears of King Darius, the son of Hystaspes, his anger against the Athenians, which had been already roused by their attack upon Sardis, waxed still fiercer, and he became more than ever eager to lead an army against Greece. Instantly he sent off messengers to

make proclamation through the several states that fresh levies were to be raised, and these at an increased rate, while ships, horses, provisions, and transports were likewise to be furnished. So the men published his commands; and now all Asia was in commotion by the space of three years, while everywhere, as Greece was to be attacked, the best and bravest were enrolled for the service, and had to make their preparations accordingly.

After this, in the fourth year, the Egyptians whom Cambyses had enslaved revolted from the Persians; whereupon Darius was more hot for war than ever, and earnestly desired to march an army against both adversaries.

2. Now, as he was about to lead forth his levies against Egypt and Athens, a fierce contention for the sovereign power arose among his sons, since the law of the Persians was that a king must not go out with his army until he has appointed one to succeed him upon the throne. Darius, before he obtained the kingdom, had had three sons born to him from his former wife, who was a daughter of Gobryas; while, since he began to reign, Atossa, the daughter of Cyrus, had borne him four. Artabazanes was the eldest of the first family, and Xerxes of the second. These two, therefore, being the sons of different mothers, were now at variance. Artabazanes claimed the crown as the eldest of all the children, because it was an established custom all over the world for the eldest to have the rule; while Xerxes, on the other hand, urged that he was sprung from Atossa, the daughter of Cyrus, and that it was Cyrus who had won the Persians their freedom.

3. Before Darius had pronounced on the matter, it happened that Demaratus, the son of Ariston, who had been deprived of his crown at Sparta, and had afterwards, of his own accord, gone into banishment, came up to Susa, and there heard of the quarrel of the princes. Hereupon, as report says, he went to Xerxes, and advised him, in addition to all that he had urged before, to plead that at the time when he was born Darius was already king, and bore rule over the Persians; but when Artabazanes came into the world, he

was a mere private person. It would therefore be neither right nor seemly that the crown should go to another in preference to himself. "For at Sparta," said Demaratus, by way of suggestion, "the law is that if a king has sons before he comes to the throne, and another son is born to him afterwards, the child so born is heir to his father's kingdom." Xerxes followed this counsel, and Darius, persuaded that he had justice on his side, appointed him his successor. For my own part I believe that, even without this, the crown would have gone to Xerxes, for Atossa was all-powerful.

4. Darius, when he had thus appointed Xerxes his heir, was minded to lead forth his armies; but he was prevented by death while his preparations were still proceeding. He died in the year following the revolt of Egypt and the matters here related [486 B.C.], after having reigned in all six-and-thirty years, leaving the revolted Egyptians and the Athenians alike unpunished. At his death the kingdom passed to his son Xerxes.

5. Now Xerxes, on first mounting the throne, was coldly disposed towards the Grecian war, and made it his business to collect an army against Egypt. But Mardonius, the son of Gobryas, who was at the court, and had more influence with him than any of the other Persians, being his own cousin, the child of a sister of Darius, plied him with discourses like the following:

"Master, it is not fitting that they of Athens escape scot-free, after doing the Persians such great injury. Complete the work which you now have in hand, and then, when the pride of Egypt is brought low, lead an army against Athens. So shall you yourself have good report among men, and others shall fear hereafter to attack your country."

Thus far it was of vengeance that he spoke; but sometimes he would vary the theme, and observe by the way, that Europe was a wondrous beautiful region, rich in all kinds of cultivated trees, and the soil excellent; that no one, save the king, was worthy to own such a land.

6. All this he said because he longed for adventures, and hoped to become satrap of Greece under the king; and after

a while he had his way, and persuaded Xerxes to do according to his desires. Other things, however, occurring about
the same time, helped his persuasions. For, in the first place,
it chanced that messengers arrived from Thessaly, sent by
the Aleuadae, Thessalian kings, to invite Xerxes into
Greece, and to promise him all the assistance which it was
in their power to give. And further, the Pisistratidae, who
had come up to Susa, held the same language as the Aleuadae, and worked upon him even more than they, by means
of Onomacritus of Athens, an oracle-monger, and the same
who set forth the prophecies of Musaeus in their order. The
Pisistratidae had previously been at enmity with this man,
but made up the quarrel before they removed to Susa. He
was banished from Athens by Hipparchus, the son of Pisistratus, because he foisted into the writings of Musaeus a prophecy that the islands which lie off Lemnos would one day disappear in the sea. Lasus of Hermione caught him in the act
of so doing. For this cause Hipparchus banished him, though
till then they had been the closest of friends. Now, however,
he went up to Susa with the Pisistratidae, and they talked
very grandly of him to the king; while he, for his part, whenever he was in the king's company, repeated to him certain
of the oracles; and while he took care to pass over all that
spoke of disaster to the barbarians, brought forward the passages which promised them the greatest success. " 'Twas
fated," he told Xerxes, "that a Persian should bridge the Hellespont, and march an army from Asia into Greece." While
Onomacritus thus plied Xerxes with his oracles, the Pisistratidae and Aleuadae did not cease to press on him their advice, till at last the king yielded, and agreed to lead forth an
expedition.

7. First, however, in the year following the death of Darius, he marched against those who had revolted from him;
and having reduced them, and laid all Egypt under a far
harder yoke than ever his father had put upon it, he gave
the government to Achaemenes, who was his own brother,
and son to Darius. This Achaemenes was afterwards slain in

his government by Inaros, the son of Psammetichus, a Libyan.

8. After Egypt was subdued, Xerxes, being about to take in hand the expedition against Athens, called together an assembly of the noblest Persians, to learn their opinions, and to lay before them his own designs. So, when the men were met, the king spoke thus to them:

"Persians, I shall not be the first to bring in among you this custom—I shall but follow one which has come down to us from our forefathers. Never yet, as our old men assure me, has our race reposed itself, since the time when Cyrus overcame Astyages, and so we Persians wrested the sceptre from the Medes. Now in all this God guides us; and we, obeying his guidance, prosper greatly. What need have I to tell you of the deeds of Cyrus and Cambyses, and my own father Darius, how many nations they conquered, and added to our dominions? You know right well what great things they achieved. But for myself, I will say that, from the day on which I mounted the throne, I have not ceased to consider by what means I may rival those who have preceded me in this post of honour, and increase the power of Persia as much as any of them. And truly I have pondered upon this, until at last I have found out a way whereby we may at once win glory, and likewise get possession of a land which is as large and as rich as our own—nay, which is even more varied in the fruits it bears—while at the same time we obtain satisfaction and revenge. For this cause I have now called you together, that I may make known to you what I design to do.

"My intent is to throw a bridge over the Hellespont and march an army through Europe against Greece, that thereby I may obtain vengeance from the Athenians for the wrongs committed by them against the Persians and against my father. Your own eyes saw the preparations of Darius against these men; but death came upon him, and balked his hopes of revenge. In his behalf, therefore, and in behalf of all the Persians, I undertake the war, and pledge myself not to rest till I have taken and burnt Athens, which has dared, unprovoked, to injure me and my father. Long since they came to Sardis with Aristagoras of Miletus, who was one of our slaves, and burnt its temples and its sacred groves; again, more lately, when we made a landing upon their coast under Datis and Artaphernes, how roughly they handled us you do not need to be told.

"For these reasons, therefore, I am bent upon this war; and I see likewise therewith united no few advantages. Once let us subdue this people, and those neighbours of theirs who hold the land of Pelops the Phrygian, and we shall extend the Persian territory as far as God's heaven reaches. The sun will then shine on no land beyond our borders; for I will pass through Europe from one end to the other, and with your aid make of all the lands which it contains one country. For thus, if what I hear be true, affairs stand: the nations whereof I have spoken once swept away, there is no city, no country left in all the world which will venture so much as to withstand us in arms. By this course then we shall bring all mankind under our yoke, alike those who are guilty and those who are innocent of doing us wrong.

"For yourselves, if you wish to please me, do as follows: when I announce the time for the army to meet together, hasten to the muster with a good will, every one of you; and know that to the man who brings with him the most gallant array I will give the gifts which our people consider the most honourable. This then is what you have to do. But to show that I am not self-willed in this matter, I lay the business before you, and give you full leave to speak your minds upon it openly."

Xerxes, having so spoken, held his peace.

9. Whereupon Mardonius took the word, and said:

"Of a truth, master, you surpass not only all living Persians, but likewise those yet unborn. Most true and right is each word that you have now uttered; but best of all your resolve not to let the Ionians who live in Europe—a worthless crew—mock us any more. It were indeed a monstrous thing if, after conquering and enslaving the Sacae, the Indians, the Ethiopians, the Assyrians, and many other mighty nations, not for any wrong that they had done us, but only to increase our empire, we should then allow the Greeks, who have done us such wanton injury, to escape our vengeance. What is it that we fear in them? Not surely their numbers? Not the greatness of their wealth? We know the manner of their battle—we know how weak their power is; already have we subdued their children who dwell in our country, the Ionians, Aeolians, and Dorians. I myself have had experience of these men when I marched against them by the orders of thy father; and though I went as far as Macedonia, and came but a little short of reaching Athens itself, yet not a soul ventured to come out against me to battle. And yet, I am told, these very Greeks are wont to wage wars against one another in the most foolish way, through sheer perversity and doltishness. For no sooner is war proclaimed than they search out the smoothest and fairest plain that is to be found in all the land, and there they assemble and fight; whence it comes to pass that even the conquerors depart with great loss: I say nothing of the conquered, for they are destroyed altogether. Now surely, as they are all of one speech, they ought to interchange heralds and messengers, and make up their differences by any means rather than battle; or, at the worst, if they must needs fight one against another, they ought to post themselves as strongly as possible, and so try their quarrels. But, notwithstanding that they have so foolish a manner of warfare, yet these Greeks, when I led my army against them to the very borders of Macedonia, did not so much as think of offering me battle.

"Who then will dare, O King, to meet you in arms, when you come with all Asia's warriors at your back, and with all her ships? For my part I do not believe the Greek people will be so foolhardy. Grant, however, that I am mistaken herein, and that they are foolish enough to meet us in open fight; in that case they will learn that there are no such soldiers in the whole world as we. Nevertheless let us spare no pains; for nothing comes without trouble; but all that men acquire is got by painstaking."

When Mardonius had in this way softened the harsh speech of Xerxes, he too held his peace.

10. The other Persians were silent; for all feared to raise their voice against the plan proposed to them. But Artabanus, the son of Hystaspes, and uncle of Xerxes, trusting to his relationship, was bold to speak. "O King," he said, "it is impossible, if no more than one opinion is uttered, to make choice of the best: a man is forced then to follow whatever advice may have been given him; but if opposite speeches are delivered, then choice can be exercised. In like manner pure gold is not recognized by itself; but when we test it along with baser ore, we perceive which is the better. I counselled your father, Darius, who was my own brother, not to attack the Scyths, a race of people who had no town in their whole land. He thought however to subdue those wandering tribes, and would not listen to me, but marched an army against them, and ere he returned home lost many of his bravest warriors. You are about, O King, to attack a people far superior to the Scyths, a people distinguished above others, it is said, both by land and sea. 'Tis fit therefore that I should tell you what danger you incur hereby.

"You say that you will bridge the Hellespont, and lead your troops through Europe against Greece. Now suppose some disaster befall you by land or sea, or by both. It may be even so; for the men are reputed valiant. Indeed one may measure their prowess from what they have already done; for when Datis and Artaphernes led their huge army against Attica, the Athenians singly defeated them. But grant they are not successful on both elements. Still, if they man their ships, and, defeating us by sea, sail to the Hellespont, and there destroy our bridge—that, sire, were a fearful hazard. And here 'tis not by my own mother wit alone that I conjecture what will happen; but I remember how narrowly we escaped disaster once, when your father, after throwing bridges over the Thracian Bosporus and the Danube, marched against the Scythians, and they tried every sort of prayer to induce the Ionians, who had charge of the bridge over the Danube, to break the passage. On that day, if

Histiaeus, the tyrant of Miletus, had sided with the other tyrants, and not set himself to oppose their views, the empire of the Persians would have come to nought. Surely a dreadful thing is this even to hear said, that the king's fortunes depended wholly on one man.

"Think then no more of incurring so great a danger when no need presses, but follow the advice I tender. Break up this meeting, and when you have well considered the matter with yourself, and settled what you will do, declare to us your resolve. I know not of aught in the world that so profits a man as taking good counsel with himself; for even if things fall out against one's hopes, still one has counselled well, though fortune has made the counsel of none effect: whereas if a man counsels ill and luck follows, he has gotten a windfall, but his counsel is none the less silly. Do you see how God with His lightning smites always the bigger animals, and will not suffer them to wax insolent, while those of a lesser bulk chafe Him not? How likewise His bolts fall ever on the highest houses and the tallest trees? So plainly does He love to bring down everything that exalts itself. Thus ofttimes a mighty host is discomfited by a few men, when God in His jealousy sends fear or storm from heaven, and they perish in a way unworthy of them. For God allows no one to have high thoughts but Himself. Again, hurry always brings about disasters, from which huge sufferings are wont to arise; but in delay lie many advantages, not apparent (it may be) at first sight, but such as in course of time are seen of all. Such then is my counsel to you, O King!

"And you, Mardonius, son of Gobryas, forbear to speak foolishly concerning the Greeks, who are men that ought not to be lightly esteemed by us. For while you revile the Greeks, you encourage the king to lead his own troops against them; and this, as it seems to me, is what you are specially striving to accomplish. May that not come to pass! For slander is of all evils the most terrible. In it two men do wrong, and one man has wrong done to him. The slanderer does wrong, forasmuch as he abuses a man behind his back; and the hearer, forasmuch as he believes what he has not searched into thoroughly. The man slandered in his absence suffers wrong at the hands of both: for one brings against him a false charge, and the other thinks him an evildoer. If, however, it must needs be that we go to war with this people, at least allow the king to abide at home in Persia. Then let you and I both stake our children on the issue. Choose out your men, and, taking with you whatever number of troops you like, lead forth our armies to battle. If things go well for the king, as you say they will, let me and my children be put to death; but if they fall out as I prophesy, let your children suffer, and yourself too, if you come back alive. But should you refuse this wager, and still resolve to march an army against Greece, sure I am that some of those whom you leave behind here will one day receive the sad tidings, that Mardonius has brought a great disaster upon the Persian people, and lies a prey to dogs and birds somewhere in the land of the Athenians, or else in that of the Lacedaemonians; unless indeed you shall have perished sooner by the way, experiencing in your own person the might of those men on whom you would fain induce the king to make war."

11. Thus spoke Artabanus. But Xerxes, full of wrath, replied to him:

"Artabanus, you are my father's brother—that shall save you from receiving the due meed of your silly words. One shame however I will lay upon you, coward and faint-hearted as you are—you shall not come with me to fight these Greeks, but shall tarry here with the women. Without your aid I will accomplish all of which I spoke. For let me not be thought the child of Darius, the son of Hystaspes, the son of Arsames, the son of Ariaramnes, the son of Teispes, the son of Cyrus, the son of Cambyses, the son of Teispes, the son of Achaemenes, if I take not vengeance on the Athenians. Full well I know that, were we to remain at rest, yet would not they, but would most certainly invade our country, if at least it be right to judge from what they have already done; for, remember, it was they who fired Sardis and attacked Asia. So now retreat is on both sides impossible, and the choice lies between doing and suffering injury; either our empire must pass under the dominion of the Greeks, or their land become the prey of the Persians; for there is no middle course left in this quarrel. It is right then that we, who have in times past received wrong, should now avenge it, and that I should thereby discover what that great risk is which I run in marching against these men—men whom Pelops the Phrygian, a slave of my forefathers, subdued so utterly that to this day both the land and the people who dwell therein alike bear the name of the conqueror!"

12. Thus far did the speaking proceed. Afterwards evening fell; and Xerxes began to find the advice of Artabanus greatly disquiet him. So he thought upon it during the night, and concluded at last that it was not for his advantage to lead an army into Greece. When he had thus made up his mind anew, he fell asleep. And now he saw in the night, as the Persians declare, a vision of this nature: he thought a tall and beautiful man stood over him and said, "Have you then changed your mind, Persian, and will you not lead your host forth against the Greeks, after commanding the Persians to gather together their levies? Be sure that you do not do well to change; nor is there a man here who will approve your conduct. The course that you determined on during the day, let that be followed." After thus speaking the man seemed to Xerxes to fly away.

13. Day dawned; and the king made no account of this dream, but called together the same Persians as before, and spoke to them as follows:

"Men of Persia, forgive me if I alter the resolve to which I came so lately. Consider that I have not yet reached to the full growth of my wisdom, and that they who urge me to engage in this war leave me not to myself for a moment. When I heard the advice of Artabanus, my young blood suddenly boiled; and I spoke words against him little befitting his years: now however I am in agreement, and am resolved to follow his counsel. Understand then that I have changed my intent with respect to carrying war into Greece, and cease to trouble yourselves."

When they heard these words, the Persians prostrated themselves, filled with joy.

14. But when night came, again the same vision stood over Xerxes as he slept, and said, "Son of Darius, it seems you have openly before all the Persians renounced the expedition, making light of my words, as though you had heard them from a nobody. Know therefore and be well assured, that unless you go forth to the war immediately, this thing shall happen to you—as you have grown mighty and powerful in a short space, so likewise will you within a little time be brought low indeed."

15. Then Xerxes, greatly frightened at the vision which he had seen, sprang from his couch, and sent a messenger to call Artabanus, who came at the summons, when Xerxes spoke to him in these words:

"Artabanus, at the moment I acted foolishly, when I gave you ill words in return for your good advice. However it was not long ere I repented, and was convinced that your counsel was such as I ought to follow. But I may not now act in this way, greatly as I desire to do so. For ever since I repented and changed my mind a dream has haunted me, which disapproves my intentions, and has now just gone from me with threats. Now if this dream is sent to me from a god, and if it is indeed his will that our troops should march against Greece, you too will have the same dream come to you and receive the same commands as myself. And this will be most sure to happen, I think, if you put on the dress which I am wont to wear, and then, after taking your seat upon my throne, lie down to sleep on my bed."

16. Such were the words of Xerxes. Artabanus would not at first yield to the command of the king, for he deemed himself unworthy to sit upon the royal throne. At the last, however, he was forced to give way, and did as Xerxes bade him; but first he spoke thus to the king:

"To me, sire, it seems to matter little whether a man is wise himself or willing to hearken to such as give good advice. In you truly both tempers are found; but the counsels of evil men lead you astray: they are like the gales of wind which vex the sea—else the most useful thing for man in the whole world—and suffer it not to follow the bent of its own nature. For myself, it irked me not so much to be reproached by you, as to observe that when two courses were placed before the Persian people, one of a nature to increase their pride, the other to humble it by showing them how hurtful it is to allow one's heart always to covet more than one at present possesses, you made choice of that which was the worse both for yourself and for the Persians.

"Now you say that from the time when you approved the better course, and gave up the thought of warring against Greece, a dream has haunted you, sent by some god, which will not suffer you to lay aside the expedition. But such things, my son, have of a truth nothing divine in them. The dreams that wander to and fro among mankind, I will tell you of what nature they are—I who have seen so many more years than you. Whatever a man has been thinking of during the day, is wont to hover round him in the visions of his dreams at night. Now we during these many days past have had our hands full of this enterprise. If however the matter be not as I suppose, but God has indeed some part therein, you have in brief declared the whole that can be said concerning it—let it appear to me as it has to you, and lay on me the same injunctions. But it ought not to appear to me any the more if I put on your clothes than if I wear my own, nor if I go to sleep in your bed than if I do so in mine—supposing, I mean, that it is about to appear at all. For this thing, be it what it may, that visits you in your sleep, surely is not so far gone in folly as to see me, and because I am dressed in your clothes, straightway to mistake me for you. Now however our business is to see if it will regard me as of small account, and not vouchsafe to appear to me, whether I wear my own clothes or yours, while it keeps on haunting you continually. If it does so, and appears often, I should myself say that it was from God. For the rest, if your mind is fixed, and it is not possible to turn you from your design, but I must needs go and sleep in your bed, well and good, let it be so; and when I have done as you wish, then let the dream appear to me. Till such time, however, I shall keep to my former opinion."

17. Thus spoke Artabanus; and when he had so said, thinking to show Xerxes that his words were nought, he did according to his orders. Having put on the garments which Xerxes was wont to wear and taken his seat upon the royal throne, he lay down to sleep. As he slept, there appeared to him the very same dream which had been seen by Xerxes; it came and stood over Artabanus, and said:

"You are the man, then, who, feigning to be tender of Xerxes, seeks to dissuade him from leading his armies against the Greeks! But you shall not escape scatheless, either now or in time to come, because you have sought to prevent that which is fated to happen. As for Xerxes, it has been plainly told to himself what will befall him, if he refuses to perform my bidding."

18. In such words, as Artabanus thought, the vision threatened him, and then endeavoured to burn out his eyes with red-hot irons. At this he shrieked, and, leaping from his couch, hurried to Xerxes, and, sitting down at his side, gave him a full account of the vision; after which he said:

"I, O King, am a man who have seen many mighty empires overthrown by weaker ones; and therefore it was that I sought to hinder you from being quite carried away by your youth; since I knew how evil a thing it is to covet much. I could remember the expedition of Cyrus against the Massagetae, and what was the issue of it; I could recollect the march of Cambyses against the Ethiopians; I had taken part in the attack of Darius upon the Scyths; bearing therefore all these things in mind, I thought with myself that if you would remain at peace, all men would deem you fortunate. But as this impulse has plainly come from above, and a heaven-sent destruction seems about to overtake the Greeks, behold, I change to another mind, and alter my thoughts upon the matter. Make known to the Persians what the god has declared, and bid them follow the orders which were first given, and prepare their levies. Be careful to act so that the bounty of the god may not be hindered by slackness on your part."

Thus these two spoke together; and Xerxes, being in good heart on account of the vision, when day broke, laid all before the Persians; while Artabanus, who had formerly been the only person openly to oppose the expedition, now showed as openly that he favoured it.

19. After Xerxes had thus determined to go forth to the war, there appeared to him in his sleep a third vision. The Magi were consulted upon it, and said that its meaning reached to the whole earth, and that all mankind would become his servants. Now the vision which the king saw was this: he dreamt that he was crowned with a branch of an olive tree, and that boughs spread out from the olive branch and covered the whole earth; then suddenly the garland, as it lay upon his brow, vanished. So when the Magi had thus interpreted the vision, straightway all the Persians who were come together departed to their several governments, each hoping to obtain for himself the gifts which had been promised. And so Xerxes gathered together his host, ransacking every corner of the continent.

20. Reckoning from the recovery of Egypt, Xerxes spent four full years in collecting his host, and making ready all things that were needful for his soldiers. It was not till the close of the fifth year [480 B.C.] that he set forth on his march, accompanied by a mighty multitude. For of all the armaments whereof any mention has reached us, this was by far the greatest; insomuch that no other expedition compared to this seems of any account, neither that which Darius undertook against the Scythians, nor the expedition of the Scythians (which the attack of Darius was designed to avenge), when they, being in pursuit of the Cimmerians, fell upon the Median territory, and subdued and held for a time almost the whole of Upper Asia; nor, again, that of the Atridae against Troy, of which we hear in story; nor that of the Mysians and Teucrians, which was still earlier, wherein these nations crossed the Bosporus into Europe, and, after

conquering all Thrace, pressed forward till they came to the Adriatic, while southward they reached as far as the river Peneus.

21. All these expeditions, and others that there were besides, are as nothing compared with this. For was there a nation in all Asia which Xerxes did not bring with him against Greece? Or was there a river, except those of unusual size, which sufficed for his troops to drink? Some nations furnished ships; others were arrayed among the foot soldiers; others had to supply horses; others, transports for the horse and men likewise for the transport service; others, long ships for the bridges; others, ships and provisions.

22. And in the first place, because the former fleet had met with so great a disaster about Athos, preparations were made, by the space of about three years, in that quarter. . . .

[Xerxes in the meantime marched with his land army to Sardis.]

32. Here his first care was to send off heralds into Greece, who were to prefer a demand for earth and water, and to require that preparations should be made everywhere to feast the king. To Athens indeed and to Sparta he sent no such demand; but, these cities excepted, his messengers went everywhere. Now the reason why he sent for earth and water to states which had already refused was this: he thought that although they had refused when Darius made the demand, they would now be too frightened to venture to say him nay. So he sent his heralds, wishing to know for certain how it would be.

33. Xerxes, after this, made preparations to advance to Abydos, where the bridge across the Hellespont from Asia to Europe was lately finished. Midway between Sestos and Madytus in the Hellespontine Chersonese, and right over against Abydos, there is a rocky tongue of land which runs out for some distance into the sea. This is the place where no long time afterwards [479 B.C.] the Athenians under Xanthippus, the son of Ariphron,[1] took Artaÿctes the Per-

---

[1] And the father of Pericles.

sian, who was at that time governor of Sestos, and nailed him living to a plank. He was the Artaÿctes who brought women into the temple of Protesilaüs at Elaeus, and there was guilty of most unholy deeds.

34. Towards this tongue of land then, the men to whom the business was assigned carried out a double bridge from Abydos; and while the Phoenicians constructed one line with cables of white flax, the Egyptians in the other used ropes made of papyrus. Now it is seven furlongs across from Abydos to the opposite coast. When, therefore, the channel had been bridged successfully, it happened that a great storm arising broke the whole work to pieces, and destroyed all that had been done.

35. So when Xerxes heard of it he was full of wrath, and straightway gave orders that the Hellespont should receive three hundred lashes, and that a pair of fetters should be cast into it. Nay, I have even heard it said, that he bade the branders take their irons and therewith brand the Helles-pont. It is certain that he commanded those who scourged the waters to utter, as they lashed them, these barbarian and wicked words: "You bitter water, your lord lays on you this punishment because you have wronged him without a cause, having suffered no evil at his hands. Verily King Xerxes will cross you, whether you will or no. Well do you deserve that no man should honour you with sacrifice; for you are of a truth a treacherous and unsavoury river." While the sea was thus punished by his orders, he likewise commanded that the overseers of the work should lose their heads. . . .

[The bridge was rebuilt and Xerxes marched his army from Sardis to Abydos.]

53. After Xerxes had thus spoken, and had sent Arta-bamus away to return to Susa [to serve as regent], he sum-moned before him all the Persians of most repute, and when they appeared, addressed them in these words:

"Persians, I have brought you together because I wished to exhort you to behave bravely, and not to sully with dis-grace the former achievements of the Persian people, which are very great and famous. Rather let us one and all, singly and jointly, exert ourselves to the uttermost; for the matter wherein we are engaged concerns the common weal. Strain every nerve, then, I beseech you, in this war. Brave warriors are the men we march against, if report says true; and such that, if we conquer them, there is not a people in all the world which will venture thereafter to withstand our arms. And now let us offer prayers to the gods who reign over the land of Persia, and then cross the channel."

54. All that day the preparations for the passage continued; and on the morrow they burnt all kinds of spices upon the bridges, and strewed the way with myrtle boughs, while they waited anxiously for the sun, which they hoped to see as he rose. And now the sun appeared; and Xerxes took a golden goblet and poured from it a libation into the sea, praying the while with his face turned to the sun, that no misfortune might befall him such as to hinder his conquest of Europe, until he had penetrated to its uttermost boundaries. After he had prayed, he cast the golden cup into the Hellespont, and with it a golden bowl, and a Persian sword of the kind which they call *acinaces*. I cannot say for certain whether it was as an offering to the sun god that he threw these things into the deep, or whether he had repented of having scourged the Hellespont, and thought by his gifts to make amends to the sea for what he had done.

55. When, however, his offerings were made, the army began to cross; and the foot soldiers, with the horsemen, passed over by one of the bridges—that (namely) which lay towards the Black Sea—while the sumpter beasts and the camp followers passed by the other, which looked on the Aegean. Foremost went the Ten Thousand Persians, all wearing garlands upon their heads; and after them a mixed multitude of many nations. These crossed upon the first day.

On the next day the horsemen began the passage; and with them went the soldiers who carried their spears with the point downwards, garlanded, like the Ten Thousand; then came the sacred horses and the sacred chariot; next Xerxes with his lancers and the thousand horse; then the rest of the army. At the same time the ships sailed over to the opposite shore. According, however, to another account which I have heard, the king crossed the last.

56. As soon as Xerxes had reached the European side, he stood to contemplate his army as they crossed under the lash. And the crossing continued during seven days and seven nights, without rest or pause. 'Tis said that here, after Xerxes had made the passage, a Hellespontian exclaimed:

"Why, O Zeus, dost thou, in the likeness of a Persian man, and with the name of Xerxes instead of thine own, lead the whole race of mankind to the destruction of Greece? It would have been as easy for thee to destroy it without them!"

57. When the whole army were about to cross, and the troops were now upon their march, a strange prodigy appeared to them, whereof the king made no account, though its meaning was not difficult to conjecture. Now the prodigy was this: a mare brought forth a hare. Hereby it was shown plainly enough that Xerxes would lead forth his host against Greece with mighty pomp and splendour, but, in order to return to his own country, he would have to run for his life. There had also been another portent, while Xerxes was still at Sardis—a mule dropped a foal having the genitals of both sexes, male and female, the former above the other.

58. Xerxes, disregarding both omens, marched forwards; and his land army accompanied him. But the fleet held an opposite course, and, sailing to the mouth of the Hellespont, made its way along the shore. Thus the fleet proceeded westward, making for Cape Sarpedon, where the orders were that it should await the coming up of the troops; but the land army marched eastward along the Chersonese, leaving on the right the tomb of Helle, the daughter of Athamas, and on the left the city of Cardia. Having passed through the town which is called Agora, they skirted the shores of the Gulf of Melas, and then crossed the river Melas, whence the gulf takes its name, the waters of which they found too scanty to supply the host. From this point their march was to the west; and after passing Aenos, an Aeolian settlement, and likewise Lake Stentoris, they came to Doriscus.

59. The name Doriscus is given to a beach and a vast plain upon the coast of Thrace, through the middle of which flows the strong stream of the Hebrus. Here was the royal fort which is likewise called Doriscus, where Darius had maintained a Persian garrison ever since the time when he attacked the Scythians. This place seemed to Xerxes a convenient spot for reviewing and numbering his soldiers, which he did. The sea captains, who had brought the fleet to Doriscus, were ordered to take the vessels to the beach adjoining, where Sale stands, a city of the Samothracians, and Zone, another city. The beach extends to Serrheum, the well-known promontory; the whole district in former times was inhabited by the Ciconians. Here then the captains were to bring their ships, and to haul them ashore for refitting, while Xerxes at Doriscus was employed in numbering the soldiers.

60. What the exact number of the troops of each nation was I cannot say with certainty—for it is not mentioned by anyone—but the whole land army together was found to amount to one million seven hundred thousand men. The manner in which the numbering took place was the following. A body of ten thousand men was brought to a certain place, and the men were made to stand as close together as possible; after which a circle was drawn around them, and the men were let go; then where the circle had been, a fence was built about the height of a man's navel, and the enclosure was filled continually with fresh troops, till the whole army had in this way been numbered. When the numbering was over, the troops were drawn up according to their several nations. . . .

100. Now when the numbering and marshalling of the host was ended, Xerxes conceived a wish to go himself throughout the forces, and with his own eyes behold everything. Accordingly he traversed the ranks seated in his chariot, and, going from nation to nation, made manifold inquiries, while his scribes wrote down the answers; till at last he had passed from end to end of the whole land army, both the horsemen and the foot. This done, he exchanged his

chariot for a Sidonian galley, and, seated beneath a golden awning, sailed along the prows of all his vessels, while he made inquiries again, as he had done when he reviewed the land force, and caused the answers to be recorded by his scribes. The captains took their ships to the distance of about four hundred feet from the shore, and there lay to, with their vessels in a single row, the prows facing the land, and with the fighting men upon the decks accoutred as if for war, while the king sailed along in the open space between the ships and the shore, and so reviewed the fleet.

101. Now after Xerxes had sailed down the whole line and was gone ashore, he sent for Demaratus the son of Ariston, who had accompanied him in his march upon Greece, and spoke to him thus:

"Demaratus, it is my pleasure at this time to ask you certain things which I wish to know. You are a Greek, and, as I hear from the other Greeks with whom I converse, no less than from your own lips, you are a native of a city which is not the weakest or the meanest in their land. Tell me, therefore, what you think. Will the Greeks lift a hand against us? My own judgement is that even if all the Greeks and all the others of the west were gathered together in one place they would not be able to abide my onset, not being really of one mind. But I should like to know what you think."

Thus Xerxes questioned; and the other replied in his turn, "O King, is it your will that I give you a true answer, or do you wish a pleasant one?"

Then the king bade him speak the plain truth, and promised that he would not on that account hold him in less favour than heretofore.

102. So Demaratus, when he heard the promise, spoke as follows:

"O King, since you bid me at all risks speak the truth, and not say what will one day prove me to have lied to you, thus I answer. Want has at all times been a fellow dweller with us in our land, while valor is an ally whom we have gained by dint of wisdom and strict laws. Her aid enables us to drive out want and escape thraldom. Brave are all the Greeks who dwell in any Dorian land; but what I am about to say does not concern all, but only the Lacedaemonians. First, then, come what may, they will never accept your terms, which would reduce Greece to slavery; and further, they are sure to join battle with you, though all the rest of the Greeks should submit to your will. As for their numbers, do not ask how many they are, that their resistance should be a possible thing; for if a thousand of them should take the field, they will meet you in battle, and so will any number, be it less or more."

103. When Xerxes heard this answer of Demaratus, he laughed and answered:

"What wild words, Demaratus! A thousand men join battle with such an army as this! Come then, will you—who were once, you say, their king—engage to fight this very day against ten men? And yet, if all your fellow citizens be indeed such as you say they are, you ought, as their king, by your own country's usages, be ready to fight twice the number. If then each one of them be a match for ten of my soldiers, I may well call upon you to be a match for twenty. Thus would you assure the truth of what you have now said. If, however, you Greeks, who vaunt yourselves so much, are of a truth men like those whom I have seen about my court, like yourself, Demaratus, and the others with whom I converse—if, I say, you are really men of this sort and size, how is the speech you have uttered more than a mere empty boast? For, to go to the very verge of likelihood—how could a thousand men, or ten thousand, or even fifty thousand, particularly if they are all alike free, and not under one lord—how could such a force, I say, stand against an army like mine? Let them be five thousand, and we shall have more than a thousand men to each one of theirs. If, indeed, like our troops, they had a single master, their fear of him might make them courageous beyond their natural bent; or they might be urged by lashes against an enemy which far outnumbered them. But left to their own free choice, assuredly they will act differently. For my part, I believe that if the Greeks had to contend with the Persians only, and the numbers were equal on both sides, the Greeks would find it hard to stand their ground. We too have among us such men as those of whom you spoke—not many indeed, but still we possess a few. For instance, some of my bodyguard would be willing to engage singly with three Greeks. But you did not know this; and therefore it was that you talked so foolishly."

104. Demaratus answered him: "I knew, O King, at the outset, that if I told you the truth my speech would displease you. But as you required me to answer with all possible truthfulness, I informed you what the Spartans will do. And in this I spoke not from any love that I bear them—for none knows better than you what my love towards them is likely to be at the present time, when they have robbed me of my rank and my ancestral honours, and made me a homeless exile, whom your father received, bestowing on me both shelter and sustenance. What likelihood is there that a man of understanding should be unthankful for kindness shown him, and not cherish it in his heart? For myself, I do not pretend to cope with ten men, nor with two—nay, had I the choice, I would rather not fight even with one. But if need appeared, or if there were any great cause urging me on, I would contend with right good will against one of those persons who boast themselves a match for any three Greeks. So likewise the Lacedaemonians, when they fight singly, are as good men as any in the world, and when they fight in a body are the bravest of all. For though they be freemen, they are not in all respects free: law is the master whom they own, and this master they fear more than your subjects fear you. Whatever he commands they do; and his commandment is always the same: it forbids them to flee in battle, whatever the number of their foes, and requires them to stand firm, and either to conquer or die. If in these words, O King, I seem to you to speak foolishly, I am content from this time forward evermore to hold my peace. I had not now spoken unless compelled by you. Certainly, I pray that all may turn out according to your wishes."

105. Such was the answer of Demaratus; and Xerxes was

not angry with him at all, but only laughed, and sent him away with words of kindness.

After this interview, and after he had made Mascames the son of Megadostes governor of Doriscus, setting aside the governor appointed by Darius, Xerxes started with his army, and marched upon Greece through Thrace. . . .

118. Now the Greeks who had to feed the army [on the march] and to entertain Xerxes were brought thereby to the very extremity of distress, insomuch that some of them were forced even to forsake house and home. When the Thasians received and feasted the host, on account of their possessions upon the mainland, Antipater, the son of Orges, one of the citizens of best repute, and the man to whom the business was assigned, proved that the cost of the meal was four hundred talents of silver.

119. And estimates almost to the same amount were made by the superintendents in other cities. For the entertainment, which had been ordered long beforehand and was reckoned to be of much consequence, was, in the manner of it, such as I will now describe. No sooner did the heralds who brought the orders give their message than in every city the inhabitants made a division of their stores of corn, and proceeded to grind flour of wheat and of barley for many months together. Besides this, they purchased the best cattle that they could find, and fattened them; and fed poultry and water fowl in ponds and buildings, to be in readiness for the army; while they likewise prepared gold and silver vases and drinking cups, and whatsoever else is needed for the service of the table. These last preparations were made for the king only, and those who sat at meat with him; for the rest of the army nothing was made ready beyond the food. On the arrival of the Persians, a tent ready pitched for the purpose received Xerxes, who took his rest therein, while the soldiers remained under the open heaven. When the dinner hour came, great was the toil of those who entertained the army; while the guests ate their fill, and then, after passing the night at the place, tore down the royal tent next morning,

and, seizing its contents, carried them all off, leaving nothing behind.

120. On one of these occasions Megacreon of Abdera wittily recommended his countrymen to go to the temples in a body, men and women alike, and there take their station as suppliants, and beseech the gods that they would in future always spare them one-half of the woes which might threaten their peace—thanking them at the same time very warmly for their past goodness in that they had caused Xerxes to be content with one meal in the day. For had the order been to provide breakfast for the king as well as dinner, the Abderites must either have fled before Xerxes came, or, if they awaited his coming, have been brought to absolute ruin. As it was, the nations, though suffering heavy pressure, complied nevertheless with the directions that had been given.

121. At Acanthus Xerxes separated from his fleet, bidding the captains sail on ahead and await his coming at Therma, on the Thermaic Gulf, the place from which the bay takes its name. Through this town lay, he understood, his shortest road. Previously, his order of march had been the following: from Doriscus to Acanthus his land force had proceeded in three bodies, one of which took the way along the sea-shore in company with the fleet, and was commanded by Mardonius and Masistes, while another pursued an inland track under Tritantaechmes and Gergis; the third, with which was Xerxes himself, marching midway between the other two, and having for its leaders Smerdomenes and Megabyzus.

122. The fleet, therefore, after leaving the king, sailed through the channel which had been cut for it by Mount Athos, and came into the bay whereon lie the cities of Assa, Pilorus, Singus, and Sarta; from all which it received contingents. . . .

124. Xerxes meanwhile with his land force left Acanthus, and started for Therma, taking his way across the land. This road led him through Paeonia and Crestonia to the

river Cheidorus, which, rising in the country of the Cresto-
nians, flows through Mygdonia, and reaches the sea near the
marsh upon the Vardar.

125. Upon this march the camels that carried the provisions of the army were set upon by lions, which left their
lairs and came down by night, but spared the men and the
sumpter beasts, while they made the camels their prey. I
marvel what may have been the cause which compelled the
lions to leave the other animals untouched and attack the
camels, when they had never seen that beast before, nor had
any experience of it.

126. That whole region is full of lions, and wild bulls
with gigantic horns which are brought into Greece. The lions
are confined within the tract lying between the river Nestus
(which flows through Abdera) on the one side, and the
Acheloüs (which waters Acarnania) on the other. No one
ever sees a lion in the fore part of Europe east of the Nestus,
nor through the entire continent west of the Acheloüs; but
in the space between these bounds lions are found.

127. On reaching Therma Xerxes halted his army, which
encamped along the coast, beginning at the city of Therma
in Mygdonia, and stretching out as far as the rivers Lydias
and Haliacmon, two streams which, mingling their waters in
one, form the boundary between Bottiaea and Macedonia.
Such was the extent of country through which the barbarians
encamped. The rivers here mentioned were all of them sufficient to supply the troops, except the Cheidorus, which was
drunk dry.

128. From Therma Xerxes beheld the Thessalian mountains, Olympus and Ossa, which are of a wonderful height.
Here, learning that there lay between these mountains a narrow gorge through which the river Peneus ran, and where
there was a road that gave an entrance into Thessaly, he
formed the wish to go by sea himself, and examine the mouth
of the river. His design was to lead his army by the upper
road through the country of the inland Macedonians, and so
to enter Perrhaebia, and come down by the city of Gonnus;

for he was told that that way was the most secure. No sooner therefore had he formed this wish than he acted accordingly. Embarking, as was his wont on all such occasions, aboard a Sidonian vessel, he gave the signal to the rest of the fleet to get under way, and, quitting his land army, set sail and proceeded to the Peneus. Here the view of the mouth caused him to wonder greatly; and sending for his guides, he asked them whether it were possible to turn the course of the stream, and make it reach the sea at any other point.

129. Now there is a tradition that Thessaly was in ancient times a lake, shut in on every side by huge hills. Ossa and Pelion—ranges which join at the foot—do in fact inclose it upon the east, while Olympus forms a barrier upon the north, Pindus upon the west, and Othrys towards the south. The tract contained within these mountains, which is a deep basin, is called Thessaly. Many rivers pour their waters into it; but five of them are of more note than the rest, namely, the Peneus, the Apidanus, the Onochonus, the Enipeus, and the Pamisus. These streams flow down from the mountains which surround Thessaly, and, meeting in the plain, mingle their waters together, and discharge themselves into the sea by a single outlet, which is a gorge of extreme narrowness. After the junction all the other names disappear, and the river is known as the Peneus. It is said that of old the gorge which allows the waters an outlet did not exist; accordingly the rivers, which were then, as well as the Lake Boebeïs, without names, but flowed with as much water as at present, made Thessaly a sea. The Thessalians tell us that the gorge through which the water escapes was caused by Poseidon; and this is likely enough; at least any man who believes that Poseidon causes earthquakes, and that chasms so produced are his handiwork, would say, upon seeing this rent, that Poseidon did it. For it plainly appeared to me that the hills had been torn asunder by an earthquake.

130. When Xerxes therefore asked the guides if there were any other outlet by which the waters could reach the sea, they, being men well informed, made answer: "O King,

there is no other passage by which this stream can empty itself into the sea save this one. For Thessaly is girt about with a circlet of hills."

Xerxes is said to have observed upon this: "Wise men truly are they of Thessaly, and good reason had they to change their minds in time and consult for their own safety. For, to pass by other matters, they must have felt that they lived in a country which may easily be brought under and subdued. Nothing more is needed than to turn the river upon their lands by an embankment which should fill up the gorge and force the stream from its present channel, and lo! all Thessaly, except the mountains, would at once be laid under water."

The king aimed in this speech at the Aleuadae, who were Thessalians, and had been the first of all the Greeks to make submission to him. He thought that they had made their friendly offers in the name of the whole people. So Xerxes, when he had viewed the place, and made the above speech, went back to Therma.

131. The stay of Xerxes in Pieria lasted for several days, during which a third part of his army was employed in cutting down the woods on the Macedonian mountain range to give his forces free passage into Perrhaebia. At this time the heralds who had been sent into Greece to require earth for the king returned to the camp, some of them empty-handed, others with earth and water.

132. Among the number of those from whom earth and water were brought were the Thessalians, Dolopians, Enianians, Perrhaebians, Locrians, Magnetians, Malians, Achaeans of Phthiotis, Thebans, and Boeotians generally, except those of Plataea and Thespiae. These are the nations against whom the Greeks that had taken up arms to resist the barbarians swore the oath which ran thus: "From all Greeks who delivered themselves up to the Persians without necessity, when their affairs are in good condition we will take a tithe of their goods, and give it to the god at Delphi." So ran the words of the Greek oath.

133. Xerxes had sent no heralds either to Athens or

Sparta to ask earth and water, for a reason which I will now relate. When Darius some time before sent messengers for the same purpose, they were thrown, at Athens, into the *barathron,* at Sparta into a well, and bidden to take therefrom earth and water for themselves, and carry it to their king. On this account Xerxes did not send to ask them. What calamity came upon the Athenians to punish them for their treatment of the heralds I cannot say, unless it were the laying waste of their city and territory; but that I believe was not on account of this crime.

134. On the Lacedaemonians, however, the wrath of Talthybius, Agamemnon's herald, fell with violence. Talthybius has a temple at Sparta; and his descendants, who are called Talthybiadae, have the privilege of being the only persons who discharge the office of herald. When therefore the Spartans had done the deed of which we speak, the victims at their sacrifices failed to give good tokens; and this failure lasted for a very long time. Then the Spartans were troubled; and, regarding what had befallen them as a grievous calamity, they held frequent assemblies of the people, and made proclamation through the town, "Is any Lacedaemonian willing to give his life for Sparta?" Upon this two Spartans, Sperthias, the son of Aneristus, and Bulis, the son of Nicolaüs, both men of good birth, and among the wealthiest in the place, came forward and freely offered themselves as an atonement to Xerxes for the heralds of Darius slain at Sparta. So the Spartans sent them away to the Medes to undergo death.

135. Nor is the courage which these men hereby displayed alone worthy of wonder; but so likewise are the following speeches which were made by them. On their road to Susa they presented themselves before Hydarnes. This Hydarnes was a Persian by birth, and had the command of all the men that dwelt along the sea-coast of Asia. He accordingly showed them hospitality, and invited them to a banquet, where, as they feasted, he said to them:

"Men of Lacedaemon, why will you not consent to be friends with the king? You have but to look at me and my fortune to see that the king knows well how to honour merit. In like manner you yourselves, were you to make your submission to him, would receive at his hands, seeing that he deems you men of merit, some government in Greece."

"Hydarnes," they answered, "you are a one-sided counsellor. You have experience of half the matter; but the other half is beyond your knowledge. You understand a slave's life; but, never having tasted liberty, you cannot tell whether it be sweet or no. Ah, had you known what freedom is, you would have bidden us fight for it, not with the spear only, but with the battle-axe."

So they answered Hydarnes.

136. And afterwards, when they were come to Susa into the king's presence, and the guards ordered them to fall down and do obeisance, and went so far as to use force to compel them, they refused, and said they would never do any such thing, even were their heads thrust down to the ground; for it was not their custom to worship men, and they had not come to Persia for that purpose. So they fought off the ceremony; and having done so, addressed the king in words much like the following:

"O King of the Medes, the Lacedaemonians have sent us hither, in the place of those heralds of yours who were slain in Sparta, to make atonement to you on their account."

Then Xerxes answered with true greatness of soul that he would not act like the Lacedaemonians, who, by killing the heralds, had broken the laws which all men hold in common. As he had blamed such conduct in them, he would never be guilty of it himself. And besides, he did not wish to free the Lacedaemonians from the stain of their former outrage by putting the two men to death in return.

137. This conduct on the part of the Spartans caused the anger of Talthybius to cease for a while, notwithstanding that Sperthias and Bulis returned home alive. But many years afterwards it awoke once more, as the Lacedaemonians themselves declare, during the war between the Peloponnesians and the Athenians.

In my judgement this was a case wherein the hand of

Heaven was most plainly manifest. That the wrath of Talthybius should have fallen upon ambassadors, and not slacked till it had full vent, so much justice required; but that it should have come upon the sons of the very men who were sent up to the Persian king on its account—upon Nicolaüs, the son of Bulis, and Aneristus, the son of Sperthias (the same who raided Halieis, the refuge of the Tirynthians, when cruising in a well-manned merchant ship)—this does seem to me to be plainly a supernatural circumstance. These two men, having been sent to Asia as ambassadors by the Lacedaemonians, were betrayed by Sitalces, the son of Teres, king of Thrace, and Nymphodorus, the son of Pythes, a native of Abdera, and being made prisoners at Bisanthe, upon the Hellespont, were conveyed to Attica, and there put to death by the Athenians, at the same time as Aristeas, the son of Adeimantus, the Corinthian. All this happened, however, very many years after the expedition of Xerxes, and I return to my subject.

138. The expedition of the Persian king, though it was in name directed against Athens, threatened really the whole of Greece. And of this the Greeks were aware some time before; but they did not all view the matter in the same light. Some of them had given the Persian earth and water, and were bold on this account, deeming themselves thereby secured against suffering hurt from the barbarian army; while others, who had refused compliance, were thrown into extreme alarm. For whereas they considered all the ships in Greece too few to engage the enemy, it was plain that the greater number of the people did not wish to take part in the war, but favoured going over to the Medes.

139. And here I feel constrained to deliver an opinion which most men, I know, will mislike, but which, as it seems to me to be true, I am determined not to withhold. Had the Athenians, from fear of the approaching danger, quitted their country, or had they without quitting it submitted to the power of Xerxes, there would certainly have been no attempt to resist the Persians by sea; in which case the course of events by land would have been the following. Though

the Peloponnesians might have carried ever so many breast-works across the Isthmus, yet their allies would have fallen off from the Lacedaemonians, not by voluntary desertion, but because town after town must have been taken by the fleet of the barbarians; and so the Lacedaemonians would at last have stood alone, and, standing alone, would have dis-played prodigies of valor, and died nobly. Either they would have done thus, or else, before it' came to that extremity, seeing one Greek state after another embrace the cause of the Medes, they would have come to terms with Xerxes; and thus, either way Greece would have been brought under Persia. For I cannot understand of what possible use the walls across the Isthmus could have been, if the king had had the mastery of the sea. If then a man should now say that the Athenians were the saviours of Greece, he would not exceed the truth. For they truly held the scales; and which-ever side they espoused must have carried the day. They too it was who, when they had determined to maintain the freedom of Greece, roused up that portion of the Greek world which had not gone over to the Medes; and so, next to the gods, *they* repulsed the invader. Even the ter-rible oracles which reached them from Delphi, and struck fear into their hearts, failed to persuade them to fly from Greece. They had the courage to remain faithful to their land, and await the coming of the foe.

140. When the Athenians, anxious to consult the oracle, sent their messengers to Delphi, hardly had the envoys com-pleted the customary rites about the sacred precinct, and taken their seats inside the sanctuary of the god, when the Pythoness, Aristonice by name, thus prophesied:

"Wretches, why sit ye here? Fly, fly to the ends of crea-tion,
  Quitting your homes, and the crags which your city crowns with her circlet.
  Neither the head nor the body is firm in its place, nor at bottom

Firm the feet, nor the hands; nor resteth the middle un-
injur'd.
All—all ruined and lost. Since fire, and impetuous Ares,
Speeding along in a Syrian chariot, hastes to destroy her.
Not alone shalt thou suffer; full many the towers he will
level,
Many the shrines of the gods he will give to a fiery
destruction.
Even now they stand with dark sweat horribly dripping.
Trembling and quaking for fear; and lo! from the high
roofs trickleth
Black blood, sign prophetic of hard distresses impending.
Get ye away from the temple; and brood on the ills that
await ye!"

141. When the Athenian messengers heard this reply,
they were filled with the deepest affliction: whereupon
Timon, the son of Androbulus, one of the men of most
mark among the Delphians, seeing how utterly cast down
they were at the gloomy prophecy, advised them to take an
olive branch, and entering the sanctuary again, consult the
oracle as suppliants. The Athenians followed this advice,
and going in once more, said, "O Lord, we pray thee reverence these boughs of supplication which we bear in our
hands, and deliver to us something more comforting concerning our country. Else we will not leave thy sanctuary,
but will stay here till we die." Upon this the priestess gave
them a second answer, which was the following:

"Pallas has not been able to soften the lord of Olympus,
Though she has often prayed him, and urged him with
excellent counsel.
Yet once more I address thee in words than adamant
firmer.
When the foe shall have taken whatever the limit of
Cecrops
Holds within it, and all which divine Cithaeron shelters,

Then far-seeing Zeus grants this to the prayers of
Athena;
Safe shall the wooden wall continue for thee and thy
children.
Wait not the tramp of the horse, nor the footmen might-
ily moving
Over the land, but turn your back to the foe, and retire
ye.
Yet shall a day arrive when ye shall meet him in battle.
Holy Salamis, thou shalt destroy the offspring of women,
When men scatter the seed, or when they gather the har-
vest."

142. This answer seemed, as indeed it was, gentler than
the former one; so the envoys wrote it down, and went back
with it to Athens. When, however, upon their arrival, they
produced it before the assembly, many and various were the
interpretations which men put on it; two, more especially,
seemed to be directly opposed to one another. Certain of the
old men were of opinion that the god meant to tell them the
Acropolis would escape; for this was anciently defended by
a palisade; and they supposed that barrier to be the "wooden
wall" of the oracle. Others maintained that the fleet was what
the god pointed at; and their advice was that nothing should
be thought of except the ships, which had best be at once
got ready. Still such as said the "wooden wall" meant the
fleet were perplexed by the last two lines of the oracle—

"Holy Salamis, thou shalt destroy the offspring of women,
When men scatter the seed, or when they gather the harvest."

These words caused great disturbance among those who took
the wooden wall to be the ships; since the interpreters understood them to mean that, if they made preparations for a sea-
fight, they would suffer a defeat off Salamis.

143. Now there was at Athens a man who had lately
made his way into the first rank of citizens: his name was
Themistocles; but he was known more generally as the son

of Neocles. This man came forward and said that the interpreters had not explained the oracle altogether aright—"For if," he argued, "the clause in question had really referred to the Athenians, it would not have been expressed so mildly; the phrase used would have been 'Luckless Salamis,' rather than 'Holy Salamis,' had those to whom the island belonged been about to perish in its neighbourhood. Rightly taken, the response of the god threatened the enemy, and not the Athenians." He therefore counselled his countrymen to make ready to fight on board their ships, since *they* were the wooden wall in which the god told them to trust. When Themistocles had thus cleared the matter, the Athenians embraced his view, preferring it to that of the interpreters. The advice of these last had been against engaging in a sea-fight; all the Athenians could do, they said was, without lifting a hand in their defence, to quit Attica, and make a settlement in some other country.

144. Themistocles had before this given a counsel which prevailed very seasonably. The Athenians, having a large sum of money in their treasury, the produce of the mines at Laureium, were about to share it among the citizens, who would have received ten drachmas apiece, when Themistocles persuaded them to forbear the distribution, and build with the money two hundred ships, to help them in their war against the Aeginetans. It was the breaking out of the Aeginetan war which was at this time the saving of Greece; for hereby were the Athenians forced to become a maritime power. The new ships were not used for the purpose for which they had been built, but became a help to Greece in her hour of need. And the Athenians had not only these vessels ready before the war, but they likewise set to work to build more; while they determined, in a council which was held after the debate upon the oracle, that, according to the advice of the god, they would embark their whole force aboard their ships, and, with such Greeks as chose to join them, give battle to the barbarian invader. Such, then, were the oracles which had been received by the Athenians.

145. The Greeks who were well affected to the Grecian

cause, having assembled in one place, and there consulted together, and interchanged pledges with each other, agreed that, before any other step was taken, the feuds and enmities which existed between the different nations should first of all be appeased. Many such there were; but one was of more importance than the rest, namely, the war which was still going on between the Athenians and the Aeginetans. When this business was concluded, understanding that Xerxes had reached Sardis with his army, they resolved to despatch spies into Asia to take note of the king's affairs. At the same time they determined to send ambassadors to the Argives, and conclude a league with them against the Persians; while they likewise despatched messengers to Gelo, the son of Deinomenes [tyrant of Syracuse], in Sicily, to the people of Corcyra, and to those of Crete, exhorting them to send help to Greece. Their wish was to unite, if possible, the entire Greek world in one, and so to bring all to join in the same plan of defence, inasmuch as the approaching dangers threatened all alike. Now the power of Gelo was said to be very great, far greater than that of any single Grecian people.

146. So when these resolutions had been agreed upon, and the quarrels between the states made up, first of all they sent into Asia three men as spies. These men reached Sardis, and took note of the king's forces, but, being discovered, were examined by order of the generals who commanded the land army, and, having been condemned to suffer death, were led out to execution. Xerxes, however, when the news reached him, disapproving the sentence of the generals, sent some of his bodyguard with instructions, if they found the spies still alive, to bring them into his presence. The messengers found the spies alive, and brought them before the king, who, when he heard the purpose for which they had come, gave orders to his guards to take them round the camp, and show them all the footmen and all the horse, letting them gaze at everything to their hearts' content; then, when they were satisfied, to send them away unharmed to whatever country they desired.

147. For these orders Xerxes gave afterwards the following reasons. Had the spies been put to death, he said, the Greeks would have continued ignorant of the vastness of his army, which surpassed the common report of it; while he would have done them a very small injury by killing three of their men. On the other hand, by the return of the spies to Greece, his power would become known; and the Greeks, he expected, would make surrender of the freedom peculiar to them before he began his march, by which means his troops would be saved all the trouble of an expedition. This reasoning was like to that which he used upon another occasion. While he was staying at Abydos, he saw some grain ships, which were passing through the Hellespont from the Black Sea, on their way to Aegina and the Peloponnesus. His attendants, hearing that they were the enemy's, were ready to capture them, and looked to see when Xerxes would give the signal. He, however, merely asked whither the ships were bound, and when they answered, "For your foes, master, with grain on board," "We too are bound thither," he rejoined, "laden, among other things, with grain. What harm is it, if they carry our provisions for us?"

148. So the spies, when they had seen everything, were dismissed, and came back to Europe. The Greeks who had banded themselves together against the Persian king, after despatching the spies into Asia, sent next ambassadors to Argos. The account which the Argives give of their own proceedings is the following. They say that they had information from the very first of the preparations which the barbarians were making against Greece. So, as they expected that the Greeks would come upon them for aid against the assailant, they sent envoys to Delphi to inquire of the god what it would be best for them to do in the matter. They had lost, not long before, six thousand citizens, who had been slain by the Lacedaemonians under Cleomenes the son of Anaxandridas; which was the reason why they now sent to Delphi. When the Pythoness heard their question, she replied:

> "Hated of all thy neighbours, beloved of the blessed Im-
>   mortals,
> Sit thou still, with thy lance drawn inward, patiently
>   watching;
> Warily guard thine head, and the head will take care of
>   the body."

This prophecy had been given them some time before the
envoys came; but still, when they afterwards arrived, it was
permitted them to enter the council-house, and there deliver
their message. And this answer was returned to their demands: "Argos is ready to do as you require, if the Lacedaemonians will first make a truce for thirty years, and will further divide with Argos the leadership of the allied army.
Although in strict right the whole command should be hers,
she will be content to have the leadership divided equally."

149. Such, they say, was the reply made by the council,
in spite of the oracle which forbade them to enter into a
league with the Greeks. For, while not without fear of dis-
obeying the oracle, they were greatly desirous of obtaining a
thirty years' truce, to give time for their sons to grow to
man's estate. They reflected that if no such truce were concluded, and it should be their lot to suffer a second calamity
at the hands of the Persians, it was likely they would fall
hopelessly under the power of Sparta. But to the demands
of the Argive council the Lacedaemonians among the envoys
made answer: They would bring before the people the question of concluding a truce; with regard to the leadership, they
had received orders what to say, and the reply was that
Sparta had two kings, Argos but one—it was not possible
that either of the two Spartans should be stripped of his dignity—but they did not oppose the Argive king having one
vote like each of them. The Argives say that they could not
brook this arrogance on the part of Sparta, and rather than
yield one jot to it, they preferred to be under the rule of the
barbarians. So they told the envoys to be gone, before sunset, from their territory, or they should be treated as
enemies.

150. Such is the account which is given of these matters by the Argives themselves. There is another story, which is told generally through Greece, of a different tenor. Xerxes, it is said, before he set forth on his expedition against Greece, sent a herald to Argos, who on his arrival spoke as follows:

"Men of Argos, King Xerxes speaks thus to you. We Persians deem that the Perses from whom we descend was the child of Perseus the son of Danaë, and of Andromeda the daughter of Cepheus. Hereby it would seem that we come of your stock and lineage. So then it neither befits us to make war upon those from whom we spring, nor can it be right for you to fight, on behalf of others, against us. Your place is to keep quiet and hold yourselves aloof. Only let matters proceed as I wish, and there is no people whom I shall have in higher esteem than you."

This address, says the story, was highly valued by the Argives, who therefore at the first neither gave a promise to the Greeks nor yet put forward a demand. Afterwards, however, when the Greeks called upon them to give their aid, they made the claim which has been mentioned, because they knew well that the Lacedaemonians would never yield it, and so they would have a pretext for taking no part in the war.

151. Some of the Greeks say that this account agrees remarkably with what happened many years afterwards. Callias, the son of Hipponicus, and certain others with him, had gone up to Susa, the city of Memnon, as ambassadors of the Athenians, upon a business quite distinct from this. While they were there, it happened that the Argives likewise sent ambassadors to Susa, to ask Artaxerxes, the son of Xerxes, if the friendship which they had formed with his father still continued, or if he looked upon them as his enemies, to which King Artaxerxes replied, "Most certainly it continues; and there is no city which I reckon more my friend than Argos."

152. For my own part I cannot positively say whether Xerxes did send the herald to Argos or not; nor whether

Argive ambassadors at Susa did really put this question to Artaxerxes about the friendship between them and him; neither do I deliver any opinion hereupon other than that of the Argives themselves. This, however, I know—that if every nation were to bring all its evil deeds to a given place, in order to make an exchange with some other nation, when they had all looked carefully at their neighbours' faults, they would be truly glad to carry their own back again. So, after all, the conduct of the Argives was not perhaps more disgraceful than that of others. For myself, my duty is to report all that is said; but I am not obliged to believe it all alike—a remark which may be understood to apply to my whole History. Some even go so far as to say that the Argives first invited the Persians to invade Greece, because of their ill success in the war with Lacedaemon, since they preferred anything to the smart of their actual sufferings.

153. Thus much concerning the Argives. Other ambassadors, among whom was Syagrus from Lacedaemon, were sent by the allies into Sicily, with instructions to confer with Gelo.

The ancestor of this Gelo, who first settled at Gela, was a native of the isle of Telos, which lies off Triopium [in Asia Minor]. When Gela was colonized by Antiphemus and the Lindians of Rhodes, he likewise took part in the expedition. In course of time his descendants became the hierophants of Demeter and Persephone—an office which they held continually, from the time that Telines, one of Gelo's ancestors, obtained it in the way which I will now mention. Certain citizens of Gela, worsted in a sedition, had found a refuge at Mactorium, a town situated on the heights above Gela. Telines reinstated these men, having no human forces, but solely the sacred objects of the cult. From whom he received them, or how he himself acquired them, I cannot say; but certain it is that, relying on their power, he brought the exiles back. For this his reward was to be the office of hierophant of these goddesses for himself and his seed for ever. It surprises me especially that such a feat should have been performed by Telines; for I have always looked upon acts of this nature as beyond the abilities of common men, and only to be achieved by such as are of a bold and manly spirit; whereas Telines is said by those who dwell about Sicily to have been a soft and womanish person. He however obtained this office in the manner above described.

154. Afterwards, on the death of Cleander the son of Pantares, who was slain by Sabyllus, a citizen of Gela, after he had held the tyranny for seven years, Hippocrates, Cleander's brother, assumed the reign. During his tyranny, Gelo, a descendant of the hierophant Telines, served with many others—of whom Aenesidemus, son of Pataïcus, was one—in his bodyguard. Within a little time his merit caused him to be raised to the command of all the horse. For when Hippocrates laid siege to Callipolis, and afterwards to Naxos, to Zancle, to Leontini, and moreover to Syracuse, and many cities of the barbarians, Gelo in every war distinguished himself above all the combatants. Of the various cities above named, there was none but Syracuse which was not reduced to slavery. The Syracusans were saved from this fate, after they had suffered defeat on the river Elorus, by the Corinthians and Corcyraeans, who made peace between them and Hippocrates, on condition of their ceding Camarina to him; for that city anciently belonged to Syracuse.

155. When, however, Hippocrates, after a reign of the same length as that of Cleander his brother, perished near the city Hybla, as he was warring with the Sicels, then Gelo, pretending to espouse the cause of the two sons of Hippocrates, Eucleides and Cleander, defeated the citizens who were seeking to recover their freedom, and, having so done, set aside the children, and himself took power. After this piece of good fortune, Gelo likewise became master of Syracuse, in the following manner. The Syracusan *gamoroi,* as they were called, had been driven from their city by the common people assisted by their own slaves, called Cyllyrians, and had fled to Casmenae. Gelo brought them back to Syracuse, and so got possession of the town; for the people surrendered themselves, and gave up their city on his approach.

156. Being now master of Syracuse, Gelo cared less to govern Gela, which he therefore entrusted to his brother Hiero, while he strengthened the defences of his new city, which indeed was now all in all to him. And Syracuse sprang up rapidly to power and became a flourishing place. For Gelo razed Camarina to the ground, and brought all the inhabitants to Syracuse, and made them citizens; he also brought thither more than half the citizens of Gela, and gave them the same rights as the Camarinaeans. So likewise with the Megarians of Sicily—after besieging their town and forcing them to surrender, he took the rich men, who, having made the war, looked now for nothing less than death at his hands, and, carrying them to Syracuse, established them there as citizens; while the common people, who, as they had not taken any share in the struggle, felt secure that no harm would be done to them, he carried likewise to Syracuse, where he sold them all as slaves to be conveyed abroad. He did the like also by the Euboeans of Sicily, making the same difference. His conduct towards both nations arose from his belief that a "people" was a most unpleasant companion. In this way Gelo became a great tyrant.

157. When the Greek envoys reached Syracuse, and were admitted to an audience, they spoke as follows:

"We have been sent hither by the Lacedaemonians and their allies, to ask you to join us against the barbarian. Doubtless you have heard of his invasion, and are aware that a Persian has thrown a bridge over the Hellespont, and, bringing with him out of Asia all the forces of the East, is about to carry war into Greece, professing indeed that he only seeks to attack Athens, but really bent on bringing all the Greeks into subjection. Do you therefore, we beseech you, aid those who would maintain the freedom of Greece, and assist to free her yourself; since the power which you wield is great, and your portion in Greece, as lord of Sicily, is no small one. For if all Greece join together in one, there will be a mighty host collected, and we shall be a match for our assailants; but if some turn traitors, and others refuse their aid, and only a small part of the whole body remain sound, then there is reason to fear that all Greece may succumb. For do not cherish a hope that the Persian, when he has conquered our country, will be content and not advance against you. Rather take your measures beforehand; and consider that you defend yourself when you give aid to us. Wise counsels, be sure, for the most part have prosperous issues."

158. Thus spoke the envoys; and Gelo replied with vehemence:

"Greeks, you have had the face to come here with selfish words, and exhort me to join in league with you against the barbarian. Yet when I erewhile asked you to join with me in fighting barbarians, what time the quarrel broke out between me and Carthage, and when I earnestly besought you to revenge on the men of Egesta their murder of Dorieus, the son of Anaxandridas, promising to assist you in setting free the trading-places, from which you receive great profits and advantages, you neither came hither to give me succour nor yet to revenge Dorieus; but, for any efforts on your part to hinder it, these countries might at this time have been entirely under the barbarians. Now, however, that matters have prospered and gone well with me, while the danger has shifted its ground and at present threatens yourselves, lo! you call Gelo to mind. But though you slighted me then, I will not imitate you now: I am ready to give you aid, and to furnish as my contribution two hundred triremes, twenty thousand men-at-arms, two thousand cavalry, and an equal number of archers, slingers, and light horsemen, together with grain for the whole Grecian army so long as the war shall last. These services, however, I promise on one condition—that you appoint me chief captain and commander of the Grecian forces during the war with the barbarian. Unless you agree to this, I will neither send succour nor come myself."

159. Syagrus, when he heard these words, was unable to contain himself, and exclaimed:

"Surely a groan would burst from Pelops' grandson, Agamemnon, did he hear that her leadership was snatched from Sparta by Gelo and the men of Syracuse. Speak then no more of any such condition, as that we should yield to you the chief command; but if you are minded to come to the aid of Greece, prepare to serve under Lacedaemonian generals. Will you not serve under a leader? Then, prithee, withhold your succour."

160. Hereupon Gelo, seeing the indignation which showed itself in the words of Syagrus, delivered to the envoys his final offer: "Spartan stranger," he said, "reproaches cast forth against a man are wont to provoke him to anger; but the insults which you have uttered in your speech shall not persuade me to outstep good breeding in my answer. Surely if you maintain so stoutly your right to the command, it is reasonable that I should be still more stiff in maintaining mine, forasmuch as I am at the head of a far larger fleet and army. Since, however, the claim which I have put forward is so displeasing to you, I will yield, and be content with less. Take, if it please you, the command of the land force, and I will be admiral of the fleet; or assume, if you prefer it, the command by sea, and I will be leader upon the land. Unless you are satisfied with these terms, you must return home by yourselves, and lose this great alliance."

161. Such was the offer which Gelo made. Hereat broke in the Athenian envoy, before the Spartan could answer, and thus addressed Gelo:

"King of the Syracusans! Greece sent us here to you to ask for an army, and not to ask for a general. You, however, do not promise to send us any army at all, if you are not made leader of the Greeks; and this command is what alone you stick for. Now when your request was to have the whole command, we were content to keep silence; for well we knew that we might trust the Spartan envoy to make answer for us both. But since, after failing in your claim to lead the whole armament, you have now put forward a request to have the command of the fleet, know that, even should the Spartan envoy consent to this, we will not consent. The command by sea, if the Lacedaemonians do not wish for it, belongs to us. While they like to keep this command, we shall raise no dispute; but we will not yield our right to it in favour of anyone else. Where would be the advantage of our having raised up a naval force greater than that of any other Greek people, if nevertheless we should suffer Syracusans to take the command away from us? From us, I say, who are Athenians, the most ancient nation in Greece, the only Greeks who have never changed their abode—the people who are said by the poet Homer to have sent to Troy the man best able of all the Greeks to array and marshal an army—so that we may be allowed to boast somewhat."

162. Gelo replied, "Athenian stranger, you have, it seems, no lack of commanders; but you are likely to lack men to receive their orders. As you are resolved to yield nothing and claim everything, you had best make haste back to Greece, and say that the spring of her year is lost to her." The meaning of this expression was the following: as the spring is manifestly the finest season of the year, so (he meant to say) were his troops the finest of the Greek army—Greece, therefore, deprived of his alliance, would be like a year with the spring taken from it.

163. Then the Greek envoys, without having any further dealings with Gelo, sailed away home. And Gelo, who feared that the Greeks would be too weak to withstand the barbarians, and yet could not anyhow bring himself to go to the Peloponnesus, and there, though tyrant of Sicily, serve under the Lacedaemonians, left off altogether to contemplate that course of action, and betook himself to quite a different plan. As soon as tidings reached him of the passage of the Hellespont by the Persians, he sent off three penteconters, under the command of Cadmus, the son of Scythes, a native of Cos, who was to go to Delphi, taking with him a large sum of money and a stock of friendly words; there he was to watch the war, and see what turn it would take: if the barbarians prevailed, he was to give Xerxes the treasure, and with it earth and water for the lands which Gelo ruled; if the Greeks won the day, he was to convey the treasure back.

164. This Cadmus had at an earlier time received from his

father the tyranny at Cos in a right good condition, and had of his own free will and without the approach of any danger, from pure love of justice, given up his power into the hands of the people at large, and departed to Sicily; where he assisted in the Samian seizure and settlement of Zancle, or Messana, as it was afterwards called. Upon this occasion Gelo chose him to send into Greece, because he was acquainted with the proofs of honesty which he had given. And now he added to his former honourable deeds an action which is not the least of his merits. With a vast sum entrusted to him and completely in his power, so that he might have kept it for his own use if he had liked, he did not touch it; but when the Greeks gained the sea fight and Xerxes fled away with his army, he brought the whole treasure back with him to Sicily.

165. They, however, who dwell in Sicily, say that Gelo, though he knew that he must serve under the Lacedaemonians, would nevertheless have come to the aid of the Greeks, had not it been for Terillus, the son of Crinippus, tyrant of Himera; who, driven from his city by Thero, the son of Aenesidemus, ruler of Agrigentum, brought into Sicily at this very time an army of three hundred thousand men, Phoenicians, Libyans, Iberians, Ligurians, Elisycians, Sardinians, and Corsicans, under the command of Hamilcar the son of Hanno, king of the Carthaginians. Terillus prevailed upon Hamilcar, partly as his sworn friend, but more through the zealous aid of Anaxilaüs the son of Cretines, tyrant of Rhegium; who, by giving his own sons to Hamilcar as hostages, induced him to make the expedition. Anaxilaüs herein served his own father-in-law; for he was married to a daughter of Terillus, by name Cydippe. So, as Gelo could not give the Greeks any aid, he sent (they say) the sum of money to Delphi.

166. They say too, that the victory of Gelo and Thero in Sicily over Hamilcar the Carthaginian fell out upon the very day that the Greeks defeated the Persians at Salamis. Hamilcar, who was a Carthaginian on his father's side only, but on his mother's a Syracusan, and who had been raised

by his merit to the throne of Carthage, after the battle and the defeat, as I am informed, disappeared from sight: Gelo made the strictest search for him, but he could not be found anywhere, either dead or alive.

167. The Carthaginians, who take probability for their guide, give the following account of this matter: Hamilcar, they say, during all the time that the battle raged between the Greeks and the barbarians, which was from early dawn till evening, remained in the camp, sacrificing and seeking favourable omens, while he burned on a huge pyre the entire bodies of the victims which he offered. Here, as he poured libations upon the sacrifices, he saw the rout of his army; whereupon he cast himself headlong into the flames, and so was consumed and disappeared. But whether Hamilcar's disappearance happened, as the Phoenicians tell us, in this way, or in some other, certain it is that the Carthaginians offer him sacrifice, and in all their colonies have monuments erected to his honour, as well as one, which is the grandest of all, at Carthage. Thus much concerning the affairs of Sicily.

168. As for the Corcyraeans, to whom the envoys that visited Sicily appealed on their way, and to whom they delivered the same message as to Gelo, their answers and actions were the following. With great readiness they promised to come and give their help to the Greeks, declaring that the ruin of Greece was a thing which they could not tamely stand by to see; for should she fall, they must the very next day submit to slavery; so that they were bound to assist her to the very uttermost of their power. But notwithstanding that they answered so smoothly, yet when the time came for the succour to be sent, they were of quite a different mind; and though they manned sixty ships, hardly had they put to sea and reached the Peloponnesus, when they lay to with their fleet, off the Lacedaemonian coast, about Pylos and Taenarum—like Gelo, watching to see what turn the war would take. For they despaired altogether of the Greeks gaining the day, and expected that the Persian would win a great battle, and then be master of the whole of Greece. They therefore acted with premeditation, in order that they

might be able to address Xerxes in words like these: "O King, though the Greeks sought to obtain our aid in their war with you, and though we had a force of no small size, and could have furnished a greater number of ships than any Greek state except Athens, yet we refused, since we would not fight against you, nor do aught to cause you annoyance." The Corcyraeans hoped that a speech like this would gain them better treatment from the Persians than the rest of the Greeks; and it would have done so, in my judgement. At the same time, they had an excuse ready to give their countrymen, which they used when the time came. Reproached by them for sending no succour, they replied, that they had fitted out a fleet of sixty triremes, but that the Etesian winds did not allow them to double Cape Malea, and this hindered them from reaching Salamis—it was not from any bad motive that they had missed the sea fight. In this way the Corcyraeans eluded the reproaches of the Greeks.

169. The Cretans, when the envoys sent to ask aid from them came and made their request, acted as follows. They despatched messengers in the name of all to Delphi and asked the god whether it would make for their welfare if they should lend succour to Greece. "Fools!" replied the Pythoness, "do you not still complain of the woes which the assisting of Menelaus cost you at the hands of angry Minos? How wroth was he, when, in spite of their having lent you no aid towards avenging his death at Camicus, you helped them to avenge the carrying off by a barbarian of a woman from Sparta!" When this answer was brought from Delphi to the Cretans, they thought no more of assisting the Greeks.

170. Minos, according to tradition, went to Sicania, or Sicily, as it is now called, in search of Daedalus, and there perished by a violent death. After a while the Cretans, warned by some god, made a great expedition into Sicania, all except the Polichnites and the Praesians, and besieged Camicus (which in my time belonged to Agrigentum) for the space of five years. At last, however, failing in their efforts to take the place, and unable to carry on the siege any longer from the pressure of hunger, they departed and

went their way. Voyaging homewards they had reached
Iapygia, when a furious storm arose and threw them upon
the [south Italian] coast. All their vessels were broken in
pieces; and so, as they saw no means of returning to Crete,
they founded the town of Hyria, where they took up their
abode, changing their name from Cretans to Messapian
Iapygians, and at the same time becoming inhabitants of the
mainland instead of islanders. From Hyria they afterwards
founded those other towns which the Tarentines at a much
later period [473 B.C.] endeavoured to take, but could not,
being defeated signally. Indeed so dreadful a slaughter of
Greeks never happened at any other time, so far as my
knowledge extends: nor was it only the Tarentines who suffered, but the men of Rhegium too, who had been forced
to go to the aid of the Tarentines by Micythus the son of
Choerus, lost here three thousand of their citizens, while the
Tarentines who fell were never counted. This Micythus
served in the household of Anaxilaüs, and was by him left in
charge of Rhegium: he is the same man who was afterwards
forced to leave Rhegium, when he settled at Tegea in
Arcadia, from which place he made his many offerings of
statues to the shrine at Olympia.

171. This account of the Rhegians and the Tarentines
is a digression from the story which I was relating. To return—the Praesians say that men of various nations now
flocked to Crete, which was stripped of its inhabitants; but
none came in such numbers as the Grecians. Three generations after the death of Minos the Trojan war took place;
and the Cretans were not the least distinguished among the
helpers of Menelaus. But on this account, when they came
back from Troy, famine and pestilence fell upon them, and
destroyed both the men and the cattle. Crete was a second
time stripped of its inhabitants, a remnant only being left;
who form, together with fresh settlers, the third people by
whom the island has been inhabited. These were the events
of which the Pythoness now reminded the men of Crete;
and thereby she prevented them from giving the Greeks aid,
though they wished to have gone to their assistance.

172. The Thessalians did not embrace the cause of the Medes until they were forced to do so; for they gave plain proof that the intrigues of the Aleuadae were not at all to their liking. No sooner did they hear that the Persian was about to cross over into Europe than they despatched envoys to the Greeks who were met to consult together at the Isthmus, whither all the states which were well inclined to the Grecian cause had sent their delegates. These envoys on their arrival thus addressed their countrymen:

"Men of Greece, it behoves you to guard the pass of Olympus; for thus will Thessaly be placed in safety, as well as the rest of Greece. We for our parts are quite ready to take our share in this work, but you must likewise send us a strong force: otherwise we give you fair warning that we shall make terms with the Persians. For we ought not to be left, exposed as we are in front of all the rest of Greece, to die in your defence alone and unassisted. If however you do not choose to send us aid, you cannot force us to resist the enemy; for there is no force so strong as inability. We shall therefore do our best to secure our own safety."

Such was the declaration of the Thessalians.

173. Hereupon the Greeks determined to send a body of foot to Thessaly by sea, which should defend the pass of Olympus. Accordingly a force was collected, which passed up the Euripus, and, disembarking at Alus, on the coast of Achaea, left the ships there, and marched by land into Thessaly. Here they occupied the defile of Tempe, which leads from Lower Macedonia into Thessaly along the course of the Peneus, having the range of Olympus on the one hand and Ossa upon the other. In this place the Greek force that had been collected, amounting to about ten thousand heavy-armed men, pitched their camp; and here they were joined by the Thessalian cavalry. The commanders were, on the part of the Lacedaemonians, Euaenetus, the son of Carenus, who had been chosen out of the polemarchs, but did not belong to the blood royal; and on the part of the Athenians, Themistocles, the son of Neocles. They did not however maintain their station for more than a few days; since envoys

came from Alexander, the son of Amyntas, the Macedonian, and counselled them to decamp from Tempe, telling
them that if they remained in the pass they would be trodden
underfoot by the invading army, whose numbers they recounted, and likewise the multitude of their ships. So when
the envoys thus counselled them, and the counsel seemed to
be good, and the Macedonian who sent it friendly, they did
even as he advised. In my opinion what chiefly wrought on
them was the fear that the Persians might enter by another
pass, whereof they now heard, which led from Upper Macedonia into Thessaly through the territory of the Perrhaebi,
and by the town of Gonnus—the pass by which soon afterwards the army of Xerxes actually made its entrance. The
Greeks therefore went back to their ships and sailed away to
the Isthmus.

174. Such were the circumstances of the expedition into
Thessaly; they took place when the king was at Abydos, preparing to pass from Asia into Europe. The Thessalians,
when their allies forsook them, no longer wavered, but
warmly espoused the side of the Medes; and afterwards, in
the course of the war, they were of the very greatest service
to Xerxes.

175. The Greeks, on their return to the Isthmus, took
counsel together concerning the words of Alexander, and
considered how and where they should conduct the war. The
opinion which prevailed was that they should guard the pass
of Thermopylae; since it was narrower than the Thessalian
defile, and at the same time nearer to them. Of the pathway
by which the Greeks who fell at Thermopylae were inter-
cepted they had no knowledge until, on their arrival at Thermopylae, it was discovered to them by the Trachinians. This
pass then it was determined that they should guard, in order
to prevent the barbarians from penetrating into Greece
through it; and at the same time it was resolved that the fleet
should proceed to Artemisium, in the region of Histiaeotis;
for, as those places are near to one another, it would be easy
for the fleet and army to hold communication. The two
places may be thus described.

176. Artemisium is where the sea of Thrace contracts into a narrow channel, running between the isle of Sciathus and the mainland of Magnesia. When this narrow strait is passed you come to the line of coast called Artemisium, which is a portion of Euboea, and contains a temple of Artemis. As for the entrance into Greece by Trachis, it is, at its narrowest point, about fifty feet wide. This however is not the place where the passage is most contracted; for it is still narrower a little above and a little below Thermopylae. At Alpeni, which is lower down than that place, it is only wide enough for a single carriage; and up above, at the river Phoenix, near the town called Anthela, it is the same. West of Thermopylae rises a lofty and precipitous hill, impossible to climb, which runs up into the chain of Oeta, while to the east the road is shut in by the sea and by marshes. In this place are the warm springs, which the natives call "The Cauldrons," and above them stands an altar sacred to Hercules. A wall had once been carried across the opening, and in this there had of old times been a gateway. These works were made by the Phocians, through fear of the Thessalians, at the time when the latter came from Thesprotia to establish themselves in the land of Aeolis, which they still occupy. As the Thessalians strove to reduce Phocis, the Phocians raised the wall to protect themselves, and likewise turned the hot springs upon the pass, that so the ground might be broken up by watercourses, using thus all possible means to hinder the Thessalians from invading their country. The old wall had been built in very remote times, and the greater part of it had gone to decay through age. Now however the Greeks resolved to repair its breaches, and here make their stand against the barbarian. At this point there is a village very nigh the road, Alpeni by name, from which the Greeks reckoned on getting grain for their troops.

177. These places, therefore, seemed to the Greeks fit for their purpose. Weighing well all that was likely to happen, and considering that in this region the barbarians could make no use of their vast numbers, nor of their cavalry, they resolved to await here the invader of Greece. And when news

reached them of the Persians being in Pieria, straightway they broke up from the Isthmus, and proceeded, some on foot to Thermopylae, others by sea to Artemisium.

178. The Greeks now made all speed to reach the two stations, and about the same time the Delphians, alarmed both for themselves and for their country, consulted the god, and received for answer a command to pray to the winds, for the winds would do Greece good service. So when this answer was given them, forthwith the Delphians sent word of the prophecy to those Greeks who were zealous for freedom, and, cheering them thereby amid the fears which they entertained with respect to the barbarian, earned their everlasting gratitude. This done, they raised an altar to the winds at Thyia (where Thyia, the daughter of Cephissus, from whom the region takes its name, has a precinct), and worshipped them with sacrifices. And even to the present day the Delphians sacrifice to the winds because of this oracle.

179. The fleet of Xerxes now departed from Therma, and ten of the swiftest sailing ships ventured to stretch across direct for Sciathus, at which place there were upon the lookout three vessels belonging to the Greeks, one a ship of Troezen, another of Aegina, and the third from Athens. These vessels no sooner saw from a distance the barbarians approaching than they all hurriedly took to flight.

180. The barbarians at once pursued, and the Troezenian ship, which was commanded by Prexinus, fell into their hands. Hereupon the Persians took the handsomest of the men-at-arms and drew him to the prow of the vessel, where they sacrificed him; for they thought it a good omen that their first Greek captive was so handsome. The man whose throat was cut was called Leon; and it may be that the name he bore [which means "lion"] helped him to his fate in some measure.

181. The Aeginetan trireme, under its captain, Asonides, gave the Persians no little trouble, one of the men-at-arms, Pythes, the son of Ischenoüs, distinguishing himself beyond all the others who fought on that day. After the ship was taken this man continued to resist till he fell quite covered with wounds. The Persians who served as men-at-arms in

the squadron, finding that he was not dead, but still breathed, and being very anxious to save his life, since he had behaved so valiantly, dressed his wounds with myrrh, and bound them up with bandages of fine linen. Then, when they were returned to their own station, they displayed their prisoner admiringly to the whole host, and behaved towards him with much kindness; but all the rest of the ship's crew were treated merely as slaves.

182. Thus did the Persians succeed in taking two of the vessels. The third, a trireme commanded by Phormus of Athens, took to flight and ran aground at the mouth of the river Peneus. The barbarians got possession of the bark, but not of the men. For the Athenians had no sooner run their vessel aground than they leapt out, and made their way through Thessaly back to Athens.

183. When the Greeks stationed at Artemisium learnt what had happened by fire-signals from Sciathus, so terrified were they, that, quitting their anchorage ground at Artemisium, and leaving scouts to watch the foe on the highlands of Euboea, they removed to Chalcis, intending to guard the Euripus.

Meantime three of the ten vessels sent forward by the barbarians advanced as far as the sunken rock between Sciathus and Magnesia, which is called "The Ant," and there set up a stone pillar which they had brought with them for that purpose. After this, their course being now clear, the barbarians set sail with all their ships from Therma, eleven days from the time that the king quitted the town. The rock, which lay directly in their course, had been made known to them by Pammon of Scyros. A day's voyage without a stop brought them to Sepias in Magnesia, and to the strip of coast which lies between the town of Casthanaea and the promontory of Sepias.

184. As far as this point then, and on land as far as Thermopylae, the armament of Xerxes had been free from mischance; and the numbers were still, according to my reckoning, of the following amount. First there was the ancient complement of the twelve hundred and seven vessels which came

with the king from Asia—the contingents of the nations severally—amounting, if we allow to each ship a crew of two hundred men, to 241,400. Each of these vessels had on board, besides native soldiers, thirty fighting men, who were either Persians, Medes, or Sacans, which gives an addition of 36,210. To these two numbers I shall further add the crews of the penteconters; which may be reckoned, one with another, at fourscore men each. Of such vessels there were (as I said before) three thousand; and the men on board them accordingly would be 240,000. This was the sea force brought by the king from Asia; and it amounted in all to 517,610 men. The number of the foot soldiers was 1,700,000; that of the horsemen 80,000; to which must be added the Arabs who rode on camels, and the Libyans who fought in chariots, whom I reckon at 20,000. The whole number, therefore, of the land and sea forces added together amounts to 2,317,610 men. Such was the force brought from Asia, without including the camp followers, or taking any account of the provision ships and the men whom they had on board.

185. To the amount thus reached we have still to add the forces gathered in Europe, concerning which I can only speak from conjecture. The Greeks dwelling in Thrace, and in the islands off the coast of Thrace, furnished to the fleet one hundred and twenty ships, the crews of which would amount to 24,000 men. Besides these, footmen were furnished by the Thracians, the Paeonians, the Eordians, the Bottiaeans, by the Chalcidean tribes, by the Brygians, the Pierians, the Macedonians, the Perrhaebians, the Enianians, the Dolopians, the Magnesians, the Achaeans, and by all the dwellers upon the Thracian sea-board; and the forces of these nations amounted, I estimate, to three hundred thousand men. These numbers, added to those of the force which came out of Asia, make the sum of the fighting men 2,641,610.

186. Such then being the number of the fighting men, it is my belief that the attendants who followed the camp, together with the crews of the supply ships, and of the other

craft accompanying the army, made up an amount rather above than below that of the fighting men. However I will not reckon them as either fewer or more, but take them at an equal number. We have therefore to add to the sum already reached an exactly equal amount. This will give 5,283,220 as the whole number of men brought by Xerxes, the son of Darius, as far as Sepias and Thermopylae.

187. Such then was the amount of the entire host of Xerxes. As for the number of the women who prepared the bread, of the concubines, and the eunuchs, no one can give any sure account of it; nor can the baggage horses and other sumpter beasts, nor the Indian hounds which followed the army, be calculated, by reason of their multitude. Hence I am not at all surprised that the water of the rivers was found too scant for the army in some instances; rather it is a marvel to me how the provisions did not fail, when the numbers were so great. For I find on calculation that if each man consumed no more than a choenix of grain a day, there must have been used daily by the army 110,340 medimni, [roughly 160,000 bushels], and this without counting what was eaten by the women, the eunuchs, the sumpter beasts, and the hounds. Among all this multitude of men there was not one who, for beauty and stature, deserved more than Xerxes himself to wield so vast a power.

188. The fleet then, on leaving Therma, sailed to the Magnesian territory, and there occupied the strip of coast between the city of Casthanaea and Cape Sepias. The ships of the first row were moored to the land, while the remainder swung at anchor further off. The beach extended but a very little way, so that they had to anchor off the shore, row upon row, eight deep. In this manner they passed the night. But at dawn of day calm and stillness gave place to a raging sea and a violent storm, which fell upon them with a strong gale from the east—a wind which the people in those parts call Hellespontias. Such of them as perceived the wind rising, and were so moored as to allow of it, forestalled the tempest by dragging their ships up on the beach, and in this way saved both themselves and their vessels. But the ships which

the storm caught out at sea were driven ashore, some of them near the place called Ipni, or "The Ovens," at the foot of Pelion; others on the strand itself; others again about Cape Sepias; while a portion were dashed to pieces near the cities of Meliboea and Casthanaea. There was no resisting the tempest.

189. It is said that the Athenians had called upon Boreas to aid the Greeks, on account of a fresh oracle which had reached them, commanding them to "seek help from their son-in-law." For Boreas, according to the tradition of the Greeks, took to wife a woman of Attica, viz., Orithyia, the daughter of Erechtheus. So the Athenians, as the tale goes, considering that this marriage made Boreas their son-in-law, and perceiving, while they lay with their ships at Chalcis of Euboea, that the wind was rising, or, it may be, even before it freshened, offered sacrifice both to Boreas and likewise to Orithyia, entreating them to come to their aid and to destroy the ships of the barbarians, as they did once before off Mount Athos. Whether it was owing to this that Boreas fell with violence on the barbarians at their anchorage I cannot say; but the Athenians declare that they had received aid from Boreas before, and that it was he who now caused all these disasters. They therefore, on their return home, built a temple to him on the banks of the Ilissus.

190. Such as put the loss of the Persian fleet in this storm at the lowest say that four hundred of their ships were destroyed, that a countless multitude of men were slain, and a vast treasure engulfed. Ameinocles, the son of Cretines, a Magnesian, who farmed land near Cape Sepias, found the wreck of these vessels a source of great gain to him; many were the gold and silver drinking-cups, cast up afterwards by the surf, which he gathered; while treasure-boxes too, which had belonged to the Persians, and golden articles of all kinds and beyond count, came into his possession. Ameinocles grew to be a man of great wealth in this way; but in other respects things did not go over well with him: he too, like other men, had his own grief—the murder of his son.

191. As for the number of the provision craft and other merchant ships which perished, it was beyond count. Indeed, such was the loss that the commanders of the sea force, fearing lest in their shattered condition the Thessalians should venture on an attack, raised a lofty barricade around their station out of the wreck of the vessels cast ashore. The storm lasted three days. At length the Magi, by offering victims to the winds, and charming them with the help of conjurers, while at the same time they sacrificed to Thetis and the Nereids, succeeded in laying the storm four days after it first began; or perhaps it ceased of itself. The reason of their offering sacrifice to Thetis was this: they were told by the Ionians that here was the place whence Peleus carried her off, and that the whole promontory was sacred to her and to her sister Nereids.

192. So the storm lulled upon the fourth day. The scouts left by the Greeks about the highlands of Euboea hastened down from their stations on the day following that whereon the storm began, and acquainted their countrymen with all that had befallen the Persian fleet. These no sooner heard what had happened than straightway they returned thanks to Poseidon the Saviour, and poured libations in his honour; after which they hastened back with all speed to Artemisium, expecting to find a very few ships left to oppose them, and, arriving there for the second time, took up their station on that strip of coast: nor from that day to the present have they ceased to address Poseidon by the name of "Saviour."

193. The barbarians, when the wind lulled and the sea grew smooth, drew their ships down to the water, and proceeded to coast along the mainland. Having then rounded the extreme point of Magnesia, they sailed straight into the bay that runs up to Pagasae. There is a place in this bay, belonging to Magnesia, where Hercules is said to have been put ashore to fetch water by Jason and his companions; who then deserted him and went on their way to Aea in Colchis, on board the ship Argo, in quest of the golden fleece. From the circumstance that they intended, after watering their vessel at this place, to quit the shore and launch forth into the

deep, it received the name of Aphetae. Here then it was that the fleet of Xerxes came to an anchor.

194. Fifteen ships, which had lagged greatly behind the rest, happening to catch sight of the Greek fleet at Artemisium, mistook it for their own, and sailing down into the midst of it, fell into the hands of the enemy. The commander of this squadron was Sandoces, the son of Thamasius, governor of Cyme, in Aeolis. He was of the number of the royal judges, and had been crucified by Darius some time before on the charge of taking a bribe to determine a cause wrongly; but while he yet hung on the cross, Darius bethought him that the good deeds of Sandoces towards the king's house were more numerous than his evil deeds; and so, confessing that he had acted with more haste than wisdom, he ordered him to be taken down and set at large. Thus Sandoces escaped destruction at the hands of Darius, and was alive at this time; but he was not fated to come off so cheaply from his second peril; for as soon as the Greeks saw the ships making towards them, they guessed their mistake, and, putting to sea, took them without difficulty.

195. Aridolis, tyrant of Alabanda in Caria, was on board one of the ships, and was made prisoner; as also was the Paphian general, Penthylus, the son of Demonoüs, who was on board another. This person had brought with him twelve ships from Paphos, and, after losing eleven in the storm off Sepias, was taken in the remaining one as he sailed towards Artemisium. The Greeks, after questioning their prisoners as much as they wished concerning the forces of Xerxes, sent them away in chains to the Isthmus of Corinth.

196. The sea force of the barbarians, with the exception of the fifteen ships commanded (as I said) by Sandoces, came safe to Aphetae. Xerxes meanwhile, with the land army, had proceeded through Thessaly and Achaea, and, three days earlier, had entered the territory of the Malians. In Thessaly, he matched his own horses against the Thessalian, which he heard were the best in Greece; but the Greek coursers were left far behind in the race. All the rivers in this region had water enough to supply his army, ex-

cept only the Onochonus; but in Achaea, the largest of the streams, the Apidanus, barely held out.

197. On his arrival at Alus in Achaea, his guides, wishing to inform him of everything, told him the tale known to the dwellers in those parts concerning the temple of the Laphystian Zeus—how that Athamas the son of Aeolus took counsel with Ino and plotted the death of Phrixus; and how that afterwards the Achaeans, warned by an oracle, laid a forfeit upon his posterity, forbidding the eldest of the race ever to enter into the court-house (which they call the *leiton*), and keeping watch themselves to see the law obeyed. If one comes within the doors, he can never go out again except to be sacrificed. Further, they told him how that many persons, expecting to be sacrificed, are seized with such fear that they flee away and take refuge in some other country; and that these, if they come back long afterwards, and are found to be the persons who entered the court-house, are led forth covered with chaplets, in a grand procession, and are sacrificed. This forfeit is paid by the descendants of Cytissorus the son of Phrixus, because, when the Achaeans, in obedience to an oracle, made Athamas the son of Aeolus their sin-offering, and were about to slay him, Cytissorus came from Aea in Colchis and rescued Athamas; by which deed he brought the anger of the god upon his own posterity. Xerxes, therefore, having heard this story, when he reached the grove of the god, avoided it, and commanded his army to do the like. He also paid the same respect to the house of the descendants of Athamas as to the sanctuary.

198. Such were the doing of Xerxes in Thessaly and in Achaea. . . .

201. King Xerxes pitched his camp in the region of Malis called Trachis, while on their side the Greeks occupied the defile. This pass the Greeks in general call Thermopylae; but the natives, and those who dwell in the neighbourhood, call it Pylae. Here then the two armies took their stand; the one master of all the region lying north of Trachis, the other of the country extending southward of that place to the verge of the continent.

202. The Greeks who at this spot awaited the coming of Xerxes were the following: from Sparta, three hundred men-at-arms; from Arcadia, a thousand Tegeans and Mantineans, five hundred of each people; a hundred and twenty Orchomenians, from the Arcadian Orchomenus; and a thousand from other cities: from Corinth, four hundred men: from Phlius, two hundred; and from Mycenae, eighty. Such was the number from the Peloponnesus. There were also present, from Boeotia, seven hundred Thespians and four hundred Thebans.

203. Besides these troops, the Locrians of Opus and the Phocians had obeyed the call of their countrymen, and sent, the former all the force they had, the latter a thousand men. For envoys had gone from the Greeks at Thermopylae among the Locrians and Phocians, to call on them for assistance, and to say that they were themselves but the vanguard of the host, sent to precede the main body, which might every day be expected to follow them. The sea was in good keeping, watched by the Athenians, the Aeginetans, and the rest of the fleet. There was no cause why they should fear; for after all the invader was not a god but a man; and there never had been, and never would be, a man who was not liable to misfortunes from the very day of his birth, and those misfortunes greater in proportion to his own greatness. The assailant therefore, being only a mortal, must needs fall from his glory. Thus urged, the Locrians and the Phocians had come with their troops to Trachis.

204. The various nations had each captains of their own under whom they served; but the one to whom all especially looked up, and who had the command of the entire force, was the Lacedaemonian, Leonidas. Now Leonidas was the son of Anaxandridas, who was the son of Leon, who was the son of Eurycratidas, who was the son of Anaxander, who was the son of Eurycrates, who was the son of Polydorus, who was the son of Alcamenes, who was the son of Telecles, who was the son of Archelaüs, who was the son of Hegesilaüs, who was the son of Doryssus, who was the son of Leobotes, who was the son of Echestratus, who was the son

of Agis, who was the son of Eurysthenes, who was the son of
Aristodemus, who was the son of Aristomachus, who was
the son of Cleodaeus, who was the son of Hyllus, who was
the son of Hercules.

Leonidas had come to be king of Sparta quite unexpectedly.

205. Having two elder brothers, Cleomenes and Dorieus,
he had no thought of ever mounting the throne. However,
when Cleomenes died without male offspring, as Dorieus
was likewise deceased, having perished in Sicily, the crown
fell to Leonidas, who was older than Cleombrotus, the
youngest of the sons of Anaxandridas, and, moreover, was
married to the daughter of Cleomenes. He had now come
to Thermopylae, accompanied by men chosen from the
three hundred and from fathers with sons living.[2] On his
way he had taken the troops from Thebes, whose number
I have already mentioned, and who were under the command of Leontiades the son of Eurymachus. The reason why
he made a point of taking troops from Thebes, and Thebes
only, was that the Thebans were strongly suspected of being
well inclined to the Medes. Leonidas therefore called on
them to come with him to the war, wishing to see whether
they would comply with his demand, or openly refuse, and
disclaim the Greek alliance. They, however, though their
wishes leant the other way, nevertheless sent the men.

206. The force with Leonidas was sent forward by the
Spartans in advance of their main body, that the sight of
them might encourage the allies to fight, and hinder them
from going over to the Medes, as it was likely they might
have done had they seen that Sparta was backward. They
intended presently, when they had celebrated the Carneian
festival, which was what now kept them at home, to leave a
garrison in Sparta, and hasten in full force to join the army.
The rest of the allies also intended to act similarly; for it
happened that the Olympic games fell exactly at this same
period. None of them looked to see the contest at Thermopy-

---

[2] The text of this sentence is uncertain.

lae decided so speedily; wherefore they were content to send forward a mere advance guard.

207. Such accordingly were the intentions of the allies. The Greek forces at Thermopylae, when the Persian army drew near to the entrance of the pass, were seized with fear; and a council was held to consider about a retreat. It was the wish of the Peloponnesians generally that the army should fall back upon the Peloponnesus, and there guard the Isthmus. But Leonidas, who saw with what indignation the Phocians and Locrians heard of this plan, gave his voice for remaining where they were, while they sent envoys to the several cities to ask for help, since they were too few to make a stand against an army like that of the Medes.

208. While this debate was going on, Xerxes sent a mounted spy to observe the Greeks, and note how many they were, and see what they were doing. He had heard, before he came out of Thessaly, that a few men were assembled at this place, and that at their head were certain Lacedaemonians, under Leonidas, a descendant of Hercules. The horseman rode up to the camp, and looked about him, but did not see the whole army; for such as were on the farther side of the wall (which had been rebuilt and was now carefully guarded) it was not possible for him to behold; but he observed those on the outside, who were encamped in front of the rampart. It chanced that at this time the Lacedaemonians held the outer guard, and were seen by the spy, some of them engaged in gymnastic exercises, others combing their long hair. At this the spy greatly marvelled, but he counted their number, and when he had taken accurate note of everything he rode back quietly; for no one pursued after him, nor paid any heed to his visit. So he returned, and told Xerxes all that he had seen.

209. Upon this Xerxes, who had no means of surmising the truth—namely, that the Spartans were preparing to die manfully—but thought it laughable that they should be engaged in such employments, sent and called to his presence Demaratus the son of Ariston, who still remained with the

army. When he appeared, Xerxes told him all that he had heard, and questioned him concerning the news, since he was anxious to understand the meaning of such behaviour on the part of the Spartans. Then Demaratus said:

"I spoke to you concerning these men long since, when we had just begun our march upon Greece; you, however, only laughed at my words, when I told you of all this, which I saw would come to pass. Earnestly do I struggle at all times to speak truth to you, O King, and now listen to it once more. These men have come to dispute the pass with us; and it is for this that they are now making ready. It is their custom, when they are about to hazard their lives, to adorn their heads with care. Be assured, however, that if you can subdue the men who are here and the Lacedaemonians who remain in Sparta, there is no other nation in all the world which will venture to lift a hand against you. You have now to deal with the first kingdom in Greece, and with the bravest men."

Then Xerxes, to whom what Demaratus said seemed altogether to surpass belief, asked further how it was possible for so small an army to contend with his.

"O King," Demaratus answered, "let me be treated as a liar if matters fall not out as I say."

210. But Xerxes was not persuaded any the more. Four whole days he suffered to go by, expecting that the Greeks would run away. When, however, he found on the fifth that they were not gone, thinking that their firm stand was mere impudence and recklessness, he grew wroth, and sent against them the Medes and Cissians, with orders to take them alive and bring them into his presence. Then the Medes rushed forward and charged the Greeks, but fell in vast numbers: others however took the places of the slain, and would not be beaten off, though they suffered terrible losses. In this way it became clear to all, and especially to the king, that though he had plenty of combatants, he had but very few warriors. The struggle, however, continued during the whole day.

211. Then the Medes, having met so rough a reception,

withdrew from the fight; and their place was taken by the band of Persians under Hydarnes, whom the king called his "Immortals"; they, it was thought, would soon finish the business. But when they joined battle with the Greeks, it was with no better success than the Median detachment—things went much as before—the two armies fighting in a narrow space, and the barbarians using shorter spears than the Greeks, and having no advantage from their numbers. The Lacedaemonians fought in a way worthy of note, and showed themselves far more skilful in fight than their adversaries, often turning their backs and making as though they were all flying away, on which the barbarians would rush after them with much noise and shouting, when the Spartans at their approach would wheel round and face their pursuers, in this way destroying vast numbers of the enemy. Some Spartans likewise fell in these encounters, but only a very few. At last the Persians, finding that all their efforts to gain the pass availed nothing, and that, whether they attacked by divisions or in any other way, it was to no purpose, withdrew to their own quarters.

212. During these assaults, it is said that Xerxes, who was watching the battle, thrice leaped from his throne. Thus they fought. Next day the barbarians had no better success. The Greeks were so few that the barbarians hoped to find them disabled, by reason of their wounds, from offering any further resistance; and so they once more attacked them. But the Greeks were drawn up in detachments according to their cities, and bore the brunt of the battle in turns—all except the Phocians, who had been stationed on the mountain to guard the pathway. So, when the Persians found no difference between that day and the preceding, they again retired to their quarters.

213. Now, as the king was in a great strait, and knew not how he should deal with the emergency, Ephialtes, the son of Eurydemus, a man of Malis, came to him and was admitted to a conference. Stirred by the hope of receiving a rich reward at the king's hands, he had come to tell him of the pathway which led across the mountain to Thermopylae; by

which disclosure he brought destruction on the band of Greeks who had there withstood the barbarians. This Ephialtes afterwards, from fear of the Lacedaemonians, fled into Thessaly; and during his exile, in an assembly of the Amphictyons held at Pylae, a price was set upon his head by the Pylagorae. When some time had gone by, he returned from exile, and went to Anticyra, where he was slain by Athenades, a native of Trachis. Athenades did not slay him for his treachery, but for another reason, which I shall mention in a later part of my history: yet still the Lacedaemonians honoured him none the less. Thus then did Ephialtes perish afterwards.

214. Besides this there is another story told, which I do not at all believe—to wit, that Onetas the son of Phanagoras, a native of Carystus, and Corydallus of Anticyra were the persons who spoke on this matter to the king, and took the Persians across the mountain. One may guess which story is true, from the fact that the deputies of the Greeks, the Pylagorae, who must have had the best means of ascertaining the truth, did not offer the reward for the heads of Onetas and Corydallus, but for that of Ephialtes of Trachis; and again from the flight of Ephialtes, which we know to have been on this account. Onetas, I allow, although he was not a Malian, might have been acquainted with the path, if he had lived much in that part of the country; but as Ephialtes was the person who actually led the Persians round the mountain by the pathway, I leave his name on record as that of the man who did the deed.

215. Great was the joy of Xerxes on this occasion; and as he approved highly of the enterprise which Ephialtes undertook to accomplish, he forthwith sent upon the errand Hydarnes, and the Persians under him. The troops left the camp about the time of the lighting of the lamps. The pathway along which they went was first discovered by the Malians of these parts, who soon afterwards led the Thessalians by it to attack the Phocians, at the time when the Phocians fortified the pass with a wall, and so put themselves

under cover from danger. But ever since, the path was not put to use by the Malians.

216. The course which it takes is the following: Beginning at the Asopus, where that stream flows through the cleft in the hills, it runs along the ridge of the mountain (which is called, like the pathway over it, Anopaea), and ends at the city of Alpenus—the first Locrian town as you come from Malis—by the stone called Melampygus and the seats of the Cercopians. Here it is as narrow as at any other point.

217. The Persians took this path, and, crossing the Asopus, continued their march through the whole of the night, having the mountains of Oeta on their right hand, and on their left those of Trachis. At dawn of day they found themselves close to the summit. Now the hill was guarded, as I have already said, by a thousand Phocian men-at-arms, who were placed there to defend the pathway, and at the same time to secure their own country. They had been given the guard of the mountain path, while the other Greeks defended the pass below, because they had volunteered for the service, and had pledged themselves to Leonidas to maintain the post.

218. The ascent of the Persians became known to the Phocians in the following manner: During all the time that they were making their way up, the Greeks remained unconscious of it, inasmuch as the whole mountain was covered with groves of oak; but it happened that the air was very still, and the leaves which the Persians stirred with their feet made, as it was likely they would, a loud rustling, whereupon the Phocians jumped up and flew to seize their arms. In a moment the barbarians came in sight, and, perceiving men arming themselves, were greatly amazed; for they had fallen in with an enemy when they expected no opposition. Hydarnes, fearing lest the Phocians might be Lacedaemonians, inquired of Ephialtes to what nation these troops belonged. Ephialtes told him the exact truth, whereupon he arrayed his Persians for battle. The Phocians, galled by the showers of arrows to which they were exposed, and imagin-

ing themselves the special object of the Persian attack, fled hastily to the crest of the mountain, and there made ready to meet death; but while their mistake continued, the Persians, with Ephialtes and Hydarnes, not thinking it worth their while to delay on account of Phocians, passed on and descended the mountain with all possible speed.

219. The Greeks at Thermopylae received the first warning of the destruction which the dawn would bring on them from the seer Megistias, who read their fate in the victims as he was sacrificing. After this deserters came in, and brought the news that the Persians were marching round by the hills: it was still night when these men arrived. Last of all, the scouts came running down from the heights, and brought in the same accounts, when the day was just beginning to break. Then the Greeks held a council to consider what they should do, and here opinions were divided: some were strong against quitting their post, while others contended to the contrary. So when the council had broken up, part of the troops departed and went their ways homeward to their several states; part however resolved to remain, and to stand by Leonidas to the last.

220. It is said that Leonidas himself sent away the troops who departed, because he tendered their safety, but thought it unseemly that either he or his Spartans should quit the post which they had been especially sent to guard. For my own part, I incline to think that Leonidas gave the order, because he perceived the allies to be out of heart and unwilling to encounter the danger to which his own mind was made up. He therefore commanded them to retreat, but said that he himself could not draw back with honour; knowing that, if he stayed, glory awaited him, and that Sparta in that case would not lose her prosperity. For when the Spartans, at the very beginning of the war, sent to consult the oracle concerning it, the answer which they received from the Pythoness was that either Sparta must be overthrown by the barbarians, or one of her kings must perish. The prophecy was delivered in hexameter verse, and ran thus:

"O ye men who dwell in the streets of broad Lacedaemon!
Either your glorious town shall be sacked by the children
     of Perseus,
Or, in exchange, must all through the whole Laconian
     country
Mourn for the loss of a king, descendant of great
     Heracles.
HE cannot be withstood by the courage of bulls nor of
     lions,
Strive as they may; he is mighty as Zeus; there is nought
     that shall stay him,
Till he have got for his prey your king, or your glorious
     city."

The remembrance of this answer, I think, and the wish to
secure the whole glory for the Spartans, caused Leonidas to
send the allies away. This is more likely than that they quarrelled with him and took their departure in such unruly fashion.

221. To me it seems no small argument in favour of this
view that the seer also who accompanied the army, Megistias, the Acarnanian—said to have been of the blood of
Melampus, and the same who was led by the appearance of
the victims to warn the Greeks of the danger which threatened them—received orders to retire (as it is certain he did)
from Leonidas, that he might escape the coming destruction. Megistias, however, though bidden to depart, refused,
and stayed with the army; but he had an only son present
with the expedition, whom he now sent away.

222. So the allies, when Leonidas ordered them to retire, obeyed him and forthwith departed. Only the Thespians and the Thebans remained with the Spartans; and of
these the Thebans were kept back by Leonidas as hostages,
very much against their will. The Thespians, on the contrary, stayed entirely of their own accord, refusing to retreat,
and declaring that they would not forsake Leonidas and his
followers. So they abode with the Spartans, and died with

them. Their leader was Demophilus, the son of Diadromes.

223. At sunrise Xerxes made libations, after which he waited until the time when the Agora is wont to fill, and then began his advance. Ephialtes had instructed him thus, as the descent of the mountain is much quicker, and the distance much shorter, than the way round the hills, and the ascent. So the barbarians under Xerxes began to draw nigh; and the Greeks under Leonidas, as they now went forth determined to die, advanced much farther than on previous days until they reached the more open portion of the pass. Hitherto they had held their station within the wall, and from this had gone forth to fight at the point where the pass was the narrowest. Now they joined battle beyond the defile, and carried slaughter among the barbarians, who fell in heaps. Behind them the captains of the squadrons, armed with whips, urged their men forward with continual blows. Many were thrust into the sea, and there perished; a still greater number were trampled to death by their own soldiers; no one heeded the dying. For the Greeks, reckless of their own safety and desperate, since they knew that, as the mountain had been crossed, their destruction was nigh at hand, exerted themselves with the most furious valour against the barbarians.

224. By this time the spears of the greater number were all shivered, and with their swords they hewed down the ranks of the Persians; and here, as they strove, Leonidas fell fighting bravely, together with many other famous Spartans, whose names I have taken care to learn on account of their great worthiness, as indeed I have those of all the three hundred. There fell too at the same time very many famous Persians: among them, two sons of Darius, Abrocomes and Hyperanthes, his children by Phratagune, the daughter of Artanes. Artanes was brother of King Darius, being a son of Hystaspes, the son of Arsames; and when he gave his daughter to the king, he made him heir likewise of all his substance; for she was his only child.

225. Thus two brothers of Xerxes here fought and fell. And now there arose a fierce struggle between the Persians and the Lacedaemonians over the body of Leonidas, in

which the Greeks four times drove back the enemy, and at last by their great bravery succeeded in bearing off the body. This combat was scarcely ended when the Persians with Ephialtes approached; and the Greeks, informed that they drew nigh, made a change in the manner of their fighting. Drawing back into the narrowest part of the pass, and retreating even behind the cross wall, they posted themselves upon a hillock, where they stood all drawn up together in one close body, except only the Thebans. The hillock whereof I speak is at the entrance of the straits, where the stone lion now stands which was set up in honour of Leonidas. Here they defended themselves to the last, such as still had swords using them, and the others resisting with their hands and teeth; till the barbarians, who in part had pulled down the wall and attacked them in front, in part had gone round and now encircled them upon every side, overwhelmed and buried the remnant which was left beneath showers of missile weapons.

226. Thus nobly did the whole body of Lacedaemonians and Thespians behave; but nevertheless one man is said to have distinguished himself above all the rest, to wit, Dieneces the Spartan. A speech which he made before the Greeks engaged the Medes remains on record. One of the Trachinians told him that such was the number of the barbarians that when they shot forth their arrows the sun would be darkened by their multitude. Dieneces, not at all frightened at these words, but making light of the Median numbers, answered, "Our Trachinian friend brings us excellent tidings. If the Medes darken the sun, we shall have our fight in the shade." Other sayings too of a like nature are reported to have been left for posterity by Dieneces the Lacedaemonian.

227. Next to him two brothers, Lacedaemonians, are reputed to have made themselves conspicuous: they were named Alpheus and Maron, and were the sons of Orsiphantus. There was also a Thespian who gained greater glory than any of his countrymen: he was a man called Dithyrambus, the son of Harmatides.

228. The slain were buried where they fell; and in their honour, nor less in honour of those who died before Leonidas sent the allies away, an inscription was set up, which said:

> "Here did four thousand men from Pelops' land
>   Against three hundred myriads bravely stand."

This was in honour of all. Another was for the Spartans alone:

> "Go, stranger, and to Lacedaemon tell
>   That here, obeying her behests, we fell."

This was for the Lacedaemonians. The seer had the following:

> "The great Megistias' tomb you here may view,
>   Whom slew the Medes, fresh from Spercheius' fords.
> Well the wise seer the coming death foreknew,
>   Yet scorned he to forsake his Spartan lords."

These inscriptions, and the pillars likewise, were all set up by the Amphictyons, except that in honour of Megistias, which was inscribed to him (on account of their sworn friendship) by [the poet] Simonides, the son of Leoprepes.

229. Two of the three hundred, it is said, Aristodemus and Eurytus, having been attacked by a disease of the eyes, had received orders from Leonidas to quit the camp; and both lay at Alpeni in the worst stage of the malady. These two men might, had they been so minded, have agreed together to return alive to Sparta; or if they did not like to return, they might have gone both to the field and fallen with their countrymen. But at this time, when either way was open to them, unhappily they could not agree, but took contrary courses. Eurytus no sooner heard that the Persians had come round the mountain than straightway he called for his armour, and, having buckled it on, bade his helot lead him to the place where his friends were fighting. The helot did so, and then turned and fled; but Eurytus plunged into the thick of the battle, and so perished. Aristodemus, on the

other hand, was faint of heart, and remained at Alpeni. It is my belief that if Aristodemus only had been sick and returned, or if both had come back together, the Spartans would have been content and felt no anger; but when there were two men with the very same excuse, and one of them was chary of his life, while the other freely gave it, they could not but be very wroth with the former.

230. This is the account which some give of the escape of Aristodemus. Others say that he, with another, had been sent on a message from the army, and, having it in his power to return in time for the battle, purposely loitered on the road, and so survived his comrades; while his fellow messenger came back in time, and fell in the battle.

231. When Aristodemus returned to Lacedaemon, reproach and disgrace awaited him; disgrace, inasmuch as no Spartan would give him a light to kindle his fire, or so much as address a word to him; and reproach, since all spoke of him as "the craven." However he wiped away all his shame afterwards at the battle of Plataea.

232. Another of the three hundred is likewise said to have survived the battle, a man named Pantites, whom Leonidas had sent on an embassy into Thessaly. He, they say, on his return to Sparta, found himself in such disesteem that he hanged himself.

233. The Thebans under the command of Leontiades remained with the Greeks, and fought against the barbarians, only so long as necessity compelled them. No sooner did they see victory inclining to the Persians, and the Greeks under Leonidas hurrying with all speed towards the hillock, than they moved away from their companions, and with hands upraised advanced towards the barbarians, exclaiming, as was indeed most true, that they for their part wished well to the Medes, and had been among the first to give earth and water to the king; force alone had brought them to Thermopylae; and so they must not be blamed for the slaughter which had befallen the king's army. These words, the truth of which was attested by the Thessalians, sufficed to obtain the Thebans the grant of their lives. However,

their good fortune was not without some drawback; for several of them were slain by the barbarians on their first approach; and the rest, who were the greater number, had the royal mark branded upon their bodies by the command of Xerxes—Leontiades, their captain, being the first to suffer. (This man's son, Eurymachus, was afterwards slain by the Plataeans, when he came with a band of four hundred Thebans and seized their city.)

234. Thus fought the Greeks at Thermopylae. And Xerxes called for Demaratus to question him, and began as follows:

"Demaratus, you are a worthy man; your true-speaking proves it. All has happened as you forewarned. Now then, tell me, how many Lacedaemonians are there left, and of those left how many are such brave warriors as these? Or are they all alike?"

"O King," replied the other, "the whole number of the Lacedaemonians is very great; and many are the cities which they inhabit. But I will tell you what you really wish to learn. There is a town of Lacedaemon called Sparta, which contains within it about eight thousand men. *They* are, one and all, equal to those who have fought here. The other Lacedaemonians are brave men, but not such warriors as these."

"Tell me now, Demaratus," rejoined Xerxes, "how we may with least trouble subdue these men. You must know all the paths of their counsels, as you were once their king."

235. Then Demaratus answered, "O King, since you ask my advice so earnestly, it is fitting that I should inform you what I consider to be the best course. Detach three hundred vessels from the body of your fleet, and send them to attack the shores of Laconia. There is an island called Cythera in those parts, not far from the coast, concerning which Chilon, our wisest man, made the remark that Sparta would gain if it were sunk to the bottom of the sea—so constantly did he expect that it would give occasion to some project like that which I now recommend to you. I mean not to say that he had a foreknowledge of your attack upon Greece; but in truth he feared all armaments. Send thy ships then to this

island, and thence affright the Spartans. If once they have a war of their own close to their doors, fear not their giving any help to the rest of the Greeks while your land force is engaged in conquering them. In this way may all Greece be subdued; and then Sparta, left to herself, will be powerless. But if you will not take this advice, I will tell you what you may look to see. When you come to the Peloponnesus, you will find a narrow neck of land, where all the Peloponnesians who are leagued against you will be gathered together; and there you will have to fight bloodier battles than any which you have yet witnessed. If, however, you will follow my plan, the Isthmus and the cities of Peloponnesus will yield to you without a battle."

236. Achaemenes, who was present, now took the word, and spoke—he was brother to Xerxes, and, having the command of the fleet, feared lest Xerxes might be prevailed upon to do as Demaratus advised—

"I perceive, O King" (he said), "that you are listening to the words of a man who is envious of your good fortune, and seeks to betray your cause. This is indeed the common temper of the Grecian people—they envy good fortune, and hate power greater than their own. If in this posture of our affairs, after we have lost four hundred vessels by shipwreck, three hundred more be sent away to make a voyage round the Peloponnesus, our enemies will become a match for us. But let us keep our whole fleet in one body, and it will be dangerous for them to venture on an attack, as they will certainly be no match for us then. Besides, while our sea and land forces advance together, the fleet and army can each help the other; but if they be parted, no aid will come either from you to the fleet, or from the fleet to you. Only order your own matters well, and trouble not yourself to inquire concerning the enemy—where they will fight, or what they will do, or how many they are. Surely they can manage their own concerns without us, as we can ours without them. If the Lacedaemonians come out against the Persians to battle, they will scarce repair the disaster which has befallen them now."

237. Xerxes replied, "Achaemenes, your counsel pleases me well, and I will do as you say. But Demaratus advised what he thought best—only his judgement was not so good as yours. Never will I believe that he does not wish well to my cause; for that is disproved both by his former counsels and also by the circumstances of the case. A citizen does indeed envy any fellow citizen who is more lucky than himself, and often hates him secretly; if such a man be called on for counsel, he will not give his best thoughts, unless indeed he be a man of very exalted virtue; and such are but rarely found. But a friend of another country delights in the good fortune of his foreign bond-friend, and will give him, when asked, the best advice in his power. Therefore I warn all men to abstain henceforth from speaking ill of Demaratus, who is my bond-friend."

238. When Xerxes had thus spoken, he proceeded to pass through the slain; and finding the body of Leonidas, whom he knew to have been the Lacedaemonian king and captain, he ordered that the head should be struck off and fastened to a stake. This proves to me most clearly what is plain also in many other ways—namely, that King Xerxes was more angry with Leonidas, while he was still in life, than with any other mortal. Certainly, he would not else have used his body so shamefully. For the Persians are wont to honour those who show themselves valiant in fight more highly than any nation that I know. They, however, to whom the orders were given, did according to the commands of the king.

239. I return now to a point in my History which at the time I left incomplete. The Lacedaemonians were the first of the Greeks to hear of the king's design against their country; and it was at this time that they sent to consult the Delphic oracle, and received the answer of which I spoke a while ago. The discovery was made to them in a very strange way. Demaratus, the son of Ariston, after he took refuge with the Medes, was not, in my judgement, which is supported by probability, a well-wisher to the Lacedaemonians. It may be questioned, therefore, whether he did what I am about to mention from good will or from insolent triumph.

It happened that he was at Susa at the time when Xerxes determined to lead his army into Greece; and in this way becoming acquainted with his design, he resolved to send tidings of it to Sparta. So as there was no other way of effecting his purpose, since the danger of being discovered was great, Demaratus framed the following contrivance. He took a double tablet, and, clearing the wax away, wrote what the king was purposing to do upon the wood of the tablets; having done this, he spread the wax once more over the writing, and so sent it. By these means, the guards placed to watch the roads, observing nothing but a blank tablet, were sure to give no trouble to the bearer. When the tablet reached Lacedaemon, there was no one, I understand, who could find out the secret, till Gorgo, the daughter of Cleomenes and wife of Leonidas, discovered it, and told the others. If they would scrape the wax off the tablet, she said, they would be sure to find writing upon the wood. The Lacedaemonians took her advice, found the writing, and read it; after which they sent it round to the other Greeks. Such then is the account which is given of this matter.

BOOK VIII

The Persian War after Marathon (Continued)

1. The Greeks engaged in the sea-service were the following. The Athenians furnished a hundred and twenty-seven vessels to the fleet, which were manned in part by the Plataeans, who, though unskilled in such matters, were led by their active and daring spirit to undertake this duty; the Corinthians furnished forty vessels; the Megarians sent twenty; the Chalcideans also manned twenty, which had been furnished to them by the Athenians; the Aeginetans came with eighteen; the Sicyonians with twelve; the Lace-

daemonians with ten; the Epidaurians with eight; the
Eretrians with seven; the Troezenians with five; the Styreans
with two; and the Ceans with two triremes and two penteconters. Last of all, the Locrians of Opus came in aid with
seven penteconters.

2. Such were the nations which furnished vessels to the
fleet now at Artemisium; and in mentioning them I have
given the number of ships furnished by each. The total number of the ships thus brought together, without counting the
penteconters, was two hundred and seventy-one; and the
captain, who had the chief command over the whole fleet,
was Eurybiades the son of Eurycleides. He was furnished by
Sparta, since the allies had said that, if a Laconian did not
take the command, they would break up the fleet, for never
would they serve under the Athenians.

3. From the first, even earlier than the time when the embassy went to Sicily to solicit alliance, there had been a talk
of intrusting the Athenians with the command at sea; but the
allies were averse to the plan, wherefore the Athenians did
not press it; for there was nothing they had so much at heart
as the salvation of Greece, and they knew that, if they quarrelled among themselves about the command, Greece would
be brought to ruin. Herein they judged rightly; for internal
strife is a thing as much worse than war carried on by a
united people, as war itself is worse than peace. The Athenians therefore, being so persuaded, did not push their
claims, but waived them, so long as they were in such great
need of aid from the other Greeks. And they afterwards
showed their motive; for at the time when the Persians had
been driven from Greece, and were now threatened by the
Greeks in their own country, they took occasion of the insolence of Pausanias to deprive the Lacedaemonians of their
leadership. This, however, happened afterwards.

4. At the present time the Greeks, on their arrival at
Artemisium, when they saw the number of the ships which
lay at anchor near Aphetae, and the abundance of troops
everywhere, feeling disappointed that matters had gone with
the barbarians so far otherwise than they had expected, and

full of alarm at what they saw, began to speak of drawing back from Artemisium towards the inner parts of their country. So when the Euboeans heard what was in debate, they went to Eurybiades, and besought him to wait a few days, while they removed their children and their slaves to a place of safety. But, as they found that they prevailed nothing, they left him and went to Themistocles, the Athenian commander, to whom they gave a bribe of thirty talents, on his promise that the fleet should remain and risk a battle in defence of Euboea.

5. And Themistocles succeeded in detaining the fleet in the way which I will now relate. He made over to Eurybiades five talents out of the thirty paid him, which he gave as if they came from himself; and having in this way gained over the admiral, he addressed himself to Adeimantus, the son of Ocytus, the Corinthian leader, who was the only remonstrant now, and who still threatened to sail away from Artemisium and not wait for the other captains. Addressing himself to this man, Themistocles said with an oath, "You forsake us? By no means! I will pay you better for remaining than the Mede would for leaving your allies," and straightway he sent on board the ship of Adeimantus three talents of silver. So these two captains were won by gifts, and came over to the views of Themistocles, who was thereby enabled to gratify the wishes of the Euboeans. He likewise made his own gain on the occasion; for he kept the rest of the money, and no one knew of it. The commanders who took the gifts thought that the sums were furnished by Athens, and had been sent to be used in this way.

6. Thus it came to pass that the Greeks stayed at Euboea and there gave battle to the enemy.

Now the battle was as follows: The barbarians reached Aphetae early in the afternoon, and then saw (as they had previously heard reported) that a fleet of Greek ships, weak in number, lay at Artemisium. At once they were eager to engage the Greeks, hoping to capture them. They did not however think it wise to make straight for the Greek station, lest the enemy should see them as they bore down and betake themselves to flight immediately; in which case night might close in before they came up with the fugitives, and so they might get clean off and make their escape from them; whereas the Persians were minded not to let a single soul slip through their hands.

7. They therefore contrived a plan, which was the following: they detached two hundred of their ships from the rest, and—to prevent the enemy from seeing them start—sent them round outside the island of Sciathos, to make the circuit of Euboea by Caphareus and Geraestus, and so to reach the Euripus. By this plan they thought to enclose the Greeks on every side; for the ships detached would block up the only way by which they could retreat, while the others would press upon them in front. With these designs therefore they dispatched the two hundred ships, while they themselves waited, since they did not mean to attack the Greeks upon that day, or until they knew, by signal, of the arrival of the detachment which had been ordered to sail round Euboea. Meanwhile they made a muster of the other ships at Aphetae.

8. Now the Persians had with them a man named Scyllias, a native of Scione, who was the most expert diver of his day. At the time of the shipwreck off Mount Pelion he had recovered for the Persians many valuables (and appropriated many for himself). He had for some time been wishing to go over to the Greeks; but no good opportunity had offered till now. In what way he contrived to reach the Greeks I am not able to say for certain: I marvel much if the tale that is commonly told be true. It is said he dived into the sea at Aphetae, and did not once come to the surface till he reached Artemisium, a distance of nearly eighty furlongs. Now many things are related of this man which are plainly false; but some of the stories seem to be true. My own opinion is that on this occasion he made the passage to Artemisium in a boat.

However this might be, Scyllias no sooner reached Artemisium than he gave the Greek captains a full account of the damage done by the storm, and likewise told them of the ships sent to make the circuit of Euboea.

9. So the Greeks on receiving these tidings held a council, whereat, after much debate, it was resolved that they should stay quiet for the present where they were, and remain at their moorings, but that after midnight they should put out to sea, and encounter the ships which were on their way round the island. Later in the day, when they found that no one meddled with them, they formed a new plan, which was to wait till near evening and then sail out against the main body of the barbarians, for the purpose of trying their mode of fight and skill in manœuvring.

10. When the Persian commanders and crews saw the Greeks thus boldly sailing towards them with their few ships, they thought them possessed with madness, and went out to meet them, expecting (as indeed seemed likely enough) that they would take all their vessels with the greatest ease. The Greek ships were so few, and their own so far outnumbered them, and sailed so much better, that they resolved, seeing their advantage, to encompass their foe on every side. And now such of the Ionians as wished well to the Grecian cause and served in the Persian fleet unwillingly, seeing their countrymen surrounded, were sorely distressed; for they felt sure that not one of them would ever make his escape, so poor an opinion had they of the strength of the Greeks. On the other hand, such as saw with pleasure the attack on Greece, now vied eagerly with each other which should be the first to make prize of an Athenian ship, and thereby to secure himself a rich reward from the king. For through both the hosts none were so much accounted of as the Athenians.

11. The Greeks, at a signal, brought the sterns of their ships together into a small compass, and turned their prows on every side towards the barbarians; after which, at a second signal, although inclosed within a narrow space, and closely pressed upon by the foe, yet they fell bravely to work, and captured thirty ships of the barbarians, at the same time taking prisoner Philaon, the son of Chersis, and

brother of Gorgus king of Salamis [in Cyprus], a man of much repute in the fleet. The first who made prize of a ship of the enemy was Lycomedes the son of Aeschraeus, an Athenian, who was afterwards adjudged the meed of valour. Victory however was still doubtful when night came on, and put a stop to the combat. The Greeks sailed back to Artemisium; and the barbarians returned to Aphetae, much surprised at the result, which was far other than they had looked for. In this battle only one of the Greeks who fought on the side of the king deserted and joined his countrymen. This was Antidorus of Lemnos, whom the Athenians rewarded for his desertion by the present of a piece of land in Salamis.[1]

12. Evening had barely closed in when a heavy rain—it was about midsummer—began to fall, which continued the whole night, with terrible thunderings and lightnings from Mount Pelion; the bodies of the slain and the broken pieces of the damaged ships were drifted in the direction of Aphetae, and floated about the prows of the vessels there, disturbing the action of the oars. The barbarians, hearing the storm, were greatly dismayed, expecting certainly to perish, as they had fallen into such a multitude of misfortunes. For before they were well recovered from the tempest and the wreck of their vessels off Mount Pelion, they had been surprised by a sea fight which had taxed all their strength, and now the sea fight was scarcely over when they were exposed to floods of rain, and the rush of swollen streams into the sea, and violent thunderings.

13. If, however, they who lay at Aphetae passed a comfortless night, far worse were the sufferings of those who had been sent to make the circuit of Euboea; inasmuch as the storm fell on them out at sea, whereby the issue was indeed calamitous. They were sailing along near the Hollows of Euboea when the wind began to rise and the rain to pour; overpowered by the force of the gale, and driven they knew not whither, at the last they fell upon rocks, Heaven so con-

[1] This Salamis is the island in the bay off Attica.

triving in order that the Persian fleet might not greatly exceed the Greek, but be brought nearly to its level.

14. This squadron, therefore, was entirely lost about the Hollows of Euboea. The barbarians at Aphetae were glad when day dawned, and remained in quiet at their station, content if they might enjoy a little peace after so many sufferings. Meanwhile there came to the aid of the Greeks a reinforcement of fifty-three ships from Attica. Their arrival, and the news (which reached Artemisium about the same time) of the complete destruction by the storm of the ships sent to sail round Euboea, greatly cheered the spirits of the Greek sailors. So they waited again till the same hour as the day before, and, once more putting out to sea, attacked the enemy. This time they fell in with some Cilician vessels, which they sank; when night came on, they withdrew to Artemisium.

15. The third day was now come, and the captains of the barbarians, ashamed that so small a number of ships should harass their fleet, and afraid of the anger of Xerxes, instead of waiting for the others to begin the battle, weighed anchor themselves, and advanced against the Greeks about the hour of noon. Now it happened that these sea fights took place on the very same days with the combats at Thermopylae; and as the aim of the struggle was in the one case to maintain the pass, so in the other it was to defend the Euripus. While the Greeks, therefore, exhorted one another not to let the barbarians burst in upon Greece, these latter shouted to their fellows to destroy the Grecian fleet, and get possession of the channel.

16. And now the fleet of Xerxes advanced in good order to the attack, while the Greeks on their side remained quite motionless at Artemisium. The Persians therefore spread themselves, and came forward in a half-moon, seeking to encircle the Greeks on all sides, and thereby prevent them from escaping. The Greeks, when they saw this, sailed out to meet their assailants; and the battle forthwith began. In this engagement the two fleets contended with no clear ad-

vantage to either, for the armament of Xerxes injured itself by its own greatness, the vessels falling into disorder, and oft-times running foul of one another; yet still they did not give way, but made a stout fight, since the crews felt it would indeed be a disgrace to turn and fly from a fleet so inferior in number. The Greeks therefore suffered much, both in ships and men; but the barbarians experienced a far larger loss of each. So the fleets separated after such a combat as I have described.

17. On the side of Xerxes the Egyptians distinguished themselves above all the combatants; for, besides performing many other noble deeds, they took five vessels from the Greeks with their crews on board. On the side of the Greeks the Athenians bore off the meed of valour; and among them the most distinguished was Clinias, the son of Alcibiades,[2] who served at his own charge with two hundred men, on board a vessel which he had himself furnished.

18. The two fleets, on separating, hastened very gladly to their anchorage grounds. The Greeks, indeed, when the battle was over, became masters of the bodies of their slain and the wrecks of the vessels; but they had been so roughly handled, especially the Athenians, one-half of whose vessels had suffered damage, that they determined to break up from their station, and withdraw to the inner parts of their country.

19. Then Themistocles, who thought that if the Ionian and Carian ships could be detached from the barbarian fleet the Greeks might be well able to defeat the rest, called the captains together. They met upon the sea-shore, where the Euboeans were now assembling their flocks and herds; and here Themistocles told them he thought that he knew of a plan whereby he could detach from the king those who were of most worth among his allies. This was all that he disclosed to them of his plan at that time. Meanwhile, looking to the circumstances in which they were, he advised them to slaughter as many of the Euboean cattle as they liked—for it was better (he said) that their own troops should enjoy

[2] And probably great-uncle of the famous Alcibiades.

them than the enemy—and to give orders to their men to kindle the fires as usual. With regard to the retreat, he said that he would take upon himself to watch the proper moment, and would manage matters so that they should return to Greece without loss. These words pleased the captains; so they had the fires lighted, and began the slaughter of the cattle.

20. The Euboeans, until now, had made light of the oracle of Bacis, as though it had been void of all significance, and had neither removed their goods from the island nor yet taken them into their strong places, as they would most certainly have done if they had believed that war was approaching. By this neglect they had brought their affairs into the very greatest danger. Now the oracle of which I speak ran as follows:

"When o'er the main shall be thrown a byblus yoke by a stranger,
Be thou ware, and drive from Euboea the goats loud-bleating."

So, as the Euboeans had paid no regard to this oracle when the evils approached and impended, now that they had arrived, the worst was likely to befall them.

21. While the Greeks were employed in the way described above, the scout who had been on the watch at Trachis arrived at Artemisium. For the Greeks had employed two watchers: Polyas, a native of Anticyra, had been stationed off Artemisium, with a rowboat at his command ready to sail at any moment, his orders being that, if an engagement took place by sea, he should convey the news at once to the Greeks at Thermopylae; and in like manner Abronichus, the son of Lysicles, an Athenian, had been stationed with a triaconter near Leonidas, to be ready, in case of disaster befalling the land force, to carry tidings of it to Artemisium. It was this Abronichus who now arrived with news of what had befallen Leonidas and those who were with him. When the Greeks heard the tidings they no longer delayed to retreat, but withdrew in the order wherein they had

been stationed, the Corinthians leading and the Athenians sailing last of all.

22. And now Themistocles chose out the swiftest sailers from among the Athenian vessels, and, proceeding to the various watering-places along the coast, cut inscriptions on the rocks, which were read by the Ionians the day following, on their arrival at Artemisium. The inscriptions ran thus: "Men of Ionia, you do wrong to fight against your own fathers, and to give your help to enslave Greece. We beseech you therefore to come over, if possible, to our side; if you cannot do this, then, we pray you, stand aloof from the contest yourselves, and persuade the Carians to do the like. If neither of these things be possible, and you are hindered, by a force too strong to resist, from venturing upon desertion, at least when we come to blows fight backwardly, remembering that you are sprung from us, and that it was through you we first provoked the hatred of the barbarian." Themistocles, in putting up these inscriptions, looked, I believe, to two chances—either Xerxes would not discover them, in which case they might bring over the Ionians to the side of the Greeks; or they would be reported to him and made a ground of accusation against the Ionians, who would thereupon be distrusted, and would not be allowed to take part in the sea fights.

23. That is what he wrote. Shortly after, a man of Histiaea went in a ship to tell the barbarians that the Greeks had fled from Artemisium. Disbelieving his report, the Persians kept the man a prisoner, while they sent some of their fastest vessels to see what had happened. These brought back word how matters stood; whereupon at sunrise the whole fleet advanced together in a body, and sailed to Artemisium, where they remained till midday; after which they went on to Histiaea. That city fell into their hands immediately; and they shortly overran the various villages upon the coast in the district of Ellopia, which was part of the Histiaean territory.

24. It was while they were at this station that a herald reached them from Xerxes, whom he had sent after making

the following dispositions with respect to the bodies of those who fell at Thermopylae. Of the twenty thousand who had been slain on the Persian side, he left one thousand upon the field while he buried the rest in trenches; and these he carefully filled up with earth, and hid with foliage, that the sailors might not see any signs of them. The herald, on reaching Histiaea, caused the whole force to be collected together, and spoke thus to them:

"Comrades, King Xerxes gives permission to all who please, to quit their posts, and see how he fights with the senseless men who think to overthrow his armies."

25. No sooner had these words been uttered, than it became difficult to get a boat, so great was the number of those who desired to see the sight. Such as went crossed the strait, and passing among the heaps of dead, in this way viewed the spectacle. Many helots were included in the slain, but everyone imagined that the bodies were all either Lacedaemonians or Thespians. However, no one was deceived by what Xerxes had done with his own dead. It was indeed most truly a laughable device—on the one side a thousand men were seen lying about the field, on the other four thousand crowded together into one spot. This day then was given up to sight-seeing; on the next the seamen embarked on board their ships and sailed back to Histiaea, while Xerxes and his army proceeded upon their march.

26. There came now a few deserters from Arcadia to join the Persians—poor men who had nothing to live on, and were in want of employment. The Persians brought them into the king's presence, and there inquired of them, by a man who acted as their spokesman, what the Greeks were doing. The Arcadians answered, "They are holding the Olympic games, seeing the athletic sports and the chariot races." "And what," said the man, "is the prize for which they contend?" "An olive wreath," returned the others, "which is given to the man who wins." On hearing this, Tritantaechmes, the son of Artabanus, uttered a speech which was in truth most noble, but which caused him to be taxed with cowardice by King Xerxes. Hearing the men say that

the prize was not money but a wreath of olive, he could not forbear from exclaiming before them all, "Good heavens! Mardonius, what manner of men are these against whom you have brought us to fight—men who contend with one another, not for money, but for honour!"

27. That is what he said then. A little before this, and just after the blow had been struck at Thermopylae, a herald was sent into Phocis by the Thessalians, who had always been on bad terms with the Phocians, and especially since their last overthrow. For it was not many years previous to this invasion of Greece by the king that the Thessalians, with their allies, entered Phocis in full force, but were defeated by the Phocians in an engagement wherein they were very roughly handled. The Phocians, who had with them as soothsayer Tellias of Elis, were blocked up in the mountain of Parnassus, when the following stratagem was contrived for them by Tellias. He took six hundred of their bravest men, and whitened their bodies and their arms with chalk; then, instructing them to slay everyone whom they should meet that was not whitened like themselves, he made a night attack upon the Thessalians. No sooner did the Thessalian sentries, who were the first to see them, behold this strange sight, than, imagining it to be a prodigy, they were all filled with affright. From the sentries the alarm spread to the army, which was seized with such a panic that the Phocians killed four thousand of them, and became masters of their dead bodies and shields. Of the shields one-half were sent as an offering to the temple at Abae, the other half were deposited at Delphi; while from the tenth part of the booty gained in the battle were made the gigantic figures which stand round the tripod in front of the Delphic shrine, and likewise the figures of the same size and character at Abae.

28. Besides this slaughter of the Thessalian foot when it was blockading them, the Phocians had dealt a blow to their horse upon its invading their territory, from which they had never recovered. There is a pass near the city of Hyampolis where the Phocians, having dug a broad trench, filled up the void with empty wine jars, after which they covered the

place with soil, so that the ground all looked alike, and then awaited the coming of the Thessalians. These, thinking to destroy the Phocians at one sweep, rushed rapidly forward, and became entangled in the wine jars, which broke the legs of their horses.

29. The Thessalians had therefore a double cause of quarrel with the Phocians, when they dispatched the herald above mentioned, who delivered this message:

"At length acknowledge, men of Phocis, that you may not think to match with us. In times past, when it pleased us to hold with the Greeks, we had always the vantage over you; and now our influence is such with the barbarian that, if we choose it, you will lose your country, and (what is even worse) you will be sold as slaves. However, though we can now do with you exactly as we like, we are willing to forget our wrongs. Quit them with a payment of fifty talents of silver, and we undertake to ward off the evils which threaten your country."

30. Such was the message which the Thessalians sent. The Phocians were the only people in these parts who had not espoused the cause of the Medes; and it is my deliberate opinion that the motive which swayed them was none other —neither more nor less—than their hatred of the Thessalians: for had the Thessalians declared in favour of the Greeks, I believe that the men of Phocis would have joined the Median side. As it was, when the message arrived, the Phocians made answer, that they would not pay anything— it was open to them, equally with the Thessalians, to make common cause with the Medes, if they only chose so to do, but they would never of their own free will become traitors to Greece.

31. On the return of this answer, the Thessalians, full of wrath against the Phocians, offered themselves as guides to the barbarian army, and led them forth from Trachinia into Doris. In this place there is a narrow tongue of Dorian territory, not more than thirty furlongs across, interposed between Malis and Phocis; it is the tract in ancient times called Dryopis; and the land, of which it is a part, is the mother

country of the Dorians in the Peloponnesus. This territory the barbarians did not plunder, for the inhabitants had espoused their side; and besides, the Thessalians wished that they should be spared.

32. From Doris they marched forward into Phocis; but here the inhabitants did not fall into their power, for some of them had taken refuge in the high grounds of Parnassus, one summit of which, called Tithorea, standing quite by itself, not far from the city of Neon, is well fitted to give shelter to a large body of men, and had now received a number of the Phocians with their movables; while the greater portion had fled to the country of the Ozolian Locrians and placed their goods in the city called Amphissa, which lies above the Crissaean plain. The land of Phocis, however, was entirely overrun, for the Thessalians led the Persian army through the whole of it; and wherever they went the country was wasted with fire and sword, the cities and even the temples being wilfully set alight by the troops.

33. The march of the army lay along the valley of the Cephissus; and here they ravaged far and wide, burning the towns of Drymus, Charadra, Erochus, Tethronium, Amphicaea, Neon, Pedieis, Triteis, Elateia, Hyampolis, Parapotamii, and Abae. At the last-named place there was a temple of Apollo, very rich, and adorned with a vast number of treasures and offerings. There was likewise an oracle there in those days, as indeed there is at the present time. This temple the Persians plundered and burnt; and here they captured a number of the Phocians before they could reach the hills, and some women, who died because of the great number who abused them.

34. After passing Parapotamii, the barbarians marched to Panopeis; and now the army separated into two bodies, whereof one, which was the more numerous and the stronger of the two, marched, under Xerxes himself, towards Athens, entering Boeotia by the country of the Orchomenians. The Boeotians had one and all embraced the cause of the Medes; and their towns were in the possession of Macedonian gar-

risons, whom Alexander had sent there to make it manifest to Xerxes that the Boeotians were on the Median side.

35. Such then was the road followed by one division of the barbarians. The other division took guides, and proceeded towards the temple of Delphi, keeping Mount Parnassus on their right hand. They too laid waste such parts of Phocis as they passed through, burning the city of the Panopeans, together with those of the Daulians and of the Aeolidae. This body had been detached from the rest of the army, and made to march in this direction, for the purpose of plundering the Delphian temple and conveying to King Xerxes the riches which were there laid up. For Xerxes, as I am informed, was better acquainted with what there was worthy of note at Delphi, than even with what he had left in his own house; so many of those about him were continually describing the treasures—more especially the offerings made by Croesus the son of Alyattes.

36. Now when the Delphians heard what danger they were in, great fear fell on them. In their terror they consulted the oracle concerning the holy treasures, and inquired if they should bury them in the ground, or carry them away to some other country. The god, in reply, bade them leave the treasures untouched—he was able, he said, without help to protect his own. So the Delphians, when they received this answer, began to think about saving themselves. And first of all they sent their women and children across the gulf into Achaea; after which the greater number of them climbed up into the tops of Parnassus and placed their goods for safety in the Corycian cave; while some effected their escape to Amphissa in Locris. In this way all the Delphians quitted the city, except sixty men, and the prophet.

37. When the barbarian assailants drew near and were in sight of the place, the prophet, who was named Aceratus, beheld, in front of the temple, a portion of the sacred armour, which it was not lawful for any mortal hand to touch, lying upon the ground, removed from the inner shrine where it was wont to hang. Then he went and told the prodigy to

the Delphians who had remained behind. Meanwhile the enemy pressed forward briskly, and had reached the shrine of Athena Pronaia, when they were overtaken by other prodigies still more wonderful than the first. Truly it was marvel enough when warlike harness was seen lying outside the temple, removed there by no power but its own; what followed, however, exceeded in strangeness all prodigies that had ever before been seen. The barbarians had just reached in their advance the chapel of Athena Pronaia when a storm of thunder burst suddenly over their heads; at the same time two crags split off from Mount Parnassus, and rolled down upon them with a loud noise, crushing vast numbers beneath their weight, while from the temple of Athena there went up the war cry and the shout of victory.

38. All these things together struck terror into the barbarians, who forthwith turned and fled. The Delphians, seeing this, came down from their hiding-places and smote them with a great slaughter, from which such as escaped fled straight into Boeotia. These men, on their return, declared (as I am told) that besides the marvels mentioned above they witnessed also other supernatural sights. Two armed warriors, they said, of a stature more than human, pursued after their flying ranks, pressing them close and slaying them.

39. These men, the Delphians maintain, were two heroes belonging to the place—by name Phylacus and Autonoüs— each of whom has a sacred precinct near the temple; one, that of Phylacus, hard by the road which runs above the temple of Pronaia; the other, that of Autonoüs, near the Castalian spring, at the foot of the peak called Hyampeia. The blocks of stone which fell from Parnassus might still be seen in my day; they lay in the precinct of Athena Pronaia, where they stopped after rolling through the host of the barbarians. Thus was this body of men forced to retire from the temple.

40. Meanwhile, the Grecian fleet, which had left Artemisium, proceeded to Salamis, at the request of the Athenians, and there cast anchor. The Athenians had begged them to take up this position in order that they might convey

their women and children out of Attica, and further might deliberate upon the course which it now behooved them to follow. Disappointed in the hopes which they had previously entertained, they were about to hold a council concerning the present posture of their affairs. For they had looked to see the Peloponnesians drawn up in full force to resist the enemy in Boeotia, but found nothing of what they had expected; nay, they learnt that the Greeks of those parts, only concerning themselves about their own safety, were building a wall across the Isthmus, and intended to guard the Peloponnesus, and let the rest of Greece take its chance. These tidings caused them to make the request whereof I spoke, that the combined fleet should anchor at Salamis.

41. So while the rest of the fleet lay to off this island, the Athenians cast anchor along their own coast. Immediately upon their arrival, proclamation was made that every Athenian should save his children and household as he best could; whereupon some sent their families to Aegina, some to Salamis, but the greater number to Troezen. This removal was made with all possible haste, partly from a desire to obey the advice of the oracle, but still more for another reason. The Athenians say that they have in their Acropolis a huge serpent, which lives in the temple, and is the guardian of the whole place. Nor do they only say this, but, as if the serpent really dwelt there, every month they lay out its food, which consists of a honey-cake. Up to this time the honey-cake had always been consumed; but now it remained untouched. So the priestess told the people what had happened; whereupon they left Athens the more readily, since they believed that the goddess had already abandoned the citadel. As soon as all was removed, the Athenians sailed back to their station.

42. And now the remainder of the Grecian sea-force, hearing that the fleet which had been at Artemisium was come to Salamis, joined it at that island from Troezen—orders having been issued previously that the ships should muster at Pogon, the port of the Troezenians. The vessels collected were many more in number than those which had

fought at Artemisium, and were furnished by more cities. The admiral was the same who had commanded before, to wit, Eurybiades, the son of Eurycleides, who was a Spartan, but not of the family of the kings; the city, however, which sent by far the greatest number of ships, and the best sailers, was Athens. . . .

49. When the captains from these various cities were come together at Salamis, a council was summoned; and Eurybiades proposed that anyone who liked to advise should say which place seemed to him the fittest, among those still in the possession of the Greeks, to be the scene of a naval combat. Attica, he said, was not to be thought of now; but he desired their counsel as to the remainder. The speakers mostly advised that the fleet should sail away to the Isthmus, and there give battle in defence of the Peloponnesus; and they urged as a reason for this that if they were worsted in a sea fight at Salamis, they would be shut up in an island where they could get no help; but if they were beaten near the Isthmus, they could escape to their homes.

50. As the captains from the Peloponnesus were thus advising, there came an Athenian to the camp, who brought word that the barbarians had entered Attica, and were ravaging and burning everything. For the division of the army under Xerxes was just arrived at Athens from its march through Boeotia, where it had burnt Thespiae and Plataea —both which cities were forsaken by their inhabitants, who had fled to the Peloponnesus—and now it was laying waste all the possessions of the Athenians. Thespiae and Plataea had been burnt by the Persians because they knew from the Thebans that neither of those cities had espoused their side.

51. Since the passage of the Hellespont and the commencement of the march upon Greece, a space of four months had gone by—one while the army made the crossing, and delayed about the region of the Hellespont, and three while they proceeded thence to Attica, which they entered in the archonship of Calliades. They found the city forsaken; a few people only remained in the temple, either

keepers of the treasures or men of the poorer sort. These persons, having fortified the Acropolis with planks and boards, held out against the enemy. It was in some measure their poverty which had prevented them from seeking shelter in Salamis; but there was likewise another reason which in part induced them to remain. They imagined themselves to have discovered the true meaning of the oracle uttered by the Pythoness, which promised that "the wooden wall" should never be taken—the wooden wall, they thought, did not mean the ships, but the place where they had taken refuge.

52. The Persians encamped upon the hill over against the Acropolis, which is called the Areopagus by the Athenians, and began the siege of the place, attacking the Greeks with arrows whereto pieces of lighted tow were attached, which they shot at the barricade. And now those who were within the citadel found themselves in a most woeful case, for their wooden rampart betrayed them; still, however, they continued to resist. It was in vain that the Pisistratidae came to them and offered terms of surrender—they thought of new modes of defence; they rolled down huge masses of stone upon the barbarians as they were mounting up to the gates: so that Xerxes was for a long time very greatly perplexed, and could not contrive any way to take them.

53. At last, however, in the midst of these many difficulties, the barbarians made discovery of an access. For it was fated, as the oracle had spoken, that the whole mainland of Attica should fall beneath the sway of the Persians. Right in front of the Acropolis, but behind the gates and the common ascent—where no watch was kept, and no one would have thought it possible that any foot of man could climb—a few soldiers mounted from the sanctuary of Aglaurus, Cecrops' daughter, notwithstanding the steepness of the precipice. As soon as the Athenians saw them upon the summit, some threw themselves headlong from the wall, and so perished, while others fled for refuge to the inner part of the temple. The Persians rushed to the gates and opened them, after

which they massacred the suppliants. When all were slain, they plundered the temple and fired every part of the citadel.

54. Xerxes, thus completely master of Athens, despatched a horseman to Susa, with a message to Artabanus, informing him of his success hitherto. The day after, he collected together all the Athenian exiles who had come into Greece in his train, and bade them go up into the citadel, and there offer sacrifice after their own fashion. I know not whether he had had a dream which made him give this order, or whether he felt some remorse on account of having set the temple on fire. However this may have been, the exiles obeyed the command given them.

55. I will now explain why I have made mention of this circumstance: there is a temple of Erechtheus the Earthborn, as he is called, in this citadel, containing within it an olive tree and a sea.[3] The tale goes among the Athenians that they were placed there as witnesses by Poseidon and Athena when they had their contention about the country. Now this olive tree had been burnt with the rest of the temple when the barbarians took the place. But when the Athenians, whom the king had commanded to offer sacrifice, went up into the temple for the purpose, they found a fresh shoot, as much as a cubit in length, thrown out from the old trunk. Such at least was the account which these persons gave.

56. Meanwhile, at Salamis, the Greeks no sooner heard what had befallen the Athenian citadel than they fell into such alarm that some of the captains did not even wait for the council to come to a vote, but embarked hastily on board their vessels, and hoisted sail as though they would take to flight immediately. The rest, who stayed at the council board, came to a vote that the fleet should give battle at the Isthmus. Night now drew on; and the captains, dispersing from the meeting, proceeded on board their respective ships.

57. Themistocles, as he entered his own vessel, was met

[3] A salt-water well.

by Mnesiphilus, an Athenian, who asked him what the council had resolved to do. On learning that the resolve was to stand away for the Isthmus, and there give battle on behalf of the Peloponnesus, Mnesiphilus exclaimed:

"If these men sail away from Salamis, you will have no fatherland for which to fight; for they will all scatter themselves to their own cities; and neither Eurybiades nor any one else will be able to hinder them, nor to stop the breaking up of the armament. Thus will Greece be brought to ruin through evil counsels. But haste now; and, if there be any possible way, seek to unsettle these resolves—perhaps you may persuade Eurybiades to change his mind, and continue here."

58. The suggestion greatly pleased Themistocles; and without answering a word, he went straight to the vessel of Eurybiades. Arrived there, he let him know that he wanted to speak with him on a matter touching the common interest. So Eurybiades bade him come on board, and say whatever he wished. Then Themistocles, seating himself at his side, went over all the arguments which he had heard from Mnesiphilus, pretending as if they were his own, and added to them many new ones besides; until at last he persuaded Eurybiades, by his importunity, to quit his ship and again collect the captains to council.

59. As soon as they were come, and before Eurybiades had opened to them his purpose in assembling them together, Themistocles, as men are wont to do when they are very anxious, spoke much to divers of them; whereupon the Corinthian captain, Adeimantus, the son of Ocytus, observed, "Themistocles, at the games they who start too soon are scourged." "True," rejoined the other in his excuse, "but they who wait too late are not crowned."

60. Thus he gave the Corinthian at this time a mild answer; and towards Eurybiades himself he did not now use any of those arguments which he had urged before, or say aught of allies betaking themselves to flight if once they broke up from Salamis; it would have been ungraceful for

him, when the confederates were present, to make accusation against any: but he had recourse to quite a new sort of reasoning, and addressed him as follows:

"It rests with you to save Greece, if you will only listen to me, and give the enemy battle here, rather than yield to the advice of those among us who would have the fleet withdrawn to the Isthmus. Listen, and judge between the two courses. At the Isthmus you will fight in an open sea, which is greatly to our disadvantage, since our ships are heavier and fewer in number than the enemy's; and further, you will in any case lose Salamis, Megara, and Aegina, even if all the rest goes well with us. The land and sea force of the Persians will advance together; and your retreat will but draw them to the Peloponnesus, and so bring all Greece into peril. If, on the other hand, you do as I advise, these are the advantages which you will secure: in the first place, as we shall fight in a narrow sea with few ships against many, if the battle follows the common course, we shall gain a great victory; for to fight in a narrow space is favorable to us—in an open sea, to them. Again, Salamis will in this case be preserved, where we have placed our wives and children. Nay, that very point by which you set most store is secured as much by this course as by the other; for whether we fight here or at the Isthmus, we shall equally give battle in defence of the Peloponnesus. Assuredly you will not do wisely to draw the Persians upon that region. For if things turn out as I anticipate, and we beat them by sea, then we shall have kept your Isthmus free from the barbarians, and they will have advanced no farther than Attica, but from thence have fled back in disorder; and we shall, moreover, have saved Megara, Aegina, and Salamis itself, where an oracle has said that we are to overcome our enemies. When men counsel reasonably, reasonable success ensues; but when in their counsels they reject reason, God does not choose to follow the wanderings of human fancies."

61. When Themistocles had thus spoken, Adeimantus the Corinthian again attacked him, and bade him be silent, since he was a man without a city; at the same time he called

on Eurybiades not to put the question at the instance of one who had no country, and urged that Themistocles should show of what state he was envoy, before he gave his voice with the rest. This reproach he made because the city of Athens had been taken and was in the hands of the barbarians. Hereupon Themistocles spoke many bitter things against Adeimantus and the Corinthians generally; and, for proof that he had a country, reminded the captains that with two hundred ships at his command, all fully manned for battle, he had both city and territory greater than theirs; since there was no Grecian state which could resist his men if they were to make a descent.

62. After this declaration he turned to Eurybiades, and addressing him with still greater warmth and earnestness, "If you stay here," he said, "and behave like a brave man, all will be well—if not, you will bring Greece to ruin. For the whole fortune of the war depends on our ships. Be persuaded by my words. If not, we will take our families on board and go, just as we are, to Siris, in Italy, which is ours from of old, and which the prophecies declare we are to colonize some day or other. You then, when you have lost allies like us, will hereafter call to mind what I have now said."

63. At these words of Themistocles, Eurybiades changed his determination; principally, as I believe, because he feared that if he withdrew the fleet to the Isthmus, the Athenians would sail away, and knew that without the Athenians, the rest of their ships could be no match for the fleet of the enemy. He therefore decided to remain and give battle at Salamis.

64. And now, the different chiefs, notwithstanding their skirmish of words, on learning the decision of Eurybiades, at once made ready for the fight. Morning broke; and, just as the sun rose, the shock of an earthquake was felt both on shore and at sea: whereupon the Greeks resolved to approach the gods with prayer, and likewise to send and invite the Aeacids to their aid. And this they did, with as much speed as they had resolved on it. Prayers were offered to all the gods, and Telamon and Ajax were invoked at once from

Salamis, while a ship was sent to Aegina to fetch Ajax himself, and the other Aeacids.

65. The following is a tale which was told by Dicaeus, the son of Theocydes, an Athenian, who was at this time an exile, and had gained a good report among the Medes. He declared that after the army of Xerxes had, in the absence of the Athenians, wasted Attica, he chanced to be with Demaratus the Lacedaemonian in the Thriasian plain, and that while there he saw a cloud of dust advancing from Eleusis, such as a host of thirty thousand men might raise. As he and his companion were wondering who the men, from whom the dust arose, could possibly be, a sound of voices reached his ear, and he thought that he recognized the mystic hymn to Bacchus. Now Demaratus was unacquainted with the rites of Eleusis, and so he inquired of Dicaeus what the voices were saying. Dicaeus made answer: "O Demaratus, beyond a doubt some mighty calamity is about to befall the king's army! For it is manifest, inasmuch as Attica is deserted by its inhabitants, that the sound which we have heard is an unearthly one, and is now upon its way from Eleusis to aid the Athenians and their confederates. If it descends upon the Peloponnesus, danger will threaten the king himself and his land army; if it moves towards the ships at Salamis, the king's fleet there faces destruction. Every year the Athenians celebrate this feast to the Mother and the Daughter [Demeter and Persephone]; and all who wish, whether they be Athenians or any other Greeks, are initiated. The sound thou hearest is the Bacchic song, which is wont to be sung at that festival." "Be still," rejoined the other, "and tell no man of this matter. For if your words be brought to the king's ear, you will assuredly lose your head because of them; neither I nor any man living can then save you. Hold your peace therefore. The gods will see to the king's army." Thus Demaratus counselled him; and they looked, and saw the dust, from which the sound arose, become a cloud, and the cloud rise up into the air and sail away to Salamis, making for the station of the Grecian fleet. Then they knew that it was the fleet of Xerxes which would suffer destruction. Such

was the tale told by Dicaeus the son of Theocydes; and he appealed for its truth to Demaratus and other eyewitnesses.

66. The men belonging to the fleet of Xerxes, after they had seen the Spartan dead at Thermopylae, and crossed the channel from Trachis to Histiaea, waited there the space of three days, and then, sailing down through the Euripus, in three more came to Phalerum. In my judgement, the Persian forces both by land and sea when they invaded Attica were not less numerous than they had been on their arrival at Sepias and Thermopylae. For against the Persian loss in the storm and at Thermopylae, and again in the sea fights off Artemisium, I set the various nations which had since joined the king—as the Malians, the Dorians, the Locrians, and the Boeotians—each serving in full force in his army except the last, who did not number in their ranks either the Thespians or the Plataeans; and together with these, the Carystians, the Andrians, the Tenians, and the other people of the islands, who all fought on this side except the five states already mentioned. For as the Persians penetrated farther into Greece, they were joined continually by fresh nations.

67. Reinforced by the contingents of all these various states, except Paros, the barbarians reached Athens. As for the Parians, they tarried at Cythnus, waiting to see how the war would go. The rest of the sea forces came safe to Phalerum; where they were visited by Xerxes, who had conceived a desire to go aboard and learn the wishes of the fleet. So he came and sat in a seat of honour; and the tyrants of the nations under his rule, and the captains of the ships, were sent for, to appear before him, and as they arrived took their seats according to the rank assigned them by the king. In the first seat sat the king of Sidon; after him, the king of Tyre; then the rest in their order. When the whole had taken their places, one after another, and were set down in orderly array, Xerxes, to try them, had Mardonius question each, whether a sea fight should be risked or no.

68. Mardonius accordingly went round the entire assemblage, beginning with the Sidonian, and asked this question;

to which all gave the same answer, advising to engage the Greeks, except only Artemisia, who spoke as follows:

"Say to the king, Mardonius, that these are my words to him: I was not the least brave of those who fought at Euboea, nor were my achievements there among the meanest; it is my right therefore, O lord, to tell you plainly what I think to be most for your advantage now. This then is my advice. Spare your ships, and do not risk a battle; for these people are as much superior to your people in seamanship as men to women. What so great need is there for you to incur hazard at sea? Are you not master of Athens, for which you undertook your expedition? Is not Greece subject to you? Not a soul now resists your advance. They who once resisted were handled even as they deserved.

"Now learn how I expect affairs will go with your adversaries. If you are not over-hasty to engage with them by sea, but will keep your fleet near the land, then, whether you abide as you are or march forward towards the Peloponnesus, you will easily accomplish all that for which you came here. The Greeks cannot hold out against you very long; you will soon part them asunder, and scatter them to their various cities. In the island where they lie, I hear they have no food in store; nor is it likely, if your land force begins its march towards the Peloponnesus, that they will remain quietly where they are—at least such as come from that region. Of a surety *they* will not greatly trouble themselves to give battle on behalf of the Athenians. On the other hand, if you are hasty to fight, I tremble lest the defeat of your sea force bring harm likewise to your land army. This, too, you should remember, O King; good masters are apt to have bad slaves, and bad masters good ones. Now, as you are the best of men, your slaves must needs be a sorry set. These Egyptians, Cypriots, Cilicians, and Pamphylians, who are counted in the number of your allies, of how little use are they!"

69. While Artemisia spoke thus to Mardonius, they who wished her well were greatly troubled concerning her words, thinking that she would suffer some hurt at the king's hands because she exhorted him not to risk a battle; they, on the

other hand, who disliked and envied her, favoured as she was by the king above all the rest of the allies, rejoiced at her declaration, expecting that her life would be the forfeit. But Xerxes, when the words of the several speakers were reported to him, was pleased beyond all others with the reply of Artemisia; and whereas even before this he had always esteemed her much, he now praised her more than ever. Nevertheless, he gave orders that the advice of the greater number should be followed; for he thought that at Euboea the fleet had not done its best, because he himself was not there to see—whereas this time he resolved that he would be an eyewitness of the combat.

70. Orders were now given to stand out to sea; and the ships proceeded towards Salamis, and took up the stations to which they were directed, without let or hindrance from the enemy. The day, however, was too far spent for them to begin the battle, since night already approached, so they prepared to engage upon the morrow. The Greeks, meanwhile, were in great distress and alarm, more especially those of the Peloponnesus, who were troubled that they had been kept at Salamis to fight on behalf of the Athenian territory, and feared that, if they should suffer defeat, they would be pent up and besieged in an island, while their own country was left unprotected.

71. The same night the land army of the barbarians began its march towards the Peloponnesus, where, however, all that was possible had been done to prevent the enemy from forcing an entrance by land. As soon as news reached the Peloponnesus of the death of Leonidas and his companions at Thermopylae, the inhabitants flocked together from the various cities and encamped at the Isthmus, under the command of Cleombrotus, son of Anaxandridas and brother of Leonidas. Here their first care was to block up the Scironian Way, after which it was determined in council to build a wall across the Isthmus. As the number assembled amounted to many tens of thousands, and there was not one who did not give himself to the work, it was soon finished. Stones, bricks, timber, baskets filled full of sand, were used

in the building; and not a moment was lost by those who gave their aid; for they laboured without ceasing either by night or day.

72. Now the Greeks who gave their aid, and who had flocked in full force to the Isthmus, were the following: the Lacedaemonians, all the Arcadians, the Eleans, the Corinthians, the Sicyonians, the Epidaurians, the Phliasians, the Troezenians, and the Hermionians. These all gave their aid, being greatly alarmed at the danger which threatened Greece. But the other inhabitants of the Peloponnesus took no part in the matter, though the Olympic and Carneian festivals were now over.

73. Seven nations inhabit the Peloponnesus. Two of them are aboriginal, and still continue in the regions where they dwelt at the first—to wit, the Arcadians and the Cynurians. A third, that of the Achaeans, has never left the Peloponnesus, but has been dislodged from its own proper country, and inhabits a district which once belonged to others. The remaining nations, four out of the seven, are all immigrants —namely, the Dorians, the Aetolians, the Dryopians, and the Lemnians. To the Dorians belong several very famous cities; to the Aetolians one only, that is, Elis; to the Dryopians, Hermione and that Asine which lies over against Cardamyle in Laconia, to the Lemnians, all the towns of the Paroreatae. The aboriginal Cynurians alone seem to be Ionians; even they, however, have, in course of time, grown to be Dorians, under the government of the argives, being Orneatae and their neighbors. All the cities of these seven nations, except those mentioned above, stood aloof from the war; and by so doing, if I may speak freely, they in fact took part with the Medes.

74. So the Greeks at the Isthmus toiled unceasingly, as though in the greatest peril, since they never imagined that any great success would be gained by the fleet. The Greeks at Salamis, on the other hand, when they heard what the rest were about, felt greatly alarmed; but their fear was not so much for themselves as for the Peloponnesus. At first they conversed together in low tones, each man with his fel-

low, secretly, and marvelled at the folly shown by Eurybiades; but presently the smothered feeling broke out, and
another assembly was held, whereat the old subjects provoked much talk from the speakers, one side maintaining
that it was best to sail to the Peloponnesus and risk battle for
that, instead of abiding at Salamis and fighting for a land already taken by the enemy; while the other, which consisted
of the Athenians, Aeginetans, and Megarians, was urgent to
remain and have the battle fought where they were.

75. Then Themistocles, when he saw that the Peloponnesians would carry the vote against him, went out secretly
from the council, and, instructing a certain man what he
should say, sent him on board a ship to the camp of the
Medes. The man's name was Sicinnus; he was one of
Themistocles' household slaves, and acted as tutor to his
sons; in after times, when the Thespians were admitting persons to citizenship, Themistocles made him a Thespian, and
a rich man to boot. The ship brought Sicinnus to the Persian
fleet, and there he delivered his message to the barbarian
leaders in these words:

"The Athenian commander has sent me to you privily,
without the knowledge of the other Greeks. He is a well-
wisher to the king's cause, and would rather success should
attend on you than on his countrymen; wherefore he bids
me tell you that fear has seized the Greeks and they are
meditating a hasty flight. Now then it is open to you to
achieve the best work that ever you wrought, if only you will
hinder their escaping. They no longer agree among themselves, so that they will not now make any resistance—nay,
it is likely you may see a fight already begun between such
as favour and such as oppose your cause." The messenger,
when he had thus expressed himself, departed and was seen
no more.

76. Then the captains, believing all that the messenger
had said, proceeded to land a large body of Persian troops
on the islet of Psyttaleia, which lies between Salamis and the
mainland; after which, about the hour of midnight, they advanced their western wing towards Salamis, so as to inclose

the Greeks. At the same time the force stationed about Ceos and Cynosura moved forward, and filled the whole strait as far as Munychia with their ships. This advance was made to prevent the Greeks from escaping by flight, and to block them up in Salamis, where it was thought that vengeance might be taken upon them for the battles fought near Artemisium. The Persian troops were landed on the islet of Psyttaleia, because, as soon as the battle began, the men and wrecks were likely to be drifted thither, as the isle lay in the very path of the coming fight, and they would thus be able to save their own men and destroy those of the enemy. All these movements were madè in silence, that the Greeks might have no knowledge of them; and they occupied the whole night, so that the men had no time to get their sleep.

77. I cannot say that there is no truth in oracles, or feel inclined to call in question those which speak with clearness, when I think of the following:

> "When they shall bridge with their ships to the sacred strand of Artemis
> Girt with the golden falchion, and eke to marine Cynosura,
> Mad hope swelling their hearts at the downfall of beautiful Athens—
> Then shall godlike Right extinguish haughty Presumption,
> Insult's furious offspring, who thinketh to overthrow all things.
> Brass with brass shall mingle, and Ares with blood shall empurple
> Ocean's waves. Then—then shall the day of Grecias freedom
> Come from Victory fair, and Cronos' son all-seeing."

When I look to this, and perceive how clearly Bacis spoke, I neither venture myself to say anything against prophecies, nor do I approve of others impugning them.

78. Meanwhile, among the captains at Salamis, the strife of words grew fierce. As yet they did not know that they

were encompassed, but imagined that the barbarians remained in the same places where they had seen them the day before.

79. In the midst of their contention, Aristides, the son of Lysimachus, who had crossed from Aegina, arrived in Salamis. He was an Athenian, and had been ostracized by the commonalty, yet I believe, from what I have heard concerning his character, that there was not in all Athens a man so worthy or so just as he. He now came to the council, and, standing outside, called for Themistocles. Now Themistocles was not his friend, but his most determined enemy. However, under the pressure of the great dangers impending, Aristides forgot their feud, and called Themistocles out of the council, since he wished to confer with him. He had heard before his arrival of the impatience of the Peloponnesians to withdraw the fleet to the Isthmus. As soon therefore as Themistocles came forth, Aristides addressed him in these words:

"Our rivalry at all times, and especially at the present season, ought to be a struggle, which of us shall most advantage our country. Let me then say to you, that so far as regards the departure of the Peloponnesians from this place, much talk and little will be found precisely alike. I have seen with my own eyes that which I now report: that, however much the Corinthians or Eurybiades himself may wish it, they cannot now retreat; for we are enclosed on every side by the enemy. Go in to them, and make this known."

80. "Your advice is excellent," answered the other; "and your tidings are also good. That which I earnestly desired to happen, your eyes have beheld accomplished. Know that what the Medes have now done was at my instance; for it was necessary, as the Greeks would not fight here of their own free will, to make them fight whether they would or no. But come now, as you have brought the good news, go in and tell it. For if I speak to them, they will think it a feigned tale, and will not believe that the barbarians have inclosed us around. Therefore you go to them, and inform them how matters stand. If they believe you, it will be for the best; but

if otherwise, it will not harm. For it is impossible that they should now flee away, if we are indeed shut in on all sides, as you say.

81. Then Aristides entered the assembly, and spoke to the captains; he had come, he told them, from Aegina, and had but barely escaped the blockading vessels—the Greek fleet was entirely inclosed by the ships of Xerxes—and he advised them to get themselves in readiness to resist the foe. Having said so much, he withdrew. And now another contest arose, for the greater part of the captains would not believe the tidings.

82. But while they still doubted, a Tenian trireme, commanded by Panaetius the son of Sosimenes, deserted from the Persians and joined the Greeks, bringing full intelligence. For this reason the Tenians were inscribed upon the tripod at Delphi among those who overthrew the barbarians. With this ship, which deserted to their side at Salamis, and the Lemnian vessel which came over before at Artemisium, the Greek fleet was brought to the full number of three hundred and eighty ships; otherwise it fell short by two of that amount.

83. The Greeks now, not doubting what the Tenians told them, made ready for the coming fight. At the dawn of day, all the men-at-arms were assembled together, and speeches were made to them, of which the best was that of Themistocles; who throughout contrasted what was noble with what was base, and bade them, in all that came within the range of man's nature and constitution, *always* to make choice of the nobler part. Having thus wound up his discourse, he told them to go at once on board their ships, which they accordingly did; and about this time the trireme, that had been sent to Aegina for the Aeacidae, returned; whereupon the Greeks put to sea with all their fleet.

84. The fleet had scarce left the land when they were attacked by the barbarians. At once most of the Greeks began to back water, and were about touching the shore, when Ameinias of Pallene, an Athenian, darted forth in front of the line and charged a ship of the enemy. The two vessels

became entangled, and could not separate, whereupon the
rest of the fleet came up to help Ameinias and engaged with
the Persians. Such is the account which the Athenians give
of the way in which the battle began; but the Aeginetans
maintain that the vessel which had been to Aegina for the
Aeacidae was the one that brought on the fight. It is also reported that a phantom in the form of a woman appeared to
the Greeks, and, in a voice that was heard from end to end
of the fleet, cheered them on to the fight, first, however, re-
buking them and saying, "Strange men, how long are you going to back water?"

85. Against the Athenians, who held the western extremity of the line towards Eleusis, were placed the Phoenicians;
against the Lacedaemonians, whose station was eastward towards the Piraeus, the Ionians. Of these last a few only followed the advice of Themistocles, to fight backwardly; the
greater number did far otherwise. I could mention here the
names of many trierarchs who took vessels from the Greeks,
but I shall pass over all excepting Theomestor, the son of
Androdamas, and Phylacus, the son of Histiaeus, both
Samians. I show this preference to them, inasmuch as for this
service Theomestor was made tyrant of Samos by the Persians, while Phylacus was enrolled among the king's benefactors and presented with a large estate in land. In the Persian tongue the king's benefactors are called *Orosangs*.

86. Far the greater number of the Persian ships engaged
in this battle were disabled, either by the Athenians or by
the Aeginetans. For as the Greeks fought in order and kept
their line, while the barbarians were in confusion and had
no plan in anything that they did, the issue of the battle could
scarce be other than it was. Yet the Persians fought far more
bravely here than at Euboea, and indeed surpassed themselves; each did his utmost through fear of Xerxes, for each
thought that the king's eye was upon himself.

87. What part the several contingents, whether Greek or
barbarian, took in the combat, I am not able to say for certain; Artemisia, however, I know, distinguished herself in
such a way as raised her even higher than she stood before

in the esteem of the king. For after confusion had spread throughout the whole of the king's fleet, and her ship was closely pursued by an Athenian trireme, she, having no way to fly, since in front of her were a number of friendly vessels, and she was nearest of all the Persians to the enemy, resolved on a measure which in fact proved her safety. Pressed by the Athenian pursuer, she bore straight against one of the ships of her own party, a Calyndian, which had Damasithymus, the Calyndian king, himself on board. I cannot say whether she had had any quarrel with the man while the fleet was at the Hellespont, or no—neither can I decide whether she of set purpose attacked his vessel, or whether it merely chanced that the Calyndian ship came in her way—but certain it is that she bore down upon his vessel and sank it, and that thereby she had the good fortune to procure herself a double advantage. For the commander of the Athenian trireme, when he saw her bear down on one of the enemy's fleet, thought immediately that her vessel was a Greek, or else had deserted from the Persians, and was now fighting on the Greek side; he therefore gave up the chase, and turned away to attack others.

88. Thus in the first place she saved her life by the action, and was enabled to get clear off from the battle; while further, it fell out that in the very act of doing the king an injury she raised herself to a greater height than ever in his esteem. For as Xerxes beheld the fight, he remarked (it is said) the destruction of the vessel, whereupon the bystanders observed to him—"Do you see, master, how well Artemisia fights, and how she has just sunk a ship of the emeny?" Then Xerxes asked if it were really Artemisia's doing; and they answered, certainly, for they knew her ensign; while all were sure that the sunken vessel belonged to the opposite side. Everything, it is said, conspired to prosper the queen—it was especially fortunate for her that not one of those on board the Calyndian ship survived to become her accuser. Xerxes, they say, in reply to the remarks made to him, observed, "My men have behaved like women, my women like men!" This is what Xerxes is supposed to have said.

89. There fell in this combat Ariabignes, a commander of the fleet, who was son of Darius and brother of Xerxes; and with him perished a vast number of men of high repute, Persians, Medes, and allies. Of the Greeks there died only a few; for, as they were able to swim, all those that were not slain outright by the enemy escaped from the sinking vessels and swam across to Salamis. But on the side of the barbarians more perished by drowning than in any other way, since they did not know how to swim. The great destruction took place when the ships which had been first engaged began to fly; for they who were stationed in the rear, anxious to display their valour before the eyes of the king, made every effort to force their way to the front, and thus became entangled with such of their own vessels as were retreating.

90. In this confusion the following event occurred: Certain Phoenicians belonging to the ships which had thus perished made their appearance before the king, and laid the blame of their loss on the Ionians, declaring that they were traitors, and had wilfully destroyed the vessels. But the upshot of this complaint was that the Ionian captains escaped the death which threatened them, while their Phoenician accusers received death as their reward. For it happened that, exactly as they spoke, a Samothracian vessel bore down on an Athenian and sank it, but was attacked and crippled immediately by one of the Aeginetan squadron. Now the Samothracians were expert with the javelin, and aimed their weapons so well that they cleared the deck of the vessel which had disabled their own, after which they sprang on board and took it. This saved the Ionians. Xerxes, when he saw the exploit, turned fiercely on the Phoenicians (he was ready, in his extreme vexation, to find fault with anyone) and ordered their heads to be cut off, to prevent them, he said, from casting the blame of their own misconduct upon braver men. During the whole time of the battle Xerxes sat at the base of the hill called Aegaleos, over against Salamis; and whenever he saw any of his own captains perform any worthy exploit he inquired concerning him; and the man's name was taken down by his scribes, together with

the names of his father and his city. Ariaramnes too, a Persian, who was a friend of the Ionians, and present at the time whereof I speak, had a share in bringing about the punishment of the Phoenicians.

91. When the rout of the barbarians began, and they sought to make their escape to Phalerum, the Aeginetans, awaiting them in the channel, performed exploits worthy to be recorded. Through the whole of the confused struggle the Athenians employed themselves in destroying such ships as either made resistance or fled to shore, while the Aeginetans dealt with those which endeavoured to escape down the strait; so that the Persian vessels were no sooner clear of the Athenians than forthwith they fell into the hands of the Aeginetan squadron.

92. It chanced here that there was a meeting between the ship of Themistocles, which was hasting in pursuit of the enemy, and that of Polycritus, son of Crius the Aeginetan, which had just charged a Sidonian trireme. The Sidonian vessel was the same that captured the Aeginetan guard-ship off Sciathus, which had Pytheas, the son of Ischenoüs, on board—that Pytheas, I mean, who fell covered with wounds, and whom the Persians kept on board their ship, from admiration of his gallantry. This man afterwards returned in safety to Aegina; for when the Sidonian vessel with its Persian crew fell into the hands of the Greeks, he was still found on board. Polycritus no sooner saw the Athenian trireme than, knowing at once whose vessel it was, as he observed that it bore the ensign of the admiral, he shouted to Themistocles jeeringly, and asked him, in a tone of reproach, if the Aeginetans did not show themselves rare friends to the Medes. At the same time, while he thus reproached Themistocles, Polycritus bore straight down on the Sidonian. Such of the barbarian vessels as escaped from the battle fled to Phalerum, and there sheltered themselves under the protection of the land army.

93. The Greeks who gained the greatest glory of all in the sea fight off Salamis were the Aeginetans, and after them the Athenians. The individuals of most distinction were

Polycritus the Aeginetan, and two Athenians, Eumenes of Anagyrus and Ameinias of Pallene; the latter of whom had pressed Artemisia so hard. And assuredly, if he had known that the vessel carried Artemisia on board, he would never have given over the chase till he had either succeeded in taking her, or else been taken himself. For the Athenian captains had received special orders touching the queen; and moreover a reward of ten thousand drachmas had been proclaimed for anyone who should make her prisoner; since there was great indignation felt that a woman should appear in arms against Athens. However, as I said before, she escaped; and so did some others whose ships survived the engagement; and these were all now assembled at the port of Phalerum.

94. The Athenians say that Adeimantus, the Corinthian commander, at the moment when the two fleets joined battle, was seized with fear, and, being beyond measure alarmed, spread his sails and hasted to fly away; on which the other Corinthians, seeing their leader's ship in full flight, sailed off likewise. They had reached in their flight that part of the coast of Salamis where stands the temple of Athena Sciras, when they met a light bark, sent by the gods: it was never discovered that anyone had sent it to them; and till it appeared they were altogether ignorant how the battle was going. That there was something beyond nature in the matter they judged from this, that when the men in the bark drew near to their ships they addressed them, saying, "Adeimantus, while you play the traitor's part, by withdrawing all these ships, and flying away from the fight, the Greeks whom you have deserted are defeating their foes as completely as they ever wished in their prayers." Adeimantus, however, would not believe what the men said, whereupon they told him he might take them with him as hostages, and put them to death if he did not find the Greeks winning. Then Adeimantus put about, both he and those who were with him; and they re-joined the fleet when the victory was already gained. Such is the tale which the Athenians tell concerning them of Corinth; these latter however do not allow its truth. On the

contrary, they declare that they were among those who distinguished themselves most in the fight. And the rest of Greece bears witness in their favour.

95. In the midst of the confusion Aristides, the son of Lysimachus, the Athenian, of whom I lately spoke as a man of the greatest excellence, performed the following service. He took a number of the Athenian heavy-armed troops, who had previously been stationed along the shore of Salamis, and, landing with them on the islet of Psyttaleia, slew all the Persians by whom it was occupied.

96. As soon as the sea fight was ended, the Greeks drew together to Salamis all the wrecks that were to be found in that quarter, and prepared themselves for another engagement, supposing that the king would renew the fight with the vessels which still remained to him. Many of the wrecks had been carried away by a westerly wind to the coast of Attica, where they were thrown upon the strip of shore called Colias. Thus not only were the prophecies of Bacis and Musaeus concerning this battle fulfilled completely, but likewise, by the place to which the wrecks were drifted, the prediction of Lysistratus, an Athenian soothsayer, uttered many years before these events, and quite forgotten at the time by all the Greeks, was fully accomplished. The words were:

"The women of Colias shall cook with oars."

Now this must have happened after the king was departed.

97. Xerxes, when he saw the extent of his loss, began to be afraid lest the Greeks might be counselled by some Ionians, or without their advice might determine to sail straight to the Hellespont and break down the bridges there; in which case he would be blocked up in Europe, and run great risk of perishing. He therefore made up his mind to fly; but, as he wished to hide his purpose alike from the Greeks and from his own people, he set to work to carry a causeway across the channel to Salamis, and began fastening a number of Phoenician freight ships together, to serve at once for a bridge and a wall. He likewise made many warlike prepara-

tions, as if he were about to engage the Greeks once more at sea. Now, when these things were seen, all grew fully persuaded that the king was bent on remaining, and intended to push the war in good earnest. Mardonius, however, was in no respect deceived; for long acquaintance enabled him to read all the king's thoughts.

98. Meanwhile, Xerxes, though engaged in this way, sent off a messenger to carry intelligence of his misfortune to Persia. Nothing mortal travels so fast as these Persian messengers. The entire plan is a Persian invention; and this is the method of it. Along the whole line of road there are men (they say) stationed with horses, in number equal to the number of days which the journey takes, allowing a man and horse to each day; and these men will not be hindered from accomplishing at their best speed the distance which they have to go, either by snow, or rain, or heat, or by the darkness of night. The first rider delivers his dispatch to the second, and the second passes it to the third; and so it is borne from hand to hand along the whole line, like the light in the torch race, which the Greeks celebrate to Hephaestus. The Persians give the riding post in this manner the name of "Angareium."

99. At Susa, on the arrival of the first message, which said that Xerxes was master of Athens, such was the delight of the Persians who had remained behind that they forthwith strewed all the streets with myrtle boughs, and burnt incense, and fell to feasting and merriment. In like manner, when the second message reached them, so sore was their dismay that they all with one accord rent their garments, and cried aloud, and wept and wailed without stint. They laid the blame of the disaster on Mardonius; and their grief on the occasion was less on account of the damage done to their ships than owing to the alarm which they felt about the safety of the king.

100. Their trouble did not cease till Xerxes himself, by his arrival, put an end to their fears. And now Mardonius, perceiving that Xerxes took the defeat of his fleet greatly to heart, and suspecting that he had made up his mind to leave

Athens and fly away, began to think of the likelihood of his being visited with punishment for having persuaded the king to undertake the war. He therefore considered that it would be the best thing for him to adventure further, and either become the conqueror of Greece—which was the result he rather expected—or else die gloriously after aspiring to a noble achievement. So with these thoughts in his mind, he said to the king:

"Do not grieve, master, or take so greatly to heart your late loss. Our hopes hang not altogether on the fate of a few planks, but on our steeds and horsemen. These fellows, whom you imagine to have conquered us, will not venture—no, not one of them—to come ashore and contend with our land army; nor will the Greeks who are upon the mainland fight our troops; such as did so have received their punishment. If it please you, we may at once attack the Peloponnesus; if you would rather wait awhile, that too is in our power. Only be not disheartened. For it is not possible that the Greeks can avoid being brought to account, alike for this and for their former injuries; nor can they anyhow escape being your slaves. You should therefore do as I have said. If, however, your mind is made up, and you are resolved to retreat and lead away your army, listen to the counsel which, in that case, I have to offer. Make not the Persians, O King, a laughing-stock to the Greeks. If your affairs have succeeded ill, it has not been by their fault; you cannot say that your Persians have ever shown themselves cowards. What matters it if Phoenicians and Egyptians, Cypriots and Cilicians, have misbehaved? Their misconduct touches not us. Since then your Persians are without fault, be advised by me. Depart home, if you are so minded, and take with you the bulk of your army; but first let me choose out three hundred thousand troops, and let it be my task to bring Greece into servitude."

101. Xerxes, when he heard these words, felt a sense of joy and delight, like a man who is relieved from care. Answering Mardonius, therefore, that he would consider his counsel, and let him know which course he might prefer,

Xerxes proceeded to consult with the chief men among the Persians; and because Artemisia on the former occasion had shown herself the only person who knew what was best to be done, he was pleased to summon her to advise him now. As soon as she arrived, he put forth all the rest, both councillors and bodyguards, and said to her:

"Mardonius wishes me to stay and attack the Peloponnesus. My Persians, he says, and my other land forces, are not to blame for the disasters which have befallen our arms; and of this he declares they would very gladly give me the proof. He therefore exhorts me, either to stay and act as I have said, or to let him choose out three hundred thousand of my troops—wherewith he undertakes to reduce Greece beneath my sway—while I myself retire with the rest of my forces, and withdraw into my own country. Do you, therefore, as you counselled me so wisely to decline the sea fight, now also advise me in this matter, and say, which course I ought to take for my own good."

102. Thus did the king ask Artemisia's counsel, and she answered as follows:

"It is a hard thing, O King, to give the best possible advice to one who asks our counsel. Nevertheless, as your affairs now stand, it seems to me that you will do right to return home. As for Mardonius, if he prefers to remain, and undertakes to do as he has said, leave him behind by all means, with the troops which he desires. If his design succeeds, and he subdues the Greeks, as he promises, yours is the conquest, master; for your slaves will have accomplished it. If, on the other hand, affairs run counter to his wishes, it is no great misfortune, so long as you are safe, and your house is in no danger. The Greeks, too, while you live and your house flourishes, must be prepared to fight full many a battle for their freedom; whereas if Mardonius fall, it matters nothing —they will have gained but a poor triumph—a victory over one of your slaves! Remember also, you go home having gained the purpose of your expedition; for you have burned Athens!"

103. The advice of Artemisia pleased Xerxes well; for

she had exactly uttered his own thoughts. I, for my part, do not believe that he would have remained had all his counsellors united to urge his stay, so great was the alarm that he felt. As it was, he gave praise to Artemisia, and entrusted certain of his children to her care, ordering her to convey them to Ephesus; for he had been accompanied by some of his natural sons.

104. He likewise sent away at this time one of the principal of his eunuchs, a man named Hermotimus, a Pedasian, who was bidden to take charge of these sons. Now the Pedasians inhabit the region above Halicarnassus; and it is related of them that in their country the following circumstance happens: When a mischance is about to befall any of their neighbours within a certain time, the priestess of Athena in their city grows a long beard. This has already taken place on two occasions.

105. This Hermotimus was, as I said, a Pedasian; and he, of all men whom we know, took the most cruel vengeance on the person who had done him an injury. He had been made a prisoner of war, and when his captors sold him he was bought by a certain Panionius, a native of Chios, who made his living by a most nefarious traffic. Whenever he could get any boys of unusual beauty, he made them eunuchs, and, carrying them to Sardis or Ephesus, sold them for large sums of money. For the barbarians value eunuchs more than others, since they regard them as more trustworthy. Many were the slaves that Panionius, who made his living by the practice, had thus treated; and among them was this Hermotimus of whom I have here made mention. However, he was not without his share of good fortune; for after a while he was sent from Sardis, together with other gifts, as a present to the king. Nor was it long before he came to be esteemed by Xerxes more highly than all his eunuchs.

106. When the king was on his way to Athens with the Persian army, and abode for a time at Sardis, Hermotimus happened to make a journey upon some business into Mysia; and there, in a district which is called Atarneus but belongs to Chios, he chanced to fall in with Panionius. Recognizing

him at once, he entered into frequent and friendly talks with him, wherein he counted up the numerous blessings he enjoyed through his means, and promised him all manner of favours in return if he would bring his household to Sardis and live there. Panionius was overjoyed, and, accepting the offer made him, came presently, and brought with him his wife and children. Then Hermotimus, when he had got Panionius and all his family into his power, addressed him in these words:

"You, who get your living by viler deeds than anyone else in the whole world, what wrong had I or any of my ancestors done to you that you should have made me, instead of a man, the nothing that I now am? Did you think that the gods took no note of your crimes? But they in their justice have delivered you, the doer of unrighteousness, into my hands; and now you cannot complain of the vengeance which I am resolved to take on you."

After these reproaches, Hermotimus commanded the four sons of Panionius to be brought, and forced the father to emasculate them with his own hands. Unable to resist, he did as Hermotimus required; and then his sons were made to treat him in the same way. So in this way there came to Panionius expiation at the hands of Hermotimus.

107. Xerxes, after charging Artemisia to convey his sons safe to Ephesus, sent for Mardonius, and bade him choose from all his army such men as he wished; and see that he made his achievements answer to his promises. During this day he did no more; but no sooner was night come than he issued his orders, and at once the captains of the ships left Phalerum, and bore away for the Hellespont, each making all the speed he could, and hasting to guard the bridges against the king's return. On their way, as they sailed by Zoster, where certain narrow points of land project into the sea, they took the cliffs for vessels, and fled far away in alarm. Discovering their mistake, however, after a time, they joined company once more, and proceeded upon their voyage.

108. Next day the Greeks, seeing the land force of the

barbarians encamped in the same place, thought that their ships must still be lying at Phalerum; and, expecting another attack from that quarter, made preparations to defend themselves. Soon however news came that the ships were all departed and gone away; whereupon it was instantly resolved to make sail in pursuit. They went as far as Andros; but, seeing nothing of the Persian fleet, they stopped at that place, and held a council of war. At this council Themistocles advised that the Greeks should follow on through the islands, still pressing the pursuit, and making all haste to the Hellespont, there to break down the bridges. Eurybiades, however, delivered a contrary opinion.

If he said, the Greeks should break down the bridges, it would be the worst thing that could possibly happen for Greece. The Persian, supposing that his retreat were cut off, and he compelled to remain in Europe, would be sure never to give them any peace. Inaction on his part would ruin all his affairs, and leave him no chance of ever getting back to Asia—nay, would even cause his army to perish by famine —whereas, if he bestirred himself, and acted vigorously, it was likely that the whole of Europe would in course of time become subject to him; since, by degrees, the various towns and tribes would either fall before his arms, or else agree to terms of submission; and in this way, his troops would find food sufficient for them, since each year the Greek harvest would be theirs. As it was, the Persian, because he had lost the sea fight, intended evidently to remain no longer in Europe. The Greeks ought to let him depart; and when he was gone from among them, and had returned into his own country, then would be the time for them to contend with him for the possession of *that*.

The other captains of the Peloponnesians declared themselves of the same mind.

109. Whereupon Themistocles, finding that the majority was against him, and that he could not persuade them to push on to the Hellespont, changed round, and, addressing himself to the Athenians, who of all the allies were the most nettled at the enemy's escape, and who eagerly desired, if

the other Greeks would not stir, to sail on by themselves to the Hellespont and break the bridges, spoke as follows:

"I have often myself witnessed occasions, and I have heard of many more from others, where men who had been conquered by an enemy, having been driven quite to desperation, have renewed the fight, and retrieved their former disasters. We have now had the great good luck to save both ourselves and all Greece by the repulse of this vast cloud of men; let us then be content and not press them too hard, now that they have begun to fly. Be sure we have not done this by our own might. It is the work of gods and heroes, who were jealous that one man should be king at once of Europe and of Asia—more especially a man like this, unholy and presumptuous, a man who esteems alike things sacred and things profane; who has cast down and burnt the very images of the gods themselves; who even caused the sea to be scourged with rods and commanded fetters to be thrown into it. At present all is well with us—let us then abide in Greece, and look to ourselves and to our families. The barbarian is clean gone—we have driven him off—let each now repair his own house, and sow his land diligently. In the spring we will take ship and sail to the Hellespont and to Ionia!"

All this Themistocles said in the hope of establishing a claim upon the king; for he wanted to have a safe retreat in case any mischance should befall him at Athens—which indeed came to pass afterwards.

110. At present, however, he dissembled; and the Athenians were persuaded by his words. For they were ready now to do whatever he advised, since they had always esteemed him a wise man, and he had lately proved himself most truly wise and well-judging. Accordingly, they came in to his views; whereupon he lost no time in sending messengers, on board a light bark, to the king, choosing for this purpose men whom he could trust to keep his instructions secret, even although they should be put to every kind of torture. Among them was the house slave Sicinnus, the same whom he had made use of previously. When the men

reached Attica, all the others stayed with the boat; but Sicinnus went up to the king, and spoke to him as follows:

"I am sent to you by Themistocles, the son of Neocles,
who is the leader of the Athenians, and the wisest and bravest man of all the allies, to bear you this message: 'Themistocles the Athenian, anxious to render you a service, has restrained the Greeks, who were impatient to pursue your
ships, and to break up the bridges at the Hellespont. Now,
therefore, return home at your leisure.' "

The messengers, when they had performed their errand,
sailed back to the fleet.

111. And the Greeks, having resolved that they would
neither proceed farther in pursuit of the barbarians, nor push
forward to the Hellespont and destroy the passage, laid siege
to Andros, wishing to destroy it. For Themistocles had required the Andrians to pay down a sum of money; and they
had refused, being the first of all the islanders who had been
approached. To his declaration that the money must needs
be paid, as the Athenians had brought with them two mighty
gods—Persuasion and Necessity—they made reply, that
Athens might well be a great and glorious city, since she was
blest with such excellent gods; but *they* were wretchedly
poor, stinted for land, and cursed with two unprofitable gods,
who always dwelt with them and would never quit their island—to wit, Poverty and Helplessness. These were the gods
of the Andrians, and therefore they would not pay the
money. For the power of Athens could not possibly be
stronger than their inability. This reply, coupled with the
refusal to pay the sum required, caused their city to be besieged by the Greeks.

112. Meanwhile Themistocles, who never ceased his pursuit of gain, sent threatening messages to the other islanders
with demands for different sums, employing the same messengers and the same words as he had used towards the
Andrians. If, he said, they did not send him the amount required, he would bring the Greek fleet upon them, and besiege them till he took their cities. By these means he collected large sums from the Carystians and the Parians, who,

when they heard that Andros was already besieged on the charge of medizing, and that Themistocles was the best esteemed of all the captains, sent the money through fear. Whether any of the other islanders did the like, I cannot say for certain; but I think some did besides those I have mentioned. However, the Carystians, though they complied, were not spared any the more; but Themistocles was softened by the Parians' gift, and therefore they received no visit from the army. In this way it was that Themistocles, operating from Andros, obtained money from the islanders, unbeknown to the other captains.

113. King Xerxes and his army waited but a few days after the sea fight, and then withdrew into Boeotia by the road which they had followed on their advance. It was the wish of Mardonius to escort the king a part of the way; and as the time of year was no longer suitable for carrying on war, he thought it best to winter in Thessaly, and wait for the spring before he attempted the Peloponnesus. After the army was come into Thessaly, Mardonius, first of all, chose the ten thousand Persians called the "Immortals," except only their leader, Hydarnes, who refused to quit the person of the king. Next, he chose the Persians who wore breastplates, and the thousand picked horse; likewise the Medes, the Sacans, the Bactrians, and the Indians, foot and horse equally. These nations he took entire; from the rest of the allies he culled a few men, taking either such as were remarkable for their appearance, or else such as had performed, to his knowledge, some valiant deed. The Persians furnished him with the greatest number of troops, men who were adorned with chains and armlets. Next to them were the Medes, who in number equalled the Persians, but in valour fell short of them. The whole army, reckoning the horsemen with the rest, amounted to three hundred thousand men.

114. At the time when Mardonius was making choice of his troops, and Xerxes still continued in Thessaly, the Lacedaemonians received an oracle from Delphi, bidding them seek satisfaction at the hands of Xerxes for the murder of

Leonidas, and take whatever he chose to give them. So the Spartans sent a herald with all speed into Thessaly, who arrived while the entire Persian army was still there. This man, being brought before the king, spoke as follows:—

"King of the Medes, the Lacedaemonians and the Heracleidae of Sparta require of you the satisfaction due for bloodshed, because you slew their king, who fell fighting for Greece."

Xerxes laughed, and for a long time spoke not a word. At last, however, he pointed to Mardonius, who was standing by him, and said, "Mardonius here shall give them the satisfaction they deserve to get." And the herald accepted the answer, and forthwith went his way.

115. Xerxes, after this, left Mardonius in Thessaly, and marched away himself, at his best speed, toward the Hellespont. In five-and-forty days he reached the place of passage, where he arrived with scarce a fraction, so to speak, of his former army. All along their line of march, in every country where they chanced to be, his soldiers seized and devoured whatever food they could find belonging to the inhabitants; while, if no grain was to be found, they gathered the grass that grew in the fields, and stripped the trees, whether cultivated or wild, alike of their bark and of their leaves, and so fed themselves. They left nothing anywhere, so hard were they pressed by hunger. Plague too and dysentery attacked the troops while still upon their march, and greatly thinned their ranks. Many died; others fell sick and were left behind in the different cities that lay upon the route, the inhabitants being strictly charged by Xerxes to tend and feed them. Of these some remained in Thessaly, others in Siris of Paeonia, others again in Macedon. Here Xerxes, on his march into Greece, had left the sacred car and steeds of Zeus, which upon his return he was unable to recover, for the Paeonians had disposed of them to the Thracians, and, when Xerxes demanded them back, they said that the Thracian tribes who dwelt about the sources of the Strymon had stolen the mares as they pastured.

116. Here too a Thracian chieftain, king of the Bisaltians

and of Crestonia, did a deed which went beyond nature. He had refused to become the willing slave of Xerxes, and had fled before him into the heights of Rhodope, at the same time forbidding his sons to take part in the expedition against Greece. But they, either because they cared little for his orders, or because they wished greatly to see the war, joined the army of Xerxes. At this time they had all returned home to him—the number of the men was six—quite safe and sound. But their father punished their offence by plucking out their eyes from the sockets. Such was their recompense.

117. The Persians, having journeyed through Thrace and reached the passage, entered their ships hastily and crossed the Hellespont to Abydos. The bridges were not found stretched across the strait, since a storm had broken and dispersed them. At Abydos the troops halted, and, obtaining more abundant provision than they had yet got upon their march, they fed without stint; from which cause, added to the change in their water, great numbers of those who had hitherto escaped perished. The remainder, together with Xerxes himself, came safe to Sardis.

118. There is likewise another account given of the return of the king. It is said that when Xerxes on his way from Athens arrived at Eïon upon the Strymon, he gave up travelling by land, and entrusting Hydarnes with the conduct of his forces to the Hellespont, embarked himself on board a Phoenician ship and so crossed into Asia. On his voyage the ship was assailed by a strong wind blowing from the mouth of the Strymon, which caused the sea to run high. As the storm increased, and the ship laboured heavily, because of the number of the Persians who had come in the king's train, and who now crowded the deck, Xerxes was seized with fear, and called out to the helmsman in a loud voice, asking him if there were any means whereby they might escape the danger. "No means, master," the helmsman answered, "unless we could be quit of these too numerous passengers." Xerxes, they say, on hearing this, addressed the Persians as follows: "Men of Persia," he said, "now is the time for you to show what love you bear your king. My safety, as it seems,

depends wholly upon you." So spoke the king; and the Persians instantly made obeisance, and then leapt over into the sea. Thus was the ship lightened, and Xerxes got safe to Asia. As soon as he had reached the shore, he sent for the helmsman, and gave him a golden crown because he had preserved the life of the king, but because he had caused the death of a number of Persians, he ordered his head to be struck from his shoulders.

119. Such is the other account which is given of the return of Xerxes; but to me it seems quite unworthy of belief, alike in other respects, and in what relates to the Persians. For had the helmsman made any such speech to Xerxes, I suppose there is not one man in ten thousand who will doubt that this is the course which the king would have followed: he would have made the men upon the ship's deck who were not only Persians, but Persians of the very highest rank, quit their place and go down below; and would have cast into the sea an equal number of the rowers, who were Phoenicians. But the truth is that the king, as I have already said, returned into Asia by the same road as the rest of the army.

120. I will add a strong proof of this. It is certain that Xerxes on his way back from Greece passed through Abdera, where he made a contract of friendship with the inhabitants, and presented them with a golden scimitar and a tiara broidered with gold. The Abderites declare—but I put no faith in this part of their story—that from the time of the king's leaving Athens, he never once loosed his girdle till he came to their city, since it was not till then that he felt himself in safety. Now Abdera is nearer to the Hellespont than Eïon and the Strymon, where Xerxes, according to the other tale, took ship.

121. Meanwhile the Greeks, finding that they could not capture Andros, sailed away to Carystus, and wasted the lands of the Carystians, after which they returned to Salamis. Arrived here, they proceeded, before entering on any other matter, to make choice of the first-fruits which should be set apart as offerings to the gods. These consisted of divers gifts; among them were three Phoenician triremes, one of

which was dedicated at the Isthmus, where it continued to my day; another at Sunium; and the third at Salamis itself, which was devoted to Ajax. This done, they made a division of the booty, and sent away the first-fruits to Delphi. Thereof was made the statue, holding in its hand the beak of a ship, which is twelve cubits high, and which stands in the same place with the golden one of Alexander the Macedonian.

122. After the first-fruits had been sent to Delphi, the Greeks made inquiry of the god, in the name of their whole body, if he had received his full share of the spoils and was satisfied therewith. The god made answer, that all the other Greeks had paid him his full due, except only the Aeginetans; on them he had still a claim for the prize of valour which they had gained at Salamis. So the Aeginetans, when they heard this, dedicated the three golden stars which stand on the top of a bronze mast in the corner near the bowl offered by Croesus.

123. When the spoils had been divided, the Greeks sailed to the Isthmus, where a prize of valour was to be awarded to the man who, of all the Greeks, had shown the most merit during the war. When the chiefs were all come, they met at the altar of Poseidon, and took the ballots wherewith they were to give their votes for the first and for the second in merit. Then each man gave himself the first vote, since each considered that he was himself the worthiest; but the second votes were given chiefly to Themistocles. In this way, while the others received but one vote apiece, Themistocles had for the second prize a large majority of the suffrages.

124. Envy, however, hindered the chiefs from coming to a decision, and they all sailed away to their homes without making any award. Nevertheless Themistocles was regarded everywhere as by far the wisest man of all the Greeks; and the whole country rang with his fame. As the chiefs who fought at Salamis, notwithstanding that he was really entitled to the prize, had withheld his honour from him, he went without delay to Lacedaemon, in the hope that he would be honoured there. And the Lacedaemonians received him handsomely, and paid him great respect. The prize of

valour indeed, which was a crown of olive, they gave to Eurybiades; but Themistocles was given a crown of olive too, as the prize of wisdom and dexterity. He was likewise presented with the most beautiful chariot that could be found in Sparta; and after receiving abundant praises, was, upon his departure, escorted as far as the borders of Tegea, by the three hundred picked Spartans, who are called the Knights. Never was it known, either before or since, that the Spartans escorted a man out of their city.

125. On the return of Themistocles to Athens, Timodemus of Aphidnae, who was one of his enemies, but otherwise a man of no repute, became so maddened with envy that he openly railed against him, and reproaching him with his journey to Sparta, said, it was not his own merit that had won him honour from the men of Lacedaemon, but the fame of Athens, his country. Then Themistocles, seeing that Timodemus repeated this phrase unceasingly, replied:

"Thus stands the case, friend. I had never got this honour from the Spartans, had I been a Belbinite—nor would you, being an Athenian." . . .

130. As for that part of the fleet of Xerxes which had survived the battle, when it had made good its escape from Salamis to the coast of Asia, and conveyed the king with his army across the strait from the Chersonesus to Abydos, it passed the winter at Cyme. On the first approach of spring, there was an early muster of the ships at Samos, where some of them indeed had remained throughout the winter. Most of the men-at-arms who served on board were Persians, or else Medes; and the command of the fleet had been taken by Mardontes, the son of Bagaeus, and Artaÿntes, the son of Artachaeus; while there was likewise a third commander, Ithamitres, the nephew of Artaÿntes, whom his uncle had advanced to the post. Further west than Samos, however, they did not venture to proceed; for they remembered what a defeat they had suffered, and there was no one to compel them to approach any nearer to Greece. They therefore remained at Samos, and kept watch over Ionia, to hinder it from breaking into revolt. The whole number of their

ships, including those furnished by the Ionians, was three hundred. It did not enter into their thoughts that the Greeks would proceed against Ionia; on the contrary, they supposed that the defence of their own country would content them, more especially as they had not pursued the Persian fleet when it fled from Salamis, but had so readily given up the chase. They despaired, however, altogether of gaining any success by sea themselves, though by land they thought that Mardonius was quite sure of victory. So they remained at Samos, and took counsel together, if by any means they might harass the enemy, at the same time that they waited eagerly to hear how matters would proceed with Mardonius.

131. The approach of spring, and the knowledge that Mardonius was in Thessaly, roused the Greeks from inaction. Their land force indeed was not yet come together; but the fleet, consisting of one hundred and ten ships, proceeded to Aegina, under the command of Leotychides. This Leotychides, who was ōoth general and admiral, was the son of Menares, the son of Hegesilaüs, the son of Hippocratides, the son of Leotychides, the son of Anaxilaüs, the son of Archidamus, the son of Anaxandrides, the son of Theopompus, the son of Nicander, the son of Charilaüs, the son of Eunomus, the son of Polydectes, the son of Prytanis, the son of Euryphon, the son of Procles, the son of Aristodemus, the son of Aristomachus, the son of Celodaeus, the son of Hyllus, the son of Hercules. He belonged to the second royal house. All his ancestors, except the two next in the above list to himself, had been kings of Sparta. The Athenian vessels were commanded by Xanthippus, the son of Ariphron.

132. When the whole fleet was collected together at Aegina, ambassadors from Ionia arrived at the Greek station; they had but just come from paying a visit to Sparta, where they had been entreating the Lacedaemonians to undertake the deliverance of Ionia. One of these ambassadors was Herodotus, the son of Basileides. Originally they were seven in number, and the whole seven had conspired to slay Strattis the tyrant of Chios; one, however, of those engaged in the plot betrayed the enterprise, and the conspiracy

being in this way discovered, the remaining six quitted Chios and went straight to Sparta, whence they had now proceeded to Aegina, their object being to beseech the Greeks that they would pass over to Ionia. It was not, however, without difficulty that they were induced to advance even so far as Delos. All beyond that seemed to the Greeks full of danger; the places were quite unknown to them, and to their fancy swarmed with Persian troops; as for Samos, it appeared to them as far off as the Pillars of Hercules. Thus it came to pass that at the very same time the barbarians were hindered by their fears from venturing any farther west than Samos, and the prayers of the Chians failed to induce the Greeks to advance any further east than Delos. Terror guarded the mid-region.

133. The Greek fleet was now on its way to Delos; but Mardonius still abode in his winter quarters in Thessaly. When he was about to leave them, he despatched a man named Mys, a Euromian by birth, to go and consult the different oracles, giving him orders to put questions everywhere to all the oracles whereof he found it possible to make trial. What it was that he wanted to know, when he gave Mys these orders, I am not able to say, for no account has reached me of the matter; but for my own part, I suppose that he sent to inquire concerning the business which he had in hand, and not for any other purpose.

134. Mys, it is certain, went to Lebadeia, and, by the payment of a sum of money, induced one of the inhabitants to go down to [the cave of] Trophonius; he likewise visited Abae of the Phocians, and there consulted the god; while at Thebes, to which place he went first of all, he not only got access to Apollo Ismenius (of whom inquiry is made by means of victims, according to the custom practised also at Olympia), but likewise prevailed on a man, who was not a Theban but a foreigner, to pass the night in the temple of Amphiaraüs. No Theban can lawfully consult this oracle, for the following reason: Amphiaraüs by an oracle gave the Thebans their choice, to have him for their soothsayer or for their ally in war; he bade them elect between the two, and

forego either one or the other; so they chose rather to have him for their ally. On this account it is unlawful for a Theban to sleep in his temple.

135. One thing which the Thebans declare to have happened at this time is to me very surprising. Mys, the Euromian, they say, after he had gone about to all the oracles, came at last to the sacred precinct of Apollo Ptoüs. The place itself bears the name of Ptoüm; it is in the country of the Thebans, and is situate on the mountain side overlooking Lake Copaïs, only a very little way from the town called Acraephia. Here Mys arrived and entered the temple, followed by three Theban citizens—picked men whom the state had appointed to take down whatever answer the god might give. No sooner was he entered than the prophet delivered him an oracle, but in a foreign tongue; so that his Theban attendants were astonished, hearing a strange language when they expected Greek, and did not know what to do. Mys, however, the Euromian, snatched from their hands the tablet which they had brought with them, and wrote down what the prophet uttered. The reply, he told them, was in the Carian language. After this, Mys departed and returned to Thessaly.

136. Mardonius, when he had read the answers given by the oracles, sent next an envoy to Athens. This was Alexander, the son of Amyntas, a Macedonian, of whom he made choice for two reasons. Alexander was connected with the Persians by family ties; for Gygaea, who was the daughter of Amyntas, and sister to Alexander himself, was married to Bubares, a Persian, and by him had a son, to wit, Amyntas of Asia; who was named after his mother's father, and enjoyed the revenues of Alabanda, a large city of Phrygia, which had been assigned him by the king. Alexander was likewise (and of this too Mardonius was well aware), both by services which he had rendered, and by formal compact of friendship, connected with Athens. Mardonius therefore thought that, by sending him, he would be most likely to gain over the Athenians to the Persian side. He had heard that they were a numerous and a valorous people, and he knew

that the disasters which had befallen the Persians by sea were mainly their work; he therefore expected that if he could form alliance with them he would easily get the mastery of the sea (as indeed he would have done, beyond a doubt), while by land he believed that he was already greatly superior; and so he thought by this alliance to make sure of overcoming the Greeks. Perhaps, too, the oracles leant this way, and counselled him to make Athens his friend; so that it may have been in obedience to them that he sent the embassy. . . .

140. When Alexander reached Athens as the ambassador of Mardonius, he spoke as follows:

"O men of Athens, these are the words of Mardonius. 'The king has sent a message to me, saying, "All the trespasses which the Athenians have committed against me I forgive. Now, then, Mardonius, act thus towards them. Restore to them their territory, and let them choose for themselves whatever land they like besides, and let them dwell therein as a free people. Build up likewise all their temples which I burnt, if on these terms they will consent to enter into a league with me." Such are the orders which I have received, and which I must needs obey, unless there be a hindrance on your part. And now I say to you, why are you so mad as to levy war against the king, whom you cannot possibly overcome, or even resist forever? You have seen the multitude and the bravery of the hosts of Xerxes; you know also how large a power remains with me in your land; suppose then you should get the better of us, and defeat this army—a thing whereof you will not, if you are wise, entertain the least hope. What follows even then but a contest with a still greater force? Do not, because you would match yourselves with the king, consent to lose your country and live in constant danger of your lives. Rather agree to make peace, which you can now do without any tarnish to your honour, since the king invites you to it. Continue free, and make an alliance with us, without fraud or deceit.'

"These are the words, O Athenians, which Mardonius has bid me speak to you. For my own part, I will say nothing of the good will I bear your nation, since you have not now for the first time to become acquainted with it. But I will beseech you to give ear to Mardonius; for I see clearly that it is impossible for you to go on forever contending against Xerxes. If that had appeared to me possible, I would not now have come hither the bearer of such a message. But the king's power surpasses that of man; and his arm reaches far. If then you do not hasten to conclude a peace when such fair terms are offered you, I tremble to think of what you will have to endure—you who of all the allies lie most directly in the path of danger, whose land will always be the chief battleground of the contending powers, and who will therefore constantly have to suffer alone. Believe me. Surely it is no small matter that the great king chooses you out from all the rest of the Greeks, to offer you forgiveness of the wrongs you have done him, and to propose himself as your friend."

141. Such were the words of Alexander. Now the Lacedaemonians, when tidings reached them that Alexander was gone to Athens to bring about a league between the Athenians and the barbarians, and when at the same time they called to mind the prophecies which declared that the Dorian race should one day be driven from the Peloponnesus by the Medes and the Athenians, were exceedingly afraid lest the Athenians might consent to the alliance with Persia. They therefore lost no time in sending envoys to Athens; and it so happened that these envoys were given their audience at the same time with Alexander, for the Athenians had waited and made delays, because they felt sure that the Lacedaemonians would hear that an ambassador was come to them from the Persians, and as soon as they heard it would with all speed send an embassy. They contrived matters therefore of set purpose, so that the Lacedaemonians might hear them deliver their sentiments on the occasion.

142. As soon as Alexander had finished speaking, the ambassadors from Sparta took the word and said:

"We are sent here by the Lacedaemonians to entreat of you that you will not do a new thing in Greece, nor agree to the terms which are offered you by the barbarian. Such conduct on the part of any of the Greeks were alike unjust and dishonourable; but in you it would be worse than in others, for divers reasons. It was by you that this war was kindled at the first among us—our wishes were in no way considered; the contest began in your defence—now the fate of Greece is involved in it. Besides it were surely an intolerable thing that the Athenians, who have always hitherto been known as a nation to which many men owed their freedom, should now become the means of bringing all other Greeks into slavery. We feel, however, for the heavy calamities which press on you—the loss of your harvest these two years, and the ruin in which your homes have lain for so long a time. We offer you, therefore, on the part of the Lacedaemonians and the allies, sustenance for your women and for the unwarlike portion of your households, so long as the war endures. Be not seduced by Alexander the Macedonian, who softens down the rough words of Mardonius. He does as is natural for him to do—a tyrant himself, he helps forward a tyrant's cause. But you should do differently, at least if you be truly wise; for you should know that with barbarians there is neither faith nor truth."

Thus spoke the envoys.

143. After which the Athenians returned this answer to Alexander:

"We know as well as you that the power of the Mede is many times greater than our own: we did not need to have *that* cast in our teeth. Nevertheless we cling so to freedom that we shall offer what resistance we may. Seek not to persuade us into making terms with the barbarian—say what you will, you will never gain our assent. Tell Mardonius that our answer to him is this: 'So long as the sun keeps his present course, we will never join alliance with Xerxes. Nay, we shall oppose him unceasingly, trusting in the aid of those gods and heroes whom he has lightly esteemed, whose houses and whose images he has burnt with fire.' And come not again to us with words like these; nor, thinking to do us a service, persuade us to unholy actions. You are the guest and friend of our nation—we would not have you receive hurt at our hands."

144. Such was the answer which the Athenians gave to Alexander. To the Spartan envoys they said:

"It was natural no doubt that the Lacedaemonians should be afraid we might make terms with the barbarian; but nevertheless it was a base fear in men who knew so well of what temper and spirit we are. Not all the gold that the whole earth contains—not the fairest and most fertile of all lands —would bribe us to take part with the Medes and help them to enslave Greece. Even could we anyhow have brought ourselves to such a thing, there are many very powerful motives which would now make it impossible. The first and chief of these is the burning and destruction of our temples and the images of our gods, which forces us to make no terms with their destroyer, but rather to pursue him with our resentment to the uttermost. Again, there is our common brotherhood with the Greeks: our common ancestry and language, the altars and the sacrifices of which we all partake, the common character which we bear—did the Athenians betray all these, of a truth it would not be well. Know then now, if you have not known it before, that while one Athenian remains alive we will never join alliance with Xerxes. We thank you, however, for your forethought on our behalf, and for your wish to give our families sustenance, now that ruin has fallen on us—the kindness is complete on your part; but for ourselves, we will endure as we may, and not be burdensome to you. Such then is our resolve. Be it your care with all speed to lead out your troops; for if we surmise aright, the barbarian will not wait long before invading our territory, but will set out so soon as he learns our answer to be that we will do none of those things which he requires of us. Now then is the time for us, before he enters Attica, to go forth ourselves into Boeotia, and give him battle."

When the Athenians had thus spoken, the ambassadors departed for Sparta.

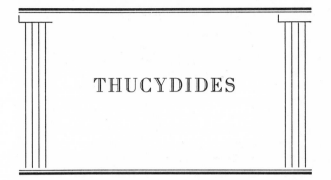

THUCYDIDES

Even less is known (or can be inferred) about the life of Thucydides than the very little which can be said about Herodotus. From the way he writes, at one point in his book, that he was old enough at the beginning of the Peloponnesian War to have maturity of judgement—a statement with unmistakably defensive overtones—it is reasonable to place his birth about 460 B.C., or a trifle later. His father had a Thracian name, Olorus, and that fact almost certainly links him with the important aristocratic family of Miltiades, the hero of Marathon, and his son Cimon, who preceded Pericles and then contended with him for leadership in Athens. Miltiades had married the daughter of a Thracian chieftain called Olorus, and that is surely why the name was carried on in Athens.

Thucydides himself stresses his Thracian connections. He owned a gold-mining concession there, he says, and in consequence he had influence over the native population in the area. Presumably, though this he himself does not say, that is why he was elected general in 424, when the most important battle was the struggle for the Greek city of Amphipolis in the Thracian sphere north of the Aegean. With his family background, Thucydides undoubtedly received not only the best available education, but also early experience in military and political affairs. There is not a shred of evidence, however, that his career was such as to warrant election to the highest office in the state (the board of ten generals) at an early age, except for the special circumstances of his involvement with Thrace at that precise stage of the war.

His failure at Amphipolis led to his exile from Athens, whether justly or unjustly. As far as we know, he spent the twenty years of his exile primarily on his history of the war. He himself says that it placed him in the advantageous position of being able to keep in touch with all parties in the conflict. Presumably his base was in Thrace, but he must have travelled widely during some of the time. He was permitted to return to Athens when the war ended, and he died not long after (five years later at the outside). Several later writers report that his tomb (or cenotaph) could be seen in the burial ground of the Cimonid family, a perfectly credible story.

Thucydides left the history of the war far from complete. The book was published posthumously, though by whom is unknown. It must have appeared very soon after his death, for an acquaintance with it is evident in various fourth-century writers, and at least five men wrote continuations in the middle or second half of the century, of which Xenophon's *Hellenica* alone survives. Nevertheless, Thucydides seems not to have been much appreciated in this period. His real popularity in antiquity came only in Roman times.

—M. I. F.

From BOOK I

The Beginnings

1. Thucydides, an Athenian, wrote the history of the war between the Peloponnesians and the Athenians, beginning at the moment that it broke out, and believing that it would be a great war, and more worthy of relation than any that had preceded it. This belief was not without its grounds. The

preparations of both the combatants were in every department in the last state of perfection; and he could see the rest of the Hellenic race taking sides in the quarrel, those who delayed doing so at once having it in contemplation. Indeed this was the greatest movement yet known in history, not only of the Hellenes, but of a large part of the barbarian world—I had almost said of mankind. For though the events of remote antiquity, and even those that more immediately precede the war, could not from lapse of time be clearly ascertained, yet the evidences, which an inquiry carried as far back as was practicable leads me to trust, all point to the conclusion that there was nothing on a great scale, either in war or in other matters.

2. For instance, it is evident that the country now called Hellas had in ancient times no settled population; on the contrary, migrations were of frequent occurrence, the several tribes readily abandoning their homes under the pressure of superior numbers. Without commerce, without freedom of communication either by land or sea, cultivating no more of their territory than the exigencies of life required, destitute of capital, never planting their land (for they could not tell when an invader might not come and take it all away, and when he did come they had no walls to stop him), thinking that the necessities of daily sustenance could be supplied at one place as well as another, they cared little for shifting their habitation, and consequently neither built large cities nor attained to any other form of greatness. The richest soils were always most subject to this change of masters, such as the district now called Thessaly, Boeotia, most of the Peloponnesus, Arcadia excepted, and the most fertile parts of the rest of Hellas. The goodness of the land favoured the aggrandizement of particular individuals, and thus created faction which proved a fertile source of ruin. It also invited invasion. Accordingly Attica, from the poverty of its soil enjoying from a very remote period freedom from faction, never changed its inhabitants. And here is no inconsiderable exemplification of my assertion that the migrations were the cause of there being no correspondent growth in other

parts. The most powerful victims of war or faction from the rest of Hellas took refuge with the Athenians as a safe retreat; and at an early period, becoming naturalized, swelled the already large population of the city to such a height that Attica became at last too small to hold them, and they had to send out colonies to Ionia.

3. There is also another circumstance that contributes not a little to my conviction of the weakness of ancient times. Before the Trojan War there is no indication of any common action in Hellas, nor indeed of the universal prevalence of the name; on the contrary, before the time of Hellen, son of Deucalion, no such appellation existed, but the country went by the names of the different tribes, in particular of the Pelasgian. It was not till Hellen and his sons grew strong in Phthiotis, and were invited as allies into the other cities, that one by one they gradually acquired from the connection the name of Hellenes; though a long time elapsed before that name could fasten itself upon all. The best proof of this is furnished by Homer. Born long after the Trojan War, he nowhere calls all of them by that name, nor indeed any of them except the followers of Achilles from Phthiotis, who were the original Hellenes: in his poems they are called Danaans, Argives, and Achaeans. He does not even use the term barbarian, probably because the Hellenes had not yet been marked off from the rest of the world by one distinctive appellation. It appears therefore that the several Hellenic communities, comprising not only those who first acquired the name, city by city, as they came to understand each other, but also those who assumed it afterwards as the name of the whole people, were before the Trojan War prevented by their want of strength and the absence of mutual intercourse from displaying any collective action. Indeed, they could not unite for this expedition till they had gained increased familiarity with the sea.

4. The first person known to us by tradition as having established a navy is Minos. He made himself master of what is now called the Hellenic sea, and ruled over the Cyclades,

into most of which he sent the first colonies, expelling the Carians and appointing his own sons governors; and thus did his best to put down piracy in those waters, a necessary step to secure the revenues for his own use.

5. For in early times the Hellenes and the barbarians of the coast and islands, as communication by sea became more common, were tempted to turn pirates, under the conduct of their most powerful men, the motives being to serve their own cupidity and to support the needy. They would fall upon a town unprotected by walls and consisting of a mere collection of villages, and would plunder it; indeed, this came to be the main source of their livelihood, no disgrace being yet attached to such an achievement, but even some glory. An illustration of this is furnished by the honour with which some of the inhabitants of the continent still regard a successful marauder, and by the question we find the old poets everywhere representing the people as asking of voyagers, "Are they pirates?" as if those who are asked the question would have no idea of disclaiming the imputation, or their interrogators of reproaching them for it. The same rapine prevailed also by land. And even at the present day many parts of Hellas still follow the old fashion, the Ozolian Locrians for instance, the Aetolians, the Acarnanians, and that region of the continent; and the custom of carrying arms is still kept up among these continentals, from the old piratical habits.

6. The whole of Hellas used once to carry arms, their habitations being unprotected and their communication with each other unsafe; indeed, to wear arms was as much a part of everyday life with them as with the barbarians. And the fact that the people in these parts of Hellas are still living in the old way points to a time when the same mode of life was once equally common to all.

The Athenians were the first to lay aside their weapons, and to adopt an easier and more luxurious mode of life; indeed, it is only lately that their rich old men left off the luxury of wearing undergarments of linen, and fastening a knot of their hair with a tie of golden grasshoppers, a fashion which spread to their Ionian kindred, and long prevailed among the old men there. On the contrary a modest style of dressing, more in conformity with modern ideas, was first adopted by the Lacedaemonians, the rich doing their best to assimilate their way of life to that of the common people. They also set the example of contending naked, publicly stripping and anointing themselves with oil in their gymnastic exercises. Formerly, even in the Olympic contests, the athletes who contended wore athletic supports about their genitals; and it is but a few years since that the practice ceased. To this day among some of the barbarians, especially in Asia, when prizes for boxing and wrestling are offered, such supports are worn by the combatants. And there are many other points in which a likeness might be shown between the life of the Hellenic world of old and the barbarian of today.

7. With respect to their towns, later on, at an era of increased facilities of navigation and a greater supply of wealth, we find the shores becoming the site of walled towns, and the isthmuses being occupied for the purposes of commerce, and defence against a neighbour. But the old towns, on account of the great prevalence of piracy, were built away from the sea, whether on the islands or the continent, and still remain in their old sites. For the pirates used to plunder one another, and indeed all coast populations, whether seafaring or not.

8. The islanders, too, were great pirates. These islanders were Carians and Phoenicians, by whom most of the islands were colonized, as was proved by the following fact. During the purification of Delos by Athens in this war [426-425 B.C.] all the graves in the island were taken up, and it was found that above half their inmates were Carians: they were identified by the fashion of the arms buried with them, and by the method of interment, which was the same as the Carians still follow. But as soon as Minos had formed his navy, communciation by sea became easier, as he colonized most of the islands, and thus expelled the malefactors. The

coast populations now began to apply themselves more closely to the acquisition of wealth, and their life became more settled; some even began to build themselves walls on the strength of their newly acquired riches. For the love of gain would reconcile the weaker to the dominion of the stronger, and the possession of resources enabled the more powerful to reduce the smaller towns to subjection. And it was at a somewhat later stage of this development that they went on the expedition against Troy.

9. What enabled Agamemnon to raise the armament was more, in my opinion, his superiority in strength than the oaths of Tyndareus, which bound Helen's suitors to follow him. Indeed, the account given by those Peloponnesians who have been the recipients of the most credible tradition is this. First of all Pelops, arriving among a needy population from Asia with vast wealth, acquired such power that, stranger though he was, the country was called after him; and this power was materially increased in the hands of his descendants. Eurystheus had been killed in Attica by the Heraclids. Atreus was his mother's brother; and to the hands of his relation, who had left his father on account of the death of Chrysippus, Eurystheus, when he set out on his expedition, had committed Mycenae and the government. As time went on and Eurystheus did not return, Atreus complied with the wishes of the Mycenaeans, who were influenced by fear of the Heraclids—besides, his power seemed considerable, and he had not neglected to court the favour of the populace— and assumed the scepter of Mycenae and the rest of the dominions of Eurystheus. And so the power of the descendants of Pelops came to be greater than that of the descendants of Perseus.

To all this Agamemnon succeeded. He had also a navy far stronger than his contemporaries, so that, in my opinion, fear was quite as strong an element as love in the formation of the confederate expedition. The strength of his navy is shown by the fact that his own was the largest contingent, and that of the Arcadians was furnished by him; this at least is what Homer says, if his testimony is deemed sufficient.

Besides, in his account of the transmission of the scepter, he calls him

> Of many an isle, and of all Argos king.

Now Agamemnon's was a continental power, and he could not have been master of any except the adjacent islands (and these would not be many) but through the possession of a fleet. And from this expedition we may infer the character of earlier enterprises.

10. Now Mycenae may have been a small place, and many of the towns of that age may appear comparatively insignificant, but no exact observer would therefore feel justified in rejecting the estimate given by the poets and by tradition of the magnitude of the armament. For I suppose if Lacedaemon were to become desolate, and the temples and the foundations of the public buildings were left, that as time went on there would be a strong disposition with posterity to refuse to accept her fame as a true exponent of her power. And yet they occupy two-fifths of Peloponnesus and lead the whole, not to speak of their numerous allies without. Still, as the city is neither built in a compact form nor adorned with magnificent temples and public edifices, but composed of villages after the old fashion of Hellas, there would be an impression of inadequacy. Whereas, if Athens were to suffer the same misfortune, I suppose that any inference from the appearance presented to the eye would make her power to have been twice as great as it is.

We have therefore no right to be sceptical, nor to content ourselves with an inspection of a town to the exclusion of a consideration of its power; but we may safely conclude that the armament in question surpassed all before it, as it fell short of modern efforts; if we can here also accept the testimony of Homer's poems, in which, without allowing for the exaggeration which a poet would feel himself licensed to employ, we can see that it was far from equalling ours. He has represented it as consisting of twelve hundred vessels, the Boeotian complement of each ship being a hundred and twenty men, that of the ships of Philoctetes fifty. By this, I conceive, he meant to convey the maximum and the minimum complement: at any rate he does not specify the amount of any others in his catalogue of the ships. That they were all rowers as well as warriors we see from his account of the ships of Philoctetes, in which all the men at the oar are bowmen. Now it is improbable that many supernumeraries sailed if we except the kings and high officers; especially as they had to cross the open sea with munitions of war, in ships, moreover, that had no decks, but were equipped in the old piratical fashion. So that if we strike the average of the largest and smallest ships, the number of those who sailed will appear inconsiderable, representing, as they did, the whole force of Hellas.

11. And this was due not so much to scarcity of men as of money. Difficulty of subsistence made the invaders reduce the numbers of the army to a point at which it might live on the country during the prosecution of the war. Even after the victory they obtained on their arrival—and a victory there must have been, or the fortifications of the naval camp could never have been built—there is no indication of their whole force having been employed; on the contrary, they seem to have turned to cultivation of the Chersonesus and to piracy from want of supplies. This was what really enabled the Trojans to keep the field for ten years against them; the dispersion of the enemy making them always a match for the detachment left behind. If they had brought plenty of supplies with them, and had persevered in the war without scattering for piracy and agriculture, they would have easily defeated the Trojans in the field; since they could hold their own against them with the division on service. In short, if they had stuck to the siege, the capture of Troy would have cost them less time and less trouble. But as want of money proved the weakness of earlier expeditions, so from the same cause even the one in question, more famous than its predecessors, may be pronounced on the evidence of what it effected to have been inferior to its renown and to the current opinion about it formed under the tuition of the poets.

12. Even after the Trojan War, Hellas was still engaged in removing and settling, and thus could not attain to the quiet which must precede growth. The late return of the Hellenes from Ilium caused many revolutions, and factions ensued almost everywhere; and it was the citizens thus driven into exile who founded the cities. Sixty years after the capture of Ilium the modern Boeotians were driven out of Arne by the Thessalians, and settled in the present Boeotia, the former Cadmeis; though there was a division of them there before, some of whom joined the expedition to Ilium. Twenty years later the Dorians and the Heraclids became masters of the Peloponnesus; so that much had to be done and many years had to elapse before Hellas could attain to a durable tranquillity undisturbed by removals, and could begin to send out colonies, as Athens did to Ionia and most of the islands, and the Peloponnesians to most of Italy and Sicily and some places in the rest of Hellas. All these places were founded subsequently to the war with Troy.

13. But as the power of Hellas grew, and the acquisition of wealth became more an object, the revenues of the states increasing, tyrannies were by their means established almost everywhere—the old form of government being hereditary monarchy with definite prerogatives—and Hellas began to fit out fleets and apply herself more closely to the sea. It is said that the Corinthians were the first to approach the modern style of naval architecture, and that Corinth was the first place in Hellas where triremes were built; and we have Ameinocles, a Corinthian shipwright, making four ships for the Samians. Dating from the end of this war, it is nearly three hundred years ago that Ameinocles went to Samos. Again, the earliest sea fight in history was between the Corinthians and Corcyraeans; this was about two hundred and sixty years ago, dating from the same time. Planted on an isthmus, Corinth had from time out of mind been an emporium; as formerly almost all communication between the Hellenes within and without the Peloponnesus was carried on overland, and the Corinthian territory was the highway through which it travelled. She had consequently great

money resources, as is shown by the epithet "wealthy" bestowed by the old poets on the place, and this enabled her, when traffic by sea became more common, to procure her navy and put down piracy; and as she could offer a mart for both branches of the trade, she acquired for herself all the power which a large revenue affords.

Subsequently the Ionians attained to great naval strength in the reign of Cyrus, the first king of the Persians, and of his son Cambyses, and while they were at war with the former commanded for a while the Ionian sea. Polycrates also, the tyrant of Samos, had a powerful navy in the reign of Cambyses with which he reduced many of the islands, and among them Rhenea, which he consecrated to the Delian Apollo. About this time also the Phocaeans, while they were founding Marseilles, defeated the Carthaginians in a sea fight.

14. These were the most powerful navies. And even these, although so many generations had elapsed since the Trojan War, seem to have been principally composed of the old penteconters and long-boats, and to have counted few triremes among their ranks. Indeed it was only shortly before the Persian war and the death of Darius the successor of Cambyses, that the Sicilian tyrants and the Corcyraeans acquired any large number of triremes. For after these there were no navies of any account in Hellas till the expedition of Xerxes; Aegina, Athens, and others may have possessed a few vessels, but they were principally penteconters. It was quite at the end of this period that the war with Aegina and the prospect of the barbarian invasion enabled Themistocles to persuade the Athenians to build the fleet with which they fought [at Salamis]; and even these vessels had not complete decks.

15. The navies, then, of the Hellenes during the period we have traversed were what I have described. All their insignificance did not prevent their being an element of the greatest power to those who cultivated them, alike in revenue and in dominion. They were the means by which the islands were reached and reduced, those of the smallest area falling the easiest prey. Wars by land there were none, none at

least by which power was acquired; we have the usual border contests, but of distant expeditions with conquest for object we hear nothing among the Hellenes. There was no union of subject cities round a great state, no spontaneous combination of equals for confederate expeditions; what fighting there was consisted merely of local warfare between rival neighbours. The nearest approach to a coalition took place in the old war between Chalcis and Eretria; this was a quarrel in which the rest of the Hellenic name did to some extent take sides.

16. Various, too, were the obstacles which the national growth encountered in various localities. The power of the Ionians was advancing with rapid strides when it came into collision with Persia, under King Cyrus, who, after having dethroned Croesus and overrun everything between the Halys and the sea, stopped not till he had enslaved the cities of the coast; the islands being only left to be subdued by Darius and the Phoenician navy.

17. Again, wherever there were tyrants in the Hellenic cities, their habit of providing simply for themselves, of looking solely to their personal comfort and family aggrandizement, made safety the great aim of their policy, and prevented anything great proceeding from them; though they would each have their affairs with their immediate neighbours. (In Sicily, however, they attained to very great power.) Thus for a long time everywhere in Hellas do we find causes which make the states alike incapable of combination for great and common ends, or of any vigorous action of their own.

18. But at last a time came when the tyrants of Athens and the far older tyrannies of the rest of Hellas were, with the exception of those in Sicily, once and for all put down by Lacedaemon; for this city, though after the settlement of the Dorians, its present inhabitants, it suffered from factions for an unparalleled length of time, still at a very early period obtained good laws, and enjoyed a freedom from tyrants which was unbroken; it has possessed the same form of government for more than four hundred years, reckoning

to the end of the late war, and has thus been in a position to arrange the affairs of the other states.

Not many years after the deposition of the tyrants, the battle of Marathon was fought between the Medes and the Athenians. Ten years afterwards the barbarian returned with the armada for the subjugation of Hellas. In the face of this great danger the command of the confederate Hellenes was assumed by the Lacedaemonians in virtue of their superior power; and the Athenians, having made up their minds to abandon their city, broke up their homes, threw themselves into their ships, and became a naval people. This coalition, after repulsing the barbarian, soon afterwards split into two sections, which included the Hellenes who had revolted from the king, as well as those who had aided him in the war. At the head of the one stood Athens, at the head of the other Lacedaemon, one the first naval, the other the first military power in Hellas. For a short time the alliance held together, till the Lacedaemonians and Athenians quarrelled, and made war upon each other with their allies, a duel into which all the Hellenes sooner or later were drawn, though some might at first remain neutral. So that the whole period from the Median War to this, with some peaceful intervals, was spent by each power in war, either with its rival or with its own revolted allies, and consequently afforded them constant practice in military matters, and that experience which is learnt in the school of danger.

19. The policy of Lacedaemon was not to exact tribute from her allies, but merely to secure their subservience to her interests by establishing oligarchies among them; Athens, on the contrary, had by degrees deprived hers of their ships, and imposed instead contributions in money on all except Chios and Lesbos. Both found their resources for this war separately to exceed the sum of their strength when the alliance flourished intact.

20. Having now given the result of my inquiries into early times, I grant that there will be a difficulty in believing every particular detail. The way that most men deal with traditions, even traditions of their own country, is to receive

them all alike as they are delivered, without applying any critical test whatever. The general Athenian public fancy that Hipparchus was tyrant when he fell by the hands of Harmodius and Aristogeiton; not knowing that Hippias, the eldest of the sons of Pisistratus, was really supreme, and that Hipparchus and Thessalus were his brothers; and that Harmodius and Aristogeiton suspecting, on the very day, nay at the very moment fixed on for the deed, that information had been conveyed to Hippias by their accomplices, concluded that he had been warned, and did not attack him, yet, not liking to be apprehended and risk their lives for nothing, fell upon Hipparchus near the Leocoreum, and slew him as he was arranging the Panathenaic procession.

There are many other unfounded ideas current among the rest of the Hellenes, even on matters of contemporary history which have not been obscured by time. For instance, there is the notion that the Lacedaemonian kings have two votes each, the fact being that they have only one; and that there is a company of Pitana, there being simply no such thing. So little pains do the vulgar take in the investigation of truth, accepting readily the first story that comes to hand.

21. On the whole, however, the conclusions I have drawn from the proofs quoted may, I believe, safely be relied on. Assuredly they will not be disturbed either by the lays of a poet displaying the exaggeration of his craft, or by the compositions of the chroniclers that are attractive at truth's expense, the subjects they treat of being out of the reach of evidence, and time having robbed most of them of historical value by enthroning them in the region of legend. Turning from these, we can rest satisfied with having proceeded upon the clearest data, and having arrived at conclusions as exact as can be expected in matters of such antiquity. To come to this war; despite the known disposition of the actors in a struggle to overrate its importance, and when it is over to return to their admiration of earlier events, yet an examination of the facts will show that it was much greater than the wars which preceded it.

22. With reference to the speeches in this history, some

were delivered before the war began, others while it was going on; some I heard myself, others I got from various quarters; it was in all cases difficult to carry them word for word in one's memory, so my habit has been to make the speakers say what was in my opinion demanded of them by the various occasions, of course adhering as closely as possible to the general sense of what they really said. And with reference to the narrative of events, far from permitting myself to derive it from the first source that came to hand, I did not even trust my own impressions, but it rests partly on what I saw myself, partly on what others saw for me, the accuracy of the report being always tried by the most severe and detailed tests possible. My conclusions have cost me some labour from the want of coincidence between accounts of the same occurrences by different eyewitnesses, arising sometimes from imperfect memory, sometimes from undue partiality for one side or the other. The absence of romance in my history will, I fear, detract somewhat from its interest; but if it be judged useful by those inquirers who desire an exact knowledge of the past as an aid to the interpretation of the future, which in the course of human things must resemble if it does not reflect it, I shall be content. In fine, I have written my work, not as an essay which is to win the applause of the moment, but as a possession for all time.

23. The Median War, the greatest achievement of past times, yet found a speedy decision in two actions by sea and two by land. The present war was prolonged to an immense length, and long as it was it was short without parallel for the misfortunes that it brought upon Hellas. Never had so many cities been taken and laid desolate, here by the barbarians, here by the parties contending (the old inhabitants being sometimes removed to make room for others); never was there so much banishing and blood-shedding, now on the field of battle, now in the strife of faction. Old stories of occurrences handed down by tradition, but scantily confirmed by experience, suddenly ceased to be incredible; there were earthquakes of unparalleled extent and violence; eclipses of the sun occurred with a frequency unrecorded

in previous history; there were great droughts in sundry places and consequent famines, and that most calamitous and awfully fatal visitation, the plague. All this came upon them with the late war, which was begun by the Athenians and Peloponnesians by the dissolution of the thirty years' truce made after the conquest of Euboea. To the question why they broke the treaty, I answer by placing first an account of their grounds of complaint and points of difference, that no one may ever have to ask the immediate cause which plunged the Hellenes into a war of such magnitude. The real cause I consider to be the one which was formally most kept out of sight. The growth of the power of Athens, and the alarm which this inspired in Lacedaemon, made war inevitable. Still it is well to give the grounds alleged by either side, which led to the dissolution of the treaty and the breaking out of the war.

24. The city of Epidamnus stands on the right of the entrance of the Ionian gulf. Its vicinity is inhabited by the barbarian Taulantians, an Illyrian people. The place is a colony from Corcyra, founded by Phalius, son of Eratocleides, of the family of the Heraclids, who had according to ancient usage been summoned for the purpose from Corinth, the mother country. The colonists were joined by some Corinthians, and others of the Dorian race. Now, as time went on, the city of Epidamnus became great and populous; but, falling a prey to factions arising, it is said, from a war with her neighbours the barbarians, she became much enfeebled, and lost a considerable amount of her power. The last act before the war was the expulsion of the nobles by the people. The exiled party joined the barbarians, and proceeded to plunder those in the city by sea and land; and the Epidamnians, finding themselves hard pressed, sent ambassadors to Corcyra beseeching their mother country not to allow them to perish, but to make up matters between them and the exiles, and to rid them of the war with the barbarians. The ambassadors seated themselves in the temple of Hera as suppliants, and made the above requests. But the Corcyraeans refused to

accept their supplication, and they were dismissed without having effected anything.

25. When the Epidamnians found that no help could be expected from Corcyra, they were in a strait what to do next. So they sent to Delphi and inquired of the god, whether they should deliver their city to the Corinthians, and endeavour to obtain some assistance from their founders. The answer he gave them was to deliver the city and place themselves under Corinthian protection. So the Epidamnians went to Corinth, and delivered over the colony in obedience to the commands of the oracle. They showed that their founder came from Corinth, and revealed the answer of the god; and they begged them not to allow them to perish, but to assist them. This the Corinthians consented to do. Believing the colony to belong as much to themselves as to the Corcyraeans, they felt it to be a kind of duty to undertake their protection. Besides, they hated the Corcyraeans for their contempt of the mother country. Instead of meeting with the usual honours accorded to the parent city by every other colony at public assemblies, such as precedence at sacrifices, Corinth found herself treated with contempt by a power which in point of wealth could stand comparison with any even of the richest communities in Hellas, which possessed great military strength, and which sometimes could not repress a pride in the high naval position of an island whose nautical renown dated from the days of its old inhabitants, the Phaeacians. This was one reason for the care that they lavished on their fleet, which became very efficient; indeed they began the war with a force of a hundred and twenty triremes.

26. All these grievances made Corinth eager to send the promised aid to Epidamnus. Advertisement was made for volunteer settlers, and a force of Ambraciots, Leucadians, and Corinthians was despatched. They marched by land to Apollonia, a Corinthian colony, the route by sea being avoided from fear of Corcyraean interruption. When the Corcyraeans heard of the arrival of the settlers and troops

in Epidamnus, and the surrender of the colony to Corinth, they took fire. Instantly putting to sea with five-and-twenty ships, which were quickly followed by others, they insolently commanded the Epidamnians to receive back the banished nobles (it must be premised that the Epidamnian exiles had come to Corcyra, and, pointing to the sepulchres of their ancestors, had appealed to their kindred to restore them) and to dismiss the Corinthian garrison and settlers. But to all this the Epidamnians turned a deaf ear. Upon this the Corcyraeans commenced operations against them with a fleet of forty sail. They took with them the exiles, with a view to their restoration, and also secured the services of the Illyrians. Sitting down before the city, they issued a proclamation to the effect that any of the natives that chose, and the foreigners, might depart unharmed, with the alternative of being treated as enemies. On their refusal the Corcyraeans proceeded to besiege the city, which stands on an isthmus.

27. The Corinthians, receiving intelligence of the investment of Epidamnus, got together an armament and proclaimed a colony to Epidamnus, equality being guaranteed to all who chose to go. Any who were not prepared to sail at once might by paying down the sum of fifty Corinthian drachmae have a share in the colony without leaving Corinth. Great numbers took advantage of this proclamation, some being ready to start directly, others paying the requisite money. In case of their passage being disputed by the Corcyraeans, several cities were asked to lend them a convoy. Megara prepared to accompany them with eight ships, Pale in Cephallenia with four; Epidaurus furnished five, Hermione one, Troezen two, Leucas ten, and Ambracia eight. The Thebans and Phliasians were asked for money, the Eleans for bottoms as well; while Corinth herself furnished thirty ships and three thousand heavy infantry.

28. When the Corcyraeans heard of their preparations they came to Corinth with envoys from Lacedaemon and Sicyon, whom they persuaded to accompany them, and bade her recall the garrison and settlers, as she had nothing to do

with Epidamnus. If, however, she had any claims to make, they were willing to submit the matter to the arbitration of such of the cities in the Peloponnesus as should be chosen by mutual agreement, and that the colony should belong to the city to whom the arbitrators might assign it. They were also willing to refer the matter to the oracle at Delphi. If, in defiance of their protestations, war was appealed to, they should be themselves compelled by this violence to seek friends in quarters where they had no desire to seek them, and to make even old ties give way to the necessity of assistance. The answer they got from Corinth was that if they would withdraw their fleet and the barbarians from Epidamnus negotiation might be possible; but, while the town was still being besieged, going before arbitrators was out of the question. The Corcyraeans retorted that if Corinth would withdraw her troops from Epidamnus they would withdraw theirs, or they were ready to let both parties remain *in statu quo,* an armistice being concluded till judgement could be given.

29. Turning a deaf ear to all these proposals, when their ships were manned and their allies had come in, the Corinthians sent a herald before them to declare war, and getting under way with seventy-five ships and two thousand heavy infantry, sailed for Epidamnus to give battle to the Corcyraeans. The fleet was under the command of Aristeus, son of Pellichas, Callicrates, son of Callias, and Timanor, son of Timanthes; the troops under that of Archetimus, son of Eurytimus, and Isarchidas, son of Isarchus. When they had reached Actium in the territory of Anactorium, at the mouth of the gulf of Ambracia, where the temple of Apollo stands, the Corcyraeans sent on a herald in a light boat to warn them not to sail against them. Meanwhile they proceeded to man their ships, all of which had been equipped for action, the old vessels being undergirded to make them seaworthy. On the return of the herald without any peaceful answer from the Corinthians, their ships being now manned, they put out to sea to meet the enemy with a fleet of eighty sail (forty were engaged in the siege of Epidamnus), formed line and

went into action, and gained a decisive victory, and destroyed fifteen of the Corinthian vessels. The same day had seen Epidamnus compelled by its besiegers to capitulate, the conditions being that the foreigners should be sold, and the Corinthians kept as prisoners of war, till their fate should be otherwise decided.

30. After the engagement the Corcyraeans set up a trophy on Leukimme, a headland of Corcyra, and slew all their captives except the Corinthians, whom they kept as prisoners of war. Defeated at sea, the Corinthians and their allies repaired home, and left the Corcyraeans masters of all the sea about those parts. Sailing to Leucas, a Corinthian colony, they ravaged their territory, and burnt Cyllene, the harbour of the Eleans, because they had furnished ships and money to Corinth. For almost the whole of the period that followed the battle they remained masters of the sea, and the allies of Corinth were harassed by Corcyraean cruisers. At last Corinth, roused by the sufferings of her allies, sent out ships and troops in the fall of the summer, who formed an encampment at Actium and about Chimerium, in Thesprotis, for the protection of Leucas and the rest of the friendly cities. The Corcyraeans on their part formed a similar station on Leukimme. Neither party made any movement, but they remained confronting each other till the end of the summer, and winter was at hand before either of them returned home.

31. Corinth, exasperated by the war with the Corcyraeans, spent the whole of the year after the engagement and that succeeding it in building ships, and in straining every nerve to form an efficient fleet, rowers being drawn from the Peloponnesus and the rest of Hellas by the inducement of pay. The Corcyraeans, alarmed at the news of their preparations, being without a single ally in Hellas (for they had not enrolled themselves either in the Athenian or in the Lacedaemonian confederacy), decided to repair to Athens in order to enter into alliance, and to endeavour to procure support from her. Corinth also, hearing of their intentions, sent

an embassy to Athens to prevent the Corcyraean navy being joined by the Athenian, and her prospect of ordering the war according to her wishes being thus impeded. An assembly was convoked, and the rival advocates appeared; the Corcyraeans spoke as follows:

32. "Athenians, when a people that have not rendered any important service or support to their neighbours in times past, for which they might claim to be repaid, appear before them as we now appear before you to solicit their assistance, they may fairly be required to satisfy certain preliminary conditions. They should show, first, that it is expedient or at least safe to grant their request; next, that they will retain a lasting sense of the kindness. But if they cannot clearly establish any of these points, they must not be annoyed if they meet with a rebuff. Now the Corcyraeans believe that with their petition for alliance they can also give you a satisfactory answer on these points, and they have therefore despatched us hither. It has so happened that our policy as regards you with respect to this request, turns out to be inconsistent, and as regards our interests, to be at the present crisis inexpedient. We say inconsistent, because a power which has never in the whole of her past history been willing to ally herself with any of her neighbours is now found asking them to ally themselves with her. And we say inexpedient, because in our present war with Corinth it has left us in a position of entire isolation, and what once seemed the wise precaution of refusing to involve ourselves in alliances with other powers, lest we should also involve ourselves in risks of their choosing, has now proved to be folly and weakness. It is true that in the late naval engagement we drove back the Corinthians from our shores single-handed. But they have now got together a still larger armament from the Peloponnesus and the rest of Hellas; and we, seeing our utter inability to cope with them without foreign aid, and the magnitude of the danger which subjection to them implies, find it necessary to ask help from you and from every other power. And we hope to be excused if we forswear our old principle of complete

political isolation, a principle which was not adopted with any sinister intention, but was rather the consequence of an error in judgement.

33. "Now there are many reasons why in the event of your compliance you will congratulate yourselves on this request having been made to you. First, because your assistance will be rendered to a power which, herself inoffensive, is a victim to the injustice of others. Secondly, because all that we most value is at stake in the present contest, and your welcome of us under these circumstances will be a proof of good will which will ever keep alive the gratitude you will lay up in our hearts. Thirdly, yourselves excepted, we are the greatest naval power in Hellas. Moreover, can you conceive a stroke of good fortune more rare in itself, or more disheartening to your enemies, than that the power whose adhesion you would have valued above much material and moral strength, should present herself self-invited, should deliver herself into your hands without danger and without expense, and should lastly put you in the way of gaining a high character in the eyes of the world, the gratitude of those whom you shall assist, and a great accession of strength for yourselves? You may search all history without finding many instances of a people gaining all these advantages at once, or many instances of a power that comes in quest of assistance being in a position to give to the people whose alliance she solicits as much safety and honour as she will receive.

"But it will be urged that it is only in the case of a war that we shall be found useful. To this we answer that if any of you imagine that that war is far off, he is grievously mistaken, and is blind to the fact that Lacedaemon regards you with jealousy and desires war, and that Corinth is powerful there—the same, remember, that is your enemy, and is even now trying to subdue us as a preliminary to attacking you. And this she does to prevent our becoming united by a common enmity, and her having us both on her hands, and also to insure getting the start of you in one of two ways, either by crippling our power or by making its strength her own.

Now it is our policy to be beforehand with her—that is, for Corcyra to make an offer of alliance and for you to accept it; in fact, we ought to form plans against her instead of waiting to defeat the plans she forms against us.

34. "If she asserts that for you to receive a colony of hers into alliance is not right, let her know that every colony that is well treated honours its parent state, but becomes estranged from it by injustice. For colonists are not sent forth on the understanding that they are to be the slaves of those that remain behind, but that they are to be their equals. And that Corinth was injuring us is clear. Invited to refer the dispute about Epidamnus to arbitration, they chose to prosecute their complaints by war rather than by a fair trial. And let their conduct towards us who are their kindred be a warning to you not to be misled by their deceit, nor to yield to their direct requests; concessions to adversaries only end in self-reproach, and the more strictly they are avoided the greater will be the chance of security.

35. "If it be urged that your reception of us will be a breach of the treaty [of 445 B.C.] existing between you and Lacedaemon, the answer is that we are a neutral state, and that one of the express provisions of that treaty is that it shall be competent for any Hellenic state that is neutral to join whichever side it pleases. And it is intolerable for Corinth·to be allowed to obtain men for her navy not only from her allies, but also from the rest of Hellas, no small number being furnished by your own subjects, while we are to be excluded both from the alliance left open to us by treaty and from any assistance that we might get from other quarters, and you are to be accused of political immorality if you comply with our request. On the other hand, we shall have much greater cause to complain of you, if you do not comply with it, if we, who are in peril, and are no enemies of yours, meet with a repulse at your hands, while Corinth, who is the aggressor and your enemy, not only meets with no hindrance from you, but is even allowed to draw material for war from your dependencies. This ought not to be, but you should either forbid her enlisting men in your domin-

ions, or you should lend us too what help you may think advisable.

"But your real policy is to afford us avowed countenance and support. The advantages of this course, as we premised in the beginning of our speech, are many. We mention one that is perhaps the chief. Could there be a clearer guarantee of our good faith than is offered by the fact that the power which is at enmity with you is also at enmity with us, and that that power is fully able to punish defection? And there is a wide difference between declining the alliance of an inland and of a maritime power. For your first endeavour should be to prevent, if possible, the existence of any naval power except your own; failing this, to secure the friendship of the strongest that does exist.

36. "And if any of you believe that what we urge is expedient, but fear to act upon this belief lest it should lead to a breach of the treaty, you must remember that on the one hand, whatever your fears, your strength will be formidable to your antagonists; on the other, whatever the confidence you derive from refusing to receive us, your weakness will have no terrors for a strong enemy. You must also remember that your decision is for Athens no less than for Corcyra, and that you are not making the best provision for her interests if, at a time when you are anxiously scanning the horizon that you may be in readiness for the breaking out of the war which is all but upon you, you hesitate to attach to your side a place whose adhesion or estrangement is alike pregnant with the most vital consequences. For it lies conveniently for the coast navigation in the direction of Italy and Sicily, being able to bar the passage of naval reinforcements from thence to the Peloponnesus, and from the Peloponnesus thither; and it is in other respects a most desirable station. To sum up as shortly as possible, embracing both general and particular considerations, let this show you the folly of sacrificing us. Remember that there are but three considerable naval powers in Hellas, Athens, Corcyra, and Corinth, and that if you allow two of these three to become one, and Corinth to secure us for herself, you will have to hold the sea against

the united fleets of Corcyra and the Peloponnesus. But if you receive us, you will have our ships to reinforce you in the struggle."

Such were the words of the Corcyraeans. After they had finished, the Corinthians spoke as follows:

37. "These Corcyraeans in the speech we have just heard do not confine themselves to the question of their reception into your alliance. They also talk of our being guilty of injustice, and their being the victims of an unjustifiable war. It becomes necessary for us to touch upon both these points before we proceed to the rest of what we have to say, that you may have a more correct idea of the grounds of our claim, and have good cause to reject their petition.

"According to them, their old policy of refusing all offers of alliance was a policy of moderation. It was in fact adopted for bad ends, not for good; indeed their conduct is such as to make them by no means desirous of having allies present to witness it, or of having the shame of asking their concurrence. Besides, their geographical situation makes them independent of others, and consequently the decision in cases where they injure any lies not with judges appointed by mutual agreement, but with themselves, because, while they seldom make voyages to their neighbours, they are constantly being visited by foreign vessels which are compelled to put in to Corcyra. In short, the object that they propose to themselves, in their specious policy of complete isolation, is not to avoid sharing in the crimes of others, but to secure a monopoly of crime to themselves—the license of outrage wherever they can compel, of fraud wherever they can elude, and the enjoyment of their gains without shame. And yet if they were the honest men they pretend to be, the less hold that others had upon them, the stronger would be the light in which they might have put their honesty by giving and taking what was just.

38. "But such has not been their conduct either towards others or towards us. The attitude of our colony towards us has always been one of estrangement, and is now one of hostility; for, say they, 'We were not sent out to be ill-treated.'

We rejoin that we did not found the colony to be insulted by them, but to be their head, and to be regarded with a proper respect. At any rate our other colonies honour us, and we are very much beloved by our colonists; and clearly, if the majority are satisfied with us, these can have no good reason for a dissatisfaction in which they stand alone, and we are not acting improperly in making war against them, nor are we making war against them without having received signal provocation. Besides, if we were in the wrong, it would be honourable in them to give way to our wishes, and disgraceful for us to trample on their moderation; but in the pride and license of wealth they have sinned again and again against us, and never more deeply than when Epidamnus, our dependency, which they took no steps to claim in its distress, upon our coming to relieve it, was by them seized, and is now held by force of arms.

39. "As to their allegation that they wished the question to be first submitted to arbitration, it is obvious that a challenge coming from the party who is safe in a commanding position cannot gain the credit due only to him who, before appealing to arms, in deeds as well as words, places himself on a level with his adversary. In their case, it was not before they laid siege to the place, but after they at length understood that we should not tamely suffer it, that they thought of the specious word arbitration. And, not satisfied with their own misconduct there, they appear here now requiring you to join with them not in alliance, but in crime, and to receive them in spite of their being at enmity with us. But it was when they stood firmest that they should have made overtures to you, and not at a time when we have been wronged, and they are in peril; nor yet at a time when you will be admitting to a share in your protection those who never admitted you to a share in their power, and will be incurring an equal amount of blame from us with those in whose offences you had no hand. No, they should have shared their power with you before they asked you to share your fortunes with them.

40. "So then the reality of the grievances we come to com-

plain of, and the violence and rapacity of our opponents, have both been proved. But that you cannot equitably receive them, this you have still to learn. It may be true that one of the provisions of the treaty is that it shall be competent for any state whose name was not down on the list to join whichever side it pleases. But this agreement is not meant for those whose object in joining is the injury of other powers, but for those whose need of support does not arise from the fact of defection, and whose adhesion will not bring to the power that is mad enough to receive them war instead of peace; which will be the case with you, if you refuse to listen to us. For you cannot become their auxiliary and remain our friend; if you join in their attack, you must share the punishment which the defenders inflict on them. And yet you have the best possible right to be neutral, or, failing this, you should on the contrary join us against them. Corinth is at least in treaty with you; with Corcyra you were never even in truce. But do not lay down the principle that defection is to be patronized. Did we on the defection of the Samians record our vote against you, when the rest of the Peloponnesian powers were divided on the question whether they should assist them? No, we told them to their face that every power has a right to punish its own allies. Why, if you make it your policy to receive and assist all offenders, you will find that just as many of your dependencies will come over to us, and the principle that you establish will press less heavily on us than on yourselves.

41. "This then is what Hellenic law entitles us to demand as a right. But we have also advice to offer and claims on your gratitude, which, since there is no danger of our injuring you, as we are not enemies, and since our friendship does not amount to very frequent intercourse, we say ought to be liquidated at the present juncture. When you were in want of ships of war for the war against the Aeginetans, before the Persian invasion, Corinth supplied you with twenty vessels. That good turn, and the line we took on the Samian question, when we were the cause of the Peloponnesians refusing to assist them, enabled you to conquer Aegina and to

punish Samos. And we acted thus at crises when, if ever, men are wont in their efforts against their enemies to forget everything for the sake of victory, regarding him who assists them then as a friend, even if thus far he has been a foe, and him who opposes them then as a foe, even if he has thus far been a friend; indeed they allow their real interests to suffer from their absorbing preoccupation in the struggle.

42. "Weigh well these considerations, and let your youth learn what they are from their elders, and let them determine to do unto us as we have done unto you. And let them not acknowledge the justice of what we say, but dispute its wisdom in the contingency of war. Not only is the straightest path generally speaking the wisest; but the coming of the war, which the Corcyraeans have used as a bugbear to persuade you to do wrong, is still uncertain, and it is not worth while to be carried away by it into gaining the instant and declared enmity of Corinth. It were, rather, wise to try and counteract the unfavourable impression which your conduct to Megara has created. For kindness opportunely shown has a greater power of removing old grievances than the facts of the case may warrant. And do not be seduced by the prospect of a great naval alliance. Abstinence from all injustice to other first-rate powers is a greater tower of strength than anything that can be gained by the sacrifice of permanent tranquillity for an apparent temporary advantage.

43. "It is now our turn to benefit by the principle that we laid down at Lacedaemon, that every power has a right to punish her own allies. We now claim to receive the same from you, and protest against your rewarding us for benefiting you by our vote by injuring us by yours. On the contrary, return us like for like, remembering that this is that very crisis in which he who lends aid is most a friend, and he who opposes is most a foe. And for these Corcyraeans—neither receive them into alliance in our despite, nor be their abettors in crime. So do, and you will act as we have a right to expect of you, and at the same time best consult your own interests."

44. Such were the words of the Corinthians.

When the Athenians had heard both out, two assemblies were held. In the first there was a manifest disposition to listen to the representations of Corinth; in the second, public feeling had changed, and an alliance with Corcyra was decided on, with certain reservations. It was to be a defensive, not an offensive alliance. It did not involve a breach of the treaty with the Peloponnesus: Athens could not be required to join Corcyra in any attack upon Corinth. But each of the contracting parties had a right to the other's assistance against invasion, whether of his own territory or that of an ally. For it began now to be felt that the coming of the Peloponnesian War was only a question of time, and no one was willing to see a naval power of such magnitude as Corcyra sacrificed to Corinth; though if they could let them weaken each other by mutual conflict, it would be no bad preparation for the struggle which Athens might one day have to wage with Corinth and the other naval powers. At the same time the island seemed to lie conveniently on the coasting passage to Italy and Sicily.

45. With these views Athens received Corcyra into alliance, and on the departure of the Corinthians not long afterwards sent ten ships to their assistance. They were commanded by Lacedaemonius, the son of Cimon, Diotimus, the son of Strombichus, and Proteas, the son of Epicles. Their instructions were to avoid collision with the Corinthian fleet except under certain circumstances. If it sailed to Corcyra and threatened a landing on her coast, or in any of her possessions, they were to do their utmost to prevent it. These instructions were prompted by an anxiety to avoid a breach of the treaty.

46. Meanwhile the Corinthians completed their preparations and sailed for Corcyra with a hundred and fifty ships. Of these Elis furnished ten, Megara twelve, Leucas ten, Ambracia twenty-seven, Anactorium one, and Corinth herself ninety. Each of these contingents had its own admiral, the Corinthian being under the command of Xenoclides, son of Euthycles, with four colleagues. Sailing from Leucas, they made land at the part of the continent opposite Corcyra.

They anchored in the harbour of Chimerium, in the territory of Thesprotis, above which, at some distance from the
sea, lies the city of Ephyre, in the Elean district. By this city
the Acherusian lake pours its waters into the sea. It gets its
name from the river Acheron, which flows through Thesprotis and falls into the lake. There also the river Thyamis
flows, forming the boundary between Thesprotis and Kes-
trine; and between these rivers rises the point of Chimerium. In this part of the continent the Corinthians now came
to anchor and formed an encampment.

47. When the Corcyraeans saw them coming, they
manned a hundred and ten ships, commanded by Meikiades,
Aisimides, and Eurybatus, and stationed themselves at one
of the Sybota isles, the ten Athenian ships being present. On
point Leukimme they posted their land forces, and a thousand heavy infantry who had come from Zacynthus to their
assistance. Nor were the Corinthians on the mainland without their allies. The barbarians flocked in large numbers to
their assistance, the inhabitants of this part of the continent
being old allies of theirs.

48. When the Corinthian preparations were completed
they took three days' provisions and put out from Chimerium
by night, ready for action. Sailing with the dawn, they
sighted the Corcyraean fleet out at sea and coming towards
them. When they perceived each other, both sides formed
in order of battle. On the Corcyraean right wing lay the
Athenian ships, the rest of the line being occupied by their
own vessels formed in three squadrons, each of which was
commanded by one of the three admirals. Such was the Corcyraean formation. The Corinthian was as follows: on the
right wing lay the Megarian and Ambraciot ships, in the centre the rest of the allies in order. But the left was composed
of the best sailers in the Corinthian navy, to encounter the
Athenians and the right wing of the Corcyraeans.

49. As soon as the signals were raised on either side, they
joined battle. Both sides had a large number of heavy infantry on their decks, and a large number of archers and darters,
the old imperfect armament still prevailing. The sea fight

was an obstinate one, though not remarkable for its science; indeed it was more like a battle by land. Whenever they charged each other, the multitude and crush of the vessels made it by no means easy to get loose; besides, their hopes of victory lay principally in the heavy infantry on the decks, who stood and fought in order, the ships remaining stationary. The manœuvre of breaking the line was not tried: in short, strength and pluck had more share in the fight than science. Everywhere tumult reigned, the battle being one scene of confusion; meanwhile the Athenian ships, by coming up to the Corcyraeans whenever they were pressed, served to alarm the enemy, though their commanders could not join in the battle from fear of their instructions.

The right wing of the Corinthians suffered most. The Corcyraeans routed it, and chased them in disorder to the continent with twenty ships, sailed up to their camp, and burnt the tents which they found empty, and plundered the stuff. So in this quarter the Corinthians and their allies were defeated, and the Corcyraeans were victorious. But where the Corinthians themselves were, on the left, they gained a decided success, the scanty forces of the Corcyraeans being further weakened by the want of the twenty ships absent on the pursuit. Seeing the Corcyraeans hard pressed, the Athenians began at length to assist them more unequivocally. At first, it is true, they refrained from charging any ships; but when the rout was becoming patent, and the Corinthians were pressing on, the time at last came when everyone set to, and all distinction was laid aside, and it came to this point, that the Corinthians and Athenians raised their hands against each other.

50. After the rout, the Corinthians, instead of employing themselves in lashing fast and hauling after them the hulls of the vessels which they had disabled, turned their attention to the men, whom they butchered as they sailed through, not caring so much to make prisoners. Some even of their own friends were slain by them, by mistake, in their ignorance of the defeat of the right wing. For the number of the ships on both sides, and the distance to which they covered

the sea, made it difficult, after they had once joined, to distinguish between the conquering and the conquered, this
battle proving far greater than any before it, any at least between Hellenes, for the number of vessels engaged. After
the Corinthians had chased the Corcyraeans to the land, they
turned to the wrecks and their dead, most of whom they succeeded in getting hold of and conveying to Sybota, the ren-
dezvous of the land forces furnished by their barbarian allies.
Sybota, it must be known, is a desert habour of Thesprotis.
This task over, they mustered anew and sailed against the
Corcyraeans, who on their part advanced to meet them with
all their ships that were fit for service and remaining to
them, accompanied by the Athenian vessels, fearing that
they might attempt a landing in their territory. It was by this
time getting late, and the paean had been sung for the attack,
when the Corinthians suddenly began to back water. They
had observed twenty Athenian ships sailing up, which had
been sent out afterwards to reinforce the ten vessels by the
Athenians, who feared, as it turned out justly, the defeat of
the Corcyraeans and the inability of their handful of ships
to protect them.

51. These ships were thus seen by the Corinthians first.
They suspected that they were from Athens, and that those
which they saw were not all, but that there were more behind; they accordingly began to retire. The Corcyraeans
meanwhile had not sighted them, as they were advancing
from a point which they could not so well see, and were
wondering why the Corinthians were backing water, when
some caught sight of them, and cried out that there were
ships in sight ahead. Upon this they also retired; for it was
now getting dark, and the retreat of the Corinthians had suspended hostilities. Thus they parted from each other, and
the battle ceased with night. The Corcyraeans were in their
camp at Leukimme, when these twenty ships from Athens,
under the command of Glaucon, the son of Leagrus, and
Andocides, son of Leogoras, bore on through the corpses
and the wrecks, and sailed up to the camp, not long after
they were sighted. It was now night, and the Corcyraeans

feared that they might be hostile vessels; but they soon knew them, and the ships came to anchor.

52. The next day the thirty Athenian vessels put out to sea, accompanied by all the Corcyraean ships that were seaworthy, and sailed to the harbour at Sybota, where the Corinthians lay, to see if they would engage. The Corinthians put out from the land and formed a line in the open sea, but beyond this made no further movement, having no intention of assuming the offensive. For they saw reinforcements arrived fresh from Athens, and themselves confronted by numerous difficulties, such as the necessity of guarding the prisoners whom they had on board, and the want of all means of refitting their ships in a desert place. What they were thinking more about was how their voyage home was to be effected; they feared that the Athenians might consider that the treaty was dissolved by the collision which had occurred, and forbid their departure.

53. Accordingly they resolved to put some men on board a boat and send them without a herald's wand to the Athenians, as an experiment. Having done so, they spoke as follows: "You do wrong, Athenians, to begin war and break the treaty. Engaged in chastising our enemies, we find you placing yourselves in our path in arms against us. Now if your intentions are to prevent us sailing to Corcyra, or anywhere else that we may wish, and if you are for breaking the treaty, first take us that are here and treat us as enemies." Such was what they said, and all the Corcyraean armament that were within hearing immediately called out to take them and kill them. But the Athenians answered as follows: "Neither are we beginning war, Peloponnesians, nor are we breaking the treaty; but these Corcyraeans are our allies, and we are come to help them. So if you want to sail anywhere else, we place no obstacle in your way; but if you are going to sail against Corcyra or any of her possessions, we shall do our best to stop you."

54. Receiving this answer from the Athenians, the Corinthians commenced preparations for their voyage home, and set up a trophy in Sybota, on the continent; while the Cor-

cyraeans took up the wrecks and dead that had been carried out to them by the current, and by a wind which rose in the night and scattered them in all directions, and set up their trophy in Sybota, on the island, as victors. The reasons each side had for claiming the victory were these. The Corinthians had been victorious in the sea fight until night, and, having thus been enabled to carry off most wrecks and dead, they were in possession of no fewer than a thousand prisoners of war, and had sunk close upon seventy vessels. The Corcyraeans had destroyed about thirty ships, and after the arrival of the Athenians had taken up the wrecks and dead on their side; they had besides seen the Corinthians retire before them, backing water on sight of the Athenian vessels, and upon the arrival of the Athenians refuse to sail out against them from Sybota. Thus both sides claimed the victory.

55. The Corinthians on the voyage home took Anactorium, which stands at the mouth of the Ambracian gulf. The place was taken by treachery, being common ground to the Corcyraeans and Corinthians. After establishing Corinthian settlers there, they retired home. Eight hundred of the Corcyraeans were slaves; these they sold; two hundred and fifty they retained in captivity and treated with great attention, in the hope that they might bring over their country to Corinth on their return, most of them being, as it happened, men of very high position in Corcyra. In this way Corcyra maintained her political existence in the war with Corinth, and the Athenian vessels left the island. This was the first cause of the war that Corinth had against the Athenians, viz., that they had fought against them with the Corcyraeans in time of treaty.

56. Almost immediately after this, fresh differences arose between the Athenians and Peloponnesians and contributed their share to the war. Corinth was forming schemes for retaliation, and Athens suspected her hostility. The Potidaeans, who inhabit the isthmus of Pallene, being a Corinthian colony, but tributary allies of Athens, were ordered to raze the wall looking towards Pallene, to give hostages, to dismiss

the Corinthian magistrates, and in future not to receive the persons sent from Corinth annually to succeed them. It was feared that they might be persuaded by Perdiccas [king of Macedon] and the Corinthians to revolt, and might draw the rest of the allies in the direction of Thrace to revolt with them. . . .

66. [In short,] the Athenians and Peloponnesians had these antecedent grounds of complaint against each other: the complaint of Corinth was that her colony of Potidaea, and Corinthian and Peloponnesian citizens within it, were being besieged; that of Athens against the Peloponnesians that they had incited a town of hers, a member of her alliance and a contributor to her revenue, to revolt, and had come and were openly fighting against her on the side of the Potidaeans. For all this, war had not yet broken out: there was still truce for a while; for this was a private enterprise on the part of Corinth.

67. But the siege of Potidaea put an end to her inaction; she had men inside it: besides, she feared for the place. Immediately summoning the allies to Lacedaemon, she came and loudly accused Athens of breach of the treaty and aggression on the Peloponnesus. With her the Aeginetans, formally unrepresented from fear of Athens, in secret proved not the least urgent of the advocates for war, asserting that they had not the independence guaranteed to them by the treaty. After extending the summons to any of their allies and others who might have complaints to make of Athenian aggression, the Lacedaemonians held their ordinary assembly and invited them to speak. There were many who came forward and made their several accusations; among them the Megarians, in a long list of grievances, called special attention to the fact of their exclusion from the ports of the Athenian empire and the market of Athens, in defiance of the treaty. Last of all the Corinthians came forward, and, having let those who preceded them inflame the Lacedaemonians, now followed with a speech to this effect:

68. "Lacedaemonians, the confidence which you feel in your constitution and social order inclines you to receive

any reflections of ours on other powers with a certain scepticism. Hence springs your moderation, but hence also the rather limited knowledge which you betray in dealing with foreign politics. Time after time was our voice raised to warn you of the blows about to be dealt us by Athens, and time after time, instead of taking the trouble to ascertain the worth of our communications, you contented yourselves with suspecting the speakers of being inspired by private interest. And so, instead of calling these allies together before the blow fell, you have delayed to do so till we are smarting under it; allies among whom we have not the worst title to speak, as having the greatest complaints to make, complaints of Athenian outrage and Lacedaemonian neglect. Now if these assaults on the rights of Hellas had been made in the dark you might be unacquainted with the facts, and it would be our duty to enlighten you. As it is, long speeches are not needed where you see servitude accomplished for some of us, meditated for others—in particular for our allies—and prolonged preparations in the aggressor against the hour of war. Or what, pray, is the meaning of their reception of Corcyra by fraud, and their holding it against us by force? what of the siege of Potidaea?—places one of which lies most conveniently for any action against the Thracian towns, while the other would have contributed a very large navy to the Peloponnesians?

69. "For all this you are responsible. You it was who first allowed them to fortify their city after the Median War, and afterwards to erect the Long Walls[1]—you who, then and now, are always depriving of freedom not only those whom they have enslaved but also those who have as yet been your allies. For the true author of the subjugation of a people is not so much the immediate agent as the power which permits it, having the means to prevent it—particularly if that power bears the glory of being the liberator of Hellas. We are at last assembled. It has not been easy to assemble, nor even now are our objects defined. We ought not to be still inquiring into the fact of our wrongs, but into the means of our de-

---

[1] These connected Athens with its harbour, the Piraeus.

fence. For the aggressors with matured plans to oppose to our indecision have cast threats aside and betaken themselves to action. And we know what are the paths by which Athenian aggression travels, and how insidious is its progress. A degree of confidence she may feel from the idea that your bluntness of perception prevents your noticing her; but it is nothing to the impulse which her advance will receive from the knowledge that you see, but do not care to interfere.

"You, Lacedaemonians, of all the Hellenes are alone inactive, and defend yourselves not by doing anything but by looking as if you would do something; you alone wait till the power of an enemy is becoming twice its original size, instead of crushing it in its infancy. And yet the world used to say that you were to be depended upon; but in your case, we fear, it said more than the truth. The Mede, we ourselves know, had time to come from the ends of the earth to the Peloponnesus, without any force of yours worthy of the name advancing to meet him. But this was a distant enemy. Well, Athens at all events is a near neighbour, and yet Athens you utterly disregard; against Athens you prefer to act on the defensive instead of on the offensive, and to make it an affair of chance by deferring the struggle till she has grown far stronger than at first. And yet you know that on the whole the rock on which the barbarian was wrecked was himself, and that if our present enemy Athens has not again and again annihilated us, we owe it more to her blunders than to your protection. Indeed, expectations from you have before now been the ruin of some whose faith induced them to omit preparation.

"We hope that none of you will consider these words of remonstrance to be rather words of hostility; men remonstrate with friends who are in error, accusations they reserve for enemies who have wronged them.

70. "Besides, we consider that we have as good a right as anyone to point out a neighbour's faults, particularly when we contemplate the great contrast between the two national characters, a contrast of which, as far as we can see, you have little perception, having never yet considered what sort

of antagonists you will encounter in the Athenians, how widely, how absolutely different from yourselves. The Athenians are addicted to innovation, and their designs are characterized by swiftness alike in conception and execution; you have a genius for keeping what you have got, accompanied by a total want of invention, and when forced to act you never go far enough. Again, they are adventurous beyond their power, and daring beyond their judgement, and in danger they are sanguine; your wont is to attempt less than is justified by your power, to mistrust even what is sanctioned by your judgement, and to fancy that from danger there is no release. Further, there is promptitude on their side against procrastination on yours; they are never at home, you are never from it: for they hope by their absence to extend their acquisitions, you fear by your advance to endanger what you have left behind. They are swift to follow up a success, and slow to recoil from a reverse. Their bodies they spend ungrudgingly in their country's cause; their intellect they jealously husband to be employed in her service. A scheme unexecuted is with them a positive loss, a successful enterprise a comparative failure. The deficiency created by the miscarriage of an undertaking is soon filled up by fresh hopes, for they alone are enabled to call a thing hoped for a thing got, by the speed with which they act upon their resolutions. Thus they toil on in trouble and danger all the days of their life, with little opportunity for enjoying, being ever engaged in getting: their only idea of a holiday is to do what the occasion demands, and to them laborious occupation is less of a misfortune than the peace of a quiet life. To describe their character in a word, one might truly say that they were born into the world to take no rest themselves and to give none to others.

71. "Such is Athens, your antagonist. And yet, Lacedaemonians, you still delay, and fail to see that peace stays longest with those who are not more careful to use their power justly than to show their determination not to submit to injustice. On the contrary, your ideal of fair dealing is based on the principle that if you do not injure others you need not risk

your own fortunes in preventing others from injuring you. Now you could scarcely have succeeded in such a policy even with a neighbour like yourselves; but in the present instance, as we have just shown, your habits are old-fashioned as compared with theirs. It is the law as in art, so in politics, that improvements ever prevail; and though fixed usages may be best for undisturbed communities, constant necessities of action must be accompanied by the constant improvement of methods. Thus it happens that the vast experience of Athens has carried her farther than you on the path of innovation.

"Here, at least, let your procrastination end. For the present, assist your allies and Potidaea in particular, as you promised, by a speedy invasion of Attica, and do not sacrifice friends and kindred to their bitterest enemies, and drive the rest of us in despair to some other alliance. Such a step would not be condemned either by the gods who received our oaths or by the men who witnessed them. The breach of a treaty cannot be laid to the people whom desertion compels to seek new relations, but to the power that fails to assist its confederate. But if you will only act, we will stand by you; it would be unnatural for us to change, and never should we meet with such a congenial ally. For these reasons choose the right course, and endeavour not to let the Peloponnesus under your supremacy degenerate from the prestige that it enjoyed under that of your ancestors."

72. Such were the words of the Corinthians. There happened to be Athenian envoys present at Lacedaemon on other business. On hearing the speeches they thought themselves called upon to come before the Lacedaemonians. Their intention was not to offer a defence on any of the charges which the cities brought against them, but to show on a comprehensive view that it was not a matter to be hastily decided on, but one that demanded further consideration. There was also a wish to call attention to the great power of Athens, and to refresh the memory of the old and enlighten the ignorance of the young, from a notion that their words might have the effect of inducing them to prefer tranquillity

to war. So they came to the Lacedaemonians and said that they too, if there was no objection, wished to speak to their assembly. They replied by inviting them to come forward. The Athenians advanced, and spoke as follows:

73. "The object of our mission here was not to argue with your allies, but to attend to the matters on which our state despatched us. However, the vehemence of the outcry that we hear against us has prevailed on us to come forward. It is not to combat the accusations of the cities (indeed you are not the judges before whom either we or they can plead), but to prevent your taking the wrong course on matters of great importance by yielding too readily to the persuasions of your allies. We also wish to show on a review of the whole indictment that we have a fair title to our possessions, and that our country has claims to consideration.

"We need not refer to remote antiquity: there we could appeal to the voice of tradition, but not to the experience of our audience. But to the Median War and contemporary history we must refer, although we are rather tired of continually bringing this subject forward. In our action during that war we ran great risk to obtain certain advantages: you had your share in the solid results, do not try to rob us of all share in the good that the glory may do us. However, the story shall be told not so much to deprecate hostility as to testify against it, and to show, if you are so ill-advised as to enter into a struggle with Athens, what sort of an antagonist she is likely to prove. We assert that at Marathon we were at the front, and faced the barbarian single-handed. That when he came the second time, unable to cope with him by land we went on board our ships with all our people, and joined in the naval action at Salamis. This prevented his taking the Peloponnesian states in detail and ravaging them with his fleet, when the multitude of his vessels would have made any combination for self-defence impossible. The best proof of this was furnished by the invader himself. Defeated at sea, he considered his power to be no longer what it had been, and retired as speedily as possible with the greater part of his army.

74. "Such, then, was the result of the matter, and it was clearly proved that it was on the fleet of Hellas that her cause depended. Well, to this result we contributed three very useful elements, viz., the largest number of ships, the ablest commander, and the most unhesitating zeal. Our contingent of ships was little less than two-thirds of the whole four hundred; the commander was Themistocles, through whom chiefly it was that the battle took place in the straits, the acknowledged salvation of our cause. Indeed, this was the reason of your receiving him with honours such as had never been accorded to any foreign visitor. While for daring zeal we had no competitors. Receiving no reinforcements by land, seeing everything in front of us already enslaved, we had the spirit, after abandoning our city, after sacrificing our property (instead of deserting the remainder of the league or depriving them of our services by dispersing), to throw ourselves into our ships and meet the danger, without a thought of resenting your neglect to assist us. We assert, therefore, that we conferred on you quite as much as we received. The cities which you had left were still filled with your homes, and you had the prospect of enjoying them again; and your coming was prompted quite as much by fear for yourselves as for us; at all events, you never appeared till we had nothing left to lose. But we left behind us a city that was a city no longer, and staked our lives for a city that had an existence only in desperate hope, and so bore our full share in your deliverance and in ours. But if we had copied others, and allowed fears for our territory to make us give in our adhesion to the Mede before you came, or if we had suffered our ruin to break our spirit and prevent us embarking in our ships, your naval inferiority would have made a sea fight unnecessary, and his objects would have been peaceably attained.

75. "Surely, Lacedaemonians, neither by the zeal that we displayed at that crisis, nor by the wisdom of our counsels, do we merit our extreme unpopularity with the Hellenes, not at least unpopularity for our empire. That empire we acquired by no violent means, but because you

were unwilling to prosecute to its conclusion the war against the barbarian, and therefore the allies attached themselves to us and spontaneously asked us to assume the command. And the nature of the case first compelled us to advance our empire to its present height; fear being our principal motive, though honour and interest afterwards came in. And at last, when almost all hated us, when some had already revolted and had been subdued, when you had ceased to be the friends that you once were, and had become objects of suspicion and dislike, it appeared no longer safe to give up our empire; especially as all who left us would fall to you. And no one can quarrel with a people for making, in matters of tremendous risk, the best provision that it can for its interest.

76. "You, at all events, Lacedaemonians, have used your supremacy to settle the states in the Peloponnesus as is agreeable to you. And if at the period of which we were speaking you had persevered to the end of the matter, and had incurred hatred in your hegemony, we are sure that you would have made yourselves just as galling to the allies, and would have been forced to choose between a strong government and danger to yourselves. It follows that it was not a very wonderful action, or contrary to the common practice of mankind, if we did accept an empire that was offered to us, and refused to give it up under the pressure of three of the strongest motives, fear, honour, and interest. And it was not we who set the example, for it has always been the law that the weaker should be subject to the stronger. Besides, we believed ourselves to be worthy of our position, and so you thought us till now, when calculations of interest have made you take up the cry of justice—a consideration which no one ever yet brought forward to hinder his ambition when he had a chance of gaining anything by might. And praise is due to all who, if not so superior to human nature as to refuse dominion, yet respect justice more than their position compels them to do. We imagine that our moderation would be best demonstrated by the conduct of others who should be placed in our position; but even our equity has very un-

reasonably subjected us to condemnation instead of approval.

77. "Our abatement of our rights in trials held under agreements with our allies, and our causing them to be decided by impartial laws at Athens, have gained us the character of being litigious. And none care to inquire why this reproach is not brought against other imperial powers, who treat their subjects with less moderation than we do; the secret being that where force can be used, courts of law are not needed. But our subjects are so habituated to associate with us as equals that any defeat whatever that clashes with their notions of justice, whether it proceeds from a legal judgement or from the power which our empire gives us, makes them forget to be grateful for being allowed to retain most of their possessions, and more vexed at a part being taken than if we had from the first cast law aside and openly gratified our covetousness. If we had done so, not even would they have disputed that the weaker must give way to the stronger. Men's indignation, it seems, is more excited by legal wrong than by violent wrong; the first looks like being cheated by an equal, the second like being compelled by a superior. At all events they contrived to put up with much worse treatment than this from the Mede, yet they think our rule severe, and this is to be expected, for the present always weighs heavy on the conquered. This at least is certain. If you were to succeed in overthrowing us and in taking our place, you would speedily lose the popularity with which fear of us has invested you, if your policy of today is at all to tally with the sample that you gave of it during the brief period of your command against the Mede. Not only is your life at home regulated by rules and institutions incompatible with those of others, but your citizens abroad act neither on these rules nor on those which are recognized by the rest of Hellas.

78. "Take time then in forming your resolution, as the matter is of great importance; and do not be persuaded by the opinions and complaints of others to bring trouble on yourselves, but consider the vast influence of accident in war,

before you are engaged in it. As it continues, it generally becomes an affair of chances, chances from which neither of us is exempt, and whose event we must risk in the dark. It is a common mistake in going to war to begin at the wrong end, to act first, and wait for disaster to discuss the matter. But we are not yet by any means so misguided, nor, so far as we can see, are you; accordingly, while it is still open to us both to choose aright, we bid you not to dissolve the treaty, or to break your oaths, but to have our differences settled by arbitration according to our agreement. Or else we take the gods who heard the oaths to witness, and if you begin hostilities, whatever line of action you choose, we will try not to be behindhand in repelling you."

79. Such were the words of the Athenians. After the Lacedaemonians had heard the complaints of the allies against the Athenians, and the observations of the latter, they made all withdraw, and consulted by themselves on the question before them. The opinions of the majority all led to the same conclusion; the Athenians were open aggressors, and war must be declared at once. But Archidamus, the Lacedaemonian king, came forward, who had the reputation of being at once a wise and a moderate man, and made the following speech:

80. "I have not lived so long, Lacedaemonians, without having had the experience of many wars, and I see those among you of the same age as myself who will not fall into the common misfortune of longing for war from inexperience or from a belief in its advantage and its safety. This, the war on which you are now debating, would be one of the greatest magnitude, on a sober consideration of the matter. In a struggle with Peloponnesians and neighbours our strength is of the same character, and it is possible to move swiftly on the different points. But a struggle with a people who live in a distant land, who have also an extraordinary familiarity with the sea, and who are in the highest state of preparation in every other department; with wealth private and public, with ships, and horses, and heavy infantry, and a population such as no one other Hellenic place can equal, and lastly

a great number of tributary allies—what can justify us in rashly beginning such a struggle? Wherein is our trust that we should rush on it unprepared? Is it in our ships? There we are inferior; while if we are to practise and become a match for them, time must intervene. Is it in our money? There we have a far greater deficiency. We neither have it in our treasury, nor are we ready to contribute it from our private funds.

81. "Confidence might possibly be felt in our superiority in heavy infantry and population, which will enable us to invade and devastate their lands. But the Athenians have plenty of other land in their empire, and can import what they want by sea. Again, if we are to attempt an insurrection of their allies, these will have to be supported with a fleet, most of them being islanders. What then is to be our war? For unless we can either beat them at sea or deprive them of the revenues which feed their navy, we shall meet with little but disaster. Meanwhile our honour will be pledged to keeping on, particularly if it be the opinion that we began the quarrel. For let us never be elated by the fatal hope of the war being quickly ended by the devastation of their lands. I fear rather that we may leave it as a legacy to our children, so improbable is it that the Athenian spirit will be the slave of their land, or Athenian experience be cowed by war.

82. "Not that I would bid you be so unfeeling as to suffer them to injure your allies and to refrain from unmasking their intrigues; but I do bid you not to take up arms at once, but to send and remonstrate with them in a tone not too suggestive of war, nor again too suggestive of submission, and to employ the interval in perfecting our own preparations. The means will be, first, the acquistion of allies, Hellenic or barbarian it matters not, so long as they are an accession to our strength, naval or pecuniary—I say Hellenic or barbarian because the odium of such an accession to all who, like us, are the objects of the designs of the Athenians is taken away by the law of self-preservation—and secondly the development of our home resources. If they listen to our

embassy, so much the better; but if not, after the lapse of two or three years our position will have become materially strengthened, and we can then attack them if we think proper. Perhaps by that time the sight of our preparations, backed by language equally significant, will have disposed them to submission, while their land is still untouched, and while their counsels may be directed to the retention of advantages as yet undestroyed. For the only light in which you can view their land is that of a hostage in your hands, a hostage the more valuable the better it is cultivated. This you ought to spare as long as possible, and not make them desperate, and so increase the difficulty of dealing with them. For if, while still unprepared, hurried away by the complaints of our allies, we are induced to lay it waste, have a care that we do not bring deep disgrace and deep perplexity upon the Peloponnesus. Complaints, whether of communities or individuals, it is possible to adjust; but war undertaken by a coalition for sectional interests, whose progress there is no means of foreseeing, does not easily admit of creditable settlement.

83. "And none need think it cowardice for a number of confederates to pause before they attack a single city. The Athenians have allies as numerous as our own, and allies that pay tribute, and war is a matter not so much of arms as of money, which makes arms of use. And this is more than ever true in a struggle between a continental and a maritime power. First, then, let us provide money, and not allow ourselves to be carried away by the talk of our allies before we have done so: as we shall have the largest share of responsibility for the consequences, be they good or bad, we have also a right to a tranquil inquiry respecting them.

84. "And the slowness and procrastination, the parts of our character that are most assailed by their criticism, need not make you blush. If we undertake the war without preparation, we should by hastening its commencement only delay its conclusion; further, a free and a famous city has through all time been ours. The quality which they condemn is really nothing but a wise moderation; thanks to its posses-

sion, we alone do not become insolent in success and give way less than others in misfortune; we are not carried away by the pleasure of hearing ourselves cheered on to risks which our judgement condemns; nor, if annoyed, are we any the more convinced by attempts to exasperate us by accusation. We are both warlike and wise, and it is our sense of order that makes us so. We are warlike, because self-control contains honour as a chief constituent, and honour bravery. And we are wise, because we are educated with too little learning to despise the laws, and with too severe a self-control to disobey them, and are brought up not to be too knowing in useless matters—such as the knowledge which can give a specious criticism of an enemy's plans in theory, but fails to assail them with equal success in practice—but are taught to consider that the schemes of our enemies are not dissimilar to our own, and that the freaks of chance are not determinable by calculation. In practice we always base our preparations against an enemy on the assumption that his plans are good; indeed, it is right to rest our hopes not on a belief in his blunders, but on the soundness of our provisions. Nor ought we to believe that there is much difference between man and man, but to think that the superiority lies with him who is reared in the severest school.

85. "These practices, then, which our ancestors have delivered to us, and by whose maintenance we have always profited, must not be given up. And we must not be hurried into deciding in a day's brief space a question which concerns many lives and fortunes and many cities, and in which honour is deeply involved, but we must decide calmly. This our strength peculiarly enables us to do. As for the Athenians, send to them on the matter of Potidaea, send on the matter of the alleged wrongs of the allies, particularly as they are prepared with legal satisfaction; and to proceed against one who offers arbitration as against a wrongdoer, law forbids. Meanwhile do not omit preparation for war. This decision will be the best for yourselves, the most terrible to your opponents."

Such were the words of Archidamus. Last came forward

Sthenelaidas, one of the ephors for that year, and spoke to the Lacedaemonians as follows:

86. "The long speech of the Athenians I do not pretend to understand. They said a good deal in praise of themselves, but nowhere denied that they are injuring our allies and the Peloponnesus. And yet if they behaved well against the Mede then, but ill towards us now, they deserve double punishment for having ceased to be good and for having become bad. We meanwhile are the same then and now, and shall not, if we are wise, disregard the wrongs of our allies, or put off till tomorrow the duty of assisting those who must suffer today. Others have much money and ships and horses, but we have good allies whom we must not give up to the Athenians, nor by lawsuits and words decide the matter, as it is anything but in word that we are harmed, but render instant and powerful help. And let us not be told that it is fitting for us to deliberate under injustice; long deliberation is rather fitting for those who have injustice in contemplation. Vote therefore, Lacedaemonians, for war, as the honour of Sparta demands, and neither allow the further aggrandizement of Athens, nor betray our allies to ruin, but with the gods let us advance against the aggressors."

87. With these words he, as ephor, himself put the question to the assembly of the Lacedaemonians. He said that he could not determine which was the loudest acclamation (their mode of decision is by acclamation, not by ballot), the fact being that he wished to make them declare their opinion openly and thus to increase their ardour for war. Accordingly he said, "All Lacedaemonians who are of opinion that the treaty has been broken, and that Athens is guilty, leave your seats and go there," pointing out a certain place; "all who are of the opposite opinion, there." They accordingly stood up and divided; and those who held that the treaty had been broken were in a decided majority. Summoning the allies, they told them that their opinion was that Athens had been guilty of injustice, but that they wished to convoke all the allies and put it to the vote, in order that they might make war, if they decided to do so, on a common resolu-

tion. Having thus gained their point, the delegates returned home at once, the Athenian envoys a little later, when they had despatched the objects of their mission. This decision of the assembly judging that the treaty had been broken was made in the fourteenth year of the thirty years' truce, which was entered into after the affair of Euboea.

88. The Lacedaemonians voted that the treaty had been broken and that war must be declared, not so much because they were persuaded by the arguments of the allies as because they feared the growth of the power of the Athenians, seeing most of Hellas already subject to them.

From BOOK II

The Funeral Oration of Pericles (*431* B.C.)

. . . . . .

34. In the same winter the Athenians gave a funeral at the public cost to those who had first fallen in this war. It was a custom of their ancestors, and the manner of it is as follows. Three days before the ceremony, the bones of the dead are laid out in a tent which has been erected; and their friends bring to their relatives such offerings as they please. In the funeral procession cypress coffins are borne in cars, one for each tribe, the bones of the deceased being placed in the coffin of their tribe. Among these is carried one empty bier decked for the missing, that is, for those whose bodies could not be recovered. Any citizen or stranger who pleases joins in the procession, and the female relatives are there to wail at the burial. The dead are laid in the public sepulchre in the beautiful suburb of the city, in which those who fall in war are always buried, with the exception of those slain at Marathon, who for their singular and extraordinary valour were interred on the spot where they fell. After the bodies

have been laid in the earth, a man chosen by the state, of approved wisdom and eminent reputation, pronounces over them an appropriate panegyric, after which all retire. Such is the manner of the burying; and throughout the whole of the war, whenever the occasion arose, the custom was observed. Meanwhile these were the first that had fallen, and Pericles, son of Xanthippus, was chosen to pronounce their eulogium. When the proper time arrived, he advanced from the sepulchre to an elevated platform in order to be heard by as many of the crowd as possible, and spoke as follows:

35. "Most of my predecessors in this place have commended him who made this speech part of the law, telling us that it is well that it should be delivered at the burial of those who fall in battle. For myself, I should have thought that the worth which had displayed itself in deeds would be sufficiently rewarded by honours also shown by deeds; such as you now see in this funeral prepared at the people's cost. And I could have wished that the reputations of many brave men were not to be imperilled in the mouth of a single individual, to stand or fall according as he spoke well or ill. For it is hard to speak properly upon a subject where it is even difficult to convince your hearers that you are speaking the truth. On the one hand, the friend who is familiar with every fact of the story may think that some point has not been set forth with that fullness which he wishes and knows it to deserve; on the other, he who is a stranger to the matter may be led by envy to suspect exaggeration if he hears anything above his own nature. For men can endure to hear others praised only so long as they can severally persuade themselves of their own ability to equal the actions recounted: when this point is passed, envy comes in and with it incredulity. However, since our ancestors have stamped this custom with their approval, it becomes my duty to obey the law and to try to satisfy your several wishes and opinions as best I may.

36. "I shall begin with our ancestors: it is both just and proper that they should have the honour of the first mention on an occasion like the present. They dwelt in the

country without break in the succession from generation to generation, and handed it down free to the present time by their valour. And if our more remote ancestors deserve praise, much more do our own fathers, who added to their inheritance the empire which we now possess, and spared no pains to be able to leave their acquisitions to us of the present generation. Lastly, there are few parts of our dominions that have not been augmented by those of us here, who are still more or less in the vigour of life, while the mother country has been furnished by us with everything that can enable her to depend on her own resources whether for war or for peace. That part of our history which tells of the military achievements which gave us our several possessions, or of the ready valour with which either we or our fathers stemmed the tide of Hellenic or foreign aggression, is a theme too familiar to my hearers for me to dilate on, and I shall therefore pass it by. But what was the road by which we reached our position, what the form of government under which our greatness grew, what the national habits out of which it sprang—these are questions which I may try to solve before I proceed to my panegyric upon these men, since I think this to be a subject upon which on the present occasion a speaker may properly dwell, and to which the whole assemblage, whether citizens or foreigners, may listen with advantage.

37. "Our constitution does not copy the laws of neighbouring states; we are rather a pattern to others than imitators ourselves. Its administration favours the many instead of the few; this is why it is called a democracy. If we look to the laws, they afford equal justice to all in their private differences; if to social standing, advancement in public life falls to reputation for capacity, class considerations not being allowed to interfere with merit; nor again does poverty bar the way—if a man is able to serve the state, he is not hindered by the obscurity of his condition. The freedom which we enjoy in our government extends also to our ordinary life. There, far from exercising a jealous surveillance over each other, we do not feel called upon to be angry with

our neighbour for doing what he likes, or even to indulge in those injurious looks which cannot fail to be offensive, although they inflict no positive penalty. But all this ease in our private relations does not make us lawless as citizens. Against this, fear is our chief safeguard, teaching us to obey the magistrates and the laws, particularly such as regard the protection of the injured, whether they are actually on the statute book or belong to that code which, although unwritten, yet cannot be broken without acknowledged disgrace.

38. "Further, we provide plenty of means for the mind to refresh itself from business. We celebrate games and sacrifices all the year round, and the elegance of our private establishments forms a daily source of pleasure and helps to banish the spleen; while the magnitude of our city draws the produce of the world into our harbour, so that to the Athenian the fruits of other countries are as familiar a luxury as those of his own.

39. "If we turn to our military policy, there also we differ from our antagonists. We throw open our city to the world, and never by alien acts exclude foreigners from any opportunity of learning or observing, although the eyes of an enemy may occasionally profit by our openness, trusting less in system and policy than to the native spirit of our citizens; while in education, where our rivals from their very cradles by a painful discipline seek after manliness, we live exactly as we please, and yet are just as ready to encounter every legitimate danger. In proof of this it may be noticed that the Lacedaemonians do not invade our country alone, but bring with them all their confederates; while we advance unsupported into the territory of a neighbour, and fighting upon a foreign soil, usually vanquish with ease men who are defending their homes. Our united force was never yet encountered by any enemy, because we have at once to attend to our marine and to despatch our citizens by land upon a hundred different services; so that, wherever they engage with some such fraction of our strength, a success against a detachment is magnified into a victory over the nation, and a

defeat into a reverse suffered at the hands of our entire people. And yet if with habits not of labour but of ease, and courage not of art but of nature, we are still willing to encounter danger, we have the double advantage of escaping the experience of hardships in anticipation and of facing them in the hour of need as fearlessly as those who are never free from them.

40. "Nor are these the only points in which our city is worthy of admiration. We cultivate refinement without stinting and knowledge without effeminacy; wealth we employ more for use than for show, and place the real disgrace of poverty not in owning to the fact but in declining the struggle against it. Our public men have, besides politics, their private affairs to attend to, and our ordinary citizens, though occupied with the pursuits of industry, are still fair judges of public matters; for, unlike any other nation, regarding him who takes no part in these duties not as unambitious but as useless, we are able to judge at all events if we cannot originate, and instead of looking on discussion as a stumbling block in the way of action, we think it an indispensable preliminary to any wise action at all. Again, in our enterprises we present the singular spectacle of daring and deliberation, each carried to its highest point, and both united in the same persons; whereas for others decision is the fruit of ignorance, hesitation of reflection. But the palm of courage will surely be adjudged most justly to those who best know the difference between hardship and pleasure and yet are never tempted to shrink from danger. In goodness we are equally singular, acquiring our friends by conferring not by receiving favours. Yet, of course, the doer of the favour is the firmer friend of the two, in order by continued kindness to keep the recipient in his debt; while the debtor feels less keenly from the very consciousness that the return he makes will be a payment, not a free gift. And it is only the Athenians who, fearless of consequences, confer their benefits not from calculations of expediency, but in the confidence of free men.

41. "In short, I say that as a city we are the school of Hellas; while I doubt if the world can produce a man who,

where he has only himself to depend upon, is equal to so many emergencies, and graced by so happy a versatility as the Athenian. And that this is no mere boast thrown out for the occasion, but plain matter of fact, the power of the state acquired by these habits proves. For Athens alone of her contemporaries is found when tested to be greater than her reputation, and alone gives no occasion to her assailants to blush at the antagonist by whom they have been worsted, or to her subjects to question her title by merit to rule. Rather, the admiration of the present and succeeding ages will be ours, since we have not left our power without witness, but have shown it by mighty proofs; and, far from needing a Homer for our panegyrist, or other of his craft whose verses might charm for the moment, only for the impression which they gave to melt at the touch of fact, we have forced every sea and land to be the highway of our daring, and everywhere, whether for evil or for good, have left imperishable monuments behind us. Such is the city for which these men, in the assertion of their resolve not to lose her, nobly fought and died; and well may every one of their survivors be ready to suffer in her cause.

42. "Indeed, if I have dwelt at some length upon the character of our country, it has been to show that our stake in the struggle is not the same as theirs who have no such blessings to lose, and also that the panegyric of the men over whom I am now speaking might be by definite proofs established. That panegyric is now in a great measure complete; for the city that I have celebrated is only what the heroism of these and their like have made her, men whose fame, unlike that of most Hellenes, will be found to be only commensurate with their deserts. And if a test of worth be wanted, it is to be found in their closing scene, and this not only in the cases in which it set the final seal upon their merit, but also in those in which it gave the first intimation of their having any. For there is justice in the claim that steadfastness in his country's battles should be as a cloak to cover a man's other imperfections; since the good action has blotted out the bad, and his merit as a citizen more than outweighed

his demerits as an individual. But none of these allowed either wealth with its prospect of future enjoyment to unnerve his spirit, or poverty with its hope of a day of freedom and riches to tempt him to shrink from danger. No, holding that vengeance upon their enemies was more to be desired than any personal blessings, and reckoning this to be the most glorious of hazards, they joyfully determined to accept the risk, to make sure of their vengeance and to let their wishes wait; and while committing to hope the uncertainty of final success, in the business before them they thought fit to act boldly and trust in themselves. Thus choosing to die resisting, rather than to live submitting, they fled only from dishonour, but met danger face to face, and after one brief moment, while at the summit of their fortune, escaped, not from their fear, but from their glory.

43. "So died these men as became Athenians. You, their survivors, must determine to have as unfaltering a resolution in the field, though you may pray that it may have a happier issue. And, not contented with ideas derived only from words of the advantages which are bound up with the defence of your country, though these would furnish a valuable text to a speaker even before an audience so alive to them as the present, you must yourselves realize the power of Athens, and feed your eyes upon her from day to day, till love of her fills your hearts; and then, when all her greatness shall break upon you, you must reflect that it was by courage, sense of duty, and a keen feeling of honour in action that men were enabled to win all this, and that no personal failure in an enterprise could make them consent to deprive their country of their valour, but they laid it at her feet as the most glorious contribution that they could offer. For this offering of their lives made in common by them all they each of them individually received that renown which never grows old, and for a sepulchre, not so much that in which their bones have been deposited, but that noblest of shrines wherein their glory is laid up to be eternally remembered upon every occasion on which deed or story shall call for its commemoration. For heroes have the whole earth for their tomb; and in

lands far from their own, where the column with its epitaph declares it, there is enshrined in every breast a record unwritten with no tablet to preserve it, except that of the heart. These take as your model, and, judging happiness to be the fruit of freedom and freedom of valour, never decline the dangers of war. For it is not the miserable that would most justly be unsparing of their lives; these have nothing to hope for; it is rather they to whom continued life may bring reverses as yet unknown, and to whom a fall, if it came, would be most tremendous in its consequences. And surely, to a man of spirit, the degradation of cowardice must be immeasurably more grievous than the unfelt death which strikes him in the midst of his strength and patriotism!

44. "Comfort, therefore, not condolence, is what I have to offer to the parents of the dead who may be here. Numberless are the chances to which, as they know, the life of man is subject; but fortunate indeed are they who draw for their lot a death so glorious as that which has caused your mourning, and to whom life has been so exactly measured as to terminate in the happiness in which it has been passed. Still I know that this is a hard saying, especially when those are in question of whom you will constantly be reminded by seeing in the homes of others blessings of which once you also boasted: for grief is felt not so much for the want of what we have never known, as for the loss of that to which we have been long accustomed. Yet you who are still of an age to beget children must bear up in the hope of having others in their stead; not only will they help you to forget those whom you have lost, but will be to the state at once a reinforcement and a security; for never can a fair or just policy be expected of the citizen who does not, like his fellows, bring to the decision the interests and apprehensions of a father. While those of you who have passed your prime must congratulate yourselves with the thought that the best part of your life was fortunate, and that the brief span that remains will be cheered by the fame of the departed. For it is only the love of honour that never grows old; and honour

it is, not gain, as some would have it, that rejoices the heart of age and helplessness.

45. "Turning to the sons or brothers of the dead, I see an arduous struggle before you. When a man is gone, all are wont to praise him, and should your merit be ever so transcendent, you will still find it difficult not merely to overtake but even to approach their renown. The living have envy to contend with, while those who are no longer in our path are honoured with a good will into which rivalry does not enter. On the other hand, if I must say anything on the subject of female excellence to those of you who will now be in widowhood, it will be all comprised in this brief exhortation. Great will be your glory in not falling short of your natural character; and greatest will be hers who is least talked of among the men whether for good or for bad.

46. "My task is now finished. I have performed it to the best of my ability, and in word, at least, the requirements of the law are now satisfied. If deeds be in question, those who are here interred have received part of their honours already, and, for the rest, their children will be brought up till manhood at the public expense: the state thus offers a valuable prize, as the garland of victory in this race of valour, for the reward both of those who have fallen and their survivors. And where the rewards for merit are greatest, there are found the best citizens.

"And now that you have brought to a close your lamentations for your relatives, you may depart."

The Plague in Athens

47. Such was the funeral that took place during this winter, with which the first year of the war came to an end. In the first days of summer the Lacedaemonians and their allies, with two-thirds of their forces as before, invaded Attica, under the command of Archidamus, son of Zeuxidamus, king of Lacedaemon, and sat down and laid waste the country. Not many days after their arrival in Attica the plague

first began to show itself among the Athenians. It was said that it had broken out in many places previously in the neighbourhood of Lemnos and elsewhere; but a pestilence of such extent and mortality was nowhere remembered. Neither were the physicians at first of any service, ignorant as they were of the proper way to treat it, but they died themselves the most thickly, as they visited the sick most often: nor did any other human art succeed any better. Supplications in the temples, divinations, and so forth were found equally futile, till the overwhelming nature of the disaster at last put a stop to them altogether.

48. It first began, it is said, in the parts of Ethiopia above Egypt, and thence descended into Egypt and Libya and into most of the king's country. Suddenly falling upon Athens, it first attacked the population in the Piraeus—which was the occasion of their saying that the Peloponnesians had poisoned the cisterns, there being as yet no fountains there— and afterwards appeared in the upper city, when the deaths became much more frequent. All speculation as to its origin and its causes, if causes can be found adequate to produce so great a disturbance, I leave to other writers, whether lay or professional; for myself, I shall simply set down its nature, and explain the symptoms by which perhaps it may be recognized by the student, if it should ever break out again. This I can the better do as I had the disease myself, and watched its operation in the case of others.

49. That year then is admitted to have been otherwise unprecedentedly free from sickness; and such few cases as occurred all ended in this. As a rule, however, there was no visible cause; but people in good health were all of a sudden attacked by violent heats in the head, and redness and inflammation in the eyes, the inward parts, such as the throat or tongue, becoming bloody and emitting an unnatural and fetid breath. These symptoms were followed by sneezing and hoarseness, after which the pain soon reached the chest, and produced a hard cough. When it settled in the heart, it upset it; and discharges of bile of every kind named by physicians ensued, accompanied by very great distress.

In most cases also an ineffectual retching followed, producing violent spasms, which in some cases ceased soon after, in others much later. Externally the body was not very hot to the touch, nor pale in its appearance, but reddish, livid, and breaking out into small pustules and ulcers. But internally it burned so that the patient could not bear to have on him clothing or linen even of the very lightest description; or indeed to be otherwise than stark naked. What they would have liked best would have been to throw themselves into cold water; as indeed was done by some of the neglected sick, who plunged into the rain-tanks in their agonies of unquenchable thirst; though it made no difference whether they drank little or much. Besides this, the miserable feeling of not being able to rest or sleep never ceased to torment them. The body meanwhile did not waste away so long as the distemper was at its height, but held out to a marvel against its ravages; so that when they succumbed, as in most cases, on the seventh or eighth day to the internal inflammation, they had still some strength in them. But if they passed this stage, and the disease descended farther into the bowels, inducing a violent ulceration there accompanied by severe diarrhoea, this brought on a weakness which was generally fatal. For the disorder first settled in the head, ran its course from thence through the whole of the body, and even where it did not prove mortal it still left its mark on the extremities; for it settled in the privy parts, the fingers, and the toes, and many escaped with the loss of these, some too with that of their eyes. Others again were seized with an entire loss of memory on their first recovery, and did not know either themselves or their friends.

50. But while the nature of the distemper was such as to baffle all description, and its attacks almost too grievous for human nature to endure, it was still in the following circumstance that its difference from all ordinary disorders was most clearly shown. All the birds and beasts that prey upon human bodies either abstained from touching them (though there were many lying unburied) or died after tasting them. In proof of this it was noticed that birds of this kind actually

disappeared; they were not about the bodies, or indeed to be seen at all. But of course the effects which I have mentioned could best be studied in a domestic animal like the dog.

51. Such then, if we pass over the varieties of particular cases, which were many and peculiar, were the general features of the distemper. Meanwhile the town enjoyed an immunity from all the ordinary disorders; or if any case occurred, it ended in this. Some died in neglect, others in the midst of every attention. No remedy was found that could be used as a specific; for what did good in one case did harm in another. Strong and weak constitutions proved equally incapable of resistance, all alike being swept away, although nursed with the utmost precaution. By far the most terrible feature in the malady was the dejection which ensued when anyone felt himself sickening, for the despair into which they instantly fell took away their power of resistance, and left them a much easier prey to the disorder; besides which there was the awful spectacle of men dying like sheep, through having caught the infection in nursing each other. This caused the greatest mortality. On the one hand, if they were afraid to visit each other, they perished from neglect; indeed many houses were emptied of their inmates for want of a nurse; on the other, if they ventured to do so, death was the consequence. This was especially the case with such as made any pretensions to virtue: honour made them unsparing of themselves in their attendance in their friends' houses, where even the members of the family were at last worn out by the moans of the dying, and succumbed to the force of the disaster. Yet it was with those who had recovered from the disease that the sick and the dying found most compassion. These knew what it was from experience, and had now no fear for themselves; for the same man was never attacked twice—never at least fatally. And such persons not only received the congratulations of others, but themselves also, in the elation of the moment, half entertained the vain hope that they were for the future safe from any disease whatsoever.

52. An aggravation of the existing calamity was the in-

flux from the country into the city, and this was especially felt by the new arrivals. As there were no houses to receive them, they had to be lodged at the hot season of the year in stifling cabins, where the mortality raged without restraint. The bodies of dying men lay one upon another, and half-dead creatures reeled about the streets and gathered round all the fountains in their longing for water. The sacred places also in which they had quartered themselves were full of corpses of persons that had died there, just as they were; for as the disaster passed all bounds, men, not knowing what was to become of them, became utterly careless of everything, whether sacred or profane. All the burial rites before in use were entirely upset, and they buried the bodies as best they could. Many, from want of the proper appliances, through so many of their friends having died already, had recourse to the most shameless sepultures: sometimes getting the start of those who had raised a pile, they threw their own dead body upon the stranger's pyre and ignited it; sometimes they tossed the corpse which they were carrying on the top of another that was burning, and so went off.

53. Nor was this the only form of lawless extravagance which owed its origin to the plague. Men now coolly ventured on what they had formerly done in a corner and not just where they pleased, seeing the rapid transitions produced by persons in prosperity suddenly dying and those who before had nothing succeeding to their property. So they resolved to spend quickly and enjoy themselves, regarding their lives and riches as alike things of a day. Perseverance in what men called honour was popular with none, it was so uncertain whether they would be spared to attain the object; but it was settled that present enjoyment, and all that contributed to it, was both honourable and useful. Fear of gods or law of man there was none to restrain them. As for the first, they judged it to be just the same whether they worshipped them or not, as they saw all alike perishing; and for the last, no one expected to live to be brought to trial for his offences, but each felt that a far severer sentence had been already passed upon them all and hung ever over their heads, and

before this fell it was only reasonable to enjoy life a little.

54. Such was the nature of the calamity, and heavily did it weigh on the Athenians, death raging within the city and devastation without. Among other things which they remembered in their distress was, very naturally, the following verse which the old men said had long ago been uttered:

A Dorian war shall come and with it death.

There had been a dispute as to whether dearth and not death had not been the word in the verse; but as the present juncture it was of course decided in favour of the latter; for the people made their recollection fit in with their sufferings. I fancy, however, that if another Dorian war should ever afterwards occur, and a dearth should happen to accompany it, the verse will probably be read accordingly. The oracle also which had been given to the Lacedaemonians was now remembered by those who knew of it. When the god was asked whether they should go to war, he answered that if they put their might into it, victory would be theirs, and that he would himself be with them. With this oracle events were supposed to tally. For the plague broke out so soon as the Peloponnesians invaded Attica, and, never entering the Peloponnesus (not at least to an extent worth noticing), committed its worst ravages at Athens, and, next to Athens, at the most populous of the other towns. Such was the history of the plague.

From BOOK III

The Mitylenian Debate

[Early in the summer of 428, the oligarchic government of Mitylene on the island of Lesbos, acting in concert with Sparta, broke away from the Athenians. Lesbos and Chios were the only members of the League who still contributed ships, under their own officers, and paid no tribute. Of the five cities on Lesbos, Mitylene was the largest, and she gained the support of three others, Antissa, Pyrrha, and Eresus, but not of Methymna. Athens promptly invested Mitylene, and in the spring of 427 the city capitulated.]

27. The Mitylenians, finding their provisions failing, while the fleet from the Peloponnesus was loitering on the way instead of appearing at Mitylene, were compelled to come to terms with the Athenians in the following manner. Salaethus [the Spartan representative], having himself ceased to expect the fleet to arrive, now armed the commons with heavy armour, which they had not before possessed, with the intention of making a sortie against the Athenians. The commons, however, no sooner found themselves possessed of arms than they refused any longer to obey their officers, and, forming in knots together, told the authorities to bring out in public the provisions and divide them amongst them all, or they would themselves come to terms with the Athenians and deliver up the city.

28. The government, aware of their inability to prevent this, and of the danger they would be in if left out of the capitulation, joined in agreeing with Paches [the Athenian commander] and the army to surrender Mitylene at discretion and to admit the troops into the town, upon the understanding that the Mitylenians should be allowed to send an embassy to Athens to plead their cause, and that Paches should not imprison, make slaves of, or put to death any of the citizens until its return. Such were the terms of the capitulation, in spite of which the chief authors of the negotiation with Lacedaemon were so completely overcome by terror when the army entered that they went and seated themselves by the altars, from which they were raised up by Paches under promise that he would do them no wrong, and lodged by him in Tenedos, until he should learn the pleasure of the Athenians concerning them. Paches also sent some triremes and seized Antissa, and took such other military measures as he thought advisable. . . .

[Paches went off in vain pursuit of the Peloponnesian fleet, and then returned to Lesbos.]

35. Arrived at Mitylene, Paches reduced Pyrrha and Eresus; and, finding the Lacedaemonian, Salaethus, in hiding in the town, sent him off to Athens, together with the Mitylenians that he had placed in Tenedos, and any other persons that he thought concerned in the revolt. He also sent back the greater part of his forces, remaining with the rest to settle Mitylene and the rest of Lesbos as he thought best.

36. Upon the arrival of the prisoners with Salaethus, the Athenians at once put the latter to death, although he offered, among other things, to procure the withdrawal of the Peloponnesians from Plataea, which was still under siege; and after deliberating as to what they should do with the former, in the fury of the moment determined to put to death not only the prisoners at Athens but the whole adult male population of Mitylene, and to make slaves of the women and children. It was remarked that Mitylene had revolted without being, like the rest, subjected to the empire; and what above all swelled the wrath of the Athenians was the fact of the Peloponnesian fleet having ventured over to Ionia to her support, a fact which was held to argue a long-meditated rebellion. They accordingly sent a trireme to communicate the decree to Paches, commanding him to lose no time in despatching the Mitylenians.

The morrow brought repentance with it and reflection on the horrid cruelty of a decree which condemned a whole city to the fate merited only by the guilty. This was no sooner perceived by the Mitylenian ambassadors at Athens and their Athenian supporters than they moved the authorities to put the question again to the vote; which they the more easily consented to do, as they themselves plainly saw that most of the citizens wished someone to give them an opportunity for reconsidering the matter. An assembly was therefore at once called, and after much expression of opinion upon both sides Cleon, son of Cleaenetus, the same who had carried the former motion of putting the Mitylenians to death, the most violent man at Athens, and at that time by far the most powerful with the commons, came forward again and spoke as follows:

37. "I have often before now been convinced that a democracy is incapable of empire, and never more so than by your present change of mind in the matter of Mitylene. Fears or plots being unknown to you in your daily relations with each other, you feel just the same with regard to your allies, and never reflect that the mistakes into which you may be led by listening to their appeals, or by giving way to your own compassion, are full of danger to yourselves, and bring you no thanks for your weakness from your allies; entirely forgetting that your empire is a tyranny and your subjects disaffected conspirators, whose obedience is insured not by your suicidal concessions but by the superiority given you by your own strength and not their loyalty. The most alarming feature in the case is the constant change of measures with which we appear to be threatened, and our seeming ignorance of the fact that bad laws which are never changed are better for a city than good ones that have no authority; that unlearned loyalty is more serviceable than quick-witted insubordination; and that ordinary men usually manage public affairs better than their more gifted fellows. The latter are always wanting to appear wiser than the laws, and to overrule every proposition brought forward, thinking that they cannot show their wit in more important matters, and by such behaviour too often ruin their country; while those who mistrust their own cleverness are content to be less learned than the laws, and less able to pick holes in the speech of a good speaker; and being fair judges rather than rival athletes, generally conduct affairs successfully. These we ought to imitate, instead of being led on by cleverness and intellectual rivalry to advise your people against our real opinions.

38. "For myself, I adhere to my former opinion, and wonder at those who have proposed to reopen the case of the Mitylenians, and who are thus causing a delay which is all in favour of the guilty by making the sufferer proceed against the offender with the edge of his anger blunted; al-

though where vengeance follows most closely upon the wrong, it best equals it and most amply requites it. I wonder also who will be the man who will maintain the contrary, and will pretend to show that the crimes of the Mitylenians are of service to us, and our misfortunes injurious to the allies. Such a man must plainly either have such confidence in his rhetoric as to adventure to prove that what has been once for all decided is still undetermined, or be bribed to try to delude us by elaborate sophisms. In such contests the state gives the rewards to others and takes the dangers for herself. The persons to blame are you who are so foolish as to institute these contests; who go to see an oration as you would to see a sight, take your facts on hearsay, judge of the practicability of a project by the wit of its advocates, and trust for the truth as to past events not to the fact which you saw more than to the clever strictures which you heard; the easy victims of new-fangled arguments, unwilling to follow received conclusions; slaves to every new paradox, despisers of the commonplace; the first wish of every man being that he could speak himself, the next to rival those who can speak by seeming to be quite up with their ideas by applauding every hit almost before it is made, and by being as quick in catching an argument as you are slow in foreseeing its consequences; asking, if I may so say, for something different from the conditions under which we live, and yet comprehending inadequately those very conditions; very slaves to the pleasure of the ear, and more like the audience of a rhetorician than the council of a city.

39. "In order to keep you from this, I proceed to show that no one state has ever injured you as much as Mitylene. I can make allowance for those who revolt because they cannot bear our empire, or who have been forced to do so by the enemy. But for those who possessed an island with fortifications; who could fear our enemies only by sea, and there had their own force of triremes to protect them; who were autonomous and held in the highest honour by you—to act as these have done, this is not revolt—revolt implies oppression; it is deliberate and wanton aggression, an attempt to

ruin us by siding with our bitterest enemies, a worse offence than a war undertaken on their own account in the acquisition of power. The fate of those of their neighbours who had already rebelled and had been subdued was no lesson to them; their own prosperity could not dissuade them from affronting danger; but blindly confident in the future, and full of hopes beyond their power though not beyond their ambition, they declared war and made their decision to prefer might to right, their attack being determined not by provocation but by the moment which seemed propitious. The truth is that great good fortune coming suddenly and unexpectedly tends to make a people insolent: in most cases it is safer for mankind to have success in reason than out of reason; and it is easier for them, one may say, to stave off adversity than to preserve prosperity.

"Our mistake has been to distinguish the Mitylenians as we have done; had they been long ago treated like the rest, they never would have so far forgotten themselves, human nature being as surely made arrogant by consideration as it is awed by firmness. Let them now therefore be punished as their crime requires, and do not, while you condemn the aristocracy, absolve the people. This is certain, that all attacked you without distinction, although they might have come over to us and been now again in possession of their city. But no, they thought it safer to throw in their lot with the aristocracy and so joined their rebellion! Consider therefore! If you subject to the same punishment the ally who is forced to rebel by the enemy, and him who does so by his own free choice, which of them, think you, is there that will not rebel upon the slightest pretext, when the reward of success is freedom, and the penalty of failure nothing so very terrible? We meanwhile shall have to risk our money and our lives against one state after another; and, if successful, shall receive a ruined town from which we can no longer draw the revenue upon which our strength depends; while, if unsuccessful, we shall have an enemy the more upon our hands, and shall spend the time that might be employed in combating our existing foes in warring with our own allies.

40. "No hope, therefore, that rhetoric may instil or money purchase, of the mercy due to human infirmity must be held out to the Mitylenians. Their offence was not involuntary, but of malice and deliberate; and mercy is only for unwilling offenders. I therefore now as before persist against your reversing your first decision, or giving way to the three failings most fatal to empire—pity, sentiment, and indulgence. Compassion is due to those who can reciprocate the feeling, not to those who will never pity us in return, but are our natural and necessary foes: the orators who charm us with sentiment may find other less important arenas for their talents, in the place of one where the city pays a heavy penalty for a momentary pleasure, themselves receiving fine acknowledgments for their fine phrases; while indulgence should be shown towards those who will be our friends in future, instead of towards men who will remain just what they were, and as much our enemies as before.

"To sum up shortly, I say that if you follow my advice you will do what is just towards the Mitylenians, and at the same time expedient; while by a different decision you will not oblige them so much as pass sentence upon yourselves. For if they were right in rebelling, you must be wrong in ruling. However, if, right or wrong, you determine to rule, you must carry out your principle and punish the Mitylenians as your interest requires, or else you must give up your empire and cultivate honesty without danger. Make up your minds, therefore, to give them like for like; and do not let the victims who escaped the plot be more insensible than the conspirators who hatched it; but reflect what they would have done if victorious over you, especially as they were the aggressors. It is they who wrong their neighbour without a cause, that pursue their victim to the death, on account of the danger which they foresee in letting their enemy survive; since the object of a wanton wrong is more dangerous, if he escape, than an enemy who has not this to complain of.

"Do not, therefore, be traitors to yourselves, but recall as nearly as possible the moment of suffering and the supreme importance which you then attached to their reduction; and now pay them back in their turn, without yielding to present weakness or forgetting the peril that once hung over you. Punish them as they deserve, and teach your other allies by a striking example that the penalty of rebellion is death. Let them once understand this and you will not have so often to neglect your enemies while you are fighting with your own confederates."

41. Such were the words of Cleon. After him Diodotus, son of Eucrates, who had also in the previous assembly spoken most strongly against putting the Mitylenians to death, came forward and spoke as follows:

42. "I do not blame the persons who have reopened the case of the Mitylenians, nor do I approve the protests which we have heard against important questions being frequently debated. I think the two things most opposed to good counsel are haste and passion; haste usually goes hand in hand with folly, passion with coarseness and narrowness of mind. As for the argument that speech ought not to be the exponent of action, the man who uses it must be either senseless or interested: senseless if he believes it possible to treat of the uncertain future through any other medium; interested if, wishing to carry a disgraceful measure and doubting his ability to speak well in a bad cause, he thinks to frighten opponents and hearers by well-aimed calumny. What is still more intolerable is to accuse a speaker of making a display in order to be paid for it. If ignorance only were imputed, an unsuccessful speaker might retire with a reputation for honesty, if not for wisdom; while the charge of dishonesty makes him suspected, if successful, and thought, if defeated, not only a fool but a rogue. The city is no gainer by such a system, since fear deprives it of its advisers; although in truth, if our speakers are to make such assertions, it would be better for the country if they could not speak at all, as we should then make fewer blunders. The good citizen ought to triumph not by frightening his opponents but by beating them fairly in argument; and a wise city, without over-distinguishing its best advisers, will nevertheless not

deprive them of their due, and far from punishing an un-
lucky counsellor will not even regard him as disgraced. In
this way successful orators would be least tempted to sacrifice their convictions to popularity, in the hope of still
higher honours, and unsuccessful speakers to resort to the
same popular arts in order to win over the multitude.

43. "This is not our way; and, besides, the moment that
a man is suspected of giving advice, however good, from
corrupt motives, we feel such a grudge against him for the
gain which after all we are not certain he will receive, that
we deprive the city of its certain benefit. Plain good advice
has thus come to be no less suspected than bad; and the advocate of the most monstrous measures is not more obliged
to use deceit to gain the people than the best counsellor is
to lie in order to be believed. We are the only city which,
owing to these refinements, can never be served openly and
without disguise, he who does serve it openly being always
suspected of serving himself in some secret way in return.
Still, considering the magnitude of the interests involved,
and the position of affairs, we orators must make it our business to look a little farther than you who judge offhand; especially as we, your advisers, are accountable, while you, our
audience, are not so. For if those who gave the advice, and
those who took it, suffered equally, you would judge more
calmly; as it is, you visit the disasters into which the whim
of the moment may have led you upon the single person of
your adviser, not upon yourselves, his numerous companions
in error.

44. "However, I have not come forward either to oppose
or to accuse in the matter of Mitylene; indeed, the question
before us as sensible men is not their guilt, but our interests.
Though I prove them ever so guilty, I shall not, therefore,
advise their death, unless it be expedient; nor, though they
should have claims to indulgence, shall I recommend it, unless it be clearly for the good of the country. I consider that
we are deliberating for the future more than for the present;
and where Cleon is so positive as to the useful deterrent
effects that will follow from making rebellion capital, I who

consider the interests of the future quite as much as he, as positively maintain the contrary. And I require you not to reject my useful considerations for his specious ones: his speech may have the attraction of seeming the more just in your present temper against Mitylene; but we are not in a court of justice, but in a political assembly; and the question is not justice, but how to make the Mitylenians useful to Athens.

45. "Now of course communities have enacted the penalty of death for many offences far lighter than this; still hope leads men to venture, and no one ever yet put himself in peril without the inward conviction that he would succeed in his design. Again, was there ever city rebelling that did not believe that it possessed either in itself or in its alliances resources adequate to the enterprise? All, states and individuals, are alike prone to err, and there is no law that will prevent them; or why should men have exhausted the list of punishments in search of enactments to protect them from evildoers? It is probable that in early times the penalties for the greatest offences were less severe, and that, as these were disregarded, the penalty of death has been by degrees in most cases arrived at, which is itself disregarded in like manner. Either then some means of terror more terrible than this must be discovered, or it must be owned that this restraint is useless, and that as long as poverty gives men the courage of necessity, or plenty fills them with the ambition which belongs to insolence and pride, and the other conditions of life remain each under the thraldom of some fatal and master passion, so long will the impulse never be wanting to drive men into danger. Hope also and cupidity, the one leading and the other following, the one conceiving the attempt, the other suggesting the facility of succeeding, cause the widest ruin, and, although invisible agents, are far stronger than the dangers that are seen. Fortune, too, powerfully helps the delusion, and, by the unexpected aid that she sometimes lends, tempts men to venture with inferior means; and this is especially the case with communities, because the stakes played for are the highest, freedom or empire, and,

when all are acting together, each man irrationally magnifies his own capacity. In fine, it is impossible to prevent, and only great simplicity can hope to prevent, human nature doing what it has once set its mind upon, by force of law or by any other deterrent force whatsoever.

46. "We must not, therefore, commit ourselves to a false policy through a belief in the efficacy of the punishment of death, or exclude rebels from the hope of repentance and an early atonement of their error. Consider a moment! At present, if a city that has already revolted perceive that it cannot succeed, it will come to terms while it is still able to refund expenses, and pay tribute afterwards. In the other case, what city think you would not prepare better than is now done, and hold out to the last against its besiegers, if it is all one whether it surrender late or soon? And how can it be otherwise than hurtful to us to be put to the expense of a siege, because surrender is out of the question; and if we take the city, to receive a ruined town from which we can no longer draw the revenue which forms our real strength against the enemy? We must not, therefore, sit as strict judges of the offenders to our own prejudice, but rather see how by moderate chastisements we may be enabled to benefit in future by the revenue-producing powers of our dependencies; and we must make up our minds to look for our protection not to legal terrors but to careful administration. At present we do exactly the opposite. When a free community, held in subjection by force, rises, as is only natural, and asserts its independence, it is no sooner reduced than we fancy ourselves obliged to punish it severely; although the right course with freemen is not to chastise them rigorously when they do rise, but rigorously to watch them before they rise, and to prevent their ever entertaining the idea, and, the insurrection suppressed, to make as few responsible for it as possible.

47. "Only consider what a blunder you would commit in doing as Cleon recommends. As things are at present, in all the cities the people is your friend, and either does not revolt with the oligarchy, or, if forced to do so, becomes

at once the enemy of the insurgents; so that in the war with the hostile city you have the masses on your side. But if you butcher the people of Mitylene, who had nothing to do with the revolt, and who, as soon as they got arms, of their own motion surrendered the town, first you will commit the crime of killing your benefactors, and next you will play directly into the hands of the higher classes, who when they induce their cities to rise will immediately have the people on their side, through your having announced in advance the same punishment for those who are guilty and for those who are not. On the contrary, even if they were guilty, you ought to seem not to notice it, in order to avoid alienating the only class still friendly to us. In short, I consider it far more useful for the preservation of our empire voluntarily to put up with injustice than to put to death, however justly, those whom it is our interest to keep alive. As for Cleon's idea that in punishment the claims of justice and expediency can both be satisfied, facts do not confirm the possibility of such a combination.

48. "Confess, therefore, that this is the wisest course, and without conceding too much either to pity or to indulgence, by neither of which motives do I any more than Cleon wish you to be influenced, upon the plain merits of the case before you, be persuaded by me to try calmly those of the Mitylenians whom Paches sent off as guilty, and to leave the rest undisturbed. This is at once best for the future, and most terrible to your enemies at the present moment; inasmuch as good policy against an adversary is superior to the blind attacks of brute force."

49. Such were the words of Diodotus. The two opinions thus expressed were the ones that most directly contradicted each other; and the Athenians, notwithstanding their change of feeling, now proceeded to a division, in which the show of hands was almost equal, although the motion of Diodotus carried the day. Another trireme was at once sent off in haste, for fear that the first might reach Lesbos in the interval and the city be found destroyed, the first ship having about a day and a night's start. Wine and barley-cakes were

provided for the vessel by the Mitylenian ambassadors, and great promises made if they arrived in time; which caused the men to use such diligence upon the voyage that they took their meals of barley-cakes kneaded with oil and wine as they rowed, and only slept by turns while the others were at the oar. Luckily they met with no contrary wind, and the first ship making no haste upon so horrid an errand, while the second pressed on in the manner described, the first arrived so little before them that Paches had only just had time to read the decree, and to prepare to execute the sentence, when the second put into port and prevented the massacre. The danger of Mitylene had indeed been great.

50. The other party whom Paches had sent off as the prime movers in the rebellion were upon Cleon's motion put to death by the Athenians, the number being rather more than a thousand. The Athenians also demolished the walls of the Mitylenians, and took possession of their ships. . . .

Sedition in Corcyra (427 B.C.)

70. The Corcyraean revolution began with the return of the prisoners taken in the sea fights off Epidamnus. These the Corinthians had released allegedly upon the security of eight hundred talents given by their *proxeni,* but in reality upon their engagement to bring over Corcyra to Corinth. These men proceeded to canvass each of the citizens, and to intrigue with the view of detaching the city from Athens. Upon the arrival of an Athenian and a Corinthian vessel, with envoys on board, discussions were held and the Corcyraeans voted to remain allies of the Athenians according to their agreement, but to be friends of the Peloponnesians as they had been formerly. Meanwhile, the returned prisoners brought Peithias, a volunteer *proxenus* of the Athenians and leader of the commons, to trial, upon the charge of enslaving Corcyra to Athens. He, being acquitted, retorted by accusing five of the richest of their number of cutting stakes in the ground sacred to Zeus and Alcinous, the

legal penalty being a stater for each stake. Upon their conviction, the amount of the penalty being very large, they seated themselves as suppliants in the temples, to be allowed to pay it by instalments; but Peithias, who was one of the senate, prevailed upon that body to enforce the law, upon which the accused, rendered desperate by the law, and also learning that Peithias had the intention, while still a member of the senate, to persuade the people to conclude a defensive and offensive alliance with Athens, banded together armed with daggers, and suddenly bursting into the senate killed Peithas and sixty others, senators and private persons, some few only of the party of Peithias taking refuge in the Athenian trireme, which had not yet departed.

71. After this outrage, the conspirators summoned the Corcyraeans to an assembly, and said that this would turn out for the best, and would save them from being enslaved by Athens; for the future, they moved to receive neither party unless they came peacefully in a single ship, treating any larger number as enemies. This motion made, they compelled it to be adopted, and instantly sent off envoys to Athens to justify what had been done and to dissuade the refugees there from any hostile proceedings which might lead to a reaction.

72. Upon the arrival of the embassy the Athenians arrested the envoys, and all who listened to them, as revolutionists, and lodged them in Aegina. Meanwhile, a Corinthian trireme arriving in the island with Lacedaemonian envoys, the controlling Corcyraean party attacked the commons and defeated them in battle. Night coming on, the commons took refuge in the Acropolis and the higher parts of the city, and concentrated themselves there, having also possession of the Hyllaic harbour, their adversaries occupying the Agora, where most of them lived, and the harbour adjoining, looking towards the mainland.

73. The next day passed in skirmishes of little importance, each party sending into the country to offer freedom to the slaves and to invite them to join them. The mass of

the slaves answered the appeal of the commons; their antagonists being reinforced by eight hundred mercenaries from
the continent.

74. After a day's interval hostilities recommenced, victory remaining with the commons, who had the advantage
in numbers and position, the women also valiantly assisting
them, pelting with tiles from the houses, and supporting the
mêlée with a fortitude beyond their sex. Towards dusk the
oligarchs in full rout, fearing that the victorious commons
might assault and carry the arsenal and put them to the
sword, fired the houses round the Agora and the lodging-
houses, in order to bar their advance; sparing neither their
own nor those of their neighbours; by which much stuff of
the merchants was consumed and the city risked total
destruction if a wind had come to help the flame by blowing
on it. Hostilities now ceasing, both sides kept quiet, passing
the night on guard, while the Corinthian ship stole out to sea
upon the victory of the commons, and most of the mercenaries passed over secretly to the continent.

75. The next day the Athenian general, Nicostratus, son
of Diitrephes, came up from Naupactus with twelve ships
and five hundred Messenian heavy infantry. He at once endeavoured to bring about a settlement and persuaded the
two parties to agree together to bring to trial ten of the ring-
leaders, who presently fled, while the rest were to live in
peace, making terms with each other and entering into a
defensive and offensive alliance with the Athenians. This
arranged, he was about to sail away, when the leaders of the
commons induced him to leave them five of his ships to
make their adversaries less disposed to move, while they
manned and sent with him an equal number of their own.
He had no sooner consented than they began to enroll their
enemies for the ships; and these, fearing that they might be
sent off to Athens, seated themselves as suppliants in the
temple of the Dioscuri. An attempt on the part of Nicostratus
to reassure them and to persuade them to rise proving unsuccessful, the commons armed upon this pretext, alleging
the refusal of their adversaries to sail with them as a proof

of the hollowness of their intentions, and took their arms out of their houses, and would have dispatched some whom they fell in with, if Nicostratus had not prevented it. The rest of the party, seeing what was going on, seated themselves as suppliants in the temple of Hera, being not less than four hundred in number; until the commons, fearing that they might adopt some desperate resolution, induced them to rise, and conveyed them over to the island in front of the temple, where provisions were sent across to them.

76. At this stage in the revolution, on the fourth or fifth day after the removal of the men to the island, the Peloponnesian ships arrived from Cyllene, where they had been stationed since their return from Ionia, fifty-three in number, still under the command of Alcidas, but with Brasidas also on board as his adviser; and, dropping anchor at Sybota, a harbour on the mainland, at daybreak made sail for Corcyra.

77. The Corcyraeans in great confusion and alarm at the state of things in the city and at the approach of the invader at once proceeded to equip sixty vessels, which they sent out, as fast as they were manned, against the enemy, in spite of the Athenians recommending them to let them sail out first, and to follow themselves afterwards with all their ships together. Upon their vessels coming up to the enemy in this straggling fashion, two immediately deserted: in others the crews were fighting among themselves, and there was no order in anything that was done; so that the Peloponnesians, seeing their confusion, placed twenty ships to oppose the Corcyraeans, and ranged the rest against the twelve Athenian ships, amongst which were the two vessels *Salaminia* and *Paralus*.

78. While the Corcyraeans, attacking without judgement and in small detachments, were already crippled by their own misconduct, the Athenians, afraid of the numbers of the enemy and of being surrounded, did not venture to attack the main body or even the centre of the division opposed to them, but fell upon its wing and sank one vessel; after which the Peloponnesians formed in a circle and the Athenians rowed round them and tried to throw them into

disorder. Perceiving this, the division opposed to the Corcyraeans, fearing a repetition of the disaster of Naupactus,
came to support their friends, and the whole fleet now
bore down, united, upon the Athenians, who retired before
it, backing water, retiring as leisurely as possible in order to
give the Corcyraeans time to escape, while the enemy was
thus kept occupied. Such was the character of this sea fight,
which lasted until sunset.

79. The Corcyraeans now feared that the enemy would
follow up their victory and sail against the town and rescue
the men in the island, or strike some other blow equally decisive, and accordingly carried the men over again to the
temple of Hera, and kept guard over the city. The Peloponnesians, however, although victorious in the sea fight, did
not venture to attack the town, but took the thirteen Corcyraean vessels which they had captured, and with them
sailed back to the continent from whence they had put out.
The next day equally they refrained from attacking the city,
although the disorder and panic were at their height, and
though Brasidas, it is said, urged Alcidas, his superior officer,
to do so, but they landed upon the promontory of Leukimme
and laid waste the country.

80. Meanwhile the commons in Corcyra, being still in
great fear of the fleet attacking them, came to a parley with
the suppliants and their friends, in order to save the town,
and prevailed upon some of them to go on board the ships,
of which they still manned thirty, against the expected attack. But the Peloponnesians after ravaging the country
until midday sailed away, and towards nightfall were informed by beacon signals of the approach of sixty Athenian
vessels from Leucas, under the command of Eurymedon, son
of Thucles; which had been sent off by the Athenians upon
the news of the revolution and of the fleet with Alcidas being
about to sail for Corcyra.

81. The Peloponnesians accordingly at once set off in
haste by night for home, coasting along shore; and, hauling
their ships across the Isthmus of Leucas, in order not to be
seen doubling it, so departed. The Corcyraeans, made aware

of the approach of the Athenian fleet and of the departure of
the enemy, brought the Messenians from outside the walls
into the town, and ordered the fleet which they had manned
to sail round into the Hyllaic harbour, and while it was so doing slew such of their enemies as they laid hands on, dis-
patching afterwards as they landed them those whom they
had persuaded to go on board the ships. Next they went to
the sanctuary of Hera and persuaded about fifty men to take
their trial, and condemned them all to death. The mass of
the suppliants who had refused to do so, on seeing what was
taking place, slew each other there in the consecrated
ground, while some hanged themselves upon the trees, and
others destroyed themselves as they were severally able.
During seven days that Eurymedon stayed with his sixty
ships, the Corcyraeans were engaged in butchering those of
their fellow citizens whom they regarded as their enemies;
and although the crime imputed was that of attempting to
put down the democracy, some were slain also for private
hatred, others by their debtors because of the monies owed
to them. Death thus raged in every shape; and, as usually
happens at such times, there was no length to which violence
did not go; sons were killed by their fathers, and suppliants
dragged from the altar or slain upon it; while some were even
walled up in the temple of Dionysus and died there.

82. So bloody was the march of the revolution, and the
impression which it made was the greater as it was the first
to occur. Later on, one may say, the whole Hellenic world
was convulsed, struggles being everywhere made by the popular chiefs to bring in the Athenians, and by the oligarchs to
introduce the Lacedaemonians. In peace there would have
been neither the pretext nor the wish to make such an invitation; but in war, with an alliance always at the command of
either faction for the hurt of their adversaries and their own
corresponding advantage, opportunities for bringing in the
foreigner were never wanting to the revolutionary parties.
The sufferings which revolution entailed upon the cities
were many and terrible, such as have occurred and always
occur, as long as the nature of mankind remains the

same; though in a severer or milder form, and varying in their symptoms, according to the variety of the particular cases. In peace and prosperity states and individuals have better sentiments, because they do not find themselves suddenly confronted with imperious necessities; but war takes away the easy supply of daily wants, and so proves a rough master, that brings most men's characters to a level with their fortunes.

Revolution thus ran its course from city to city, and the places which it arrived at last, from having heard what had been done before, carried to a still greater excess the refinement of their inventions, as manifested in the cunning of their enterprises and the atrocity of their reprisals. Words had to change their ordinary meaning and to take that which was now given them. Reckless audacity came to be considered the courage of a loyal ally; prudent hesitation, specious cowardice; moderation was held to be a cloak for unmanliness; ability to see all sides of a question inaptness to act on any. Frantic violence became the attribute of manliness, cautious plotting, a justifiable means of self-defence. The advocate of extreme measures was always trustworthy, his opponent a man to be suspected. To succeed in a plot was to have a shrewd head, to divine a plot a still shrewder; but to try to provide against having to do either was to break up your party and to be afraid of your adversaries. In fine, to forestall an intending criminal, or to suggest the idea of a crime where it was wanting, was equally commended, until even blood became a weaker tie than party, from the superior readiness of those united by the latter to dare everything without reserve; for such associations had not in view the blessings derivable from established institutions but were formed by ambition for their overthrow; and the confidence of their members in each other rested less on any religious sanction than upon complicity in crime. The fair proposals of an adversary were met with jealous precautions by the stronger of the two, and not with a generous confidence. Revenge also was held of more account than self-preservation. Oaths of reconciliation, being proffered on either side only to meet an immediate difficulty, held good only so long as no other weapon was at hand; but when opportunity offered, he who first ventured to seize it and to take his enemy off his guard, thought this perfidious vengeance sweeter than an open one, since, considerations of safety apart, success by treachery won him the palm of superior intelligence. Indeed it is generally the case that men are readier to call rogues clever than simpletons honest, and are as ashamed of being the second as they are proud of being the first.

The cause of all these evils was the lust for power arising from greed and ambition; and from these passions proceeded the violence of parties once engaged in contention. The leaders in the cities, each provided with the fairest professions, on the one side with the cry of political equality of the people, on the other of a moderate aristocracy, sought prizes for themselves in those public interests which they pretended to cherish, and, recoiling from no means in their struggles for ascendancy, engaged in the direst excesses; in their acts of vengeance they went to even greater lengths, not stopping at what justice or the good of the state demanded, but making the party caprice of the moment their only standard, and invoking with equal readiness the condemnation of an unjust verdict or the authority of the strong arm to glut the animosities of the hour. Thus morality was in honour with neither party; but the use of fair phrases to arrive at guilty ends was in high reputation. Meanwhile the moderate part of the citizens perished between the two, either for not joining in the quarrel or because envy would not suffer them to escape.

83. Thus every form of iniquity took root in the Hellenic countries by reason of the troubles. The ancient simplicity into which honour so largely entered was laughed down and disappeared; and society became divided into camps in which no man trusted his fellow. To put an end to this, there was neither promise to be depended upon nor oath that could command respect; but all parties, dwelling rather in their calculation upon the hopelessness of a permanent state of things, were more intent upon self-defence than capable

of confidence. In this contest the blunter wits were most successful. Apprehensive of their own deficiencies and of the cleverness of their antagonists, they feared to be worsted in debate and to be surprised by the combinations of their more versatile opponents, and so at once boldly had recourse to action; while their adversaries, arrogantly thinking that they should know in time, and that it was unnecessary to secure by action what policy afforded, often fell victims to their want of precaution.

From BOOK VI

The War in Sicily

1. The same winter [416-415 B.C.] the Athenians resolved to sail again to Sicily, with a greater armament than that under Laches and Eurymedon, and, if possible, to conquer the island; most of them being ignorant of its size and of the number of its inhabitants, Hellenic and barbarian, and of the fact that they were undertaking a war not much inferior to that against the Peloponnesians. For the voyage round Sicily in a merchantman is not far short of eight days; and yet, large as the island is, there are only two miles of sea to prevent its being mainland.

2. It was settled originally as follows, and the peoples that occupied it are these. The earliest inhabitants spoken of in any part of the country are the Cyclopes and Laestrygones; but I cannot tell of what race they were, or whence they came or whither they went, and must leave my readers to what the poets have said of them and to what may be generally known concerning them. The Sicanians appear to have been the next settlers, although they pretend to have been the first of all and aborigines; but the facts show that they were Iberians, driven by the Ligurians from the river Sicanus in Iberia. It was from them that the island, before called

Trinacria, took its name of Sicania, and to the present day they inhabit the west of Sicily.

On the fall of Ilium, some of the Trojans escaped from the Achaeans, came in ships to Sicily, and settled next to the Sicanians under the general name of Elymi; their towns being called Eryx and Egesta. With them settled some of the Phocians carried on their way from Troy by a storm, first to Libya, and afterwards from thence to Sicily. The Sicels crossed over to Sicily from their first home Italy, flying from the Opicans, as tradition says and as seems not unlikely, upon rafts, having watched till the wind set down the strait to effect the passage; although perhaps they may have sailed over in some other way. Even at the present day there are still Sicels in Italy; and the country got its name of Italy from Italus, a king of the Sicels, so called. These went with a great host to Sicily, defeated the Sicanians in battle, and forced them to remove to the south and west of the island, which thus came to be called Sicily instead of Sicania, and after they crossed over continued to enjoy the richest parts of the country for near three hundred years before any Hellenes came to Sicily; indeed they still hold the centre and north of the island.

There were also Phoenicians living all round Sicily, who had occupied promontories upon the sea-coasts and the islets adjacent for the purpose of trading with the Sicels. But when the Hellenes began to arrive in considerable numbers by sea, the Phoenicians abandoned most of their stations and, drawing together, took up their abode in Motye, Soloeis, and Panormus, near the Elymi, partly because they confided in their alliance, and also because these are the nearest points, for the voyage between Carthage and Sicily. . . .

[There follows a rapid account of the Greek settlements.]

6. Such is the list of the peoples, Hellenic and barbarian, inhabiting Sicily, and such the magnitude of the island which the Athenians were now bent upon invading, being ambitious in real truth of conquering the whole, although they had also the specious design of succouring their kindred and other allies in the island. But they were especially incited by

envoys from Egesta, who had come to Athens and invoked their aid more urgently than ever. The Egestaeans had gone to war with their neighbours the Selinuntines upon questions of marriage and disputed territory, and the Selinuntines had procured the alliance of the Syracusans, and pressed Egesta hard by land and sea. The Egestaeans now reminded the Athenians of the alliance made in the time of Laches, during the former Leontine war, and begged them to send a fleet to their aid, and among a number of other considerations urged as a capital argument that if the Syracusans were allowed to go unpunished for their depopulation of Leontini, to ruin the allies still left to Athens in Sicily, and to get the whole power of the island into their hands, there would be a danger of their one day coming with a large force, as Dorians, to the aid of their Dorian brethren, and as colonists, to the aid of the Peloponnesians who had sent them out, and joining these in pulling down the Athenian power. The Athenians would, therefore, do well to unite with the allies still left to them, and to make a stand against the Syracusans; especially as they, the Egestaeans, were prepared to furnish money sufficient for the war. The Athenians, hearing these arguments constantly repeated in their assemblies by the Egestaeans and their supporters, voted first to send envoys to Egesta, to see if there was really the money that they talked of in the treasury and temples, and at the same time to ascertain in what posture was the war with the Selinuntines.

7. The envoys of the Athenians were accordingly despatched to Sicily. The same winter the Lacedaemonians and their allies, the Corinthians excepted, marched into the Argive territory, and ravaged a small part of the land, and took some yokes of oxen and carried off some corn. They also settled the Argive exiles at Orneae, and left them a few soldiers taken from the rest of the army; and, after making a truce for a certain while, according to which neither Orneatae nor Argives were to injure each other's territory, returned home with the army. Not long afterwards the Athe-

nians came with thirty ships and six hundred heavy infantry, and the Argives joining them with all their forces, marched out and besieged the men in Orneae for one day; but the garrison escaped by night, the besiegers having bivouacked some way off. The next day the Argives, discovering it, razed Orneae to the ground and went back again, after which the Athenians went home in their ships. Meanwhile the Athenians took by sea to Methone on the Macedonian border some cavalry of their own and the Macedonian exiles that were at Athens, and plundered the country of Perdiccas. Upon this the Lacedaemonians sent to the Thracian Chalcidians, who had a truce with Athens with a ten-day clause, urging them to join Perdiccas in the war, which they refused to do. And the winter ended, and with it ended the sixteenth year of this war of which Thucydides is the historian.

8. Early in the spring of the following summer the Athenian envoys arrived from Sicily, and Egestaeans with them, bringing sixty talents of uncoined silver as a month's pay for sixty ships, which they were to ask to have sent them. The Athenians held an assembly, and after hearing from the Egestaeans and their own envoys a report, as attractive as it was untrue, upon the state of affairs generally, and in particular as to the money, of which, it was said, there was abundance in the temples and the treasury, voted to send sixty ships to Sicily, under the command of Alcibiades, son of Clinias, Nicias, son of Niceratus, and Lamachus, son of Xenophanes, who were appointed with full powers; they were to help the Egestaeans against the Selinuntines, to restore Leontini upon gaining any advantage in the war, and to order all other matters in Sicily as they should deem best for the interests of Athens. Five days after this a second assembly was held, to consider the speediest means of equipping the ships, and to vote whatever else might be required by the generals for the expedition; and Nicias, who had been chosen to the command against his will, and who thought that the state was not well advised, but upon a slight and specious pretext was aspiring to the conquest of the whole

of Sicily, a great matter to achieve, came forward in the hope of diverting the Athenians from the enterprise, and gave them the following counsel:

9. "Although this assembly was convened to consider the preparations to be made for sailing to Sicily, I think, notwithstanding, that we have still this question to examine, whether it be better to send out the ships at all, and that we ought not to give so little consideration to a matter of such moment, or let ourselves be persuaded by foreigners into undertaking a war with which we have nothing to do. And yet, individually, I gain in honour by such a course, and fear as little as other men for my person—not that I think a man need be any the worse citizen for taking some thought for his person and estate; on the contrary, such a man would for his own sake desire the prosperity of his country more than others —nevertheless, as I have never spoken against my convictions to gain honour, I shall not begin to do so now, but shall say what I think best. Against your character any words of mine would be weak enough; if I were to advise your keeping what you have got, and not risking what is actually yours for advantages which are dubious in themselves, and which you may or may not attain. I will, therefore, content myself with showing that your ardour is out of season, and your ambition not easy of accomplishment.

10. "I affirm, then, that you leave many enemies behind you here to go yonder and bring more back with you. You imagine, perhaps, that the treaty which you have made can be trusted; a treaty that will continue to exist nominally, as long as you keep quiet—for nominal it has become, owing to the practices of certain men here and at Sparta—but which in the event of a serious reverse in any quarter would not delay our enemies a moment in attacking us; first, because the convention was forced upon them by disaster and was less honourable to them than to us; and secondly, because in this very convention there are many points that are still disputed. Again, some of the most powerful states have never yet accepted the arrangement at all. Some of these are at open war with us; others (as the Lacedaemonians do not

yet move) are restrained by truces with ten-day clauses, and it is only too probable that if they found our power divided, as we are hurrying to divide it, they would attack us vigorously with the Sicilians, whose alliance they would have in the past valued as they would that of few others. A man ought, therefore, to consider these points, and not to think of running risks with a country placed so critically, or of grasping at another empire before we have secured the one we have already; for in fact the Thracian Chalcidians have been all these years in revolt from us without being yet subdued, and others on the continents yield us but a doubtful obedience. Meanwhile the Egestaeans, our allies, have been wronged, and we run to help them, while the rebels who have so long wronged us still wait for punishment.

11. "And yet the latter, if brought under, might be kept under; while the Sicilians, even if conquered, are too far off and too numerous to be ruled without difficulty. Now it is folly to go against men who could not be kept under even if conquered, while failure would leave us in a very different position from that which we occupied before the enterprise. The Sicilians, again, to take them as they are at present, in the event of a Syracusan conquest (the favourite bugbear of the Egestaeans), would to my thinking be even less dangerous to us than before. At present they might possibly come here as separate states for love of Lacedaemon; in the other case one empire would scarcely attack another; for after joining the Peloponnesians to overthrow ours, they could only expect to see the same hands overthrow their own in the same way. The Hellenes in Sicily would fear us most if we never went there at all, and, next to this, if after displaying our power we went away again as soon as possible. We all know that that which is farthest off and the reputation of which can least be tested, is the object of admiration; at the least reverse they would at once begin to look down upon us, and would join our enemies here against us. You have yourselves experienced this with regard to the Lacedaemonians and their allies, whom your unexpected success, as compared with what you feared at first, has made you sud-

denly despise, tempting you further to aspire to the conquest of Sicily. Instead, however, of being puffed up by the misfortunes of your adversaries, you ought to think of breaking their spirit before giving yourselves up to confidence, and to understand that the one thought awakened in the Lacedaemonians by their disgrace is how they may even now, if possible, overthrow us and repair their dishonour; inasmuch as military reputation is their oldest and chiefest study. Our struggle, therefore, if we are wise, will not be for the barbarian Egestaeans in Sicily, but how to defend ourselves most effectually against the oligarchical machinations of Lacedaemon.

12. "We should also remember that we are but now enjoying some respite from a great pestilence and from war, to the no small benefit of our estates and persons, and that it is right to employ these at home on our own behalf, instead of using them on behalf of these exiles whose interest it is to lie as fairly as they can, who do nothing but talk themselves and leave the danger to others, and who if they succeed will show no proper gratitude, and if they fail will drag down their friends with them. And if there be any man here, overjoyed at being chosen to command, who urges you to make the expedition, merely for ends of his own—especially if he be still too young to command—who seeks to be admired for his stud of horses, but on account of its heavy expenses hopes for some profit from his appointment, do not allow such a one to maintain his private splendour at his country's risk, but remember that such persons injure the public fortune while they squander their own, and that this is a matter of importance, and not for young men to decide or hastily to take in hand.

13. "When I see such persons now sitting here at the side of that same individual and summoned by him, alarm seizes me; and I, in my turn, summon any of the older men that may have such a person sitting next him, not to let himself be shamed down, for fear of being thought a coward if he do not vote for war, but, remembering how rarely success is got by wishing and how often by forecast, to leave to them

the mad dream of conquest, and as a true lover of his country, now threatened by the greatest danger in its history, to hold up his hand on the other side; to vote that the Sicilians be left in the limits now existing between us, limits of which no one can complain (the Ionian sea for the coasting voyage, and the Sicilian across the open main), to enjoy their own possessions and to settle their own quarrels; that the Egestaeans, for their part, be told to end by themselves with the Selinuntines the war which they began without consulting the Athenians; and that for the future we do not enter into alliance, as we have been used to do, with people whom we must help in their need, and who can never help us in ours.

14. "And you, Mr. President, if you think it your duty to care for the commonwealth, and if you wish to show yourself a good citizen, put the question to the vote, and take a second time the opinions of the Athenians. If you are afraid to move the question again, consider that a violation of the law cannot carry any prejudice with so many abettors, that you will be the physician of your misguided city, and that the virtue of men in office is briefly this, to do their country as much good as they can, or in any case no harm that they can avoid."

15. Such were the words of Nicias. Most of the Athenians that came forward spoke in favour of the expedition, and of not annulling what had been voted, although some spoke on the other side. By far the warmest advocate of the expedition was, however, Alcibiades, son of Clinias, who wished to thwart Nicias both as his political opponent and also because of the attack he had made upon him in his speech, and who was, besides, exceedingly ambitious of a command by which he hoped to reduce Sicily and Carthage, and personally to gain in wealth and reputation by means of his successes. For the position he held among the citizens led him to indulge his tastes beyond what his real means would bear, both in keeping horses and in the rest of his expenditure; and this later on had not a little to do with the ruin of the Athenian state. Alarmed at the greatness of his license in his own life and habits, and of the ambition which he showed in all

things soever that he undertook, the mass of the people set him down as a pretender to the tyranny, and became his enemies; and although publicly his conduct of the war was as good as could be desired, individually, his habits gave offence to everyone, and caused them to commit affairs to other hands, and thus before long to ruin the city. Meanwhile he now came forward and gave the following advice to the Athenians:

16. "Athenians, I have a better right to command than others—I must begin with this as Nicias has attacked me—and at the same time I believe myself to be worthy of it. The things for which I am abused bring fame to my ancestors and to myself, and to the country profit besides. The Hellenes, after expecting to see our city ruined by the war, concluded it to be even greater than it really is, by reason of the magnificence with which I participated in the Olympic games, when I sent into the lists seven chariots, a number never before entered by any private person, and won the first prize, and was second and fourth, and took care to have everything else in a style worthy of my victory. Custom regards such displays as honourable, and they cannot be made without leaving behind them an impression of power. Again, any splendour that I may have exhibited at home in providing choruses or otherwise is naturally envied by my fellow citizens, but in the eyes of foreigners has an air of strength as in the other instance. And this is no useless folly, when a man at his own private cost benefits not himself only, but his city: nor is it unfair that he who prides himself on his position should refuse to be upon an equality with the rest. He who is badly off has his misfortunes all to himself, and as we do not see men courted in adversity, on the like principle a man ought to accept the insolence of prosperity; or else let him first mete out equal measure to all, and then demand to have it meted out to him. What I know is that persons of this kind and all others that have attained to any distinction, although they may be unpopular in their lifetime in their relations with their fellow men and especially with their equals, leave to posterity the desire of claiming connection with

them even without any ground, and are vaunted by the country to which they belonged, not as strangers or ill-doers, but as fellow countrymen and heroes. Such are my aspirations, and, however I am abused for them in private, the question is whether anyone manages public affairs better than I do. Having united the most powerful states of the Peloponnesus, without great danger or expense to you, I compelled the Lacedaemonians to stake their all upon the issue of a single day at Mantinea; and, although victorious in the battle, they have never since fully recovered confidence.

17. "Thus did my youth and so-called monstrous folly find fitting arguments to deal with the power of the Peloponnesians, and by its ardour win their confidence and prevail. And do not be afraid of my youth now, but while I am still in its flower, and Nicias appears fortunate, avail yourselves to the utmost of the services of us both. Neither rescind your resolution to sail to Sicily, on the ground that you would be going to attack a great power. The cities in Sicily are peopled by motley rabbles, and easily change their institutions and adopt new ones in their stead; and consequently the inhabitants, being without any feeling of patriotism, are not provided with arms for their persons, and have not regularly established themselves on the land; every man thinks that either by fair words or by party strife he can obtain something at the public expense, and then in the event of a catastrophe settle in some other country, and makes his preparations accordingly. From a mob like this you need not look for either unanimity in counsel or concert in action; but they will probably one by one come in as they get a fair offer, especially if they are torn by civil strife as we are told. Moreover, they have not so many heavy infantry as they boast; just as the Hellenes generally did not prove so numerous as each state reckoned itself, but Hellas greatly over-estimated their numbers, and has hardly had an adequate force of heavy infantry throughout this war.

"The states in Sicily, therefore, from all that I can hear, will be found as I say, and I have not pointed out all our advantages, for we shall have the help of many barbarians, who from their hatred of the Syracusans will join us in attacking them; nor will the powers at home prove any hindrance, if you judge rightly. Our fathers with these very adversaries, which it is said we shall now leave behind us when we sail, and the Mede as their enemy as well, were able to win the empire, depending solely on their superiority at sea. The Peloponnesians had never so little hope against us as at present; and, let them be ever so sanguine, although strong enough to invade our country even if we stay at home, they can never hurt us with their navy, as we leave one of our own behind us that is a match for them.

18. "In this state of things what reason can we give to ourselves for holding back, or what excuse can we offer to our allies in Sicily for not helping them? They are our confederates, and we are bound to assist them without objecting that they have not assisted us. We did not take them into alliance to have them to help us in Hellas, but that they might so annoy our enemies in Sicily as to prevent them from coming over here and attacking us. It is thus that empire has been won, both by us and by all others that have held it, by a constant readiness to support all, whether barbarians or Hellenes, that invite assistance; since if all were to keep quiet or to pick and choose whom they ought to assist, we should make but few new conquests, and should imperil those we have already won. Men do not rest content with parrying the attacks of a superior, but often strike the first blow to prevent the attack being made. And we cannot fix the exact point at which our empire shall stop; we have reached a position in which we must not be content with retaining but must scheme to extend it, for, if we cease to rule others, we are in danger of being ruled ourselves. Nor can you look at inaction from the same point of view as others, unless you are prepared to change your habits and make them like theirs.

"Be convinced then that we shall augment our power at home by this adventure abroad, and let us make the expedition, and so humble the pride of the Peloponnesians by sailing off to Sicily, and letting them see how little we care for the peace that we are now enjoying; and at the same time we shall either become masters, as we very easily may, of the whole of Hellas through the accession of the Sicilian Hellenes, or in any case ruin the Syracusans, to the no small advantage of ourselves and our allies. The faculty of staying if successful, or of returning, will be secured to us by our navy, as we shall be superior at sea to all the Sicilians put together. And do not let the do-nothing policy which Nicias advocates, or his setting of the young against the old, turn you from your purpose, but in the good old fashion by which our fathers, old and young together, by their united counsels brought our affairs to their present height, do you endeavour still to advance them; understanding that neither youth nor old age can do anything the one without the other, but that levity, sobriety, and deliberate judgement are strongest when united, and that, by sinking into inaction, the city, like everything else, will wear itself out, and its skill in everything decay; while each fresh struggle will give it fresh experience, and make it more used to defend itself not in word but in deed. In short, my conviction is that a city not inactive by nature could not choose a quicker way to ruin itself than by suddenly adopting such a policy, and that the safest rule of life is to take one's character and institutions for better and for worse, and to live up to them as closely as one can."

19. Such were the words of Alcibiades. After hearing him and the Egestaeans and some Leontine exiles, who came forward reminding them of their oaths and imploring their assistance, the Athenians became more eager for the expedition than before. Nicias, perceiving that it would be now useless to try to deter them by the old line of argument, but thinking that he might perhaps alter their resolution by the extravagance of his estimates, came forward a second time and spoke as follows:

20. "I see, Athenians, that you are thoroughly bent upon the expedition, and therefore hope that all will turn out as we wish, and proceed to give you my opinion at the present juncture. From all that I hear we are going against cities that are great and not subject to one another, or in need of

change, so as to be glad to pass from enforced servitude to an easier condition, or in the least likely to accept our rule in exchange for freedom; and, to take only the Hellenic towns, they are very numerous for one island. Besides Naxos and Catana, which I expect to join us from their connection with Leontini, there are seven others armed at all points just like our own power, particularly Selinus and Syracuse, the chief objects of our expedition. These are full of heavy infantry, archers, and darters, have triremes in abundance and crowds to man them; they have also money, partly in the hands of private persons, partly in the temples at Selinus, and at Syracuse first-fruits from some of the barbarians as well. But their chief advantage over us lies in the number of their horses, and in the fact that they grow their grain at home instead of importing it.

21. "Against a power of this kind it will not do to have merely a weak naval armament, but we shall want also a large land army to sail with us, if we are to do anything worthy of our ambition, and are not to be shut out from the country by a numerous cavalry; especially if the cities should take alarm and combine, and we should be left without friends (except the Egestaeans) to furnish us with horse to defend ourselves with. It would be disgraceful to have to retire under compulsion, or to send back for reinforcements, owing to want of reflection at first: we must therefore start from home with a competent force, seeing that we are going to sail far from our country, and upon an expedition not like any which you may have undertaken in the quality of allies, among your subject states here in Hellas, where any additional supplies needed were easily drawn from the friendly territory; but we are cutting ourselves off, and going to a land entirely strange, from which during four months in winter it is not even easy for a messenger to get to Athens.

22. "I think, therefore, that we ought to take great numbers of heavy infantry, both from Athens and from our allies, and not merely from our subjects, but also any we may be able to get for love or for money in the Peloponnesus, and great numbers also of archers and slingers, to make head

against the Sicilian horse. Meanwhile we must have an overwhelming superiority at sea, to enable us the more easily to carry in what we want; and we must take our own grain in transport vessels, that is to say, wheat and parched barley, and bakers from the mills compelled to serve for pay in the proper proportion; in order that in case of our being weatherbound the armament may not want provisions, as it is not every city that will be able to entertain numbers like ours. We must also provide ourselves with everything else as far as we can, so as not to be dependent upon others; and above all we must take with us from home as much money as possible, as the sums talked of as ready at Egesta are readier, you may be sure, in talk than in any other way.

23. "Indeed, even if we leave Athens with a force not only equal to that of the enemy except in the number of heavy infantry in the field, but even at all points superior to him, we shall still find it difficult to conquer Sicily or save ourselves. We must not disguise from ourselves that we go to found a city among strangers and enemies, and that he who undertakes such an enterprise should be prepared to become master of the country the first day he lands, or failing in this to find everything hostile to him. Fearing this, and knowing that we shall have need of much good counsel and more good fortune—a hard matter for mortal men to aspire to—I wish as far as may be to make myself independent of fortune before sailing, and when I do sail, to be as safe as a strong force can make me. This I believe to be surest for the country at large, and safest for us who are to go on the expedition. If anyone thinks differently I resign to him my command."

24. With this Nicias concluded, thinking that he should either disgust the Athenians by the magnitude of the undertaking, or, if obliged to sail on the expedition, would thus do so in the safest way possible. The Athenians, however, far from having their taste for the voyage taken away by the burdensomeness of the preparations, became more eager for it than ever; and just the contrary took place of what Nicias had thought, as it was held that he had given good advice,

and that the expedition would be the safest in the world. All alike fell in love with the enterprise. The older men thought that they would either subdue the places against which they were to sail, or at all events, with so large a force, meet with no disaster; those in the prime of life felt a longing for foreign sights and spectacles, and had no doubt that they should come safe home again; while the idea of the common people and the soldiery was to earn wages at the moment, and make conquests that would supply a never-ending fund of pay for the future. With this enthusiasm of the majority, the few that liked it not feared to appear unpatriotic by holding up their hands against it, and so kept quiet.

25. At last one of the Athenians came forward and called upon Nicias and told him that he ought not to make excuses or put them off, but say at once before them all what forces the Athenians should vote him. Upon this he said, not without reluctance, that he would advise upon that matter more at leisure with his colleagues; as far however as he could see at present, they must sail with at least one hundred triremes —the Athenians providing as many transports as they might determine, and sending for others from the allies—not less than five thousand heavy infantry in all, Athenian and allied, and if possible more; and the rest of the armament in proportion; archers from home and from Crete, and slingers, and whatever else might seem desirable, being got ready by the generals and taken with them.

26. Upon hearing this the Athenians at once voted that the generals should have full powers in the matter of the numbers of the army and of the expedition generally, to do as they judged best for the interests of Athens. After this the preparations began; messages being sent to the allies and the rolls drawn up at home. And as the city had just recovered from the plague and the long war, and a number of young men had grown up and capital had accumulated by reason of the truce, everything was the more easily provided.

27. In the midst of these preparations all the stone Hermae in the city of Athens, that is to say the customary square figures so common in the doorways of private houses

and temples, had in one night most of them their faces muti-
lated. No one knew who had done it, but large public rewards were offered to find the authors; and it was further
voted that anyone who knew of any other act of impiety having been committed should come and give information without fear of consequences, whether he were citizen, alien, or
slave. The matter was taken up the more seriously, as it was
thought to be ominous for the expedition, and part of a conspiracy to bring about a revolution and to upset the democracy.

28. Information was given accordingly by some resident
aliens and body servants, not about the Hermae but about
some previous mutilations of other images perpetrated by
young men in a drunken frolic, and of mock celebrations of
the mysteries, averred to take place in private houses. Alcibiades being implicated in this charge, it was taken hold of
by those who could least endure him, because he stood in
the way of their obtaining the undisturbed direction of the
people, and who thought that if he were once removed the
first place would be theirs. These accordingly magnified the
matter and loudly proclaimed that the affair of the mysteries
and the mutilation of the Hermae were part and parcel of a
scheme to overthrow the democracy, and that nothing of all
this had been done without Alcibiades; the proofs alleged
being the general and undemocratic license of his life and
habits.

29. Alcibiades repelled on the spot the charges in question, and also before going on the expedition, the preparations for which were now complete, offered to stand his trial,
that it might be seen whether he was guilty of the acts imputed to him, desiring to be punished if found guilty, but,
if acquitted, to take the command. Meanwhile he protested
against their receiving slanders against him in his absence,
and begged them rather to put him to death at once if he
were guilty, and pointed out the imprudence of sending him
out at the head of so large an army, with so serious a charge
still undecided. But his enemies feared that he would have
the army for him if he were tried immediately, and that the

people might relent in favour of the man whom they already caressed as the cause of the Argives and some of the Mantineans joining in the expedition, and did their utmost to get this proposition rejected, putting forward other orators who said that he ought at present to sail and not delay the departure of the army, and be tried on his return within a fixed number of days; their plan being to have him sent for and brought home for trial upon some graver charge, which they would the more easily get up in his absence. Accordingly it was decreed that he should sail.

30. After this the departure for Sicily took place, it being now about midsummer. Most of the allies, with the food transports and the smaller craft and the rest of the expedition, had already received orders to muster at Corcyra, to cross the Ionian sea from thence in a body to the Iapygian promontory. But the Athenians themselves, and such of their allies as happened to be with them, went down to the Piraeus upon a day appointed at daybreak, and began to man the ships for putting out to sea. With them also went down the whole population, one may say, of the city, both citizens and foreigners; the inhabitants of the country each escorting those that belonged to them, their friends, their relatives, or their sons, with hope and lamentation upon their way, as they thought of the conquests which they hoped to make, or of the friends whom they might never see again, considering the long voyage which they were going to make from their country.

31. Indeed, at this moment, when they were now upon the point of parting from one another, the danger came more home to them than when they voted for the expedition; although the strength of the armament, and the profuse provision which they remarked in every department, was a sight that could not but comfort them. As for the foreigners and the rest of the crowd, they simply went to see a sight worth looking at and passing all belief.

Indeed this armament that first sailed out was by far the most costly and splendid Hellenic force that had ever been sent out by a single city up to that time. In mere number of ships and heavy infantry that against Epidaurus under Pericles, and the same when going against Potidaea under Hagnon, was not inferior; containing as it did four thousand Athenian heavy infantry, three hundred horse, and one hundred triremes accompanied by fifty Lesbian and Chian vessels and many allies besides. But these were sent upon a short voyage and with a scanty equipment. The present expedition was formed in contemplation of a long term of service by land and sea alike, and was furnished with ships and troops so as to be ready for either as required. The fleet had been elaborately equipped at great cost to the captains and the state; the treasury giving a drachma a day to each seaman, and providing empty ships, sixty men of war and forty transports, and manning these with the best crews obtainable; while the captains gave a bounty in addition to the pay from the treasury to the *thranite* and crews generally, besides spending lavishly upon figureheads and equipments, and one and all making the utmost exertions to enable their own ships to excel in beauty and fast sailing. Meanwhile the land forces had been picked from the best muster-rolls, and vied with each other in paying great attention to their arms and personal accoutrements.

From this resulted not only a rivalry among themselves in their different departments, but an idea that it was more a display of power and resources to the rest of the Hellenes than an armament against an enemy. For if anyone had counted up the public expenditure of the state, and the private outlay of individuals—that is to say, the sums which the state had already spent upon the expedition and was sending out in the hands of the generals, and those which individuals had expended upon their personal outfit, or as captains of triremes had laid out and were still to lay out upon their vessels; and if he had added to this the journey money which each was likely to have provided himself with, independently of the pay from the treasury, for a voyage of such length, and what the soldiers or traders took with them for the purpose of exchange—it would have been found that many talents in all were being taken out of the city. Indeed the expedition became not less famous for its wonderful boldness and for the splendour of its appearance than for its overwhelming strength as compared with the peoples against whom it was directed, and for the fact that this was the longest passage from home hitherto attempted, and the most ambitious in its objects considering the resources of those who undertook it.

32. The ships being now manned, and everything put on board with which they meant to sail, the trumpet commanded silence, and the prayers customary before putting out to sea were offered, not in each ship by itself, but by all together to the voice of a herald; and bowls of wine were mixed through all the armament, and libations made by the soldiers and their officers in gold and silver goblets. In their prayers joined also the crowds on shore, the citizens and all others that wished them well. The paean sung and the libations finished, they put out to sea, and first sailing out in column then raced each other as far as Aegina, and so hastened to reach Corcyra, where the rest of the allied forces were also assembling.

Meanwhile at Syracuse news came in from many quarters of the expedition, but for a long while met with no credence whatever. Indeed, an assembly was held in which speeches, as will be seen, were delivered by different orators, believing or contradicting the report of the Athenian expedition; among whom Hermocrates, son of Hermon, came forward, being persuaded that he knew the truth of the matter, and gave the following counsel:

33. "Although I shall perhaps be no better believed than others have been when I speak upon the reality of the expedition, and although I know that those who either make or repeat statements thought not worthy of belief not only gain no converts, but are thought fools for their pains, I shall certainly not be frightened into holding my tongue when the state is in danger, and when I am persuaded that I can speak with more authority on the matter than other persons.

"Much as you wonder at it, the Athenians nevertheless have set out against us with a large force, naval and military, professedly to help the Egestaeans and to restore Leontini, but really to conquer Sicily, and above all our city, which once gained, the rest, they think, will easily follow. Make up your minds, therefore, to see them speedily here, and see how you can best repel them with the means under your hand, and do not be taken off your guard through despising the news, or neglect the common weal through disbelieving it.

"Meanwhile those who believe me need not be dismayed at the force or daring of the enemy. They will not be able to do us more hurt than we shall do them; nor is the greatness of their armament altogether without advantage to us. Indeed, the greater it is the better, with regard to the rest of the Sicilians, whom dismay will make more ready to join us; and if we defeat or drive them away, disappointed of the objects of their ambition (for I do not fear for a moment that they will get what they want), it will be a most glorious exploit for us, and in my judgement by no means an unlikely one. Few indeed have been the large armaments, either Hellenic or barbarian, that have gone far from home and been successful. They cannot be more numerous than the people of the country and their neighbours, all of whom fear leagues together; and if they miscarry for want of supplies in a foreign land, to those against whom their plans were laid none the less they leave renown, although they may themselves have been the main cause of their own discomfort. Thus these very Athenians rose by the defeat of the Mede, in a great measure due to accidental causes, from the mere fact that Athens had been the object of his attack; and this may very well be the case with us also.

34. "Let us, therefore, confidently begin preparations here; let us send and confirm some of the Sicels, and obtain the friendship and alliance of others, and despatch envoys to the rest of Sicily to show that the danger is common to all, and to Italy to get them to become our allies, or at all events to refuse to receive the Athenians. I also think that it would be best to send to Carthage as well; they are by no means there without apprehension, but it is their constant fear that

the Athenians may one day attack their city, and they may perhaps think that they might themselves suffer by letting Sicily be sacrificed, and be willing to help us secretly if not openly, in one way if not in another. They are the best able to do so, if they will, of any of the present day, as they possess most gold and silver, by which war, like everything else, flourishes. Let us also send to Lacedaemon and Corinth, and ask them to come here and help us as soon as possible, and to keep alive the war in Hellas.

"But the true thing of all others, in my opinion, to do at the present moment, is what you, with your constitutional love of quiet, will be slow to see, and what I must nevertheless mention. If we Sicilians, all together, or at least as many as possible besides ourselves, would only launch the whole of our actual navy with two months' provisions, and meet the Athenians at Tarentum and the Iapygian promontory, and show them that before fighting for Sicily they must first fight for their passage across the Ionian sea, we should strike dismay into their army, and set them on thinking that we have a base for our defensive—for Tarentum is ready to receive us—while they have a wide sea to cross with all their armament, which could with difficulty keep its order through so long a voyage, and would be easy for us to attack as it came on slowly and in small detachments. On the other hand, if they were to lighten their vessels, and draw together their fast sailers and with these attack us, we could either fall upon them when they were wearied with rowing, or, if we did not choose to do so, we could retire to Tarentum; while they, having crossed with few provisions just to give battle, would be hard put to it in desolate places, and would either have to remain and be blockaded, or to try to sail along the coast, abandoning the rest of their armament, and being further discouraged by not knowing for certain whether the cities would receive them.

"In my opinion this consideration alone would be sufficient to deter them from putting out from Corcyra; and, what with deliberating and reconnoitring our numbers and whereabouts, they would let the season go on until winter was upon them, or, confounded by so unexpected a circumstance, would break up the expedition, especially as their most experienced general has, as I hear, taken the command against his will, and would grasp at the first excuse offered by any serious demonstration of ours. We should also be reported, I am certain, as more numerous than we really are, and men's minds are affected by what they hear, and besides the first to attack, or to show that they mean to defend themselves against an attack, inspire greater fear because men see that they are ready for the emergency. This would just be the case with the Athenians at present. They are now attacking us in the belief that we shall not resist, having a right to judge us severely because we did not help the Lacedaemonians in crushing them; but if they were to see us showing a courage for which they are not prepared, they would be more dismayed by the surprise than they could ever be by our actual power.

"I could wish to persuade you to show this courage; but if this cannot be, at all events lose not a moment in preparing generally for the war; and remember all of you that contempt for an assailant is best shown by bravery in action, but that for the present the best course is to accept the preparations which fear inspires as giving the surest promise of safety, and to act as if the danger was real. That the Athenians are coming to attack us, and are already upon the voyage, and all but here—this is what I am sure of."

35. Thus far spoke Hermocrates. Meanwhile the people of Syracuse were at great strife among themselves, some contending that the Athenians had no idea of coming and that there was no truth in what he said, some asking if they did come what harm they could do that would not be repaid them tenfold in return, while others made light of the whole affair and turned it into ridicule. In short, there were few that believed Hermocrates and feared for the future. Meanwhile Athenagoras, the leader of the people and very powerful at that time with the masses, came forward and spoke as follows:

36. "For the Athenians, he who does not wish that they

may be as misguided as they are supposed to be, and that they may come here to become our subjects, is either a coward or a traitor to his country; while as for those who carry such tidings and fill you with so much alarm, I wonder less at their audacity than at their folly if they flatter themselves that we do not see through them. The fact is that they have their private reasons to be afraid, and wish to throw the city into consternation to have their own terrors cast into the shade by the public alarm. In short, this is what these reports are worth; they do not arise of themselves, but are concocted by men who are always causing agitation here in Sicily. However, if you are well advised, you will not be guided in your calculation of probabilities by what these persons tell you, but by what shrewd men and of large experience, as I esteem the Athenians to be, would be likely to do. Now it is not likely that they would leave the Peloponnesians behind them, and before they have well ended the war in Hellas wantonly come in quest of a new war quite as arduous in Sicily; indeed, in my judgement, they are only too glad that we do not go and attack them, being so many and so great cities as we are.

37. "However, if they should come as is reported, I consider Sicily better able to go through with the war than the Peloponnesus, as being at all points better prepared, and our city by itself far more than a match for this pretended army of invasion, even were it twice as large again. I know that they will not have horses with them, or get any here, except a few perhaps from the Egestaeans; or be able to bring a force of heavy infantry equal in number to our own, in ships which will already have enough to do to come all this distance, however lightly laden, not to speak of the transport of the other stores required against a city of this magnitude, which will be no slight quantity. In fact, so strong is my opinion upon the subject that I do not well see how they could avoid annihilation if they brought with them another city as large as Syracuse, and settled down and carried on war from our frontier; much less can they hope to succeed with all Sicily hostile to them, as all Sicily will be, and with only a

camp pitched from the ships, and composed of tents and bare necessaries, from which they would not be able to stir far for fear of our cavalry.

38. "But the Athenians see this as I tell you, and, as I have reason to know, are looking after their possessions at home, while persons here invent stories that neither are true nor ever will be. Nor is this the first time that I see these persons, when they cannot resort to deeds, trying by such stories and by others even more abominable to frighten your people and get into their hands the government: it is what I see always. And I cannot help fearing that trying so often they may one day succeed, and that we, as long as we do not feel the smart, may prove too weak for the task of prevention, or, when the offenders are known, of pursuit. The result is that our city is rarely at rest, but is subject to constant troubles and to contests as frequent against herself as against the enemy, not to speak of occasional tyrannies and infamous cabals. However, I will try, if you will support me, to let nothing of this happen in our time, by gaining you, the people, and by chastising the authors of such machinations, not merely when they are caught in the act—a difficult feat to accomplish—but also for what they have the wish though not the power to do; as it is necessary to punish an enemy not only for what he does, but also beforehand for what he intends to do, if the first to relax precaution would not be also the first to suffer. I shall also reprove, watch, and on occasion warn the oligarchs—the most effectual way, in my opinion, of turning them from their evil courses. And after all, as I have often asked, what would you have, young men? Would you hold office at once? The law forbids it, a law enacted rather because you are not competent than to disgrace you when competent. Would you rather not be on a footing of legal equality with the masses? But how can it be right that citizens of the same state should be held unworthy of the same privileges?

39. "It will be said, perhaps, that democracy is neither wise nor equitable, but that the holders of property are also the best fitted to rule. I say, on the contrary, first, that the

word *demos,* or people, includes the whole state, oligarchy only a part; next, that if the best guardians of property are the rich, and the best counsellors the wise, none can hear and decide so well as the many; and that all these talents, severally and collectively, have their just place in a democracy. But an oligarchy gives the many their share of the danger, and not content with the largest part takes and keeps the whole of the profit; and this is what the powerful and young among you aspire to, but in a great city cannot possibly obtain.

40. "But even now, foolish men, most senseless of all the Hellenes that I know, if you have no sense of the wickedness of your designs, or most criminal if you have that sense and still dare to pursue them—even now, if it is not a case for repentance, you may still learn wisdom, and thus advance the interest of the country, the common interest of us all. Reflect that in the country's prosperity the men of merit in your ranks will have a share and a larger share than the great mass of your fellow countrymen, but that if you have other designs you run a risk of being deprived of all; and desist from reports like these, as the people know your object and will not put up with it. If the Athenians arrive, this city will repulse them in a manner worthy of itself; we have, moreover, generals who will see to this matter. And if nothing of this be true, as I incline to believe, the city will not be thrown into a panic by your intelligence, or impose upon itself a self-chosen servitude by choosing you for its rulers; the city itself will look into the matter, and will judge your words as if they were acts, and, instead of allowing itself to be deprived of its liberty by listening to you, will strive to preserve that liberty, by taking care to have always at hand the means of making itself respected."

41. Such were the words of Athenagoras. One of the generals now stood up and stopped any other speakers coming forward, adding these words of his own with reference to the matter in hand: "It is not well for speakers to utter calumnies against one another, or for their hearers to entertain them;

we ought rather to look to the intelligence that we have received, and see how each man by himself and the city as a whole may best prepare to repel the invaders. Even if there be no need, there is no harm in the state being furnished with horses and arms and all other insignia of war; and we will undertake to see to and order this, and to send round to the cities to reconnoitre and do all else that may appear desirable. Part of this we have seen to already, and whatever we discover shall be laid before you." After these words from the general, the Syracusans departed from the assembly.

42. In the meantime the Athenians with all their allies had now arrived at Corcyra. Here the generals began by again reviewing the armament, and made arrangements as to the order in which they were to anchor and encamp, and, dividing the whole fleet into three divisions, allotted one to each of their number, to avoid sailing all together and being thus embarrassed for water, harbourage, or provisions at the stations which they might touch at, and at the same time to be generally better ordered and easier to handle, by each squadron having its own commander. Next they sent on three ships to Italy and Sicily to find out which of the cities would receive them, with instructions to meet them on the way and let them know before they put in to land.

43. After this the Athenians weighed from Corcyra, and proceeded to cross to Sicily with an armament now consisting of one hundred and thirty-four triremes in all (besides two Rhodian penteconters), of which one hundred were Athenian vessels—sixty men-of-war and forty troopships— and the remainder from Chios and the other allies; five thousand and one hundred heavy infantry in all, that is to say, fifteen hundred Athenian citizens from the rolls at Athens and seven hundred thetes[1] shipped as marines, and the rest allied troops, some of them Athenian subjects, and besides these five hundred Argives, and two hundred and fifty Mantineans serving for hire; four hundred and eighty archers in all, eighty of whom were Cretans; seven hundred

[1] Citizens of the lowest property rating.

slingers from Rhodes; one hundred and twenty light-armed exiles from Megara; and one horse-transport carrying thirty horses.

44. Such was the strength of the first armament that sailed over for the war. The supplies for this force were carried by thirty ships of burden laden with supplies, which conveyed the bakers, stone-masons and carpenters, and the tools for raising fortifications, accompanied by one hundred boats, like the former pressed into the service, besides many other boats and ships of burden which followed the armament voluntarily for purposes of trade; all of which now left Corcyra and struck across the Ionian sea together. The whole force making land at the Iapygian promontory and Tarentum, with more or less good fortune, coasted along the shores of Italy, the cities shutting their markets and gates against them, and according them nothing but water and anchorage, and Tarentum and Locris not even that, until they arrived at Rhegium, the extreme point of Italy. Here at length they reunited, and not gaining admission within the walls pitched a camp outside the city in the precinct of Artemis, where a market was also provided for them, and drew their ships on shore and kept quiet. Meanwhile they opened negotiations with the Rhegians, and called upon them as Chalcidians to assist their Leontine kinsmen; to which the Rhegians replied that they would not side with either party, but should await the decision of the rest of the Italiots, and do as they did. Upon this the Athenians now began to consider what would be the best action to take in the affairs of Sicily, and meanwhile waited for the ships sent on to come back from Egesta, in order to know whether there was really there the money mentioned by the messengers at Athens.

45. In the meantime came in from all quarters to the Syracusans, as well as from their own scouts, the positive tidings that the fleet was at Rhegium, upon which they laid aside their incredulity and threw themselves heart and soul into the work of preparation. Guards or envoys, as the case might be, were sent round to the Sicels, garrisons put into the posts of the Peripoli in the country, horses and arms re-

viewed in the city to see that nothing was wanting, and all other steps taken to prepare for a war which might be upon them at any moment.

46. Meanwhile the three ships that had been sent on came from Egesta to the Athenians at Rhegium, with the news that so far from there being the sums promised, all that could be produced was thirty talents. The generals were not a little disheartened at being thus disappointed at the outset, and by the refusal to join in the expedition of the Rhegians, the people they had first tried to gain and had had most reason to count upon, from their relationship to the Leontines and constant friendship for Athens. If Nicias was prepared for the news from Egesta, his two colleagues were taken completely by surprise. The Egestaeans had had recourse to the following stratagem, when the first envoys from Athens came to inspect their resources. They took the envoys in question to the temple of Aphrodite at Eryx and showed them the treasures deposited there: bowls, flagons, censers, and a large number of other pieces of plate, which from being in silver gave an impression of wealth quite out of proportion to their really small value. They also privately entertained the ships' crews, and collected all the cups of gold and silver that they could find in Egesta itself or could borrow in the neighbouring Phoenician and Hellenic towns, and each brought them to the banquets as their own; and as all used pretty nearly the same, and everywhere a great quantity of plate was shown, the effect was most dazzling upon the Athenian sailors, and made them talk loudly of the riches they had seen when they got back to Athens. The dupes in question—who had in their turn persuaded the rest —when the news got abroad that there was not the money supposed at Egesta, were much blamed by the soldiers.

47. Meanwhile the generals consulted upon what was to be done. The opinion of Nicias was to sail with all the armament to Selinus, the main object of the expedition, and if the Egestaeans could provide money for the whole force, to advise accordingly; but if they could not, to require them to supply provisions for the sixty ships that they had asked

for, to stay and settle matters between them and the Selinuntines either by force or by agreement, and then to coast past the other cities, and after displaying the power of Athens and proving their zeal for their friends and allies, to sail home again (unless they should have some sudden and unexpected opportunity of serving the Leontines, or of bringing over some of the other cities), and not to endanger the state by wasting its home resources.

48. Alcibiades said that a great expedition like the present must not disgrace itself by going away without having done anything; heralds must be sent to all the cities except Selinus and Syracuse, and efforts be made to make some of the Sicels revolt from the Syracusans, and to obtain the friendship of others, in order to have food and troops; and first of all to gain the Messinese, who lay right in the passage and entrance to Sicily, and would afford an excellent harbour and base for the army. Thus, after bringing over the towns and knowing who would be their allies in the war, they might at length attack Syracuse and Selinus; unless the latter came to terms with Egesta and the former ceased to oppose the restoration of Leontini.

49. Lamachus, on the other hand, said that they ought to sail straight to Syracuse, and fight their battle at once under the walls of the town while the people were still unprepared, and the panic at its height. Every armament was most terrible at first; if it allowed time to run on without showing itself, men's courage revived, and they saw it appear at last almost with indifference. By attacking suddenly, while Syracuse still trembled at their coming, they would have the best chance of gaining a victory for themselves and of striking a complete panic into the enemy by the aspect of their numbers—which would never appear so considerable as at present—by the anticipation of coming disaster, and above all by the immediate danger of the engagement. They might also count upon surprising many in the fields outside, incredulous of their coming; and at the moment that the enemy was carrying in his property the army would not want for booty if it sat down in force before the city. The rest of

the Sicilians would thus be immediately less disposed to enter into alliance with the Syracusans, and would join the Athenians, without waiting to see which were the strongest. They must make Megara their naval station as a place to retreat to and a base from which to attack: it was an uninhabited place at no great distance from Syracuse either by land or by sea.

50. After speaking to this effect, Lamachus nevertheless gave his support to the opinion of Alcibiades. After this Alcibiades sailed in his own vessel across to Messina with proposals of alliance, but met with no success, the inhabitants answering that they could not receive him within their walls, though they would provide him with a market outside. Upon this he sailed back to Rhegium. Immediately upon his return the generals manned and victualled sixty ships out of the whole fleet and coasted along to Naxos, leaving the rest of the armament behind them at Rhegium with one of their number. Received by the Naxians, they then coasted on to Catana, and, being refused admittance by the inhabitants, there being a Syracusan party in the town, went on to the river Terias. Here they bivouacked, and the next day sailed in single file to Syracuse with all their ships except ten which they sent on in front to sail into the great harbour and see if there was any fleet launched, and to proclaim by herald from shipboard that the Athenians were come to restore the Leontines to their country, as being their allies and kinsmen, and that such of them, therefore, as were in Syracuse should leave it without fear and join their friends and benefactors the Athenians. After making this proclamation and reconnoitring the city and the harbours, and the features of the country which they would have to make their base of operations in the war, they sailed back to Catana.

51. An assembly being held here, the inhabitants refused to receive the armament, but invited the generals to come in and say what they desired; and while Alcibiades was speaking and the citizens were intent on the assembly, the soldiers broke down an ill-walled-up postern-gate without being observed, and getting inside the town, flocked into the market-

place. The Syracusan supporters in the town no sooner saw the army inside than they became frightened and withdrew, not being at all numerous; while the rest voted for an alliance with the Athenians and invited them to fetch the rest of their forces from Rhegium. After this the Athenians sailed to Rhegium, and put off, this time with all the armament, for Catana, and fell to work at their camp immediately upon their arrival.

52. Meanwhile word was brought them from Camarina that if they went there the town would go over to them, and also that the Syracusans were manning a fleet. The Athenians accordingly sailed along shore with all their armament, first to Syracuse, where they found no fleet manning, and so always along the coast to Camarina, where they brought to at the beach, and sent a herald to the people, who, however, refused to receive them, saying that their oaths bound them to receive the Athenians only with a single vessel, unless they themselves sent for more. Disappointed here, the Athenians now sailed back again, and, after landing and plundering on Syracusan territory and losing some stragglers from their light infantry through the coming up of the Syracusan horse, so got back to Catana.

53. There they found the Salaminia come from Athens for Alcibiades, with orders for him to sail home to answer the charges which the state brought against him, and for certain others of the soldiers who with him were accused of sacrilege in the matter of the mysteries and of the Hermae. For the Athenians, after the departure of the expedition, had continued as active as ever in investigating the facts of the mysteries and of the Hermae, and, instead of testing the informers, in their suspicious temper welcomed all indifferently, arresting and imprisoning the best citizens upon the evidence of rascals, and preferring to sift the matter to the bottom sooner than to let an accused person of good character pass unquestioned, owing to the rascality of the informer. The commons had heard how oppressive the tyranny of Pisistratus and his sons had become before it ended, and further that that tyranny had been put down at last, not

by themselves and Harmodius, but by the Lacedaemonians, and so were always in fear and took everything suspiciously.

54. Indeed, the daring action of Aristogeiton and Harmodius was undertaken in consequence of a love affair, which I shall relate at some length, to show that the Athenians are not more accurate than the rest of the world in their accounts of their own tyrants and of the facts of their own history. Pisistratus dying at an advanced age in possession of the tyranny, was succeeded by his eldest son, Hippias, and not Hipparchus, as is vulgarly believed. Harmodius was then in the flower of youthful beauty, and Aristogeiton, a citizen in the middle rank, was his lover and possessed him. Solicited without success by Hipparchus, son of Pisistratus, Harmodius told Aristogeiton, and the enraged lover, afraid that the powerful Hipparchus might take Harmodius by force, immediately formed a design, such as his condition permitted, for overthrowing the tyranny. In the meantime Hipparchus, after a second solicitation of Harmodius, attended with no better success, unwilling to use violence, arranged to insult him in some covert way.

Indeed, generally their government was not grievous to the multitude, or in any way odious in practice; and these tyrants cultivated wisdom and virtue as much as any, and, without exacting from the Athenians more than a twentieth of their income, splendidly adorned their city, and carried on their wars, and provided sacrifices for the temples. For the rest, the city was left in full enjoyment of its existing laws, except that care was always taken to have one office in the hands of someone of the family. Among those of them that held the yearly archonship at Athens was Pisistratus, son of the tyrant Hippias, and named after his grandfather, who dedicated during his term of office the altar to the twelve gods in the Agora, and that of Apollo in the Pythian precinct. The Athenian people afterwards built on to and lengthened the altar in the Agora, and obliterated the inscription; but that in the Pythian precinct can still be seen, though in faded letters, and is to the following effect:

Pisistratus, the son of Hippias,
Set up this record of his archonship
In precinct of Apollo Pythias.

55. That Hippias was the eldest son and succeeded to the government is what I positively assert as a fact upon which I have had more exact accounts than others, and may be also ascertained by the following circumstance. He is the only one of the legitimate brothers that appears to have had children; as the altar shows, and the pillar placed in the Athenian Acropolis, commemorating the crime of the tyrants, which mentions no child of Thessalus or of Hipparchus, but five of Hippias, which he had by Myrrhine, daughter of Callias, son of Hyperechides; and naturally the eldest would have married first. Again, his name comes first on the pillar after that of his father; and this too is quite natural, as he was the eldest after him, and the reigning tyrant. Nor can I ever believe that Hippias would have obtained the tyranny so easily if Hipparchus had been in power when he was killed, and he, Hippias, had had to establish himself upon the same day; but he had no doubt been long accustomed to overawe the citizens, and to be obeyed by his mercenaries, and thus not only conquered, but conquered with ease, without experiencing any of the embarrassment of a younger brother unused to the exercise of authority. It was the sad fate which made Hipparchus famous that got him also the reputation with posterity of having been tyrant.

56. To return to Harmodius; Hipparchus, having been repulsed in his solicitations, insulted him as he had resolved, by first inviting a sister of his, a young girl, to come and bear a basket in a certain procession, and then rejecting her on the plea that she had never been invited at all owing to her unworthiness. If Harmodius was indignant at this, Aristogeiton for his sake now became more exasperated than ever; and, having arranged everything with those who were to join them in the enterprise, they only waited for the feast of the Greater Panathenaea, the sole day upon which the citizens forming part of the procession could meet together in arms

without suspicion. Aristogeiton and Harmodius were to begin, but were to be supported immediately by their accomplices against the bodyguard. The conspirators were not many, for better security, besides which they hoped that those not in the plot would be carried away by the example of a few daring spirits, and use the arms in their hands to recover their liberty.

57. At last the festival arrived, and Hippias with his bodyguard was outside the city in the Ceramicus, arranging how the different parts of the procession were to proceed. Harmodius and Aristogeiton had already their daggers and were getting ready to act, when seeing one of their accomplices talking familiarly with Hippias, who was easy of access to everyone, they took fright, and concluded that they were discovered and on the point of being taken; and eager if possible to be revenged first upon the man who had wronged them and for whom they had undertaken all this risk, they rushed, as they were, within the gates, and meeting with Hipparchus by the Leocorium recklessly fell upon him at once, infuriated, Aristogeiton by love, and Harmodius by insult, and smote him and slew him. Aristogeiton escaped the guards at the moment, through the crowd running up, but was afterwards taken and dispatched in no merciful way; Harmodius was killed on the spot.

58. When the news was brought to Hippias in the Ceramicus, he at once proceeded not to the scene of action but to the armed men in the procession before they, being some distance away, knew anything of the matter, and composing his features for the occasion, so as not to betray himself, pointed to a certain spot, and bade them repair thither without their arms. They withdrew accordingly, fancying he had something to say; upon which he told the mercenaries to remove the arms, and there and then picked out the men he thought guilty and all found with daggers, the shield and spear being the usual weapons for a procession.

59. In this way offended love first led Harmodius and Aristogeiton to conspire, and the alarm of the moment to commit the rash action recounted. After this the tyranny

pressed harder on the Athenians, and Hippias, now grown more fearful, put to death many of the citizens, and at the same time began to turn his eyes abroad for a refuge in case of revolution. Thus, although an Athenian, he gave his daughter, Archedice, to Aeantides, son of Hippoclos the tyrant of Lampsacus, seeing that they had great influence with Darius. And there is her tomb in Lampsacus with this inscription:

> Archedice lies buried in this earth,
> Hippias her sire, and Athens gave her birth;
> Unto her bosom pride was never known,
> Though daughter, wife, and sister to the throne.

Hippias, after reigning three years longer over the Athenians, was deposed in the fourth by the Lacedaemonians and the banished Alcmaeonids, and went with a safe conduct to Sigeum, and to Aeantides at Lampsacus, and from thence to King Darius; from whose court he set out twenty years after, in his old age, and came with the Medes to Marathon.

60. With these events in their minds, and recalling everything they knew by hearsay on the subject, the Athenian people grew difficult of humour and suspicious of the persons charged in the affair of the mysteries, and persuaded that all that had taken place was part of an oligarchical and tyrannical conspiracy. In the state of irritation thus produced, many persons of consideration had been already thrown into prison, and, far from showing any signs of abating, public feeling grew daily more savage, and more arrests were made; until at last one of those in custody, thought to be the most guilty of all, was induced by a fellow prisoner to make a revelation, whether true or not is a matter on which there are two opinions, no one having been able, either then or since, to say for certain who did the deed. However this may be, the other found arguments to persuade him that even if he had not done it he ought to save himself by gaining a promise of impunity, and free the state of its present suspicions; as he would be surer of safety if he confessed after promise of impunity than if he denied and were brought to trial. He

accordingly made a revelation, affecting himself and others in the affair of the Hermae; and the Athenian people, glad at last, as they supposed, to get at the truth, and furious until then at not being able to discover those who had conspired against the commons, at once let go the informer and all the rest whom he had not denounced, and bringing the accused to trial executed as many as were apprehended, and condemned to death such as had fled, and set a price upon their heads. In this it was, after all, not clear whether the sufferers had been punished unjustly, while in any case the rest of the city received immediate and manifest relief.

61. To return to Alcibiades: public feeling was very hostile to him, being worked on by the same enemies who had attacked him before he went out; and now that the Athenians fancied that they had got at the truth of the matter of the Hermae, they believed more firmly than ever that the affair of the mysteries also, in which he was implicated, had been contrived by him in the same intention and was connected with the plot against the democracy. Meanwhile it so happened that, just at the time of this agitation, a small force of Lacedaemonians had advanced as far as the Isthmus, in pursuance of some scheme with the Boeotians. It was now thought that this had come by appointment, at his instigation, and not on account of the Boeotians, and that if the citizens had not acted on the information received, and forestalled them by arresting the prisoners, the city would have been betrayed. The citizens went so far as to sleep one night armed in the Theseum within the walls. The friends also of Alcibiades at Argos were just at this time suspected of a design to attack the commons; and the Argive hostages deposited in the islands were given up by the Athenians to the Argive people to be put to death upon that account; in short, everywhere something was found to create suspicion against Alcibiades. It was therefore decided to bring him to trial and execute him, and the Salaminia was sent to Sicily for him and the others named in the information, with instructions to order him to come and answer the charges against him, but not to arrest him, because they wished to avoid causing any agi-

tation in the army or among the enemy in Sicily, and above all to retain the services of the Mantineans and Argives, who, it was thought, had been induced to join by his influence.

Alcibiades, with his own ship and his fellow accused, accordingly sailed off with the Salaminia from Sicily, as though to return to Athens, and went with her as far as Thurii, and there they left the ship and disappeared, being afraid to go home for trial with such a prejudice existing against them. The crew of the Salaminia stayed some time looking for Alcibiades and his companions, and at length, as they were nowhere to be found, set sail and departed. Alcibiades, now an outlaw, crossed in a boat not long after from Thurii to the Peloponnesus; and the Athenians passed sentence of death by default upon him and those in his company.

62. The Athenian generals left in Sicily now divided the armament into two parts, and, each taking one by lot, sailed with the whole for Selinus and Egesta, wishing to know whether the Egestaeans would give the money, and to look into the question of Selinus and ascertain the state of the quarrel between her and Egesta. Coasting along Sicily, with the shore on their left, on the side towards the Tyrrhenian Gulf, they touched at Himera, the only Hellenic city in that part of the island, and being refused admission resumed their voyage. On their way they took Hyccara, a petty Sicanian seaport, nevertheless at war with Egesta, and making slaves of the inhabitants gave up the town to the Egestaeans, some of whose horse had joined them; after which the army proceeded through the territory of the Sicels until it reached Catana, while the fleet sailed along the coast with the slaves on board. Meanwhile Nicias sailed straight from Hyccara along the coast and went to Egesta, and after transacting his other business and receiving thirty talents, rejoined the forces. They now sold their slaves for the sum of one hundred and twenty talents, and sailed round to their Sicel allies to urge them to send troops; and meanwhile went with half their own force to the hostile town of Hybla in the territory

of Gela, but did not succeed in taking it. Summer was now over.

63. The winter following, the Athenians at once began to prepare for moving on Syracuse, and the Syracusans on their side for marching against them. From the moment when the Athenians failed to attack them instantly as they at first feared and expected, every day that passed did something to revive their courage; and when they saw them sailing far away from them on the other side of Sicily, and going to Hybla only to fail in their attempts to storm it, they thought less of them than ever, and called upon their generals, as the multitude is apt to do in its moments of confidence, to lead them to Catana, since the enemy would not come to them. Parties also of the Syracusan horse employed in reconnoitring constantly rode up to the Athenian armament, and among other insults asked them whether they had not really come to settle with the Syracusans in a foreign country rather than to resettle the Leontines in their own.

64. Aware of this, the Athenian generals determined to draw them out in mass as far as possible from the city, and themselves in the meantime to sail by night along shore, and take up at their leisure a convenient position. This they knew they could not so well do if they had to disembark from their ships in front of a force prepared for them, or to go by land openly. The numerous cavalry of the Syracusans (a force which they were themselves without), would then be able to do the greatest mischief to their light troops and the crowd that followed them; but this plan would enable them to take up a position in which the horse could do them no hurt worth speaking of, some Syracusan exiles with the army having told them of the spot near the Olympieum which they afterwards occupied. In pursuance of their idea, the generals imagined the following stratagem. They sent to Syracuse a man devoted to them, and by the Syracusan generals thought to be no less in their interest; he was a native of Catana, and said he came from persons in that place, whose names the Syracusan generals were acquainted with,

and whom they knew to be among the members of their party still left in the city. He told them that the Athenians passed the night in the town, at some distance from their arms, and that if the Syracusans would name a day and come with all their people at daybreak to attack the armament, they, their friends, would close the gates upon the troops in the city, and set fire to the vessels, while the Syracusans would easily take the camp by an attack upon the stockade. In this they would be aided by many of the Catanians, who were already prepared to act, and from whom he himself came.

65. The generals of the Syracusans, who did not want confidence, and who had intended even without this to march on Catana, believed the man without any sufficient inquiry, fixed at once a day upon which they would be there, and dismissed him, and, the Selinuntines and others of their allies having now arrived, gave orders for all the Syracusans to march out in mass. Their preparations completed, and the time fixed for their arrival being at hand, they set out for Catana, and passed the night upon the river Symaethus, in the Leontine territory. Meanwhile the Athenians no sooner knew of their approach than they took all their forces and such of the Sicels or others as had joined them, put them on board their ships and boats, and sailed by night to Syracuse. Thus when morning broke the Athenians were landing opposite the Olympieum ready to seize their camping ground, and the Syracusan horse, having ridden up first to Catana and found that all the armament had put to sea, turned back and told the infantry, and then all turned back together, and went to the relief of the city.

66. In the meantime, as the march before the Syracusans was a long one, the Athenians quietly sat down their army in a convenient position, where they could begin an engagement when they pleased, and where the Syracusan cavalry would have least opportunity of annoying them, either before or during the action, being fenced off on one side by walls, houses, trees, and by a marsh, and on the other by cliffs. They also felled the neighbouring trees and carried

them down to the sea, and formed a palisade alongside of their ships, and with stones which they picked up and wood hastily raised a fort at Daskon, the most vulnerable point of their position, and broke down the bridge over the Anapus. These preparations were allowed to go on without any interruption from the city, the first hostile force to appear being the Syracusan cavalry, followed afterwards by all the foot together. At first they came close up to the Athenian army, and then, finding that they did not offer to engage, crossed the Helorine road and encamped for the night.

67. The next day the Athenians and their allies prepared for battle, their dispositions being as follows: Their right wing was occupied by the Argives and Mantineans, the centre by the Athenians, and the rest of the field by the other allies. Half their army was drawn up eight deep in advance, half close to their tents in a hollow square, formed also eight deep, which had orders to look out and be ready to go to the support of the troops hardest pressed. The camp followers were placed inside this reserve. The Syracusans, meanwhile, formed their heavy infantry sixteen deep, consisting of the mass-levy of their own people, and such allies as had joined them, the strongest contingent being that of the Selinuntines; next to them the cavalry of the Geloans, numbering two hundred in all, with about twenty horse and fifty archers from Camarina. The cavalry was posted on their right, full twelve hundred strong, and next to it the darters. As the Athenians were about to begin the attack, Nicias went along the lines and addressed these words of encouragement to the army and the nations composing it:

68. "Soldiers, a long exhortation is little needed by men like ourselves, who are here to fight in the same battle, the force itself being, to my thinking, more fit to inspire confidence than a fine speech with a weak army. Where we have Argives, Mantineans, Athenians, and the first of the islanders in the ranks together, it were strange indeed, with so many and so brave companions in arms, if we did not feel confident of victory; especially when we have mass-levies opposed to our picked troops, and what is more, Sicilians,

who may disdain us but will not stand against us, their skill not being at all commensurate to their rashness. You may also remember that we are far from home and have no friendly land near, except what your own swords shall win you; and here I put before you a motive just the reverse of that which the enemy are appealing to, their cry being that they shall fight for their country, mine that we shall fight for a country that is not ours, where we must conquer or hardly get away, as we shall have their horse upon us in great numbers. Remember, therefore, your renown, and go boldly against the enemy, thinking the present strait and necessity more terrible than they."

69. After this address Nicias at once led on the army. The Syracusans were not at that moment expecting an immediate engagement, and some had even gone away to the town, which was close by; these now ran up as hard as they could, and, though behind time, took their places here or there in the main body as fast as they joined it. Want of zeal or daring was certainly not the fault of the Syracusans, either in this or the other battles, but although not inferior in courage, so far as their military science might carry them, when this failed them they were compelled to give up their resolution also. On the present occasion, although they had not supposed that the Athenians would begin the attack, and although constrained to stand upon their defence at short notice, they at once took up their arms and advanced to meet them. First, the stone-throwers, slingers, and archers of either army began skirmishing, and routed or were routed by one another, as might be expected between light troops; next, soothsayers brought forward the usual victims, and trumpeters urged on the heavy infantry to the charge; and thus they advanced, the Syracusans to fight for their country, and each individual for his safety that day and liberty hereafter; in the enemy's army, the Athenians to make another's country theirs and to save their own from suffering by their defeat; the Argives and autonomous allies to help them in getting what they came for, and to earn by victory another sight of the country they had left behind; while the subject

allies owned most of their ardour to the desire of self-preservation, which they could only hope for if victorious; next to which, as a secondary motive, came the chance of serving on easier terms, after helping the Athenians to a fresh conquest.

70. The armies now came to close quarters, and for a long while fought without either giving ground. Meanwhile there occurred some claps of thunder with lightning and heavy rain, which did not fail to add to the fears of the party fighting for the first time and very little acquainted with war; while to their more experienced adversaries these phenomena appeared to be produced by the time of year, and much more alarm was felt at the continued resistance of the enemy. At last the Argives drove in the Syracusan left, and after them the Athenians routed the troops opposed to them, and the Syracusan army was thus cut in two and betook itself to flight. The Athenians did not pursue far, being held in check by the numerous and undefeated Syracusan horse, who attacked and drove back any of their heavy infantry whom they saw pursuing in advance of the rest; in spite of which the victors followed so far as was safe in a body, and then went back and set up a trophy. Meanwhile the Syracusans rallied at the Helorine road, where they re-formed as well as they could under the circumstances, and even sent a garrison of their own citizens to the Olympieum, fearing that the Athenians might lay hands on some of the treasures there. The rest returned to the town.

71. The Athenians, however, did not go to the temple, but collected their dead and laid them upon a pyre, and passed the night upon the field. The next day they gave the enemy back their dead under truce, to the number of about two hundred and sixty, Syracusans and allies, and gathered together the bones of their own, some fifty, Athenians and allies, and, taking the spoils of the enemy, sailed back to Catana. It was now winter; and it did not seem possible for the moment to carry on the war before Syracuse until horse should have been sent for from Athens and levied among the allies in Sicily—to do away with their utter inferiority in

cavalry—and money should have been collected in the country and received from Athens, and until some of the cities, which they hoped would be now more disposed to listen to them after the battle, should have been brought over, and wheat and all other necessaries provided, for a campaign in the spring against Syracuse.

72. With this intention they sailed off to Naxos and Catana for the winter. Meanwhile the Syracusans buried their dead, and then held an assembly, in which Hermocrates, son of Hermon, a man who with a general ability of the first order had given proofs of military capacity and brilliant courage in the war, came forward and encouraged them, and told them not to let what had occurred make them give way, since their spirit had not been conquered, but their want of discipline had done the mischief. Still they had not been beaten by so much as might have been expected especially as they were, one might say, novices in the art of war, an army of amateurs opposed to the most practised soldiers in Hellas. What had also done great mischief was the number of the generals (there were fifteen of them) and the quantity of orders given, combined with the disorder and anarchy of the troops. But if they were to have a few skilful generals, and used this winter in preparing their heavy infantry, finding arms for such as had not got any, so as to make them as numerous as possible, and forcing them to attend to their training generally, they would have every chance of beating their adversaries, courage being already theirs and discipline in the field having thus been added to it. Indeed, both these qualities would improve, since danger would exercise them in discipline, while their courage would be led to surpass itself by the confidence which skill inspires. The generals should be few and elected with full powers, and an oath should be taken to leave them entire discretion in their command: if they adopted this plan, their secrets would be better kept, all preparations would be properly made, and there would be no room for excuses.

73. The Syracusans heard him, and voted everything as he advised, and elected three generals, Hermocrates him-

self, Heraclides, son of Lysimachus, and Sicanus, son of Execestes. They also sent envoys to Corinth and Lacedaemon to procure a force of allies to join them, and to induce the Lacedaemonians for their sakes openly to address themselves in real earnest to the war against the Athenians, that they might either have to leave Sicily or be less able to send reinforcements to their army there.

74. The Athenian forces at Catana now at once sailed against Messina, in the expectation of its being betrayed to them. The intrigue, however, after all came to nothing: Alcibiades, who was in the secret, when he left his command upon the summons from home, foreseeing that he would be outlawed, gave information of the plot to the friends of the Syracusans in Messina, who had at once put to death its authors, and now rose in arms against the opposite faction with those of their way of thinking, and succeeded in preventing the admission of the Athenians. The latter waited for thirteen days, and then, as they were exposed to the weather and without provisions, and met with no success, went back to Naxos, where they made places for their ships to lie in, erected a palisade round their camp, and retired into winter quarters; meanwhile they sent a trireme to Athens for money and cavalry to join them in the spring. . . .

88. . . . In the meantime, while Syracuse pursued her preparations for war, the Athenians were encamped at Naxos, and tried by negotiation to gain as many of the Sicels as possible. Those more in the low lands, and subjects of Syracuse, mostly held aloof; but the peoples of the interior who had never been otherwise than independent, with few exceptions, at once joined the Athenians, and brought down supplies to the army, and in some cases even money. The Athenians marched against those who refused to join, and forced some of them to do so; in the case of others they were stopped by the Syracusans sending garrisons and reinforcements. Meanwhile the Athenians moved their winter quarters from Naxos to Catana, and reconstructed the camp burnt by the Syracusans, and stayed there the rest of the winter. They also sent a trireme to Carthage, with proffers

of friendship, on the chance of obtaining assistance, and another to Tyrrhenia; some of the cities there having spontaneously offered to join them in the war. They also sent round to the Sicels and to Egesta, desiring them to send them as many horses as possible, and meanwhile prepared bricks, iron, and all other things necessary for the work of circumvallation, intending by the spring to begin hostilities.

In the meantime the Syracusan envoys despatched to Corinth and Lacedaemon tried as they passed along the coast to persuade the Italians to interfere with the proceedings of the Athenians, which threatened Italy quite as much as Syracuse, and having arrived at Corinth made a speech calling on the Corinthians to assist them on the ground of their common origin. The Corinthians voted at once to aid them heart and soul themselves, and then sent on envoys with them to Lacedaemon, to help them to persuade her also to prosecute the war with the Athenians more openly at home and to send aid to Sicily. The envoys from Corinth having reached Lacedaemon found there Alcibiades with his fellow refugees, who had at once crossed over in a trading vessel from Thurii, first to Cyllene in Elis, and afterwards from thence to Lacedaemon, upon the Lacedaemonians' own invitation, after first obtaining a safe conduct, as he feared them for the part he had taken in the affair of Mantinea. The result was that the Corinthians, Syracusans, and Alcibiades, pressing all the same request in the assembly of the Lacedaemonians, succeeded in persuading them; but as the ephors and the authorities, although resolved to send envoys to Syracuse to prevent their surrendering to the Athenians, showed no disposition to send them any assistance, Alcibiades now came forward and inflamed and stirred the Lacedaemonians by speaking as follows:

89. "I am forced first to speak to you of the prejudice with which I am regarded, in order that suspicion may not make you disinclined to listen to me upon public matters. The connection with you as your *proxenoi,* which the ancestors of our family by reason of some discontent renounced, I personally tried to renew by my good offices towards you,

in particular upon the occasion of the disaster at Pylos. But although I maintained this friendly attitude, you yet chose to negotiate the peace with the Athenians through my enemies, and thus to strengthen them and to discredit me. You had therefore no right to complain if I turned to the Mantineans and Argives, and seized other occasions of thwarting and injuring you; and the time has now come when those among you, who in the bitterness of the moment may have been then unfairly angry with me, should look at the matter in its true light, and take a different view. Those again who judged me unfavourably, because I leaned rather to the side of the commons, must not think that their dislike is any better founded. We have always been hostile to tyrants, and all who oppose arbitrary power are called commons; hence we continued to act as leaders of the multitude; besides which, as democracy was the government of the city, it was necessary in most things to conform to established conditions. However, we endeavoured to be more moderate than the licentious temper of the times; and while there were others, formerly as now, who tried to lead the multitude astray, the same who banished me, our party was that of the whole people, our creed being to do our part in preserving the form of government under which the city enjoyed the utmost greatness and freedom, and which we had found existing. As for democracy, the men of sense among us knew what it was, and I perhaps as well as any, as I have the more cause to complain of it; but there is nothing new to be said of a patent absurdity—meanwhile we did not think it safe to alter it under the pressure of your hostility.

90. "So much then for the prejudices with which I am regarded: I now can call your attention to the questions you must consider, and upon which superior knowledge perhaps permits me to speak. We sailed to Sicily first to conquer, if possible, the Sicilians, and after them the Italians also, and finally to assail the empire and city of Carthage. In the event of all or most of these schemes succeeding, we were then to attack the Peloponnesus, bringing with us the entire force of the Hellenes lately acquired in those parts, and taking a

number of barbarians into our pay, such as the Iberians and others in those countries, confessedly the most warlike known, and building numerous triremes in addition to those which we had already, timber being plentiful in Italy; and with this fleet blockading the Peloponnesus from the sea and assailing it with our armies by land, taking some of the cities by storm, drawing works of circumvallation round others, we hoped without difficulty to effect its reduction, and after this to rule the whole of the Hellenic name. Money and food meanwhile for the better execution of these plans were to be supplied in sufficient quantities by the newly acquired places in those countries, independently of our revenues here at home.

91. "You have thus heard the history of the present expedition from the man who most exactly knows what our objects were; and the remaining generals will, if they can, carry these out just the same. But that the states in Sicily must succumb if you do not help them, I will now show. Although the Sicilians, with all their inexperience, might even now be saved if their forces were united, the Syracusans alone, beaten already in one battle with all their people and blockaded from the sea, will be unable to withstand the Athenian armament that is now there. But if Syracuse falls, all Sicily falls also, and Italy immediately afterwards; and the danger which I just now spoke of from that quarter will before long be upon you. None need therefore fancy that Sicily only is in question; the Peloponnesus will be so also, unless you speedily do as I tell you, and send on board ship to Syracuse troops that shall be able to row their ships themselves, and serve as heavy infantry the moment that they land; and—what I consider even more important than the troops—a Spartan as commanding officer to discipline the forces already on foot and to compel recusants to serve. The friends that you have already will thus become more confident, and the waverers will be encouraged to join you.

"Meanwhile you must carry on the war here more openly, that the Syracusans, seeing that you do not forget them, may put heart into their resistance, and that the Athenians may be less able to reinforce their armament. You must fortify Decelea in Attica, the blow of which the Athenians are always most afraid and the only one that they think they have not experienced in the present war; the surest method of harming an enemy being to find out what he most fears, and to choose this means of attacking him, since everyone naturally knows best his own weak points and fears accordingly. The fortification in question, while it benefits you, will create difficulties for your adversaries, of which I shall pass over many, and shall only mention the chief. Whatever property there is in the country will most of it become yours, either by capture or surrender; and the Athenians will at once be deprived of their revenues from the silver mines at Laurium, of their present gains from their land and from the law courts, and above all of the revenue from their allies, which will be paid less regularly, as they lose their awe of Athens, and see you addressing yourselves with vigour to the war. The zeal and speed with which all this shall be done depends, Lacedaemonians, upon yourselves; as to its possibility, I am quite confident, and I have little fear of being mistaken.

92. "Meanwhile I hope that none of you will think any the worse of me if, after having hitherto passed as a lover of my country, I now actively join its worst enemies in attacking it, or will suspect what I say as the fruit of an outlaw's enthusiasm. I am an outlaw from the iniquity of those who drove me forth, not, if you will be guided by me, from your service: my worst enemies are not you who only harmed your foes, but they who forced their friends to become enemies; and love of country is what I do not feel when I am wronged, but what I felt when secure in my rights as a citizen. Indeed I do not consider that I am now attacking a country that is still mine; I am rather trying to recover one that is mine no longer; and the true lover of his country is not he who consents to lose it unjustly rather than attack it, but he who longs for it so much that he will go all lengths to recover it. For myself, therefore, Lacedaemonians, I beg you to use me without scruple for danger and trouble of

every kind, and to remember the argument in everyone's mouth, that if I did you great harm as an enemy, I could likewise do you good service as a friend, inasmuch as I know the plans of the Athenians, while I only guessed yours. For yourselves I entreat you to believe that your most capital interests are now under deliberation; and I urge you to send without hesitation the expeditions to Sicily and Attica; by the presence of a small part of your forces you will save important cities in that island, and you will destroy the power of Athens both present and prospective; after this you will dwell in security and enjoy the supremacy over all Hellas, resting not on force but upon consent and affection."

93. Such were the words of Alcibiades. The Lacedaemonians, who had themselves before intended to march against Athens, but were still waiting and looking about them, at once became much more in earnest when they received this particular information from Alcibiades, and considered that they had heard it from the man who best knew the truth of the matter. Accordingly they now turned their attention to the fortifying of Decelea and sending immediate aid to the Sicilians; and, naming Gylippus, son of Cleandridas, to the command of the Syracusans, bade him consult with that people and with the Corinthians and arrange for help reaching the island, in the best and speediest way possible under the circumstances. Gylippus desired the Corinthians to send him at once two ships to Asine, and to prepare the rest that they intended to send, and to have them ready to sail at the proper time. Having settled this, the envoys departed from Lacedaemon.

In the meantime arrived the Athenian trireme from Sicily sent by the generals for money and cavalry; and the Athenians, after hearing what they wanted, voted to send the supplies for the armament and the cavalry. And the winter ended, and with it ended the seventeenth year of the present war of which Thucydides is the historian.

From BOOK VII

The Sicilian Disaster (*413* B.C.)

· · · · ·

36. Meanwhile the Syracusans, hearing of their approach, resolved to make a second attempt with their fleet and their other forces on shore, which they had been collecting for this very purpose in order to do something before their arrival. In addition to other improvements suggested by the former sea fight which they now adopted in the equipment of their navy, they cut down their prows to a smaller compass to make them more solid and made their cheeks stouter, and from these let stays into the vessel's sides for a length of six cubits within and without, in the same way as the Corinthians had altered their prows before engaging the squadron at Naupactus. The Syracusans thought that they would thus have an advantage over the Athenian vessels, which were not constructed with equal strength, but were slight in the bows, from their being more used to sail round and charge the enemy's side than to meet him prow to prow, and that the battle being in the great harbour, with a great many ships in not much room, was also a fact in their favour. Charging prow to prow, they would stave in the enemy's bows by striking with solid and stout beaks against hollow and weak ones; and secondly, the Athenians for want of room would be unable to use their favourite manœuvre of breaking the line or of sailing round, as the Syracusans would do their best not to let them do the one, and want of room would prevent their doing the other. This charging prow to prow, which had hitherto been thought want of skill in a helmsman, would be the Syracusans' chief manœuvre, as being that which they should find most useful, since the Athenians,

if repulsed, would not be able to back water in any direction except towards the shore, and that only for a little way, and in the little space in front of their own camp. The rest of the harbour would be commanded by the Syracusans; and the Athenians, if hard pressed, by crowding together in a small space and all to the same point, would run foul of one another and fall into disorder, which was, in fact, the thing that did the Athenians most harm in all the sea fights, they not having, like the Syracusans, the whole harbour to retreat over. As to their sailing round into the open sea, this would be impossible with the Syracusans in possession of the way out and in, especially as Plemmyrium would be hostile to them, and the mouth of the harbour was not large.

37. With these contrivances to suit their skill and ability, and now more confident after the previous sea fight, the Syracusans attacked by land and sea at once. The town force Gylippus led out a little first and brought them up to the wall of the Athenians, where it looked towards the city, while the force from the Olympieum, that is to say, the heavy infantry that were there with the horse and the light troops of the Syracusans, advanced against the wall from the opposite side, the ships of the Syracusans and allies sailing out immediately afterwards. The Athenians at first fancied that they were to be attacked by land only, and it was not without alarm that they saw the fleet suddenly approaching as well; and while some were forming upon the walls and in front of them against the advancing enemy, and some marching out in haste against the numbers of horse and darters coming from the Olympieum and from outside, others manned the ships or rushed down to the beach to oppose the enemy, and when the ships were manned put out with seventy-five sail against about eighty of the Syracusans.

38. After spending a great part of the day in advancing and retreating and skirmishing with each other, without either being able to gain any advantage worth speaking of, except that the Syracusans sank one or two of the Athenian vessels, they parted, the land force at the same time retiring from the lines. The next day the Syracusans remained quiet,

and gave no signs of what they were going to do; but Nicias, seeing that the battle had been a drawn one, and expecting that they would attack again, compelled the captains to refit any of the ships that had suffered, and moored merchant vessels before the stockade which they had driven into the sea in front of their ships, to serve instead of an enclosed harbour, at about two hundred feet from each other, in order that any ship that was hard pressed might be able to retreat in safety and sail out again at leisure. These preparations occupied the Athenians all day until nightfall.

39. The next day the Syracusans began operations at an earlier hour, but with the same plan of attack by land and sea. A great part of the day the rivals spent as before, confronting and skirmishing with each other; until at last Ariston, son of Pyrrhicus, a Corinthian, the ablest helmsman in the Syracusan service, persuaded their naval commanders to send to the officials in the city, and tell them to move the market as quickly as they could down to the sea, and oblige everyone to bring whatever eatables he had and sell them there, thus enabling the commanders to land the crews and dine at once close to the ships, and shortly afterwards, the selfsame day, to attack the Athenians again when they were not expecting it.

40. In compliance with this advice a messenger was sent and the market got ready, upon which the Syracusans suddenly backed water and withdrew to the town, and at once landed and took their dinner upon the spot; while the Athenians, supposing that they had returned to the town because they felt they were beaten, disembarked at their leisure and set about getting their dinners and about their other occupations, under the idea that they had done with naval fighting for that day. Suddenly the Syracusans manned their ships and again sailed against them; and the Athenians, in great confusion and most of them fasting, got on board, and with great difficulty put out to meet them. For some time both parties remained on the defensive without engaging, until the Athenians at last resolved not to let themselves be worn out by waiting where they were, but to attack without delay,

and, giving a cheer, went into action. The Syracusans received them, and, charging prow to prow as they had intended, stove in a great part of the Athenian foreships by the strength of their beaks; the darters on the decks also did great damage to the Athenians, but still greater damage was done by the Syracusans who went about in small boats, ran in upon the oars of the Athenian triremes, and sailed against their sides, and discharged from thence their darts upon the sailors.

41. At last, fighting hard in this fashion, the Syracusans gained the victory, and the Athenians turned and fled between the merchantmen to their own station. The Syracusan ships pursued them as far as the merchantmen, where they were stopped by the beams armed with dolphins suspended from those vessels over the passage. Two of the Syracusan vessels went too near in the excitement of victory and were smashed, one of them being taken with its crew. After sinking seven of the Athenian vessels and disabling many, and taking most of the men prisoners and killing others, the Syracusans retired and set up trophies for both the engagements, being now confident of having a decided superiority by sea, and by no means despairing of equal success by land.

92. In the meantime, while the Syracusans were preparing for a second attack upon both elements, Demosthenes and Eurymedon arrived with reinforcements from Athens, consisting of about seventy-three ships, including the foreigners; nearly five thousand heavy infantry, Athenian and allied; a large number of darters, Hellenic and barbarian; and slingers and archers and everything else upon a corresponding scale. The Syracusans and their allies were for the moment not a little dismayed at the idea that there was to be no term or ending to their dangers, seeing, in spite of the fortification of Decelea, a new army arrive nearly equal to the former, and the power of Athens proving so great in every quarter. On the other hand, the first Athenian armament regained a certain confidence in the midst of its misfortunes.

Demosthenes, seeing how matters stood, felt that he could

not drag on and fare as Nicias had done, who by wintering in Catana instead of at once attacking Syracuse had allowed the terror of his first arrival to evaporate in contempt, and had given time to Gylippus to arrive with a force from the Peloponnesus, which the Syracusans would never have sent for if he had attacked immediately; for they fancied that they were a match for him by themselves, and would not have discovered their inferiority until they were already invested, and even if they then sent for help, they would no longer have been equally able to profit by their arrival. Recollecting this, and well aware that it was now on the first day after his arrival that he like Nicias was most formidable to the enemy, Demosthenes determined to lose no time in drawing the utmost profit from the consternation at the moment inspired by his army; and seeing that the counterwall of the Syracusans, which hindered the Athenians from investing them, was a single one, and that he who should become master of the way up to Epipolae, and afterwards of the camp there, would find no difficulty in taking it, as no one would even wait for his attack, made all haste to attempt the enterprise. This he took to be the shortest way of ending the war, as he would either succeed and take Syracuse or would lead back the armament instead of frittering away the lives of the Athenians engaged in the expedition and the resources of the country at large.

First therefore the Athenians went out and laid waste the lands of the Syracusans about the Anapus and carried all before them as at first by land and by sea, the Syracusans not offering to oppose them upon either element, unless it were with their cavalry and darters from the Olympieum.

43. Next Demosthenes resolved to attempt the counterwall first by means of engines. As however the engines that he brought up were burnt by the enemy fighting from the wall, and the rest of the forces repulsed after attacking at many different points, he determined to delay no longer, and, having obtained the consent of Nicias and his fellow commanders, proceeded to put in execution his plan of attacking Epipolae. As by day it seemed impossible to ap-

proach and get up without being observed, he ordered provisions for five days, took all the masons and carpenters, and other things, such as arrows, and everything else that they could want for the work of fortification if successful; and after the first watch set out with Eurymedon and Menander and the whole army for Epipolae, Nicias being left behind in the lines. Having come up by the hill of Euryelus (where the former army had ascended at first), unobserved by the enemy's guards, they went up to the fort which the Syracusans had there, and took it, and put to the sword part of the garrison. The greater number, however, escaped at once and gave the alarm to the camps, of which there were three upon Epipolae, defended by outworks, one of the Syracusans, one of the other Sicilians, and one of the allies; and also to the six hundred Syracusans forming the original garrison for this part of Epipolae. These at once advanced against the assailants, and falling in with Demosthenes and the Athenians, were routed by them after a sharp resistance, the victors immediately pushing on, eager to achieve the objects of the attack without giving time for their ardour to cool; meanwhile others from the very beginning were taking the counterwall of the Syracusans, which was abandoned by its garrison, and pulling down the battlements. The Syracusans and the allies, and Gylippus with the troops under his command, advanced to the rescue from the outworks, but engaged in some consternation (a night attack being a piece of audacity which they had never expected), and were at first compelled to retreat. But while the Athenians, flushed with their victory, now advanced with less order, wishing to make their way as quickly as possible through the whole force of the enemy not yet engaged, without relaxing their attack or giving them time to rally, the Boeotians made the first stand against them, attacked them, routed them, and put them to flight.

44. The Athenians now fell into great disorder and perplexity, so that it was not easy to get from one side or the other any detailed account of the affair. By day certainly the combatants have a clearer notion, though even then by no

means of all that takes place, no one knowing much of anything that does not go on in his own immediate neighbourhood; but in a night engagement (and this was the only one that occurred between great armies during the war) how could anyone know anything for certain? Although there was a bright moon they saw each other only as men do by moonlight, that is to say, they could distinguish the form of the body, but could not tell for certain whether it was a friend or an enemy. Both had great numbers of heavy infantry moving about in a small space. Some of the Athenians were already defeated, while others were coming up yet unconquered for their first attack. A large part also of the rest of their forces either had only just got up or were still ascending, so that they did not know which way to march.

Owing to the rout that had taken place, all in front was now in confusion, and the noise made it difficult to distinguish anything. The victorious Syracusans and allies were cheering each other on with loud cries, by night the only possible means of communication, and meanwhile receiving all who came against them; while the Athenians were seeking for one another, taking all in front of them for enemies, even although they might be some of their now flying friends; and by constantly asking for the watchword, which was their only means of recognition, not only caused great confusion among themselves by asking all at once, but also made it known to the enemy, whose own they did not so readily discover, as the Syracusans were victorious and not scattered, and thus less easily mistaken. The result was that if the Athenians fell in with a party of the enemy that was weaker than they, it escaped them through knowing their watchword; while if they themselves failed to answer they were put to the sword. But what hurt them as much, or indeed more than anything else, was the singing of the paean, from the perplexity which it caused by being nearly the same on either side: the Argives and Corcyraeans and any other Dorian peoples in their own army struck terror into the Athenians whenever they raised their paean, no less than did the enemy.

Thus, after being once thrown into disorder, they ended

by coming into collision with each other in many parts of the field, friends with friends, and citizens with citizens, and not only terrified one another, but even came to blows and could only be parted with difficulty. In the pursuit many perished by throwing themselves down the cliffs, the way down from Epipolae being narrow; and of those who got down safely into the plain, although many, especially those who belonged to the first armament, escaped through their better acquaintance with the locality, some of the newcomers lost their way and wandered over the country, and were cut off in the morning by the Syracusan cavalry and killed.

45. The next day the Syracusans set up two trophies, one upon Epipolae where the ascent had been made, and the other on the spot where the first check was given by the Boeotians; and the Athenians took back their dead under truce. A great many of the Athenians and allies were killed, although still more arms were taken than could be accounted for by the number of the dead, as some of those who were obliged to leap down from the cliffs without their shields escaped with their lives and did not perish like the rest.

46. After this the Syracusans, recovering their old confidence at such an unexpected stroke of good fortune, despatched Sicanus with fifteen ships to Agrigentum where there was a revolution, to induce if possible the city to join them; while Gylippus again went by land into the rest of Sicily to bring up reinforcements, being now in hope of taking the Athenian lines by storm, after the result of the affair on Epipolae.

47. In the meantime the Athenian generals consulted upon the disaster which had happened, and upon the general weakness of the army. They saw themselves unsuccessful in their enterprises, and the soldiers disgusted with their stay, disease being rife among them owing to its being the sickly season of the year, and to the marshy and unhealthy nature of the spot in which they were encamped, and the state of their affairs generally being thought desperate. Accordingly, Demosthenes was of opinion that they ought not to stay any longer; but agreeably to his original idea in risk-

ing the attempt upon Epipolae, now that this had failed, he gave his vote for going away without further loss of time, while the sea might yet be crossed, and their late reinforcement might give them the superiority at all events on that element. He also said that it would be more profitable for the state to carry on the war against those who were building fortifications in Attica than against the Syracusans whom it was no longer easy to subdue, besides which it was not right to squander large sums of money to no purpose by going on with the siege.

48. This was the opinion of Demosthenes. Nicias, without denying the bad state of their affairs, was unwilling to avow their weakness, or to have it reported to the enemy that the Athenians in full council were openly voting for retreat; for in that case they would be much less likely to effect it when they wanted without discovery. Moreover, his own particular information still gave him reason to hope that the affairs of the enemy would soon be in a worse state than their own, if the Athenians persevered in the siege; as they would wear out the Syracusans by want of money, especially with the more extensive command of the sea now given them by their present navy. Besides this, there was a party in Syracuse who wished to betray the city to the Athenians, and kept sending him messages and telling him not to raise the siege.

Accordingly, knowing this and really waiting because he hesitated between the two courses and wished to see his way more clearly, in his public speech on this occasion he refused to lead off the army, saying he was sure the Athenians would never approve of their returning without a vote of theirs. Those who would vote upon their conduct, instead of judging the facts as eyewitnesses like themselves and not from what they might hear from hostile critics, would simply be guided by the calumnies of the first clever speaker; while many, indeed most, of the soldiers on the spot, who now so loudly proclaimed the danger of their position, when they reached Athens would proclaim just as loudly the opposite, and would say that their generals had been bribed to betray them and return. For himself, therefore, who knew the Athenian temper, sooner than perish under a dishonourable charge and by an unjust sentence at the hands of the Athenians, he would rather take his chance and die, if die he must, a soldier's death at the hand of the enemy. Besides, after all, the Syracusans were in a worse case than themselves. What with paying mercenaries, spending upon fortified posts, and now for a full year maintaining a large navy, they were already at a loss and would soon be at a standstill: they had already spent two thousand talents and incurred heavy debts besides, and could not lose even ever so small a fraction of their present force through not paying it, without ruin to their cause; depending as they did more upon mercenaries than upon soldiers obliged to serve, like their own. He therefore said that they ought to stay and carry on the siege, and not depart defeated in point of money, in which they were much superior.

49. Nicias spoke positively because he had exact information of the financial distress at Syracuse, and also because of the strength of the Athenian party there which kept sending him messages not to raise the siege; besides which he had more confidence than before in his fleet, and felt sure at least of its success. Demosthenes, however, would not hear for a moment of continuing the siege, but said that if they could not lead off the army without a decree from Athens, and if they were obliged to stay on, they ought to remove to Thapsus or Catana; where their land forces would have a wide extent of country to overrun, and could live by plundering the enemy, and would thus do them damage; while the fleet would have the open sea to fight in, that is to say, instead of a narrow space which was all in the enemy's favour, a wide sea-room where their science would be of use, and where they could retreat or advance without being confined or circumscribed either when they put out or put in. In any case he was altogether opposed to their staying on where they were, and insisted on removing at once, as quickly and with as little delay as possible; and in this judgement Eurymedon agreed. Nicias however still objecting, a certain diffidence

and hesitation came over them, with a suspicion that Nicias might have some further information to make him so positive. The Athenians therefore lingered on without moving from where they were.

50. Gylippus and Sicanus now arrived at Syracuse. Sicanus had failed to gain Agrigentum, the party friendly to the Syracusans having been driven out while he was still at Gela; but Gylippus was accompanied not only by a large number of troops raised in Sicily, but by the heavy infantry sent off in the spring from the Peloponnesus in the merchantmen, who had arrived at Selinus from Libya. They had been carried to Libya by a storm, and, having obtained two triremes and pilots from the Cyrenians, on their voyage along shore had taken sides with the Euesperitae and had defeated the Libyans who were besieging them, and from thence coasting on to Neapolis, a Carthaginian mart, and the nearest point to Sicily, from which it is only two days' and a night's voyage, there crossed over and came to Selinus. Immediately upon their arrival the Syracusans prepared to attack the Athenians again by land and sea at once. The Athenian generals, seeing a fresh army come to the aid of the enemy, and that their own circumstances, far from improving, were becoming daily worse, and above all distressed by the sickness of the soldiers, now began to repent of not having removed before; and Nicias no longer offering the same opposition, except by urging that there should be no open voting, they gave orders as secretly as possible for all to be prepared to sail out from the camp at a given signal. All was at last ready, and they were on the point of sailing away, when an eclipse of the moon, which was then at the full, took place. Most of the Athenians, deeply impressed by this occurrence, now urged the generals to wait; and Nicias, who was somewhat over-addicted to divination and practices of that kind, refused from that moment even to take the question of departure into consideration until they had waited the thrice nine days prescribed by the soothsayers.

51. The besiegers were thus condemned to stay in the country; and the Syracusans, getting wind of what had hap-

pened, became more eager than ever to press the Athenians, who had now themselves acknowledged that they were no longer their superiors either by sea or by land, as otherwise they would never have planned to sail away. Besides which the Syracusans did not wish them to settle in any other part of Sicily, where they would be more difficult to deal with, but desired to force them to fight at sea as quickly as possible in a position favourable to themselves. Accordingly they manned their ships and practised for as many days as they thought sufficient. When the moment arrived they assaulted on the first day the Athenian lines, and, upon a small force of heavy infantry and horse sallying out against them by certain gates, cut off some of the former and routed and pursued them to the lines, where, as the entrance was narrow, the Athenians lost seventy horses and some few of the heavy infantry.

52. Drawing off their troops for this day, on the next the Syracusans went out with a fleet of seventy-six sail, and at the same time advanced with their land forces against the lines. The Athenians put out to meet them with eighty-six ships, came to close quarters, and engaged. The Syracusans and their allies first defeated the Athenian center and then caught Eurymedon, the commander of the right wing, who was sailing out from the line more towards the land in order to surround the enemy, in the hollow and recess of the harbour, and killed him and destroyed the ships accompanying him; after which they now chased the whole Athenian fleet before them and drove them ashore.

53. Gylippus, seeing the enemy's fleet defeated and carried ashore beyond their stockades and camp, ran down to the breakwater with some of his troops, in order to cut off the men as they landed and make it easier for the Syracusans to tow off the vessels near a shore that was friendly. The Tyrrhenians who guarded this point for the Athenians, seeing them come on in disorder, advanced out against them and attacked and routed their van, hurling it into the marsh of Lysimeleia. Afterwards the Syracusan and allied troops arrived in greater numbers, and the Athenians fearing

for their ships came up also to the rescue and engaged them, and defeated and pursued them to some distance and killed a few of their heavy infantry. They succeeded in rescuing most of their ships and brought them down by their camp; eighteen however were taken by the Syracusans and their allies, and all the men killed. The rest the enemy tried to burn by means of an old merchantman which they filled with faggots and pine-wood, set on fire, and let drift down the wind which blew full on the Athenians. The Athenians, however, alarmed for their ships, contrived means for stopping it and putting it out, and, checking the flames and the nearer approach of the merchantman, thus escaped the danger.

54. After this the Syracusans set up a trophy for the sea fight and for the heavy infantry whom they had cut off up at the lines, where they took the horses; and the Athenians for the rout of the foot driven by the Tyrrhenians into the marsh, and for their own victory with the rest of the army.

55. The Syracusans had now gained a decisive victory at sea, where until now they had feared the reinforcement brought by Demosthenes, and deep, in consequence, was the despondency of the Athenians, and great their disappointment, and greater still their regret for having come on the expedition. These were the only cities that they had yet encountered, similar to their own in character, under democracies like themselves, which had ships and horses, and were of considerable magnitude. They had been unable to divide and bring them over by holding out the prospect of changes in their governments, or to crush them by their great superiority in force, but had failed in most of their attempts, and, being already in perplexity, had now been defeated at sea, where defeat could never have been expected, and were thus plunged deeper in embarrassment than ever.

56. Meanwhile the Syracusans immediately began to sail freely along the harbour, and determined to close up its mouth, so that the Athenians might not be able to steal out in future even if they wished. Indeed, the Syracusans no

longer thought only of saving themselves, but also how to hinder the escape of the enemy; thinking, and thinking rightly, that they were now much the strongest, and that to conquer the Athenians and their allies by land and sea would win them great glory in Hellas. The rest of the Hellenes would thus immediately be either freed or released from apprehension, as the remaining forces of Athens would be henceforth unable to sustain the war that would be waged against her; while they, the Syracusans, would be regarded as the authors of this deliverance, and would be held in high admiration, not only with all men now living but also with posterity. Nor were these the only considerations that gave dignity to the struggle. They would thus conquer not only the Athenians but also their numerous allies, and conquer not alone, but with their companions-in-arms, commanding side by side with the Corinthians and Lacedaemonians, having offered their city to stand in the van of danger, and having been in a great measure the pioneers of naval success. Indeed, there were never so many peoples assembled before a single city, if we except the grand total gathered together in this war under Athens and Lacedaemon. . . .

59. . . . It was no wonder, therefore, if the Syracusans thought that it would win them great glory if they could follow up their recent victory in the sea fight by the capture of the whole Athenian armada, without letting it escape either by sea or by land. They began at once to close up the great harbour by means of boats, merchant vessels, and triremes moored broadside across its mouth, which is nearly a mile wide, and made all their other arrangements for the event of the Athenians again venturing to fight at sea. There was, in fact, nothing little in either their plans or their ideas.

60. The Athenians, seeing them closing up the harbour and perceiving their further designs, called a council of war. The generals and taxiarchs assembled and discussed the difficulties of the situation, the point which pressed most being that they no longer had provisions for immediate use (having sent on to Catana to tell them not to send any, in the

belief that they were going away), and that they would not have any in future unless they could command the sea. They therefore determined to evacuate their upper lines, to enclose with a cross-wall and garrison a small space close to the ships, only just sufficient to hold their stores and sick, and manning all the ships, seaworthy or not, with every man that could be spared from the rest of their land forces, to fight it out at sea, and if victorious, to go to Catana, if not, to burn their vessels, form in close order, and retreat by land for the nearest friendly place they could reach, Hellenic or barbarian. This was no sooner settled than carried into effect: they descended gradually from the upper lines and manned all their vessels, compelling all to go on board who were of age to be in any way of use. They thus succeeded in manning about one hundred and ten ships in all, on board of which they embarked a large number of archers and darters taken from the Acarnanians and from the other foreigners, making all other provisions allowed by the nature of their plan and by the necessities which imposed it. All was now nearly ready, and Nicias, seeing the soldiery disheartened by their unprecedented and decided defeat at sea, and by reason of the scarcity of provisions eager to fight it out as soon as possible, called them all together, and first addressed them, speaking as follows:

61. "Soldiers of the Athenians and of the allies, we have all an equal interest in the coming struggle, in which life and country are at stake for us quite as much as they can be for the enemy; since if our fleet wins the day, each can see his native city again, wherever that city may be. You must not lose heart, or be like men without any experience who fail in a first essay and ever afterwards fearfully forebode a future as disastrous. But let the Athenians among you who have already had experience of many wars, and the allies who have joined us in so many expeditions, remember the surprises of war, and, with the hope that fortune will not be always against us, prepare to fight again in a manner worthy of the number which you see yourselves to be.

62. "Now, whatever we thought would be of service

against the crush of vessels in such a narrow harbour, and against the force upon the decks of the enemy, from which we suffered before, has all been considered with the helmsmen, and, as far as our means allowed, provided. A number of archers and darters will go on board, and a multitude that we should not have employed in an action in the open sea, where our science would be crippled by the weight of the vessels; but in the present land fight that we are forced to make from shipboard all this will be useful. We have also discovered the changes in construction that we must make to meet theirs; and against the thickness of their cheeks, which did us the greatest mischief, we have provided grappling-irons, which will prevent an assailant backing water after charging, if the soldiers on deck here do their duty; since we are absolutely compelled to fight a land battle from the fleet, and it seems to be our interest neither to back water ourselves, nor to let the enemy do so, especially as the shore, except so much of it as may be held by our troops, is hostile ground.

63. "You must remember this and fight on as long as you can, and must not let yourselves be driven ashore, but once alongside must make up your minds not to part company until you have swept the heavy infantry from the enemy's deck. I say this more for the heavy infantry than for the seamen, as it is more the business of the men on deck; and our land forces are even now on the whole the strongest. The sailors I advise, and at the same time implore, not to be too much daunted by their misfortunes, now that we have our decks better armed and a greater number of vessels. Bear in mind how well worth preserving is the pleasure felt by those of you who through your knowledge of our language and imitation of our manners were always considered Athenians, even though not so in reality, and as such were honoured throughout Hellas, and had your full share of the advantages of our empire, and more than your share in the respect of our subjects and in protection from ill treatment. You, therefore, with whom alone we freely share our empire, we now justly require not to betray that empire in its

extremity, and in scorn of Corinthians, whom you have often conquered, and of Sicilians, none of whom so much as presumed to stand against us when our navy was in its prime, we ask you to repel them, and to show that even in sickness and disaster your skill is more than a match for the fortune and vigour of any other.

64. "For the Athenians among you, I add once more this reflection: you left behind you no more such ships in your docks as these, no more heavy infantry in their flower; if you do aught but conquer, our enemies here will immediately sail thither, and those that are left of us at Athens will become unable to repel their home assailants, reinforced by these new allies. Here you will fall at once into the hands of the Syracusans—I need not remind you of the intentions with which you attacked them—and your countrymen at home will fall into those of the Lacedaemonians. Since the fate of both thus hangs upon this single battle, now, if ever, stand firm, and remember, each and all, that you who are now going on board are the army and navy of the Athenians, and all that is left of the state and the great name of Athens, in whose defence if any man has any advantage in skill or courage, now is the time for him to show it, and thus serve himself and save all."

65. After this address Nicias at once gave orders to man the ships. Meanwhile Gylippus and the Syracusans could perceive by the preparations which they saw going on that the Athenians meant to fight at sea. They had also notice of the grappling-irons, against which they specially provided by stretching hides over the prows and much of the upper part of their vessels, in order that the irons when thrown might slip off without taking hold. All being now ready, the generals and Gylippus addressed them in the following terms:

66. "Syracusans and allies, the glorious character of our past achievements and the no less glorious results at issue in the coming battle are, we think, understood by most of you, or you would never have thrown yourselves with such ardour into the struggle; and if there be anyone not as fully

aware of the facts as he ought to be, we will declare them to him. The Athenians came to this country first to effect the conquest of Sicily, and after that, if successful, of the Peloponnesus and the rest of Hellas, possessing already the greatest empire yet known, of present or former times, among the Hellenes. Here for the first time they found in you men who faced their navy which made them masters everywhere; you have already defeated them in the previous sea fights, and will in all likelihood defeat them again now. When men are once checked in what they consider their special excellence, their whole opinion of themselves suffers more than if they had not at first believed in their superiority, the unexpected shock to their pride causing them to give way more than their real strength warrants; and this is probably now the case with the Athenians.

67. "With us it is different. The original estimate of ourselves which gave us courage in the days of our unskilfulness has been strengthened, while the conviction super-added to it that we must be the best seamen of the time, if we have conquered the best, has given a double measure of hope to every man among us; and, for the most part, where there is the greatest hope, there is also the greatest ardour for action. The means to combat us which they have tried to find in copying our armament are familiar to us and will be met by proper provisions; while they will never be able to have a number of heavy infantry on their decks, contrary to their custom, and a number of darters (born landsmen, one may say, Acarnanians and others, embarked afloat, who will not know how to discharge their weapons when they have to keep still), without hampering their vessels and falling all into confusion among themselves through fighting not according to their own tactics. For they will gain nothing by the number of their ships—I say this to those of you who may be alarmed by having to fight against odds—as a quantity of ships in a confined space will only be slower in executing the movements required, and most exposed to injury from our means of offence. Indeed, if you would know the plain truth, as we are credibly informed, the excess of their

sufferings and the necessities of their present distress have made them desperate; they have no confidence in their force, but wish to try their fortune in the only way they can, and either to force their passage and sail out, or after this to retreat by land, it being impossible for them to be worse off than they are.

68. "The fortune of our greatest enemies having thus betrayed itself, and their disorder being what I have described, let us engage in anger, convinced that, as between adversaries, nothing is more legitimate than to claim to sate the whole wrath of one's soul in punishing the aggressor, and nothing more sweet, as the proverb has it, than the vengeance upon an enemy, which it will now be ours to take. That enemies they are and mortal enemies you all know, since they came here to enslave our country, and if successful had in reserve for our men all that is most dreadful, and for our children and wives all that is most dishonourable, and for the whole city the name which conveys the greatest reproach. None should therefore relent or think it gain if they go away without further danger to us. This they will do just the same, even if they get the victory; while if we succeed, as we may expect, in chastising them, and in handing down to all Sicily her ancient freedom strengthened and confirmed, we shall have achieved no mean triumph. And the rarest dangers are those in which failure brings little loss and success the greatest advantage."

69. After the above address to the soldiers on their side, the Syracusan generals and Gylippus now perceived that the Athenians were manning their ships, and immediately proceeded to man their own also. Meanwhile Nicias, appalled by the position of affairs, realizing the greatness and the nearness of the danger now that they were on the point of putting out from shore, and thinking, as men are apt to think in great crises, that when all has been done they have still something left to do, and when all has been said that they have not yet said enough, again called on the trierachs one by one, addressing each by his father's name and by his own, and by that of his tribe, and adjured them not to belie their

own personal renown, or to obscure the hereditary virtues for which their ancestors were illustrious; he reminded them of their country, the freest of the free, and of the unfettered discretion allowed in it to all to live as they pleased; and added other arguments such as men would use at such a crisis, and which, with little alteration, are made to serve on all occasions alike—appeals to wives, children, and national gods—without caring whether they are thought common-place, but loudly invoking them in the belief that they will be of use in the consternation of the moment. Having thus admonished them, not, he felt, as he would, but as he could, Nicias withdrew and led the troops to the sea, and ranged them in as long a line as he was able, in order to aid as far as possible in sustaining the courage of the men afloat; while Demosthenes, Menander, and Euthydemus, who took the command on board, put out from their own camp and sailed straight to the barrier across the mouth of the harbour and to the passage left open, to try to force their way out.

70. The Syracusans and their allies had already put out with about the same number of ships as before, a part of which kept guard at the outlet, and the remainder all round the rest of the harbour, in order to attack the Athenians on all sides at once; while the land forces held themselves in readiness at the points at which the vessels might put in to the shore. The Syracusan fleet was commanded by Sicanus and Agatharchus, who had each a wing of the whole force, with Pythen and the Corinthians in the centre. When the rest of the Athenians came up to the barrier, with the first shock of their charge they overpowered the ships stationed there, and tried to undo the fastenings; after this, as the Syracusans and allies bore down upon them from all quarters, the action spread from the barrier over the whole harbour, and was more obstinately disputed than any of the preceding ones.

On either side the rowers showed great zeal in bringing up their vessels at the boatswains' orders, and the helmsmen great skill in manœuvring, and great emulation one with another; while, the ships once alongside, the soldiers on board did their best not to let the service on deck be outdone by the others; in short, every man strove to prove himself the first in his particular department. And as many ships were engaged in a small compass (for these were the largest fleets fighting in the narrowest space ever known, being together little short of two hundred), the regular attacks with the beak were few, there being no opportunity of backing water or of breaking the line; while the collisions caused by one ship chancing to run foul of another, either in flying from or attacking a third, were more frequent. So long as a vessel was coming up to the charge the men on the decks rained darts and arrows and stones upon her; but once alongside, the heavy infantry tried to board each other's vessel, fighting hand to hand. In many quarters also it happened, by reason of the narrow room, that a vessel was charging an enemy on one side and being charged herself on another, and that two or sometimes more ships had perforce got entangled round one, obliging the helmsmen to attend to defence here, offence there, not to one thing at once, but to many on all sides; while the huge din caused by the number of ships crashing together not only spread terror, but made the orders of the boatswains inaudible. The boatswains on either side in the discharge of their duty and in the heat of the conflict shouted incessantly orders and appeals to their men; the Athenians they urged to force the passage out, and now if ever to show their mettle and lay hold of a safe return to their country; to the Syracusans and their allies they cried that it would be glorious to prevent the escape of the enemy, and, conquering, to exalt the countries that were theirs. The generals, moreover, on either side, if they saw any in any part of the battle backing ashore without being forced to do so, called out to the trierarch by name and asked him—the Athenians, whether they were retreating because they thought the thrice hostile shore more their own than that sea which had cost them so much labour to win; the Syracusans, whether they were flying from the flying Athenians, whom they well knew to be eager to escape in whatever way they could.

71. Meanwhile the two armies on shore, while victory hung in the balance, were a prey to the most agonizing and conflicting emotions, the natives thirsting for more glory than they had already won, while the invaders feared to find themselves in even worse plight than before. Since all the Athenians were set upon their fleet, their fear for the event was like nothing they had ever felt; while their view of the struggle was necessarily as checkered as the battle itself. Close to the scene of action and not all looking at the same point at once, some saw their friends victorious and took courage, and fell to calling upon heaven not to deprive them of salvation, while others who had their eyes turned upon the losers wailed and cried aloud, and, although spectators, were more overcome than the actual combatants. Others, again, were gazing at some spot where the battle was evenly disputed; as the strife was protracted without decision, their swaying bodies reflected the agitation of their minds, and they suffered the worst agony of all, ever just within reach of safety or just on the point of destruction. In short, in that one Athenian army as long as the sea fight remained doubtful there was every sound to be heard at once, shrieks, cheers, 'We win,' 'We lose,' and all the other manifold exclamations that a great host would necessarily utter in great peril.

And with the men in the fleet it was nearly the same, until at last the Syracusans and their allies, after the battle had lasted a long while, put the Athenians to flight, and with much shouting and cheering chased them in open rout to the shore. The naval force, one one way, one another, as many as were not taken afloat, now ran ashore and rushed from on board their ships to their camp; while the army, no more divided, but carried away by one impulse, all with shrieks and groans deplored the event, and ran down, some to help the ships, others to guard what was left of their wall, while the remaining and most numerous part already began to consider how they should save themselves. Indeed, the panic of the present moment had never been surpassed. They now suffered very nearly what they had inflicted at Pylos; as then the Lacedaemonians with the loss of their fleet lost also the men who had crossed over to the island, so now the Athenians had no hope of escaping by land without the help of some extraordinary accident.

72. The sea fight having been a severe one, and many ships and lives having been lost on both sides, the victorious Syracusans and their allies now picked up their wrecks and dead, and sailed off to the city and set up a trophy. The Athenians, overwhelmed by their misfortune, never even thought of asking leave to take up their dead or wrecks, but wished to retreat that very night. Demosthenes, however, went to Nicias and gave it as his opinion that they should man the ships they had left and make another effort to force their passage out next morning; saying that they had still left more ships fit for service than the enemy, the Athenians having about sixty remaining as against less than fifty of their opponents. Nicias was quite of his mind; but when they wished to man the vessels, the sailors refused to go on board, being so utterly overcome by their defeat as no longer to believe in the possibility of success. Accordingly they all now made up their minds to retreat by land.

73. Meanwhile the Syracusan Hermocrates suspecting their intention, and impressed by the danger of allowing a force of that magnitude to retire by land, establish itself in some other part of Sicily, and from thence renew the war, went and stated his views to the authorities, and pointed out to them that they ought not to let the enemy get away by night, but that all the Syracusans and their allies should at once march out and block up the roads and seize and guard the passes. The authorities were entirely of his opinion, and thought that it ought to be done, but on the other hand felt sure that the people, who had given themselves over to rejoicing and were taking their ease after a great battle at sea, would not be easily brought to obey; besides, they were celebrating a festival, having on that day a sacrifice to Heracles, and most of them in their rapture at the victory had fallen to drinking at the festival, and would probably consent to anything sooner than to take up their arms and march out at that moment. For these reasons the thing appeared impracticable

to the magistrates; and Hermocrates, finding himself unable to do anything further with them, had now recourse to the following stratagem of his own. What he feared was that the Athenians might quietly get the start of them by passing the most difficult places during the night; and he therefore sent, as soon as it was dusk, some friends of his own to the camp with some horsemen who rode up within earshot and called out to some of the men, as though they were well-wishers of the Athenians, and told them to tell Nicias (who had in fact some correspondents who informed him of what went on inside the town), not to lead off the army by night as the Syracusans were guarding the roads, but to make his preparations at his leisure and to retreat by day. After saying this they departed; and their hearers informed the Athenian generals.

74. The generals put off going for that night on the strength of this message, not doubting its sincerity. Then, since they had not set out at once, they determined to stay also the following day to give time to the soldiers to pack up as well as they could the most useful articles, and, leaving everything else behind, to start only with what was strictly necessary for their personal subsistence. Meanwhile the Syracusans and Gylippus marched out and blocked up the roads through the country by which the Athenians were likely to pass, and kept guard at the fords of the streams and rivers, posting themselves so as to receive them and stop the army where they thought best; while their fleet sailed up to the beach and towed off the ships of the Athenians. Some few were burned by the Athenians themselves as they had intended; the rest the Syracusans lashed on to their own at their leisure as they had been thrown up on shore, without anyone trying to stop them, and conveyed to the town.

75. After this, Nicias and Demosthenes now thinking that enough had been done in the way of preparation, the removal of the army took place upon the second day after the sea fight. It was a lamentable scene, not merely from the single circumstance that they were retreating after having lost all their ships, their great hopes gone, and themselves

and the state in peril; but also in leaving the camp there were things most grievous for every eye and heart to contemplate. The dead lay unburied, and each man as he recognized a friend among them shuddered with grief and horror; while the living whom they were leaving behind, wounded or sick, were to the living far more shocking than the dead, and more to be pitied than those who had perished. These fell to entreating and bewailing until their friends knew not what to do, begging them to take them and loudly calling to each individual comrade or relative whom they could see, hanging upon the necks of their tent-fellows in the act of departure, and following as far as they could, and when their bodily strength failed them calling again and again upon heaven and shrieking aloud as they were left behind. So that the whole army being filled with tears and distracted after this fashion found it not easy to go, even from an enemy's land, where they had already suffered evils too great for tears and in the unknown future before them feared to suffer more.

Dejection and self-condemnation were also rife among them. Indeed they could only be compared to a starved-out town, and that no small one, escaping, the whole multitude upon the march being not less than forty thousand men. All carried anything they could which might be of use, and the heavy infantry and troopers, contrary to their wont, while under arms carried their own victuals, in some cases for want of servants, in others through not trusting them, as they had long been deserting and now did so in greater numbers than ever. Yet even thus they did not carry enough, as there was no longer food in the camp. Moreover their disgrace generally, and the universality of their sufferings, however to a certain extent alleviated by being borne in company, were still felt at the moment a heavy burden, especially when they contrasted the splendour and glory of their setting out with the humiliation in which it had ended. For this was by far the greatest reverse that ever befell an Hellenic army. They had come to enslave others, and were departing in fear of being enslaved themselves: they had sailed out with prayer and paeans, and now started to go back with omens directly contrary, travelling by land instead of by sea, and trusting not in their fleet but in their heavy infantry. Nevertheless the greatness of the danger still impending made all this appear tolerable.

76. Nicias, seeing the army dejected and greatly altered, passed along the ranks and encouraged and comforted them as far as was possible under the circumstances, raising his voice still higher and higher as he went from one company to another in his earnestness, and in his anxiety that the benefit of his words might reach as many as possible:

77. "Athenians and allies, even in our present position we must still hope on, since men have ere now been saved from worse straits than this; and you must not condemn yourselves too severely either because of your disasters or because of your present unmerited sufferings. I myself who am not superior to any of you in strength—indeed you see how I am in my sickness—and who in the gifts of fortune am, I think, whether in private life or otherwise, the equal of any, am now exposed to the same danger as the meanest among you; and yet my life has been one of much devotion toward the gods, and of much justice and without offence toward men. I have, therefore, still a strong hope for the future, and our misfortunes do not terrify me as much as they might. Indeed we may hope that they will be lightened: our enemies have had good fortune enough; and if any of the gods was offended at our expedition, we have been already amply punished. Others before us have attacked their neighbours and have done what men will do without suffering more than they could bear; and we may now justly expect to find the gods more kind, for we have become fitter objects for their pity than their jealousy. And then look at yourselves, mark the numbers and efficiency of the heavy infantry marching in your ranks, and do not give way too much to despondency, but reflect that you are yourselves at once a city wherever you sit down, and that there is no other in Sicily that could easily resist your attack, or expel you when once established.

"The safety and order of the march is for yourselves to

look to, the one thought of each man being that the spot on which he may be forced to fight must be conquered and held as his country and stronghold. Meanwhile we shall hasten on our way night and day alike, as our provisions are scanty; and if we can reach some friendly place of the Sicels, whom fear of the Syracusans still keeps true to us, you may forthwith consider yourselves safe. A message has been sent on to them with directions to meet us with supplies of food. To sum up, be convinced, soldiers, that you must be brave, as there is no place near for your cowardice to take refuge in, and that if you now escape from the enemy, you may all see again what your hearts desire, while those of you who are Athenians will raise up again the great power of the state, fallen though it be. Men make the city and not walls or ships without men in them."

78. As he made this address, Nicias went along the ranks and brought back to their place any of the troops that he saw straggling out of the line; while Demosthenes did as much for his part of the army, addressing them in words very similar. The army marched in a hollow square, the division under Nicias leading, and that of Demosthenes following, the heavy infantry being outside and the baggage-carriers and the bulk of the army in the middle. When they arrived at the ford of the river Anapus they there found drawn up a body of the Syracusans and allies, and, routing these, made good their passage and pushed on, harassed by the charge of the Syracusan horse and by the missiles of their light troops. On that day they advanced about four miles and a half, halting for the night upon a certain hill. On the next they started early and got on about two miles farther, and descended into a place in the plain and there encamped, in order to procure some eatables from the houses, as the place was inhabited, and to carry on with them water from thence, as for many furlongs in front, in the direction in which they were going, it was not plentiful. The Syracusans meanwhile went on and fortified the pass in front, where there was a steep hill with a rocky ravine on each side of it, called the Acrean cliff. The next day the Athenians advancing found

themselves impeded by the missiles and charges of the horse and darters, both very numerous, of the Syracusans and allies; and, after fighting for a long while, at length retired to the same camp, where they had no longer provisions as before, it being impossible to leave their position by reason of the cavalry.

79. Early next morning they started afresh and forced their way to the hill, which had been fortified, where they found before them the enemy's infantry drawn up many shields deep to defend the fortification, the pass being narrow. The Athenians assaulted the work, but were greeted by a storm of missiles from the hill, which told with the greater effect through its being a steep one, and, unable to force the passage, retreated again and rested. Meanwhile occurred some claps of thunder and rain, as often happens towards autumn, which still further disheartened the Athenians, who thought all these things to be omens of their approaching ruin. While they were resting Gylippus and the Syracusans sent a part of their army to throw up works in their rear on the way by which they had advanced; however, the Athenians immediately sent some of their men and prevented them, after which they retreated more towards the plain and halted for the night. When they advanced the next day the Syracusans surrounded and attacked them on every side, and disabled many of them, falling back if the Athenians advanced and coming on if they retired, and in particular assaulting their rear, in the hope of routing them in detail, and thus striking a panic into the whole army. For a long while the Athenians persevered in this fashion, but after advancing for four or five furlongs halted to rest in the plain, the Syracusans also withdrawing to their own camp.

80. During the night Nicias and Demosthenes, seeing the wretched condition of their troops, now in want of every kind of necessary, and numbers of them disabled in the numerous attacks of the enemy, determined to light as many fires as possible, and to lead off the army, no longer by the same route as they had intended, but towards the sea in the opposite direction to that guarded by the Syracusans. The

whole of this route was leading the army not to Catana but to the other side of Sicily, towards Camarina, Gela, and the other Hellenic and barbarian towns in that quarter. They accordingly lit a number of fires and set out by night. Now all armies, and the greatest most of all, are liable to fears and alarms, especially when they are marching by night through an enemy's country and with the enemy near; and the Athenians falling into one of these panics, the leading division, that of Nicias, kept together and got on a good way in front, while that of Demosthenes, comprising rather more than half the army, got separated and marched on in some disorder. By morning, however, they reached the sea, and getting into the Helorine Road, pushed on in order to reach the river Cacyparis, and to follow the stream up through the interior, where they hoped to be met by the Sicels whom they had sent for. Arrived at the river, they found there also a Syracusan party engaged in barring the passage of the ford with a wall and a palisade, and, forcing this guard, crossed the river and went on to another called the Erineus, according to the advice of their guides.

81. Meanwhile, when day came and the Syracusans and allies found that the Athenians were gone, most of them accused Gylippus of having let them escape on purpose, and, hastily pursuing by the road which they had no difficulty in finding that they had taken, overtook them about dinner-time. They first came up with the troops under Demosthenes, who were behind and marching somewhat slowly and in disorder, owing to the night-panic above referred to, and at once attacked and engaged them, the Syracusan horse surrounding them with more ease now that they were separated from the rest, and hemming them in on one spot. The division of Nicias was five or six miles on in front, as he led them more rapidly, thinking that under the circumstances their safety lay not in staying and fighting, unless obliged, but in retreating as fast as possible, and fighting only when forced to do so. On the other hand, Demosthenes was, generally speaking, harassed more incessantly, as his post in the rear left him the first exposed to the attacks of the enemy;

and now, finding that the Syracusans were in pursuit, he omitted to push on, in order to form his men for battle, and so lingered until he was surrounded by his pursuers, and himself and the Athenians with him placed in the most distressing position, being huddled into an enclosure with a wall all round it, a road on this side and on that, and olive trees in great number, where missiles were showered in upon them from every quarter. This mode of attack the Syracusans had with good reason adopted in preference to fighting at close quarters, as to risk a struggle with desperate men was now more for the advantage of the Athenians than for their own; besides, their success had now become so certain that they began to spare themselves a little in order not to be cut off in the moment of victory, thinking too that, as it was, they would be able in this way to subdue and capture the enemy.

82. In fact, after plying the Athenians and allies all day long from every side with missiles, they at length saw that they were worn out with their wounds and other sufferings; and Gylippus and the Syracusans and their allies made a proclamation, offering their liberty to any of the islanders who chose to come over to them; and some few cities went over. Afterwards capitulation was agreed upon for all the rest with Demosthenes, to lay down their arms on condition that no one was to be put to death either by violence or imprisonment or want of the necessaries of life. Upon this they surrendered to the number of six thousand in all, laying down all the money in their possession, which filled the hollows of four shields, and were immediately conveyed by the Syracusans to the town. Meanwhile Nicias with his division arrived that day at the river Erineus, crossed over, and posted his army upon some high ground upon the other side.

83. The next day the Syracusans overtook him and told him that the troops under Demosthenes had surrendered, and invited him to follow their example. Incredulous of the fact, Nicias asked for a truce to send a horseman to see, and, upon the return of the messenger with the tidings that they had surrendered, sent a herald to Gylippus and the Syra-

cusans, saying that he was ready to agree with them on behalf of the Athenians to repay whatever money the Syracusans had spent upon the war if they would let his army go; and offered until the money was paid to give Athenians as hostages, one for every talent. The Syracusans and Gylippus rejected this proposition, and attacked this division as they had the other, standing all round and plying them with missiles until the evening. Food and necessaries were as miserably wanting to the troops of Nicias as they had been to their comrades; nevertheless they watched for the quiet of the night to resume their march. But as they were taking up their arms the Syracusans perceived it and raised their paean, upon which the Athenians, finding that they were discovered, laid them down again, except about three hundred men who forced their way through the guards and went on during the night as they were able.

84. As soon as it was day Nicias put his army in motion, pressed, as before, by the Syracusans and their allies, pelted from every side by their missiles, and struck down by their javelins. The Athenians pushed on for the Assinarus, impelled by the attacks made upon them from every side by a numerous cavalry and the swarm of other arms, fancying that they should breathe more freely if once across the river, and driven on also by their exhaustion and craving for water. Once there they rushed in, and all order was at an end, each man wanting to cross first, and the attacks of the enemy making it difficult to cross at all; forced to huddle together, they fell against and trod down one another, some dying immediately upon the javelins, others getting entangled together and stumbling over the articles of baggage, without being able to rise again. Meanwhile the opposite bank, which was steep, was lined by the Syracusans, who showered missiles down upon the Athenians, most of them drinking greedily and heaped together in disorder in the hollow bed of the river. The Peloponnesians also came down and butchered them, especially those in the water, which was thus immediately spoiled, but which they went on drinking just the same, mud and all, bloody as it was, most even fighting to have it.

85. At last, when many dead now lay piled one upon another in the stream, and part of the army had been destroyed at the river, and the few that escaped from thence cut off by the cavalry, Nicias surrendered himself to Gylippus, whom he trusted more than he did the Syracusans, and told him and the Lacedaemonians to do what they liked with him, but to stop the slaughter of the soldiers. Gylippus, after this, immediately gave orders to make prisoners, upon which the rest were brought together alive, except a large number secreted by the soldiery, and a party was sent in pursuit of the three hundred who had got through the guard during the night, and who were now taken with the rest. The number of the enemy collected as public property was not considerable, but that secreted was very large, and all Sicily was filled with them, no convention having been made in their case as for those taken with Demosthenes. Besides this, a large portion were killed outright, the carnage being very great, and not exceeded by any in this Sicilian war. In the numerous other encounters upon the march, not a few also had fallen. Nevertheless many escaped, some at the moment, others served as slaves, and then ran away subsequently. These found refuge at Catana.

86. The Syracusans and their allies now mustered and took up the spoils and as many prisoners as they could, and went back to the city. The rest of their Athenian and allied captives were deposited in the quarries, this seeming the safest way of keeping them; but Nicias and Demosthenes were butchered, against the will of Gylippus, who thought that it would be the crown of his triumph if he could take the enemy's generals to Lacedaemon. One of them, as it happened, Demosthenes, was one of her greatest enemies, on account of the affair of the island and of Pylos; while the other, Nicias, was for the same reasons one of her greatest friends, owing to his exertions to procure the release of the prisoners by persuading the Athenians to make peace. For these reasons the Lacedaemonians felt kindly towards him; and it was in this that Nicias himself mainly confided when he surrendered to Gylippus. But some of the Syracusans who had been

in correspondence with him were afraid, it was said, of his being put to the torture and troubling their success by his revelations; others, especially the Corinthians, of his escaping, as he was wealthy, by means of bribes, and living to do them further mischief; and these persuaded the allies and put him to death. This or the like was the cause of the death of a man who, of all the Hellenes in my time, least deserved such a fate, seeing that the whole course of his life had been regulated with strict attention to virtue.

87. The prisoners in the quarries were at first hardly treated by the Syracusans. Crowded in a narrow hole, without any roof to cover them, the heat of the sun and the stifling closeness of the air tormented them during the day, and then the nights, which came on autumnal and chilly, made them ill by the violence of the change; besides, as they had to do everything in the same place for want of room, and the bodies of those who died of their wounds or from the variation in the temperature, or from similar causes, were left heaped together one upon another, intolerable stenches arose; while hunger and thirst never ceased to afflict them, each man during eight months having only half a pint of water and a pint of grain given him daily. In short, no single suffering to be apprehended by men thrust into such a place was spared them. For some seventy days they thus lived all together, after which all, except the Athenians and any Sicilians or Italians who had joined in the expedition, were sold. The total number of prisoners taken it would be difficult to state exactly, but it could not have been less than seven thousand.

This was the greatest Hellenic achievement of any in this war, or, in my opinion, in Hellenic history; at once most glorious to the victors, and most calamitous to the conquered. They were beaten at all points and altogether; all that they suffered was great; they were destroyed, as the saying is, with a total destruction, their fleet, their army—everything was destroyed, and few out of many returned home.

XENOPHON

Xᴇɴᴏᴘʜᴏɴ was born in the first years of the Peloponnesian War, in an Athenian family of sufficient means to procure him an education with the sophists. In his youth three interests emerged which were to play a very large part in his long career as man of affairs and as writer: his passion for horsemanship and military matters, his interest in philosophy, and his great love for Sparta (which made him a major contributor to what a French scholar has called "the Spartan mirage").

Our first knowledge of Xenophon comes in the spring of 401 when, against the advice of Socrates, whose friend and (in a very minor way) disciple he had become, he joined a Greek mercenary force recruited by Cyrus. The latter had for some years been Sparta's chief ally in Persian circles and he was now hoping to seize the throne from his older brother Artaxerxes. Cyrus was killed in battle and the Greek mercenaries had a long and difficult struggle back from Persian territory, more or less under Xenophon's leadership. He subsequently wrote an account of the expedition, and this work, known as the *Anabasis,* is surely his most attractive. Curiously enough, in the *Hellenica* he attributes the *Anabasis* to Themistogenes of Syracuse, an undoubtedly mythical figure. Plutarch suggests, in explanation, that Xenophon sacrificed the glory of authorship in order to obtain more credence for the picture he drew of himself in the book. And that is likely enough: there is nothing modest about the way in which Xenophon's wisdom, leadership, and general indispensability are portrayed in the *Anabasis*.

The abortive coup by Cyrus helped bring Sparta and Persia to a state of war, and Xenophon next appears in 396 in the camp of Agesilaus, the Spartan king who commanded the forces plundering the Persian satrapies in Asia Minor. Two years later he fought on the Spartan side at Coronea against an Athenian–Theban coalition. For this (or possibly even earlier because of his direct participation in Spartan military activities) the Athenians exiled him. He went to Sparta, where his two sons were educated. The Spartans gave him an estate in Scillus, in Elean territory near Olympia, where he lived some twenty years. He was forced to leave in 371, driven out by the Eleans then at war with Sparta, and after some wandering he settled in Corinth.

In 367 or thereabouts the Athenians revoked the old decree of exile. It is possible, at the very least, that the motive was a political one. The constantly shifting political alignment in Greece had now brought Athens and Sparta into alliance against Thebes, and Xenophon, who presumably had already acquired considerable fame as a writer, was therefore an asset. The only note in his *Hellenica,* the history of Greece which he wrote in continuation of Thucydides', which is as strong as his liking for Sparta is his hatred of Thebes. Whether Xenophon ever returned to Athens is unknown, although his sons fought in her army at the battle of Mantinea in 362, where one was killed. Xenophon died in the later 350s, probably, and one tradition has him in Corinth then.

From the time he moved to Scillus, Xenophon apparently abandoned all military and direct political activity, and devoted himself to his writing. He was the first polygraph in Greek history, and it is sufficient measure of his continuing popularity that every one of his works, so far as we know, has survived in full, a fate almost without parallel among Greek writers. Apart from his historical and biographical works (which include an encomium of Agesilaus), his longest and most significant books can be classified as popular philosophy (in the pejorative sense), notably the *Memorabilia of Socrates* and the *Cyropaedia,* a lengthy disquisition on morals thinly disguised as a biography of Cyrus.

—M. I. F.

THE ANABASIS

From BOOK I

. . . . . .

9.1. Thus then died Cyrus, a man who, of all the Persians since Cyrus the elder, was the most princely and most worthy of rule, as is agreed by all who appear to have had personal knowledge of him. 2. In the first place, while he was yet a boy, and when he was receiving his education with his brother and the other youths, he was thought to surpass them all in everything. 3. For all the sons of the Persian nobles are educated at the gates of the king, where they may learn many a lesson of virtuous conduct, but can see or hear nothing disgraceful. 4. Here the boys see some honoured by the king, and others disgraced, and hear of them, so that in their very childhood they learn to govern and to obey.

5. Here Cyrus, first of all, showed himself most remarkable for modesty among those of his own age, and for paying more ready obedience to his elders than even those who were inferior to him in station; and next, he was noted for his fondness for horses, and for managing them in a superior manner. They found him, too, very desirous of learning, and most assiduous in practising, the warlike exercises of archery, and hurling the javelin. 6. When it suited his age, he grew extremely fond of the chase, and of braving dangers in encounters with wild beasts. On one occasion, he did not shrink from a she-bear that attacked him, but, in grappling with her, was dragged from off his horse, and received some wounds, the scars of which were visible on his body, but at

last killed her. The person who first came to his assistance he made a happy man in the eyes of many.

7. When he was sent down by his father, as satrap of Lydia and Great Phrygia and Cappadocia, and was also appointed commander of all the troops whose duty it is to muster in the plain of Castolus, he soon showed that if he made a league or compact with anyone, or gave a promise, he deemed it of the utmost importance not to break his word. 8. Accordingly the states that were committed to his charge, as well as individuals, had the greatest confidence in him; and if anyone had been his enemy, he felt secure that if Cyrus entered into a treaty with him, he should suffer no infraction of the stipulations. 9. When, therefore, he waged war against Tissaphernes, all the cities, of their own accord, chose to adhere to Cyrus in preference to Tissaphernes, except the Milesians; but they feared him, because he would not abandon the cause of the exiles; 10. for he both showed by his deeds and declared in words that he would never desert them, since he had once become a friend to them, not even though they should grow still fewer in number, and be in a worse condition than they were.

11. Whenever anyone did him a kindness or an injury, he showed himself anxious to go beyond him in those respects; and some used to mention a wish of his that he desired to live long enough to outdo both those who had done him good, and those who had done him ill, in the requital that he should make. 12. Accordingly to him alone of the men of our days were so great a number of people desirous of committing the disposal of their property, their cities, and their own persons.

13. Yet no one could with truth say this of him, that he suffered the criminal or unjust to deride his authority; for he of all men inflicted punishment most unsparingly; and there were often to be seen, along the most frequented roads, men deprived of their feet, or hands, or eyes; so that in Cyrus's dominions, it was possible for anyone, Greek or barbarian, who did no wrong, to travel without fear withersoever

he pleased, and having with him whatever might suit his convenience.

14. To those who showed ability for war, it is acknowledged that he paid distinguished honour. His first war was with the Pisidians and Mysians; and, marching in person into these countries, he made those whom he saw voluntarily hazarding their lives in his service governors over the territory that he subdued, and distinguished them with rewards in other ways. 15. So that the brave appeared to be the most fortunate of men, while the cowardly were deemed fit only to be their slaves. There were, therefore, great numbers of persons who voluntarily exposed themselves to danger, wherever they thought that Cyrus would become aware of their exertions.

16. With regard to justice, if any appeared to him inclined to display that virtue, he made a point of making such men richer than those who sought to profit by injustice. 17. Accordingly, while in many other respects his affairs were administered judiciously, he likewise possessed an army worthy of the name. For it was not for money that generals and captains came from foreign lands to enter into his service, but because they were persuaded that to serve Cyrus well would be more profitable than any amount of monthly pay. 18. Besides, if anyone executed his orders in a superior manner, he never suffered his diligence to go unrewarded; consequently, in every undertaking, the best-qualified officers were said to be ready to assist him.

19. If he noticed anyone that was a skilful manager, with strict regard to justice, stocking the land of which he had the direction, and securing income from it, he would never take anything from such a person, but was ever ready to give him something in addition; so that men laboured with cheerfulness, acquired property with confidence, and made no concealment from Cyrus of what each possessed; for he did not appear to envy those who amassed riches openly, but to endeavour to bring into use the wealth of those who concealed it.

20. Whatever friends he made, and felt to be well disposed to him, and considered to be capable of assisting him in anything that he might wish to accomplish, he is acknowledged by all to have been most successful in attaching them to him. 21. For, on the very same account on which he thought that he himself had need of friends, namely, that he might have cooperators in his undertakings, did he endeavour to prove an efficient assistant to his friends in whatever he perceived any of them desirous of effecting.

22. He received, for many reasons, more presents than perhaps any other single individual; and these he outdid everyone else in distributing amongst his friends, having a view to the character of each, and to what he perceived each most needed. 23. Whatever presents anyone sent him of articles of personal ornament, whether for warlike accoutrement, or merely for dress, concerning these, they said, he used to remark that he could not decorate his own person with them all, but that he thought friends well equipped were the greatest ornament a man could have. 24. That he should outdo his friends, indeed, in conferring great benefits, is not at all wonderful, since he was so much more able; but that he should surpass his friends in kind attentions, and an anxious desire to oblige appears to me far more worthy of admiration. 25. Frequently, when he had wine served him of a peculiarly fine flavour, he would send half-emptied flagons of it to some of his friends, with a message to this effect: "Cyrus has not for some time met with pleasanter wine than this; and he has therefore sent some of it to you, and begs you will drink it today, with those whom you love best." 26. He would often, too, send geese partly eaten, and the halves of loaves, and other such things, desiring the bearer to say, in presenting them, "Cyrus has been delighted with these, and therefore wishes you also to taste of them."

27. Wherever provender was scarce, but he himself, from having many attendants, and from the care which he took, was able to procure some, he would send it about, and desire his friends to give that provender to the horses that carried them, so that hungry steeds might not carry his friends.

28. Whenever he rode out, and many were likely to see him, he would call to him his friends, and hold earnest conversation with them, that he might show whom he held in honour; so that, from what I have heard, I should think that no one was ever beloved by a greater number of persons, either Greeks or barbarians. 29. Of this fact the following is a proof —that no one deserted to the king from Cyrus, though only a subject (except that Orontes attempted to do so, but he soon found the person whom he believed faithful to him, more a friend to Cyrus than to himself), while many came over to Cyrus from the king, after they became enemies to each other; and these, too, men who were greatly beloved by the king; for they felt persuaded that if they proved themselves brave soldiers under Cyrus they would obtain from him more adequate rewards for their services than from the king.

30. What occurred also at the time of his death is a great proof, as well that he himself was a man of merit, as that he could accurately distinguish such as were trustworthy, well disposed, and constant in their attachment. 31. For when he was killed, all his friends and the partakers of his table who were with him, fell fighting in his defence, except Ariaeus, who had been posted, in command of the cavalry, on the left; and, when he learned that Cyrus had fallen in the battle, he took to flight, with all the troops which he had under his command.

10.1. The head and right hand of Cyrus were then cut off. The king, and the troops that were with him, engaging in pursuit, fell upon the camp of Cyrus; when the soldiers of Ariaeus no longer stood their ground, but fled through their camp to the station whence they had last started, which was said to be four parasangs distant. 2. The king and his followers seized upon many other things, and also captured the Phocaean woman, the concubine of Cyrus, who was said to be both accomplished and beautiful. 3. The younger Milesian woman, being taken by some of the king's soldiers, fled for refuge, without her outer garment, to the party of Greeks, who were stationed under arms to guard the baggage, and who, drawing themselves up for defence, killed several of the pillagers; and some of their own number also fell; yet they did not flee, but saved not only the woman but all the rest of the property and people that were in their quarters.

4. The king and the main body of Greeks were now distant from each other about thirty stadia, the Greeks pursuing those that had been opposed to them, as if they had conquered all; the Persians engaged in plundering, as if they were wholly victorious. 5. But when the Greeks found that the king with his troops was amongst their baggage, and the king, on the other hand, heard from Tissaphernes that the Greeks had routed that part of his line which had been opposed to them, and were gone forward in pursuit, the king, on his part, collected his forces and formed them in line again; while Clearchus, on the other side, calling to him Proxenus, who happened to be nearest to him, consulted with him whether they should send a detachment to the camp, or proceed, all of them together, to relieve it. 6. In the meantime, the king was observed again approaching them, as it seemed, in their rear. The Greeks, wheeling round, prepared to receive him, in the belief that he would attack them on that quarter; the king, however, did not lead his troops that way, but led them off by the same route by which he had before passed on the outside of their left wing, taking with him both those who had deserted to the Greeks during the engagement and Tissaphernes with the troops under his command.

7. Tissaphernes had not fled at the commencement of the engagement, but had charged through the Greek peltasts, close to the banks of the river. In breaking through, however, he killed not a single man, for the Greeks, opening their ranks, struck his men with their swords, and hurled their javelins at them. Episthenes of Amphipolis had the command of the peltasts, and was said to have proved himself an able captain. 8. Tissaphernes, therefore, when he thus came off with disadvantage, did not turn back again, but, proceeding onwards to the Grecian camp, met the king

there; and thence they now returned together, with their
forces united in battle array. 9. When they were opposite the
left wing of the Greeks, the Greeks feared lest they should
attack them on that wing, and, enclosing them on both sides,
should cut them off; they therefore thought it advisable to
draw back this wing, and to put the river in their rear. 10.
While they were planning this manœuvre, the king, having
passed beyond them, presented his force opposite to them
in the same form in which he had at first come to battle; and
when the Greeks saw their enemies close at hand, and drawn
up for fight, they again sang the paean, and advanced upon
them with much greater spirit than before. 11. The barbarians, on the other hand, did not await their onset, but fled
sooner than at first; and the Greeks pursued them as far as
a certain village, where they halted; 12. for above the village was a hill, upon which the king's troops had checked
their flight, and though there were no longer any infantry
there, the height was filled with cavalry; so that the Greeks
could not tell what was doing. They said that they saw the
royal standard, a golden eagle upon a spear, with expanded
wings.

13. But as the Greeks were on the point of proceeding
thither, the cavalry too left the hill, not indeed in a body,
but some in one direction and some in another; and thus the
hill was gradually thinned of cavalry, till at last they were
all gone. 14. Clearchus, however, did not march up the hill,
but, stationing his force at its foot, sent Lycius the Syracusan
and another up the hill, and ordered them, after taking a
view from the summit, to report to him what was passing on
the other side. 15. Lycius accordingly rode thither, and having made his observations, brought word that the enemy
were fleeing with precipitation. Just as these things took
place, the sun set.

16. Here the Greeks halted and, piling their arms, took
some rest; and at the same time they wondered that Cyrus
himself nowhere made his appearance, and that no one else
came to them from him; for they did not know that he was
killed, but conjectured that he either was gone in pursuit of

the enemy or had pushed forward to secure some post. 17. They then deliberated whether they should remain in that spot and fetch their baggage thither, or return to the camp; and it was resolved to return, and they arrived at the tents about supper-time. 18. Such was the conclusion of this day.

They found almost all their baggage, and whatever food and drink was with it, plundered and wasted; the wagons, too, full of barley-meal and wine, which Cyrus had provided, in order that, if ever a great scarcity of provisions should fall upon the army, he might distribute them amongst the Grecian troops (and the wagons, as was said, were four hundred in number)—these also the king's soldiers had plundered. 19. Most of the Greeks consequently remained supperless; and they had also been without dinner, for before the army had halted for dinner, the king made his appearance. In this state they passed the ensuing night.

From BOOK II

1. . . . . 2. When it was day, the generals met together and expressed their surprise that Cyrus had neither sent any person to give directions how they should act, nor had made his appearance himself. It seemed best to them, therefore, to pack up what baggage they had, and, arming themselves, to march forward till they could effect a junction with Cyrus. 3. But when they were on the point of starting, just as the sun was rising, there came to them Procles, the governor of Teuthrania (who was descended from Damaratus the Lacedaemonian) and with him Glus, the son of Tamos, who told them that Cyrus was dead, and that Ariaeus, having fled, was with the rest of the barbarians at the station whence they started the day before; and that he said he would wait for the Greeks that day, if they would come to him; but on the morrow, he said, he should set off for Ionia, from whence he had come.

4. The generals, on hearing this intelligence, and the other Greeks, on learning it from them, were grievously afflicted; and Clearchus spoke thus: "Would that Cyrus were still alive; but since he is no more, carry back word to Ariaeus that we at least are victorious over the king, and that, as you see, no enemy any longer offers us battle; and, if you had not come, we should have marched against the king; and we promise Ariaeus that, if he will come hither, we will seat him on the royal throne; for to those who conquer, it belongs also to rule." 5. Saying this, he dismissed the messengers, and sent with them Cheirisophus the Lacedaemonian and Menon the Thessalian; for Menon himself desired to go, as he was connected with Ariaeus by ties of friendship and hospitality.

6. While they departed on their mission Clearchus waited where he was; and the troops supplied themselves with food, as well as they could, from the carcases of their baggage-cattle, slaughtering their oxen and asses; and, going a little way in front of the line to the place where the battle was fought, they collected and used as fuel not only the arrows, which lay in great quantities, and which the Greeks had compelled the deserters from the king to throw down, but also the wicker shields of the Persians, and the wooden ones of the Egyptians; and there were also many other light shields, and wagons emptied of their contents, to be taken away; using all which materials to cook the meat, they appeased their hunger for that day.

7. It was now about the middle of the forenoon, when some heralds arrived from the king and Tissaphernes, all of them barbarians, except one, a Greek named Phalinus, who chanced to be with Tissaphernes, and was highly esteemed by him, for he had pretensions to skill in the arrangement of troops and in the exercise of heavy arms. 8. These persons, having approached and asked to speak with the commanders of the Greeks, told them that the king, since he had gained the victory and slain Cyrus, required the Greeks to deliver up their arms, and go to the gates of the king, and try to obtain, if they could, some favour from him.

9. Thus spoke the king's heralds; and the Greeks heard them with no small concern; but Clearchus only said that it was not the part of conquerors to deliver up their arms. "But," he continued, "do you, fellow captains, give these men such an answer as you think most honourable and proper, and I will return immediately"; for one of the attendants just then called him away to inspect the entrails which had been taken out of the victim, as he happened to be engaged in sacrifice. 10. Cleanor the Arcadian, the oldest of them, then answered that they would die before they would deliver up their arms. "For my part," said Proxenus the Theban, "I wonder, Phalinus, whether it is as conqueror that the king asks for our arms, or as gifts in friendship; for if as conqueror, why should he ask for them at all, and not rather come and take them? But if he wishes to get them from us by means of persuasion, let him say what will be left to the soldiers, if they gratify him in this particular." 11. To this Phalinus replied, "The king considers himself the conqueror, since he has slain Cyrus. For who is there now that disputes the sovereignty with him? And he also looks upon yourselves as his captives, having you here in the middle of his dominions, and enclosed within impassable rivers; and being able to lead such multitudes against you, as, though he gave them into your power, it would be impossible for you to destroy."

12. After him, Theopompus, an Athenian, spoke thus: "O Phalinus, we have now, as you see, nothing to avail us except our arms and our valour. While we retain our arms, we may hope to profit by our valour; but if we were to give them up, we should expect to be deprived also of our lives. Do not suppose, therefore, that we shall give up to you the only things of value that we possess; but, with these in our hands, we will even fight for whatever of value you possess." 13. On hearing him speak thus, Phalinus laughed and said, "You seem like a philosopher, young man, and express yourself not without grace; but be assured that you are out of your senses if you imagine that your valour will prove victorious over the might of the king." 14. But it was reported that certain others of the generals, giving way to their fears,

said that they had been faithful to Cyrus, and might likewise prove of great service to the king, if he were willing to become their friend; and that whether he might wish to employ them in any other service or in an expedition against Egypt, they would assist him in reducing it."

15. In the meantime Clearchus returned, and asked whether they had yet given their answer. Phalinus, in reply, said, "Your companions, O Clearchus, give each a different answer; and now tell us what you have to say." 16. Clearchus then said, "I was glad to see you, O Phalinus, and so, I dare say, were all the rest of us; for you are a Greek, as we also are; and, being so many in number as you see, and placed in such circumstances, we would advise with you how we should act with regard to the message that you bring. 17. Give us then, I entreat you by the gods, such advice as seems to you most honourable and advantageous, and such as will bring you honour in time to come, when it is related that Phalinus, being once sent from the king to require the Greeks to deliver up their arms, gave them, when they consulted him, such-and-such counsel; for you know that whatever counsel you do give will necessarily be reported in Greece."

18. Clearchus craftily threw out this suggestion with the desire that the very person who came as an envoy from the king should advise them not to deliver up their arms, in order that the Greeks might be led to conceive better hopes. But Phalinus, adroitly evading the appeal, spoke, contrary to his expectation, as follows: 19. "If, out of ten thousand hopeful chances, you have any single one of saving yourselves by continuing in arms against the king, I advise you not to deliver up your arms; but if you have not a single hope of safety in opposing the king's pleasure, I advise you to save yourselves in the only way in which it is possible." 20. Clearchus rejoined, "Such, then, is your advice; but on our part return this answer, that we are of opinion that, if we are to be friends with the king, we shall be more valuable friends if we retain our arms than if we surrender them to another; but that if we must make war against him, we should make

war better if we retain our arms than if we give them up to another." 21. Phalinus said, "This answer, then, we will report; but the king desired us also to inform you that while you remain in this place a truce is to be considered as existing between him and you; but, if you advance or retreat, there is to be war. Give us, therefore, your answer on this point also, whether you will remain here, and a truce is to exist, or whether I shall announce from you that there is war." 22. Clearchus replied, "Report, therefore, on this point also, that our resolution is the same as that of the king." "And what is that?" said Phalinus. Clearchus replied, "If we stay here, a truce; but if we retreat or advance, war." 23. Phalinus again asked him, "Is it a truce or war that I shall report?" Clearchus again made the same answer: "A truce, if we stay; and if we retreat or advance, war." But of what he intended to do he gave no intimation.

2. 1. Phalinus and his companions departed; and there now returned, from their interview with Ariaeus, Procles and Cheirisophus; Menon had remained there with Ariaeus. They reported that Ariaeus said that there were many Persians, of superior rank to himself, who would not endure that he should be king. " 'But,' he adds, 'if you wish to return with him, he desires you to come to him this very night; if you do not, he says that he will set out by himself early in the morning.' 2. Clearchus rejoined, "And we must certainly do as you say, if we determine to go to him; but if not, adopt for yourselves such measures as you may think most for your advantage"; for not even to them did he disclose what he intended to do.

3. But afterwards, when the sun was setting, having assembled the generals and captains, he spoke as follows: "My friends, when I offered a sacrifice with reference to marching against the king, the signs of the victims were not favourable, and indeed it was with good cause that they were not so; for, as I now learn, there is between us and the king the river Tigris, a navigable river, which we could not cross without vessels; and vessels we have none. Yet it is not pos-

sible to remain here, for we have no means of procuring provisions. But for going to the friends of Cyrus, the sacrifices were extremely favourable. 4. We must accordingly proceed thus: when we separate, we must sup, each of us on what he has; when the signal is given with the horn as if for going to rest, proceed to pack up your baggage; when it sounds the second time, place it on your baggage-cattle; and, at the third signal, follow him who leads the way, keeping your baggage-cattle next the river, and the heavy-armed troops on the outside." 5. The generals and captains, after listening to this address, went away, and did as he directed; and thenceforth he commanded, and the others obeyed, not indeed having elected him commander, but perceiving that he alone possessed such qualifications as a leader ought to have, and that the rest of them were comparatively inexperienced. . . .

7. Here, as soon as it was dark, Miltocythes the Thracian deserted to the king, with about forty horse that he commanded, and nearly three hundred of the Thracian infantry. 8. Clearchus led the way for the rest, in the prescribed order; and they followed, and arrived at the first halting place, to join Ariaeus and his troops about midnight; and the generals and captains of the Greeks, having drawn up their men under arms, went in a body to Ariaeus; when the Greeks on the one hand, and Ariaeus and his principal officers on the other, took an oath not to betray each other, and to be true allies; and the barbarians took another oath, that they would lead the way without treachery. 9. These oaths they took after sacrificing a bull, a boar, and a ram over a shield, the Greeks dipping a sword, and the barbarians a lance, into the blood.

10. When these pledges of mutual fidelity were given, Clearchus said, "Since then, Ariaeus, our route and yours is now the same, tell us what is your opinion with respect to our course—whether we shall return the way we came or whether you consider that you have thought of a better way." 11. Ariaeus replied, "If we were to return the way we came, we should all perish of hunger, for we have now no

supply of provisions; and for the last seventeen days' march, even when we were coming hither, we could procure nothing from the country through which we passed; or, if anything was to be found there, we consumed it ourselves in our passage. But now we propose to take a longer road, but one in which we shall not want for provisions. 12. We must make the first days' marches as long as we can, that we may remove ourselves to the greatest possible distance from the king's army; for if we once escape two or three days' journey from him, the king will no longer be able to overtake us; since he will not dare to pursue us with a small force; and, with a numerous army, he will not be able to march fast enough, and will probably experience a scarcity of provisions. Such is my opinion."

13. This scheme for conducting the army was calculated for nothing else than to effect an escape, clandestinely or openly, by flight. But fortune proved a better leader, for as soon as it was day they began their march, with the sun on their right, expecting to arrive about sunset at some villages in the Babylonian territory; and in this expectation they were not disappointed. 14. But, in the afternoon, they thought that they perceived some of the enemy's cavalry; and those of the Greeks who happened not to be in their ranks ran to their places in the ranks; and Ariaeus (for he was riding in a wagon because he had been wounded) came down and put on his armour, as did those who were with him. 15. But while they were arming themselves, the scouts that had been sent forward returned, and reported that they were not cavalry, but baggage-cattle grazing; and everyone immediately concluded that the king was encamped somewhere near. Smoke also was seen rising from some villages not far distant. 16. Clearchus however did not lead his troops against the enemy (for he was aware that his soldiers were tired and in want of food, and besides it was now late); yet he did not turn out of his way, taking care not to appear to flee, but continued his march in a direct line, and took up his quarters with his vanguard, just at sunset, in the nearest villages, from which even the woodwork of the houses had been carried off by

the king's troops. 17. These, therefore, who were in advance, encamped with some degree of regularity; but those who followed, coming up in the dark, took up with such quarters as they chanced to find, and made so much noise in calling to each other that even the enemy heard them; and those of the enemy who were stationed the nearest fled from their encampments. 18. That this had been the case became apparent on the following day, for there was no longer a single beast of burden to be seen, nor any camp, nor smoke anywhere near. The king had been alarmed, as it seemed, by the sudden approach of the Grecian army; and of this he gave proof by what he did on the following day.

19. However, in the course of this night a panic fell upon the Greeks themselves, and there arose such noise and commotion in their camp as usually ensues on the occurrence of sudden terror. 20. Upon this, Clearchus ordered Tolmides, an Eleian, whom he happened to have with him, the best herald of his time, to command silence and proclaim, "The generals give notice that whoever will give information of the person who turned the ass among the arms, shall receive a reward of a talent of silver." 21. On this proclamation being made, the soldiers were convinced that their alarm was groundless, and their generals were safe. At break of day, Clearchus issued orders for the Greeks to form themselves under arms, in the same order in which they had been when the battle took place.

3.1. What I just now stated, that the king was alarmed at the approach of the Greeks, became evident by what followed; for though, when he sent to them on the preceding day, he desired them to deliver up their arms, he now, at sunrise, sent heralds to negotiate a truce. 2. These heralds, upon arriving at the outposts, requested to speak with the commanders. Their request being reported by the guards, Clearchus, who happened then to be inspecting the several divisions, told the guards to desire the heralds to wait till he should be at leisure. 3. When he had arranged the army in such a manner as to present on every side the fair appearance of a compact phalanx, and so that none of the unarmed were to be seen, he called for the heralds and came forward himself, having about him the best-armed and best-looking of his soldiers, and told the other leaders to do the same. 4. When he drew near the messengers, he asked them what they wanted. They replied that they came to negotiate a truce, with full powers to communicate with the Greeks on behalf of the king, and with the king on behalf of the Greeks. 5. Clearchus answered, "Tell the king, then, that we must come to battle first, for we have no breakfast; and there is no one who will dare to talk to the Greeks of a truce without first supplying them with breakfast."

6. On hearing this answer, the messengers departed, but soon returned, from whence it was apparent that the king, or some other person to whom a commission had been given to conduct the negotiation, was somewhere near. They brought word that the king thought what they said was reasonable, and that they now came with guides, who, in case the truce should be settled, would conduct the Greeks to a place where they might procure provisions. 7. Clearchus then inquired whether the king would grant the benefit of the truce to those only who went to him, on their way thither and back, or whether the truce would be with the rest as well. The messengers replied, "With all; until what you have to say is communicated to the king." 8. When they had said this, Clearchus, directing them to withdraw, deliberated with the other officers, and they proposed to conclude the truce at once, and to go after the provisions at their ease, and supply themselves. 9. And Clearchus said, "I too am of that opinion. I will not, however, announce our determination immediately, but will wait till the messengers begin to be uneasy lest we should determine not to conclude the truce. And yet," said he, "I suspect that a similar apprehension will arise among our own soldiers." When he thought therefore that the proper time had arrived, he announced to the messengers that he agreed to the truce, and desired them to conduct him forthwith to the place where the provisions were.

10. They accordingly led the way, and Clearchus pro-

ceeded to conclude the truce, keeping his army however in battle array; the rear he brought up himself. They met with ditches and canals so full of water that they could not cross without bridges; but they made crossings of the palm trees which had fallen, and others which they cut down. 11. Here it might be seen how Clearchus performed the duties of a commander, holding his spear in his right hand, and a staff in his left; and if any of those ordered to the work seemed to him to loiter at it, he would select a fit object for punishment, and give him a beating, and would lend his assistance himself, leaping into the midst, so that all were ashamed not to share his industry. 12. The men of thirty and under only had been appointed by him to the work, but the older men, when they saw Clearchus thus busily employed, gave their assistance likewise. 13. Clearchus made so much the more haste, as he suspected that the ditches were not always so full of water (for it was not the season for irrigating the ground); but thought that the king had let out the water upon the plain, in order that even now there might appear to the Greeks to be many difficulties in the march.

14. Proceeding on their way, they arrived at some villages, from which the guides signified that they might procure provisions. In these villages there was great plenty of grain, and wine made from date palms, and an acidulous drink obtained from them by boiling. 15. As to the dates themselves, such as those we see in Greece were here put aside for the use of the servants; but those which were laid by for their masters were choice fruit, remarkable for beauty and size; their colour was not unlike that of amber; and some of these they dried and preserved as sweetmeats. These were a pleasant accompaniment to drink, but apt to cause headache. 16. Here too the soldiers for the first time tasted the cabbage from the top of the palm tree, and most of them were agreeably struck both with its external appearance and the peculiarity of its sweetness. But this also was exceedingly apt to give headache. The palm tree out of which the cabbage had been taken soon withered throughout.

17. In this place they remained three days, when Tissa-

phernes arrived from the Great King, and with him the brother of the king's wife, and three other Persians; and many slaves attended them. The generals of the Greeks having met them on their arrival, Tissaphernes first spoke by an interpreter, to the following effect: 18. "I myself dwell, O Greeks, in the neighbourhood of your country; and when I perceived you fallen into many troubles and difficulties, I thought it a piece of good fortune if I could in any way press a request upon the king to allow me to conduct you in safety back to Greece. For I think that such a service would be attended with no want of gratitude either from yourselves or from Greece in general. 19. With these considerations, I made my request to the king, representing to him that he might reasonably grant me this favour, because I had been the first to give him intelligence that Cyrus was marching against him, and at the same time that I brought him the intelligence had come to him with an auxiliary force; because I alone, of all those opposed to the Greeks, did not flee, but, on the contrary, charged through the midst of them, and joined the king in your camp, whither he came after he had slain Cyrus; and because, together with these who are now present with me, and who are his most faithful servants, I engaged in pursuit of the barbarian part of Cyrus's army. 20. The king promised to consider my request; and in the meantime desired me to come and ask you on what account it was that you took the field against him, and I advise you to answer with moderation, in order that it may be easier for me to secure you whatever advantage I can from the king."

21. The Greeks then withdrew, and, after some deliberation, gave their answer, Clearchus speaking for them: "We neither formed ourselves into a body with the view of making war upon the king, nor, when we set out, was our march directed against him; but Cyrus, as you yourself are well aware, devised many pretences for his proceedings, that he might both take you by surprise and lead us up hither. 22. But when we afterwards saw him in danger, we were ashamed, in the face of gods and men, to desert him, as we

had before allowed him to bestow favours upon us. 23. As Cyrus, however, is now dead, we neither dispute the sovereignty with the king, nor is there any reason why we should desire to do harm to the king's territory; nor would we wish to kill him, but would proceed homeward, if no one molest us; but we will endeavour, with the aid of the gods, to avenge ourselves on anyone that may do us an injury; while, if any-one does us good, we shall not be behind-hand in requiting him to the utmost of our power." 24. Thus spoke Clearchus. Tissaphernes, having heard him, said, "I will report your answer to the king, and bring back to you his reply; and till I return, let the truce remain in force; and we will provide a market for you."

25. On the following day he did not return, so that the Greeks began to be anxious; but on the third day he came, and said that he returned after having obtained the king's permission to be allowed to save the Greeks; although many spoke against it, saying that it did not become the king to suffer men to escape who had engaged in war against him. 26. In conclusion he said, "You may now receive from us solemn promises that we will render the country through which you will pass friendly to you; and will, without treachery, conduct you back to Greece, affording you opportunities of purchasing provisions; and wheresoever we do not afford you an opportunity of purchasing, we will allow you to take for yourselves necessaries from the adjacent country. 27. On the other hand, it will be incumbent upon you to swear to us that you will march as through a friendly territory, without doing harm, only taking a supply of meat and drink, whenever we do not give you an opportunity of purchasing, but that if we give you such opportunity, you will procure your supplies by purchase." 28. These conditions were assented to, and they took the oaths, and Tissaphernes and the brother of the king's wife gave their right hands to the generals and captains of the Greeks, and received from the Greeks theirs in return. 29. After this, Tissaphernes said, "And now I shall go back to the king; and as soon as I have accomplished what I wish, I will come again, after making

the necessary preparations, for the purpose of conducting you back to Greece, and returning myself to my province."

4. 1. After these occurrences, the Greeks and Ariaeus, encamping near each other, waited for Tissaphernes more than twenty days, in the course of which there came to visit Ariaeus both his brothers and other relations, and certain other Persians, to see his companions and gave them encouraging hopes; some too were the bearers of assurances from the king that he would not remember to their disadvantage their expedition against him under Cyrus, or anything else that was past. 2. On these things taking place, the followers of Ariaeus evidently began to pay the Greeks less attention, so that, on this account, they rendered most of the Greeks dissatisfied with them; and many of them, going to Clearchus and the other generals, said, 3. "Why do we remain here? are we not aware that the king would wish above all things to destroy us, in order that a dread of going to war with the great king may fall upon the rest of the Greeks? For the present he craftily protracts our stay, because his forces are dispersed; but, when his army is reassembled, it is not possible but that he will attack us. 4. Perhaps, too, he is digging some trench, or building some wall, that the way may be rendered impassable; for he will never consent, at least willingly, that we should go back to Greece and relate how so small a number as we are have defeated the king at his own gates and returned after setting him at nought."

5. To those who thus addressed him, Clearchus answered, "I have been considering all these things as well; but I think that, if we now go away, we shall be thought to go with a view to war, and to act contrary to the terms of the truce. Moreover, in the first place, there will be no one to provide us a market, or any means of procuring provisions; and, in the next place, there will be no one to guide us; besides, the moment that we do this, Ariaeus will separate himself from us, so that not a friend will be left us; and, what is more, our former friends will then become our enemies. 6. Whether there is any other river for us to cross, I do not

know; but as for the Euphrates, we know that it is impossible to cross that, if the enemy try to prevent us. Nor yet, if it should be necessary to fight, have we any horse to support us; while the enemy's cavalry is most numerous and efficient; so that, though we were victorious, how many of our enemies should we be able to kill? And, if we were defeated, it would not be possible for a man of us to escape. 7. With regard to the king, therefore, who is aided by so many advantages, I know not, if he wishes to effect our destruction, why he should swear, and give his right hand, and perjure himself before the gods, and render his pledges faithless both to Greeks and barbarians." He said much besides to the same effect.

8. In the meantime Tissaphernes arrived with his army, as if with the view of returning home; and Orontes came with his army. Orontes also brought with him the king's daughter, whom he had received in marriage. 9. From hence they now proceeded on their march, Tissaphernes being their guide, and securing them opportunities of buying provisions; Ariaeus also, with the barbarian troops of Cyrus, marched in company with Tissaphernes and Orontes, and encamped in common with them. 10. But the Greeks, conceiving a suspicion of these men, began to march by themselves, taking guides of their own; and they always encamped at the distance of a parasang, or little less, from each other; and both parties kept on their guard against one another, as if they had been enemies, and this consequently increased their distrust. 11. More than once, too, as they were gathering fuel, or collecting fodder and other such things in the same quarter, they came to blows with each other; and this was an additional source of animosity between them.

12. After marching three days, they arrived at the wall of Media, as it is called, and passed to the other side of it. This wall was built of burnt bricks, laid in bitumen; it was twenty feet in thickness and a hundred in height, and the length of it was said to be twenty parasangs; and it was not far distant from Babylon. 13. Hence they proceeded, in two days' march, the distance of eight parasangs, crossing two canals,

the one by a permanent bridge, the other by a temporary one formed of seven boats. These canals were supplied from the river Tigris; and from one to the other of them were cut ditches across the country, the first of considerable size, and the next smaller; and at last diminutive drains, such as are cut in Greece through the millet fields. They then arrived at the Tigris, near which there was a large and populous city, called Sitace, distant from the banks of the river only fifteen stadia. 14. In the neighbourhood of this city the Greeks encamped, close to an extensive and beautiful park, thickly planted with all kinds of trees. The barbarians, though they had but just crossed the Tigris, were no longer in sight.

15. After supper Proxenus and Xenophon happened to be walking in front of the place where the arms were piled, when a man approached and inquired of the sentinels where he could see Proxenus or Clearchus. But he did not ask for Menon, though he came from Ariaeus, Menon's intimate friend. 16. Proxenus replying, "I am the person whom you seek," the man said, "Ariaeus and Artaozus, the faithful friends of Cyrus, who are interested for your welfare, have sent me to you, and exhort you to beware lest the barbarians should fall upon you in the night; for there is a considerable body of troops in the adjoining park. 17. They also advise you to send a guard to the bridge over the Tigris, as Tissaphernes designs to break it down in the night, if he can, in order that you may not be able to cross the river, but may be hemmed in between the river and the canal." 18. On hearing the man's message, they conducted him to Clearchus and told him what he had said. When Clearchus heard it he was greatly agitated and alarmed.

19. But a young man, one of those who were present, after reflecting a little on the matter, observed that the imputed designs of making an attack, and of breaking down the bridge, were not consistent. "For," said he, "if they attack us, they must certainly either conquer or be conquered; if then they are to conquer us, why should they break down the bridge? for even though there were many bridges, we have no place where we could save ourselves by flight; 20. but if,

on the other hand, we should conquer them, then, if the bridge is broken down, they will have no place of retreat; nor will any of their friends on the other side of the river, however numerous, be able to come to their assistance when the bridge is destroyed." 21. After listening to these observations, Clearchus asked the messenger what was the extent of the country that lay between the Tigris and the canal. He replied that it was of considerable extent, and that there were several villages and large towns in it. 22. It was then immediately concluded that the barbarians had sent this man with an underhand object, being afraid lest the Greeks, having taken to pieces the bridge, should remain in the island, where they would have, as defences, the river Tigris on the one side, and the canal on the other; and might procure a sufficient supply of provisions from the country which lay between, and which was extensive and fertile, with people in it to cultivate it, and which would also serve as a place of refuge to any that might be inclined to annoy the king.

23. They then prepared for rest, but did not neglect, however, to send a guard to the bridge; but neither did anyone attempt to attack them on any quarter, nor did any of the enemies come near the bridge, as those who were stationed on guard there reported.

24. As soon as it was day they crossed the bridge, which was constructed of thirty-seven boats, with every precaution in their power; for some of the Greeks, who came from Tissaphernes, stated that the enemy meant to attack them as they were crossing; but this report was also false. However, as they were going over, Glus made his appearance, with some others, watching to see if they were crossing the river; and when they saw they were, he immediately rode away.

25. From the Tigris they proceeded, in four days' march, a distance of twenty parasangs, to the river Physcus, which was a plethrum in breadth, and over which was a bridge. Here was situated a large town called Opis, near which an illegitimate brother of Cyrus and Artaxerxes, who was leading a numerous army from Susa and Ecbatana with the intention of assisting the king, met the Greeks, and, ordering his

troops to halt, took a view of the Greeks as they passed by. 26. Clearchus marched his men two abreast, and halted occasionally on the way; and as long as the van of the army halted, so long there was necessarily a halt through the whole of the line, so that even to the Greeks themselves their army seemed very large, and the Persian was amazed at the sight of it.

27. Hence they proceeded through Media, six days' march through a desert country, a distance of thirty parasangs, when they arrived at the villages of Parysatis, the mother of Cyrus and the king; which Tissaphernes, in mockery of Cyrus, gave permission to the Greeks to plunder of everything except the slaves. There was found in them a great quantity of grain and cattle, and other property. 28. Hence they advanced in a march of four days more through the desert, a distance of twenty parasangs, having the Tigris on their left. At the end of the first day's march there was situated on the opposite bank of the river a large and opulent city, called Caenae, whence the barbarians brought over, on rafts made of hide, a supply of bread, cheese, and wine.

5.1. Soon after, they arrived at the river Zabatus, the breadth of which was four plethra. Here they remained three days; during which the same suspicions continued, but no open indication of treachery appeared. 2. Clearchus therefore resolved to have a meeting with Tissaphernes, and, if it was at all possible, to put a stop to these suspicions before open hostilities should arise from them. He accordingly sent a person to say that he wished to have a meeting with Tissaphernes; who at once requested him to come. 3. When they met, Clearchus spoke as follows: "I am aware, Tissaphernes, that oaths have been taken and right hands pledged between us that we will do no injury to each other: nevertheless, I observe you on your guard against us, as though we were enemies; and we, perceiving this, stand on our guard against you. 4. But since, upon attentive observation, I can neither detect you in any attempt to injure us, and since, as I am certain, we have no such intentions towards you, it seemed proper for me to come to a conference with you, that we may put an end, if we can, to our distrust of one another. 5. For I have, before now, known instances of men, who, being in fear of another, some through direct accusations, and others through mere suspicion, have, in their eagerness to act before they suffered, inflicted irremediable evils upon those who neither intended nor wished anything of the kind. 6. Thinking, therefore, that such misunderstandings may be best cleared up by personal communications, I have come here, and am desirous to convince you that you have no just ground for mistrusting us. 7. In the first and principal place, the oaths, which we have sworn by the gods, forbid us to be enemies to each other; and I should never consider him to be envied who is conscious of having disregarded such obligations; for from the vengeance of the gods I know not with what speed anyone could flee so as to escape, or into what darkness he could steal away, or how he could retreat into any stronghold, since all things, in all places, are subject to the gods, and they have power over all everywhere alike. 8. Such are my sentiments respecting the gods, and the oaths which we swore by them, in whose keeping we deposited the friendship that we cemented; but among human advantages, I, for my own part, consider you to be the greatest that we at present possess; 9. for with your assistance, every road is easy, every river is passable, and there will be no want of provisions; but without you all our way would lie through darkness (for we know nothing of it), every river would be difficult to pass, and every multitude of men would be terrible, but solitude most terrible of all, as it is full of extreme perplexity.

10. "And even if we should be so mad as to kill you, what else would be the consequence than that, having slain our benefactor, we should have, to contend with the king as your most powerful avenger? For my own part, of how many and how great expectations I should deprive myself if I attempted to do you any injury, I will make you acquainted. 11. I was desirous that Cyrus should be my friend, as I thought him, of all the men of his time, the most able to ben-

efit those whom he wished to favour. But I now see that you are in the possession both of the power and the territory of Cyrus, while you still retain your own province, and that the power of the king, which was opposed to Cyrus, is ready to support you. 12. Such being the case, who is so mad as not to wish to be your friend?

"But I will mention also the circumstances from which I derive hopes that you will yourself desire to be our friend. 13. I am aware that the Mysians give you much annoyance, and these, I have no doubt, I should be able, with my present force, to render subservient to you; I am aware also that the Pisidians molest you, and I hear that there are many such nations besides, which I think I could prevent from ever disturbing your tranquillity. As for the Egyptians, against whom I perceive you are most of all incensed, I do not see what auxiliary force you could use to chastise them better than that which I now have with me. 14. If, again, among the states that lie around you, you were desirous to become a friend to anyone, you might prove the most powerful of friends; and if any of them gave you any annoyance, you might, by our instrumentality, deal with them as a master, as we should serve you not for the sake of pay merely, but from gratitude, which we should justly feel towards you if we are saved by your means. 15. When I consider all these things, it appears to me so surprising that you should distrust us, that I would most gladly hear the name of him who is so persuasive a speaker as to make you believe that we are forming designs against you."

Thus spoke Clearchus. Tissaphernes replied as follows: 16. "I am delighted, Clearchus, to hear your judicious observations, for, with these sentiments, if you were to meditate anything to my injury, you would appear to be at the same time your own enemy. But that you may be convinced that you have no just cause for distrusting either the king or me, listen to me in your turn. 17. If we wished to destroy you, do we appear to you to be deficient in numbers either of cavalry or infantry, or in warlike equipments, with the aid of which we might be able to do you injury without danger

of suffering any in return? 18. Or do we seem to you likely
to be in want of suitable places to make an attack upon you?
Are there not so many plains which, as the inhabitants of them are friendly to us, you traverse with exceeding
toil? See you not so many mountains before you to be
crossed, which we might, by pre-occupying them, render impassable to you? Or are there not so many rivers at which
we might parcel you out, as many at a time as we might be
willing to engage? Some of these rivers, indeed, you could
not cross at all unless we secured you a passage. 19. But
even supposing that we were baffled in all these points, yet
fire at least would prove its power over the produce of the
soil, by burning which, we could set famine in array against
you, which, though you were the bravest of the brave, you
would find it difficult to withstand. 20. How then, having so
many means of waging war with you, and none of them
attended with danger to ourselves, should we select from
amongst them all this mode, the only one that is impious in
the sight of the gods, the only one that is disgraceful in the
sight of men?

21. "It belongs, altogether, to men who are destitute of
means, deprived of every resource, and under the coercion
of necessity, and at the same time devoid of principle, to
seek to effect their purposes by perjury towards the gods and
breach of faith towards men. We, Clearchus, are not so foolish or so inconsiderate; 22. or why, when we have the opportunity of effecting your destruction, have we made no such
attempt? Be well assured that the cause of this was my desire
to prove myself faithful to the Greeks, and, in consequence
of doing them service, to return supported by that very body
of foreign troops to whom Cyrus, when he went up, trusted
only on account of the pay that he gave them. 23. As to the
particulars in which you will be of service to me, some of
them you have enumerated, but of the greatest of all I am
myself fully conscious; for though it is permitted to the king
alone to wear the turban upright on the head, yet perhaps
another than he may, with your assistance, wear that upright which is on the heart."

24. Tissaphernes, in speaking thus, seemed to Clearchus to speak with sincerity, and he replied, "Do not those, then, who endeavour by calumny to make us enemies, when there are such strong inducements to friendship between us, deserve the severest of punishment?" 25. "Well, then," said Tissaphernes, "if you will come to me, as well generals as captains, in a public manner, I will inform you who they are that tell me that you are forming plots against me and my army." 26. "I will bring them all," said Clearchus, "and, on my part, will let you know the quarter whence I hear reports respecting you." 27. After this conversation, Tissaphernes, behaving to Clearchus with much courtesy, desired him to stay with him, and made him his guest at supper.

On the following day, when Clearchus returned to the camp, he plainly showed that he considered himself to be on the most friendly footing with Tissaphernes, and stated what he had proposed; and he said that those must go to Tissaphernes, whose presence he required, and that whoever of the Greeks should be proved guilty of uttering the alleged calumnies must be punished as traitors and persons ill-affected to the Greeks. 28. It was Menon that he suspected of making the charges, as he knew that he had had an interview with Tissaphernes in company with Ariaeus, and was forming a party and intriguing against himself, in order that, having gained the whole army over to his own interests, he might secure the friendship of Tissaphernes. 29. Clearchus likewise wished the whole army to have their affections fixed on himself, and troublesome rivals to be removed out of his way.

Some of the soldiers urged, in opposition to his advice, that all the captains and generals should not go, and that they ought to place no confidence in Tissaphernes. 30. But Clearchus pressed his proposal with great vehemence, till he at length succeeded in getting five generals and twenty captains to go; and some of the other soldiers followed them, to the number of about two hundred, as if for the purpose of marketing.

31. When they had arrived at the entrance of Tissa-

phernes' tent, the generals, who were Proxenus the Boeotian, Menon the Thessalian, Agias the Arcadian, Clearchus the Lacedaemonian, and Socrates the Achaean, were invited to enter; but the captains waited at the door. 32. Not long after, at one and the same signal, those within were seized, and those without massacred; and immediately afterwards a body of barbarian cavalry, riding through the plain, killed every Greek, slave or freeman, that they met.

33. The Greeks, observing the motions of these cavalry from the camp, were filled with astonishment, and wondered what they could be doing, till Nicarchus, an Arcadian, came fleeing thither, wounded in the belly and holding his intestines in his hands, and related all that had occurred. 34. The Greeks, in consequence, ran to their arms in a state of general consternation, expecting that the enemy would immediately march upon the camp. 35. They however did not all come, but only Ariaeus and Artaozus and Mithridates, who had been Cyrus's most confidential friends; and the interpreter of the Greeks said that he saw with them, and recognized, the brother of Tissaphernes. Other Persians, equipped with corslets, to the number of three hundred, were in attendance on them. 36. As they approached the camp, they called for whatever general or captain of the Greeks might be there to come out to them, that they might deliver a message from the king. 37. There accordingly went forth to them, with much caution, Cleanor the Orchomenian, and Sophaenetus the Stymphalian, generals of the Greeks, and with them Xenophon the Athenian, that he might learn news of Proxenus. As for Cheirisophus, he happened to be absent at some village looking for provisions.

38. When they had stopped just within hearing, Ariaeus said to them, "Clearchus, O Greeks, having been found guilty of perjury, and of violating the truce, has received his just punishment, and is dead; Proxenus and Menon, as having denounced his treachery, are in great honour; but the king demands of you your arms; for he says that they are his, as they belonged to Cyrus his slave." 39. To this the Greeks answered (Cleanor the Orchomenian spoke for

them), "Ariaeus, most wicked of men, and the rest of you, as many as were the friends of Cyrus, have you no regard either for gods or men, that, after having sworn that you would consider our friends and enemies to be likewise yours, you have thus, after treacherously deserting us in concert with Tissaphernes, the most godless and most unprincipled of human beings, murdered the very men to whom you swore alliance, and, abandoning us who are left, have come against us in conjunction with our enemies?" 40. Ariaeus replied, "Clearchus had been previously detected in treacherous designs against Tissaphernes and Orontes, and all of us who accompany them." 41. To this Xenophon rejoined, "Clearchus, then, if he infringed the truce in violation of his oath, is deservedly punished; for it is just that those who violate their oaths should suffer death; but as for Proxenus and Menon, as they are your benefactors and our generals, send them hither; for it is clear that, being friends to both parties, they will endeavour to advise what is best both for you and for us." 42. The barbarians, after conversing among themselves for some time, departed without making any answer to this proposal.

6.1. The generals who were thus made prisoners were taken up to the king and put to death by being beheaded.

One of them, Clearchus, by the general consent of all who were acquainted with him, appears to have been a man well qualified for war, and extremely fond of military enterprise. 2. For as long as the Lacedaemonians were at war with the Athenians, he remained in the service of his country; but when the peace took place, having induced his government to believe that the Thracians were committing ravages on the Greeks, and having gained his point, as well as he could, with the ephors, he sailed from home to make war upon the Thracians that lie above the Chersonesus and Perinthus. 3. But when the ephors, after he was gone, having for some reason changed their mind, took measures to oblige him to turn back from the Isthmus, he then no longer paid obedience to their commands but sailed away to the Hellespont, 4. and was in consequence condemned to death for disobedience by the chief magistrates at Sparta. Being then an exile, he went to Cyrus; and by what methods he conciliated the favour of Cyrus has been told in another place. Cyrus presented him with ten thousand darics; 5. and he, on receiving that sum, did not give himself up to idleness, but, having collected an army with the money, made war upon the Thracians, and conquered them in battle, and from that time plundered and laid waste their country, and continued this warfare till Cyrus had need of his army; when he went to him for the purpose of again making war in concert with him.

6. These seem to me to have been the proceedings of one fond of war, who, when he might have lived in peace without disgrace or loss, chose war in preference; when he might have spent his time in idleness, voluntarily underwent toil for the sake of military adventure; and when he might have enjoyed riches in security, chose rather, by engaging in warfare, to diminish their amount. He was indeed led by inclination to spend his money in war, as he might have spent it in pursuits of gallantry, or any other pleasure; to such a degree was he fond of war. 7. He appears also to have been qualified for military undertakings, as he liked perilous adventure, was ready to march day and night against the enemy, and was possessed of great presence of mind in circumstances of difficulty, as those who were with him on all such occasions were universally ready to acknowledge.

8. For commanding troops he was said to be qualified in as great a degree as was consistent with his temper; for he was excelled by no one in ability to contrive how an army might have provisions, and to procure them; and he was equally fitted to impress on all around him the necessity of obeying Clearchus. 9. This he effected by severity, for he was of a stern countenance and harsh voice, and he always punished violently, and sometimes in anger, so that he occasionally repented of what he had done. He punished too on principle, for he thought that there could be no efficiency in an army undisciplined by chastisement. 10. He is also re-

ported to have said that a soldier ought to fear his commander more than the enemy, if he would either keep guard well, or abstain from doing injury to friends, or march without hesitation against foes. 11. In circumstances of danger, accordingly, the soldiers were willing to obey him implicitly, and wished for no other leader; for they said that the sternness in his countenance then assumed an appearance of cheerfulness, and that what was severe in it seemed undauntedness against the enemy; so that it appeared indicative of safety and not of austerity. 12. But when they were out of danger, and were at liberty to betake themselves to other chiefs, they deserted him in great numbers; for he had nothing attractive in him, but was always forbidding and repulsive, so that the soldiers felt towards him as boys towards their master. 13. Hence it was that he never had anyone who followed him out of friendship and attachment to his person; though such as followed him from being appointed to the service by their country, or from being compelled by want or other necessity, he found extremely submissive to him. 14. And when they began under his command to gain victories over the enemy, there were many important circumstances that concurred to render his troops excellent soldiers; for their perfect confidence against the enemy had its effect, and their dread of punishment from him rendered them strictly observant of discipline. 15. Such was his character as a commander. But he was said to have been by no means willing to be commanded by others. When he was put to death, he was about fifty years of age.

16. Proxenus the Boeotian from his earliest youth felt a desire to become a man capable of great undertakings; and through this desire paid Gorgias of Leontini for instruction. 17. When he had passed some time with him, and thought himself capable of command, and, if honoured with the friendship of the great, of making no inadequate return for their favours, he proceeded to take a part in this enterprise with Cyrus; and expected to acquire in it a great name, extensive influence, and abundant wealth. 18. But though he earnestly wished for these things, he at the same time plainly

showed that he was unwilling to acquire any of them by injustice, but that he thought he ought to obtain them by just and honourable means, or otherwise not at all.

19. He was indeed able to command orderly and well-disposed men but incapable of inspiring ordinary soldiers with either respect or fear for him; he stood even more in awe of those under his command than they of him; and evidently showed that he was more afraid of being disliked by his soldiers, than his soldiers of being disobedient to him. 20. He thought it sufficient, both for being and appearing capable of command, to praise him who did well, and withhold his praise from the offender. Such, therefore, of his followers as were of honourable and virtuous character were much attached to him, but the unprincipled formed designs upon him as a man easy to manage. He was about thirty years old when he was put to death.

21. As for Menon the Thessalian, he ever manifested an excessive desire for riches, being desirous of command that he might receive greater pay, and desirous of honours that he might obtain greater perquisites; and he wished to be well with those in power, in order that when he did wrong he might not suffer punishment. 22. To accomplish what he desired, he thought that the shortest road lay through perjury, falsehood, and deceit; while sincerity and truth he regarded as no better than folly. 23. He evidently had no affection for any man; and as for those to whom he professed to be a friend, he was unmistakably plotting mischief against them. He never ridiculed an enemy, but always used to talk with his associates as if ridiculing all of them. 24. He formed no designs on the property of his enemies, for he thought it difficult to take what belonged to such as were on their guard against him, but looked upon himself as the only person sensible how very easy it was to invade the unguarded property of friends.

25. Those whom he saw given to perjury and injustice he feared as men well armed, but sought to practise on those who were pious and observant of truth as imbeciles. 26. As another might take a pride in religion, and truth, and justice,

so Menon took a pride in being able to deceive, in devising falsehoods, in sneering at friends; and thought the man who was guileless was to be regarded as deficient in knowledge of the world. He believed that he must conciliate those in whose friendship he wished to stand first by calumniating such as already held the chief place in their favour. 27. The soldiers he tried to render obedient to him by being an accomplice in their dishonesty. He expected to be honoured and courted by showing that he had the power and the will to inflict the greatest injuries. When anyone deserted him, he spoke of it as a favour on his own part that, while he made use of his services, he did not work his destruction.

28. As to such parts of his history as are little known, I might, if I were to speak of them, say something untrue of him; but those which everyone knows are these. While yet in the prime of youth he obtained, at the hands of Aristippus, the command of his corps of mercenaries. He was also, in his prime, most intimate with Ariaeus, though a barbarian, as Ariaeus delighted in beautiful youths. He himself, too, while yet a beardless youth, made a favourite of Tharypas, who had arrived at manhood.

29. When his fellow officers were put to death, because they had served with Cyrus against the king, he, though he had done the same, was not put to death with them; but after the death of the other generals, he died under a punishment inflicted by the king, not like Clearchus and the other commanders, who were beheaded (which appears to be the speediest kind of death), but after living a year in torture, like a malefactor, he is said at length to have met his end.

30. Agias the Arcadian and Socrates the Achaean were also put to death. These no one ever derided as wanting courage in battle, or blamed for their conduct towards their friends. They were both about five-and-thirty years of age.

From BOOK III

1. . . . . 4. There was in the army a certain Xenophon, an Athenian, who accompanied it neither in the character of general nor captain nor common soldier, but it had happened that Proxenus, an old guest-friend of his, had sent for him from home, giving him a promise that if he came he would recommend him to the friendship of Cyrus, whom he considered, he said, as a greater object of regard than his own country. 5. Xenophon, on reading the letter, consulted Socrates the Athenian as to the propriety of making the journey; and Socrates, fearing that if he attached himself to Cyrus it might prove a ground for accusation against him with his country, because Cyrus was thought to have zealously assisted the Lacedaemonians in their war with Athens, advised Xenophon to go to Delphi and consult the god respecting the expedition. 6. Xenophon, having gone thither accordingly, inquired of Apollo to which of the gods he should sacrifice and pray, in order most honourably and successfully to perform the journey which he contemplated, and, after prosperously accomplishing it, to return in safety. Apollo indicated to him the gods to whom to sacrifice. 7. When he returned, he repeated the oracle to Socrates, who, on hearing it, blamed him for not asking Apollo in the first place whether it were better for him to go or stay at home; whereas, having settled with himself that he would go, he only asked how he might best go. "But since you have," said he, "put the question thus, you must do what the god has directed."

8. Xenophon, therefore, having sacrificed to the gods that Apollo commanded, set sail, and found Proxenus and Cyrus at Sardis, just setting out on their march up the country, and was presented to Cyrus. 9. Proxenus desiring that he should remain with them, Cyrus joined in the same de-

sire, and said that as soon as the expedition was ended he would send him home again. The expedition was said to be intended against the Pisidians. 10. Xenophon accordingly joined in the enterprise, being thus deceived, but not by Proxenus; for he did not know that the movement was against the king, nor did any other of the Greeks, except Clearchus. When they arrived in Cilicia, however, it appeared manifest to everyone that it was against the king that their force was directed; but, though they were afraid of the length of the journey, and unwilling to proceed, yet the greater part of them, out of respect both for one another and for Cyrus, continued to follow him, of which number was Xenophon.

11. When this perplexity occurred,[1] Xenophon was distressed as well as the other Greeks, and unable to rest, but, having at length got a little sleep, he had a dream in which, in the midst of a thunder-storm, a bolt seemed to him to fall upon his father's house, and the house in consequence became all in a blaze. 12. Being greatly frightened, he immediately awoke, and considered his dream as in one respect favourable, inasmuch as, being in troubles and dangers, he seemed to behold a great light from Zeus; but in another respect he was alarmed, because the dream appeared to him to be from Zeus the King, and the fire to blaze all around him, lest he should be unable to escape from the king's territories, but should be hemmed in on all sides by inextricable difficulties.

13. What it betokens, however, to see such a dream, we may conjecture from the occurrences that happened after the dream. What immediately followed was this. As soon as he awoke, the thought that first occurred to him was, "Why do I lie here? The night is passing away. With daylight it is probable that the enemy will come upon us; and if we once fall into the hands of the king, what is there to prevent us from being put to death with ignominy after witnessing the most grievous sufferings among our comrades, and enduring every

---

[1] After this brief digression introducing himself, Xenophon now returns to his narrative.

severity of torture ourselves? 14. Yet no one concerts measures, or takes thought, for our defence, but we lie still, as if we were at liberty to enjoy repose. From what city, then, do I expect a leader to undertake our defence? What age am I waiting for to come to myself? Assuredly I shall never be older, if I give myself up to the enemy today."

15. After these reflections he arose, and called together, in the first place, the captains that were under Proxenus. When they were assembled, he said, "For my part, captains, I cannot sleep, nor, I should think, can you, nor can I lie still any longer, when I consider in what circumstances we are placed; 16. for it is plain that the enemy did not openly manifest hostility towards us until they thought that they had judiciously arranged their plans; but on our side no one takes any thought how we may best maintain a contest with them. 17. Yet if we prove remiss, and fall into the power of the king, what may we not expect to suffer from a man who cut off the head and hand of his own brother by the same mother, even after he was dead, and fixed them upon a stake? What may not we expect to suffer, who have no relative to take our part, and who have marched against him to make him a subject instead of a monarch, and to put him to death if it should lie in our power? 18. Will he not proceed to every extremity, that by reducing us to the last degree of ignominious suffering he may inspire all men with a dread of ever taking the field against him? We must however try every expedient not to fall into his hands. 19. For myself, I never ceased, while the truce lasted, to consider ourselves as objects of pity, and to regard the king and his people as objects of envy, as I contemplated how extensive and valuable a country they possessed, how great an abundance of provisions, how many slaves and cattle, and how vast a quantity of gold and raiment; 20. while, on the other hand, when I reflected on the condition of our own soldiers, that we had no share in any of all these blessings, unless we bought it, and knew that few of us had any longer money to buy, and that our oaths restrained us from getting provisions, otherwise than by buying, I sometimes, on taking all these

circumstances into consideration, feared the continuance of peace more than I now fear war.

21. "But since they have put an end to peace, their own haughtiness and our mistrust seem likewise to be brought to an end; for the advantages which I have mentioned lie now as prizes between us, for whichsoever of us shall prove the better men; and the gods are the judges of the contest, who, as is just, will be on our side. 22. The enemy have offended them by perjury, while we, though seeing many good things to tempt us, have resolutely abstained from all of them through regard to our oaths; so that, as it seems to me, we may advance to the combat with much greater confidence than they can feel. 23. We have bodies, moreover, better able than theirs to endure cold and heat and toil; and we have, with the help of the gods, more resolute souls; while the enemy, if the gods, as before, grant us success, will be found more vulnerable to wounds and death than we are. 24. But possibly others of you entertain the same thoughts; let us not, then, in the name of heaven, wait for others to come and exhort us to noble deeds, but let us be ourselves the first to excite others to exert their valour. Prove yourselves the bravest of the captains, and more worthy to lead than those who are now leaders. 25. As for me, if you wish to take the start in the course, I am willing to follow you, or, if you appoint me to be a leader, I shall not make my youth an excuse, but shall think myself sufficiently mature to defend myself against harm."

26. Thus spoke Xenophon; and the captains, on hearing his observations, all desired him to be their leader, except a certain Apollonides, a Boeotian in his manner of speaking. This man said that whoever asserted they could gain safety by any other means than by obtaining, if he could, the king's consent to it, talked absurdly; and at the same time began to enumerate the difficulties surrounding them. 27. But Xenophon, interrupting him, said, "O most wonderful of men, you neither understand what you see, nor remember what you hear. Yet you were on the same spot with those here present, when the king, after Cyrus was dead, being in high spir-

its at the circumstance, sent to demand that we should deliver up our arms; 28. and when we, refusing to deliver them
up, and appearing in full armour, went and encamped over
against him, what means did he not try, sending deputies,
asking for a truce, and supplying us with provisions until he
obtained a truce? 29. But when, on the other hand, our generals and captains went to confer with the barbarians, as you
now advise us to do, without their arms, and relying on the
truce, were they not beaten, goaded, outraged, and were
they not unable, wretched men, to die, though, I should
think, greatly longing for death? And do you, knowing all
these occurrences, say that those who exhort us to defend
ourselves talk absurdly, and advise us to go again to try persuasion? 30. To me, men, it seems that we should no longer
admit this man into the same service with ourselves, but
take from him his captaincy, and, laying baggage on his
back, make use of him in that capacity; for he disgraces both
his own country and all Greece, inasmuch as, being a Greek,
he is of such a character." 31. Here Agasias of Stymphalus,
proceeding to speak, said, "But this man, assuredly, has
nothing to do either with Boeotia or with Greece at all, for
I have observed that he has both his ears bored, like a
Lydian." Such indeed was the case; and they accordingly expelled him.

32. The rest, proceeding to the different divisions of the
troops, called up the general wherever there was a general
surviving, and the lieutenant general where the general was
dead, and the captain wherever there was a captain surviving. 33. When they were all come together, they sat down
before the place where the arms were piled, and the generals and captains assembled were about a hundred in all.
The time when the meeting took place was about midnight.
34. Hieronymus, a native of Elis, the oldest of all the captains that had served under Proxenus, was the first to speak,
as follows: "It has seemed proper to us, generals and
captains, on contemplating the present state of our affairs,
to meet together ourselves, and to call upon you to join us,
that we may determine, if we can, on some plan for our

benefit. But do you, Xenophon, first represent to the assembly what you have already observed to us."

35. Xenophon accordingly said, "We are all aware that the king and Tissaphernes have made prisoners of as many of us as they could; and it is evident that they are forming designs against the rest of us, that they may put us to death if they can. But on our parts I think that every means should be adopted in order that we may not fall into the barbarians' hands, but rather that they, if we can accomplish it, may fall into ours. 36. Be well assured then, that you, who have now met together in such numbers, have upon you a most important responsibility; for all the soldiers look to you, and if they see you dispirited they will themselves lose courage, but if both you yourselves appear well prepared to meet the enemy, and exhort others to be equally prepared, be certain that they will follow you, and strive to imitate you. 37. Perhaps, too, it is right that you should show some superiority over them; for you are their generals, their officers, and their captains, and, when there was peace, you enjoyed advantages over them in money and honour; and now, in consequence, when war arises, you ought to prove yourselves preeminent over the multitude, and to take the lead in forming plans for them, and, should it ever be necessary, in toiling for them. 38. And, in the first place, I think that you will greatly benefit the army if you take care that generals and captains be chosen as soon as possible in place of those whom we have lost; for without commanders nothing honourable or advantageous can be achieved, I may say in one word, anywhere, but least of all in the field of battle. Good order conduces to safety, but want of order has already proved fatal to many.

39. "Again, when you have appointed as many commanders as are requisite, I consider that if you were to assemble and encourage the rest of the soldiers, you would act very suitably to the occasion; 40. for you perhaps observe, as well as myself, how dejectedly they have now come to the place of arms, and how dejectedly they go upon guard, so that, while they are in such a condition, I know not for

what service anyone could employ them, whether required by night or by day. 41. But if anyone could change the direction of their thoughts, so that they may contemplate not merely what they are likely to suffer but what they may be able to do, they will become much more eager for action; 42. for you know that it is neither numbers nor strength which gives the victory in war, but that whichsoever side, with the aid of the gods, advances on the enemy with the more resolute courage, their opponents, in general, cannot withstand their onset. 43. I have also remarked, men, that such as are eager in the field to preserve their lives at any rate, for the most part perish wretchedly and ignominiously, while I see that such as reflect that death is to all men common and inevitable, and seek in battle only to fall with honour, more frequently, from whatever cause, arrive at old age, and live, while they live, with greater happiness. 44. Being aware, then, of these facts, it behoves us, such are the circumstances in which we are placed, both to prove ourselves to be brave soldiers, and to exhort others to be so likewise." 45. Having spoken thus, he stopped.

After him Cheirisophus said, "Till the present moment, Xenophon, I knew nothing of you, except having heard that you were an Athenian, but now I have to praise you both for what you say and what you do, and could wish that there were very many like you; for it would be a general good. 46. And now," he added, "let us not delay, men, but proceed at once to choose commanders, since you need them, and when you have elected them, come to the centre of the camp, and bring those that are chosen; and we will then call the rest of the soldiers together here. And let Tolmides the herald," said he, "come with us." 47. As he said this, he rose up, that the necessary measures might not be delayed, but carried at once into execution. There were accordingly chosen commanders, Timasion a Dardanian in place of Clearchus, Xanthicles an Achaean in that of Socrates, Cleanor an Arcadian in that of Agias, Philesius an Achaean in that of Menon, and Xenophon of Athens in that of Proxenus.

From BOOK IV

. . . . . .

4.1. When they had crossed the river, and had ranged themselves in order about noon, they proceeded through the country of Armenia, consisting wholly of plains and gently sloping hills, a distance of not less than five parasangs; for there were no villages near the river, in consequence of the hostilities with the Carduchi. 2. The village, however, at which they at length arrived, was of considerable size, and contained a palace for the satrap; upon most of the houses there were towers, and provisions were in great plenty.

3. Hence they proceeded, two days' journey, a distance of ten parasangs, until they passed round the sources of the river Tigris. From hence they advanced, three days' journey, fifteen parasangs, to the river Teleboas, a stream not large, indeed, but of much beauty; and there were many villages on its banks. 4. This part of the country was called Western Armenia. The governor of it was Tiribazus, who was an intimate friend of the king; and no one else, when he was present, assisted the king to mount his horse. 5. He now rode up with a body of cavalry, and, sending forward an interpreter, said that he wished to speak with the commanders. The generals thought proper to hear what he had to say, and advancing within hearing, asked what he wanted. 6. He replied that he wished to make a treaty with them on the conditions that he himself should not hurt the Greeks, and that the Greeks should not burn the houses, but should be at liberty to take such provisions as they required. This proposal was agreeable to the generals, and they concluded a treaty upon these terms.

7. Hence they proceeded, three days' march, a distance of fifteen parasangs, through a plain; and Tiribazus followed them with his troops, keeping at the distance of about

ten stadia. They then came to a palace, with several villages around it stored with abundance of provisions. 8. While they were encamped, there fell a great quantity of snow in the night; and in the morning it was thought advisable that the companies and officers should take up their quarters in the neighbouring villages; for they perceived no enemy, and it appeared to be safe on account of the quantity of the snow. 9. Here they found all kinds of excellent provisions, cattle, wheat, old wines of great fragrance, dried grapes, and vegetables of all kinds.

Some of the soldiers, however, who had strolled away from the camp, brought word that many fires had been visible during the night. 10. The generals thought it unsafe, therefore, for the troops to quarter apart, and resolved to bring the whole army together again. They accordingly assembled, for it seemed to be clearing up. 11. But as they were passing the night here, there fell a vast quantity of snow, so that it covered both the arms and the men as they lay on the ground. The snow cramped the baggage-cattle, and many men were very reluctant to rise; for, as they lay, the snow that had fallen upon them served to keep them warm, when it had not dropped off. 12. But when Xenophon was hardy enough to rise without his outer garment, and to cleave wood, someone else then rose, and taking the wood from him, cleft it himself. Soon after, the rest got up, and lighted fires and anointed themselves; 13. for abundance of ointment was found there, made of hog's lard, sesamum, bitter almonds, and turpentine, which they used instead of olive oil. Of the same materials also a perfumed unguent was found.

14. After this it was resolved to quarter again throughout the villages, under shelter; and the soldiers went off with great shouting and delight to the cottages and provisions. Those who had set fire to the houses, when they quitted them before, paid the penalty of having to encamp uncomfortably in the open air. 15. Hence they despatched in the night Democrates of Temenos, giving him a detachment of men, to the hills where the stragglers said that they

had seen the fires; they selected him because he was thought on several former occasions to have brought exact information concerning such matters, reporting what was, just as it appeared, and what was not, as not existing. 16. Having gone, he said that he saw no fires, but he brought with him a captive that he had taken, having a Persian bow and quiver, and a short battle-axe, such as the Amazons have. 17. Being asked of what country he was, he said that he was a Persian, and that he was going from the army of Tiribazus to get provisions. They then asked him how large the army was, and for what purpose it was assembled. 18. He said that Tiribazus had his own troops, and some mercenaries from the Chalybes and Taochians; and that he was prepared to attack the Greeks in their passage over the mountains, at a narrow defile through which lay their only road.

19. The generals, on hearing this, resolved to collect the army, and, leaving a guard, with Sophaenetus the Stymphalian as commander over those who stayed behind, proceeded to march without delay, taking the man that had been captured for their guide. 20. After they had passed the mountains, the peltasts, who went before the rest, and were the first to discover the enemy's camp, did not wait for the heavy-armed men, but ran forward with a shout to attack it. 21. The barbarians, hearing the noise, did not stand their ground, but fled; some of them however were killed, and about twenty horses taken, as was also the tent of Tiribazus, and in it some couches with silver feet, and drinking-cups, and some prisoners, who said that they were bakers and cupbearers. 22. When the officers of the heavy-armed troops heard what had taken place, they resolved upon marching back as fast as possible to their own camp, lest any attempt should be made on those who had been left there. Calling in the men immediately, therefore, by sound of trumpet, they returned to the camp the same day.

5.1. The next day it was thought necessary to march away as fast as possible, before the enemy's force should be reassembled and get possession of the passes. Collecting their baggage at once, therefore, they set forward through a deep snow, taking with them several guides; and, having the same day passed the height on which Tiribazus had intended to attack them, they encamped. 2. Hence they proceeded three days' journey through a desert tract of country, a distance of fifteen parasangs, to the river Euphrates, and passed it without being wet higher than the middle. The sources of the river were said not to be far off. 3. From hence they advanced three days' march, through much snow and a level plain, a distance of fifteen parasangs; the third day's march was extremely troublesome, as the north wind blew full in their faces, completely parching up everything and benumbing the men. 4. One of the seers, in consequence, advised that they should sacrifice to the wind; and a sacrifice was accordingly offered; when the vehemence of the wind appeared to everyone manifestly to abate. The depth of the snow was a fathom, so that many of the baggage-cattle and slaves perished, with about thirty of the soldiers. 5. They continued to burn fires through the whole night, for there was plenty of wood at the place of encampment. But those who came up late could get no wood; those therefore who had arrived before, and had kindled fires, would not admit the latecomers to the fire unless they gave them a share of the wheat or other provisions that they had brought. 6. Thus they shared with each other what they respectively had. In the places where the fires were made, as the snow melted, there were formed large pits that reached down to the ground; and here there was accordingly opportunity to measure the depth of the snow.

7. From hence they marched through snow the whole of the following day, and many of the men contracted the *bulimia*. Xenophon, who commanded in the rear, finding in his way such of the men as had fallen down with it, knew not what disease it was. 8. But as one of those acquainted with it told him that they were evidently affected with *bulimia,* and that they would get up if they had something to eat, he went round among the baggage, and, wherever he saw anything eatable, he gave it out, and sent such as were able to

run to distribute it among those diseased, who, as soon as they had eaten, rose up and continued their march. 9. As they proceeded, Cheirisophus came, just as it grew dark, to a village, and found, at a spring in front of the rampart, some women and girls belonging to the place fetching water. 10. The women asked them who they were; and the interpreter answered, in the Persian language, that they were people going from the king to the satrap. They replied that he was not there, but about a parasang off. However, as it was late, they went with the water-carriers within the rampart to the head man of the village. 11. And here Cheirisophus, and as many of the troops as could come up, encamped; but of the rest, such as were unable to get to the end of the journey spent the night on the way without food or fire; and some of the soldiers lost their lives on that occasion. 12. Some of the enemy too, who had collected themselves into a body, pursued our rear, and seized any of the baggage-cattle that were unable to proceed, fighting with one another for the possession of them. Such of the soldiers, also, as had lost their sight from the effects of the snow, or had had their toes mortified by the cold, were left behind. 13. It was found to be a relief to the eyes against the snow if the soldiers kept something black before them on the march, and to the feet if they kept constantly in motion and allowed themselves no rest, and if they took off their shoes in the night. 14. But as to such as slept with their shoes on, the straps worked into their feet, and the soles were frozen about them; for when their old shoes had failed them, shoes of raw hides had been made by the men themselves from the newly skinned oxen.

15. From such unavoidable sufferings, some of the soldiers were left behind, who, seeing a piece of ground of a black appearance, from the snow having disappeared there, conjectured that it must have melted; and it had in fact melted in the spot from the effect of a fountain, which was sending up vapour in a woody hollow close at hand. Turning aside thither, they sat down and refused to proceed farther. 16. Xenophon, who was with the rear guard, as soon as

he heard this, tried to prevail on them by every art and means not to be left behind, telling them, at the same time, that the enemy were collected and pursuing them in great numbers. At last he grew angry, and they told him to kill them, as they were quite unable to go forward. 17. He then thought it the best course to strike terror, if possible, into the enemy that were behind, lest they should fall upon the exhausted soldiers. It was now dark, and the enemy were advancing with a great noise, quarrelling about the booty that they had taken; 18. when such of the rear guard as were not disabled started up and rushed towards them, while the tired men, shouting as loud as they could, clashed their spears against their shields. The enemy, struck with alarm, threw themselves among the snow into the hollow, and no one of them afterwards made themselves heard from any quarter.

19. Xenophon, and those with him, telling the sick men that a party should come to their relief next day, proceeded on their march, but before they had gone four stadia they found other soldiers resting by the way in the snow, and covered up with it, no guard being stationed over them. They roused them up, but they said that the head of the army was not moving forward. 20. Xenophon, going past them, and sending on some of the ablest of the peltasts, ordered them to ascertain what it was that hindered their progress. They brought word that the whole army was in that manner taking rest. 21. Xenophon and his men, therefore, stationing such a guard as they could, took up their quarters there without fire or supper. When it was near day, he sent the youngest of his men to the sick, telling them to rouse them and oblige them to proceed. 22. At this juncture Cheirisophus sent some of his people from the villages to see how the rear were faring. The young men were rejoiced to see them, and gave them the sick to conduct to the camp, while they themselves went forward, and, before they had gone twenty stadia, found themselves at the village in which Cheirisophus was quartered. 23. When they came together, it was thought safe enough to lodge the troops up and down in the villages. Cheirisophus accordingly remained where he was, and the

other officers, appropriating by lot the several villages that they had in sight, went to their respective quarters with their men.

24. Here Polycrates, an Athenian captain, requested leave to advance, and, taking with him the most active of his men, and hastening to the village which Xenophon had been allotted, surprised all the villagers, and their head man, in their houses, together with seventeen colts that were bred as a tribute for the king, and the head man's daughter, who had been but nine days married; her husband was gone out to hunt hares, and was not found in any of the villages. 25. Their houses were under ground, the entrance like the mouth of a well, but spacious below; there were passages dug into them for the cattle, but the people descended by ladders. In the houses were goats, sheep, cows, and fowls, with their young; all the cattle were kept on fodder within the walls. 26. There was also wheat, barley, leguminous vegetables, and barley wine in large bowls; the grains of barley floated in it even with the brims of the vessels, and reeds also lay in it, some larger and some smaller, without joints; 27. and these, when anyone was thirsty, he was to take in his mouth, and suck. The liquor was very strong, unless one mixed water with it, and a very pleasant drink to those accustomed to it.

28. Xenophon made the chief man of his village sup with him, and told him to be of good courage, assuring him that he should not be deprived of his children, and that they would not go away without filling his house with provisions in return for what they took, if he would but prove himself the author of some service to the army till they should reach another tribe. 29. This he promised, and, to show his good will, pointed out where some wine was buried. This night, therefore, the soldiers rested in their several quarters in the midst of great abundance, setting a guard over the chief, and keeping his children at the same time under their eye. 30. The following day Xenophon took the head man and went with him to Cheirisophus, and wherever he passed by a village he turned aside to visit those who were quartered in it,

and found them in all parts feasting and enjoying themselves; nor would they anywhere let them go till they had set refreshments before them. 31. And they placed everywhere upon the same table lamb, kid, pork, veal, and fowl, with plenty of bread both of wheat and barley. 32. Whenever any person, to pay a compliment, wished to drink to another, he took him to the large bowl, where he had to stoop down and drink, sucking like an ox. The chief they allowed to take whatever he pleased, but he accepted nothing from them; where he found any of his relatives, however, he took them with him.

33. When they came to Cheirisophus, they found his men also feasting in their quarters, crowned with wreaths made of hay, and Armenian boys in their barbarian dress, waiting upon them, to whom they made signs what they were to do as if they had been deaf and dumb. 34. When Cheirisophus and Xenophon had saluted one another, they both asked the chief man, through the interpreter who spoke the Persian language, what country it was. He replied that it was Armenia. They then asked him for whom the horses were bred; and he said that they were a tribute for the king, and added that the neighbouring country was that of the Chalybes, and told them in what direction the road lay. 35. Xenophon then went away, conducting the chief back to his family, giving him the horse that he had taken, which was rather old, to fatten and offer in sacrifice (for he had heard that it had been consecrated to the sun), being afraid, indeed, that it might die, as it had been injured by the journey. He then took some of the young horses, and gave one of them to each of the other generals and captains. 36. The horses in this country were smaller than those of Persia, but far more spirited. The chief instructed the men to tie little bags round the feet of the horses and other cattle when they drove them through the snow, for without such bags they sank up to their bellies.

6.1. When the eighth day was come, Xenophon committed the guide to Cheirisophus. He left the chief all the members of his family except his son, a youth just coming to puberty; him he gave in charge to Episthenes of Amphipolis, in order that if the father should conduct them properly, he might return home with him. At the same time they carried to his house as many provisions as they could, and then broke up their camp and resumed their march. 2. The chief conducted them through the snow, walking at liberty. When he came to the end of the third day's march, Cheirisophus was angry at him for not guiding them to some villages. He said that there were none in that part of the country. Cheirisophus then struck him, but did not confine him; 3. and in consequence he ran off in the night, leaving his son behind him. This affair, the ill-treatment and neglect of the guide, was the only cause of dissension between Cheirisophus and Xenophon during the march. Episthenes conceived an affection for the youth, and, taking him home, found him extremely attached to him.

4. After this occurrence they proceeded seven days' journey, five parasangs each day, along the river Phasis, the breadth of which is a plethrum. 5. Hence they advanced two days' journey, ten parasangs; when, on the pass that led over the mountains into the plain, the Chalybes, Taochi, and Phasians were drawn up to oppose their progress. 6. Cheirisophus, seeing these enemies in possession of the height, came to a halt, at the distance of about thirty stadia, that he might not approach them while leading the army in a column. He accordingly ordered the other officers to bring up their companies, that the whole force might be formed in line.

7. When the rear guard was come up, he called together the generals and captains, and spoke to them as follows: "The enemy, as you see, are in possession of the pass over the mountains; and it is proper for us to consider how we may encounter them to the best advantage. 8. It is my opinion, therefore, that we should direct the troops to get their dinner, and that we ourselves should hold a council, in the meantime, whether it is advisable to cross the mountain today or tomorrow." 9. "It seems best to me," exclaimed

Cleanor, "to march at once, as soon as we have dined and resumed our arms, against the enemy; for if we waste the present day in inaction, the enemy who are now looking down upon us will grow bolder, and it is likely that, as their confidence is increased, others will join them in geater numbers."

10. After him Xenophon said, "I am of opinion that, if it is necessary to fight, we ought to make our arrangements so as to fight with the greatest advantage; but that, if we propose to pass the mountains as easily as possible, we ought to consider how we may incur the fewest wounds and lose the fewest men. 11. The range of hills, as far as we see, extends more than sixty stadia in length; but the people nowhere seem to be watching us except along the line of road; and it is therefore better, I think, to endeavour to try to seize unobserved some part of the unguarded range, and to get possession of it, if we can, beforehand, than to attack a strong post and men prepared to resist us. 12. For it is far less difficult to march up a steep ascent without fighting than along a level road with enemies on each side; and, in the night, if men are not obliged to fight, they can see better what is before them than by day if engaged with enemies; while a rough road is easier to the feet to those who are marching without molestation than a smooth one to those who are pelted on the head with missiles. 13. Nor do I think it at all impracticable for us to steal a way for ourselves, as we can march by night, so as not to be seen, and can keep at such a distance from the enemy as to allow no possibility of being heard. We seem likely, too, in my opinion, if we make a pretended attack on this point, to find the rest of the range still less guarded; for the enemy will so much the more probably stay where they are.

14. "But why should I speak doubtfully about stealing? For I hear that you Lacedaemonians, Cheirisophus, such of you at least as are of full citizen status, practise stealing from your boyhood, and it is not a disgrace, but an honour, to steal whatever the law does not forbid; 15. while, in order that you may steal with the utmost dexterity, and strive to

escape discovery, it is appointed by law that, if you are caught stealing, you are scourged. It is now high time for you, therefore, to give proof of your education, and to take care that we are not caught stealing a bit of the mountain so we may not receive many stripes."

16. "But I hear that you Athenians also," rejoined Cheirisophus, "are very clever at stealing the public money, though great danger threatens him that steals it; and that your best men steal it most, if indeed your best men are thought worthy to be your magistrates; so that it is time for you likewise to give proof of your education."

17. "I am then ready," exclaimed Xenophon, "to march with the rear guard, as soon as we have supped, to take possession of the hills. I have guides too, for our light-armed men captured some of the marauders following us by lying in ambush; and from them I learn that the mountains are not impassable, but are grazed over by goats and oxen, so that if we once gain possession of any part of the range, there will be tracks also for our baggage-cattle. 18. I expect also that the enemy will no longer keep their ground when they see us upon a level with them on the heights, for they will not now come down to be upon a level with us." 19. Cheirisophus then said, "But why should you go, and leave the charge of the rear? Rather send others, unless some volunteers present themselves." 20. Upon this Aristonymus of Methydria came forward with his heavy-armed men, and Aristeas of Chios and Nicomachus of Oeta with their light-armed; and they made an arrangement that as soon as they should reach the top they should light a number of fires. 21. Having settled these points, they went to dinner; and after dinner Cheirisophus led forward the whole army ten stadia towards the enemy, that he might appear to be fully resolved to march against them on that quarter.

22. When they had taken their supper, and night came on, those appointed for the service went forward and got possession of the hills; the other troops rested where they were. The enemy, when they saw the heights occupied, kept watch and burned a number of fires all night. 23. As soon as it was

day, Cheirisophus, after having offered sacrifice, marched forward along the road, while those who had gained the heights advanced by the ridge. 24. Most of the enemy, meanwhile, stayed at the pass, but a part went to meet the troops coming along the heights. But before the main bodies came together, those on the ridge closed with one another, and the Greeks had the advantage, and put the enemy to flight. 25. At the same time the Greek peltasts ran up from the plain to attack the enemy drawn up to receive them, and Cheirisophus followed at a quick pace with the heavy-armed men. 26. The enemy at the pass, however, when they saw those above defeated, took to flight. Not many of them were killed, but a great number of shields were taken, which the Greeks, by hacking them with their swords, rendered useless. 27. As soon as they had gained the ascent, and had sacrificed and erected a trophy, they went down into the plain before them, and arrived at a number of villages stored with abundance of excellent provisions.

7.1. From hence they marched five days' journey, thirty parasangs, to the country of the Taochi, where provisions began to fail them, for the Taochi inhabited strong fastnesses, in which they had laid up all their supplies. 2. Having at length, however, arrived at one place which had no city or houses attached to it, but in which men and women and a great number of cattle were assembled, Cheirisophus, as soon as he came before it, made it the object of an attack; and when the first division that assailed it began to be tired, another succeeded, and then another; for it was not possible for them to surround it in a body, as there was a river about it. 3. When Xenophon came up with his rear guard, peltasts, and heavy-armed men, Cheirisophus exclaimed, "You come seasonably, for we must take this place, as there are no provisions for the army unless we take it."

4. They then deliberated together, and Xenophon asking what hindered them from taking the place, Cheirisophus replied, "The only approach to it is the one which you see; but when any of our men attempt to pass along it, the enemy

roll down stones over yonder impending rock, and whoever is struck is treated as you behold"; and he pointed, at the same moment, to some of the men who had had their legs and ribs broken. 5. "But if they expend all their stones," rejoined Xenophon, "is there anything else to prevent us from advancing? For we see in front of us only a few men, and but two or three of them armed. 6. The space, too, through which we have to pass under exposure to the stones, is, as you see, only about a hundred and fifty feet in length; and of this about a hundred feet is covered with large pine trees in groups, against which if the men place themselves, what would they suffer either from the flying stones or the rolling ones? The remaining part of the space is not above fifty feet, over which, when the stones cease, we must pass at a running pace." 7. "But," said Cheirisophus, "the instant we offer to go to the part covered with trees, the stones fly in great numbers." "That," cried Xenophon, "would be the very thing we want, for thus they will exhaust their stones the sooner. Let us then advance, if we can, to the point whence we shall have but a short way to run, and from which we may, if we please, easily retreat."

8. Cheirisophus and Xenophon, with Callimachus of Parrhasia, one of the captains, who had that day the lead of all the other captains of the rear guard, then went forward, all the rest of the captains remaining out of danger. Next, about seventy of the men advanced under the trees, not in a body, but one by one, each sheltering himself as he could. 9. Agasias of Stymphalus and Aristonymus of Methydria, who were also captains of the rear guard, with some others, were at the same time standing behind, without the trees, for it was not safe for more than one company to stand under them. 10. Callimachus then adopted the following stratagem: he ran forward two or three paces from the tree under which he was sheltered, and, when the stones began to be hurled, hastily drew back; and at each of his sallies more than ten cart-loads of stones were spent. 11. Agasias, observing what Callimachus was doing, and that the eyes of the whole army were upon him, and fearing that he himself

might not be the first to enter the place, began to advance alone, calling neither to Aristonymus who was next him, nor to Eurylochus of Lusia, both of whom were his intimate friends, nor to any other person, and passed by all the rest. 12. Callimachus, seeing him rushing by, caught hold of the rim of his shield, and at that moment Aristonymus of Methydria ran past them both, and after him Eurylochus of Lusia, for all these sought distinction for valour, and were rivals to one another; and thus, in mutual emulation, they got possession of the place, for when they had once rushed in, not a stone was hurled from above. 13. But a dreadful spectacle was then to be seen; for the women, flinging their children over the precipice, threw themselves after them, and the men followed their example. Aeneas of Stymphalus, a captain, seeing one of them, who had on a rich garment, running to throw himself over, caught hold of it with intent to stop him. 14. But the man dragged him forward, and they both went rolling down the rocks together, and were killed. Thus very few prisoners were taken, but a great number of oxen, asses, and sheep.

15. Hence they advanced, seven days' journey, a distance of fifty parasangs, through the country of the Chalybes. These were the most warlike people of all that they passed through, and came to close combat with them. They had linen cuirasses, reaching down to the groin, and, instead of skirts, thick cords twisted. 16. They had also greaves and helmets, and at their girdles a short falchion, as large as a Spartan crooked dagger, with which they cut the throats of all whom they could master, and then, cutting off their heads, carried them away with them. They sang and danced when the enemy were likely to see them. They carried also a spear of about fifteen cubits in length, having one spike. 17. They stayed in their villages till the Greeks had passed by, when they pursued and perpetually harassed them. They had their dwellings in strong places, in which they had also laid up their provisions, so that the Greeks could get nothing from that country, but lived upon the cattle which they had taken from the Taochi.

18. The Greeks next arrived at the river Harpasus, the breadth of which was four plethra. Hence they proceeded through the territory of the Scythini, four days' journey, making twenty parasangs, over a level tract, until they came to some villages, in which they halted three days and collected provisions. 19. From this place they advanced four days' journey, twenty parasangs, to a large, rich, and populous city, called Gymnias, from which the governor of the country sent the Greeks a guide, to conduct them through a region at war with his own people. 20. The guide, when he came, said that he would take them in five days to a place whence they should see the sea; if not, he would consent to be put to death. When, as he proceeded, he entered the country of their enemies, he exhorted them to burn and lay waste the lands, whence it was evident that he had come for this very purpose, and not from any good will to the Greeks. 21. On the fifth day they came to the mountain; and the name of it was Theches. When the men who were in the front had mounted the height, and looked down upon the sea, a great shout proceeded from them; 22. and Xenophon and the rear guard, on hearing it, thought that some new enemies were assailing the front, for in the rear, too, the people from the country that they had burnt were following them, and the rear guard, by placing an ambuscade, had killed some, and taken others prisoners, and had captured about twenty shields made of raw ox-hides with the hair on. 23. But as the noise still increased as they drew nearer, and as those who came up from time to time kept running at full speed to join those who were continually shouting, the cries becoming louder as the men became more numerous, it appeared to Xenophon that it must be something of very great moment. 24. Mounting his horse, therefore, and taking with him Lycius and the cavalry, he hastened forward to give aid, when presently they heard the soldiers shouting, "The sea, the sea!" and cheering on one another. They then all began to run, the rear guard as well as the rest, and the baggage-cattle and horses were put to their speed; 25. and when they had all arrived at the top, the men embraced

one another, and their generals and captains, with tears in their eyes. Suddenly, whoever it was that suggested it, the soldiers brought stones, and raised a large mound, 26. on which they laid a number of raw ox-hides, staves, and shields taken from the enemy. The shields the guide himself hacked in pieces, and exhorted the rest to do the same. 27. Soon after, the Greeks sent away the guide, giving him presents from the common stock, a horse, a silver cup, a Persian robe, and ten darics, but he showed most desire for the rings on their fingers, and obtained many of them from the soldiers. Having then pointed out to them a village where they might take up their quarters, and the road by which they were to proceed to the Macrones, when the evening came on he departed, pursuing his way during the night.

POLYBIUS

IN THE centuries after Alexander the Great, the political center of gravity in Greece shifted from Athens, Sparta, and Thebes to the two leagues, the Achaean and the Aetolian, and to Macedon. Polybius was born to leadership in the Achaean League, his father Lycortas being a wealthy landowner and active politician. However, in 168, when he was scarcely over thirty years of age and had only begun his political career, he fell victim to Rome's final triumph over the Macedonians at the battle of Pydna. Polybius was one of the thousand well-born Achaeans carried to Rome as hostages in punishment for the League's part in the Third Macedonian War. There he quickly was taken up by Aemilius Paullus and the young Scipio Aemilianus, and for the next twenty or twenty-five years his life was spent in the closest association with the so-called Scipionic circle. He travelled widely in Italy, Africa, Spain, and Gaul, and he was with Scipio when the latter destroyed Carthage in 146.

For a man who undertook to write a "universal history" narrating and analyzing in minute detail Rome's conquest of the world from 220 to 168 (a date which he later shifted to 144 in order to include the final conquest of Spain, Africa, and Greece), the circumstances of his life could hardly have been improved upon. He knew, and knew well, most of the chief actors both in Rome and in Greece. He also knew the places, and for the later years he witnessed some of the events. In the end his travels included that rare experience, for his time, of a voyage on the Atlantic along both the African and Portuguese coasts, and visits to Egypt and Asia Minor. He had access to archives, and he read very widely in the pertinent historical and biographical literature. He also pretended, I might add, to a considerable knowledge of philosophy, but his Stoicism is palpably shallow and derivative.

All this knowledge and experience were assembled in a vast work of forty books, of which only the first five survive in full, the rest merely in extracts preserved by later anthologies and epitomes. Nothing in what we have points explicitly beyond the year 144, and, apart from some possible (and very veiled) hints in Book VI on the Roman constitution, nothing gives warning that a decade later, with the Gracchi, Rome would enter a full century of civil strife and revolution. As usual, we are completely uninformed about the date or circumstances of the actual publication. It is worth noting, however, that if the tradition is accurate that Polybius died at the age of eighty-two, then he was alive in the tribunates of both Tiberius and Gaius Gracchus.

—M. I. F.

From BOOK I

Introduction

1. Had the praise of history been passed over by former chroniclers it would perhaps have been incumbent upon me to urge the choice and special study of histories of this sort, as knowledge of the past is the readiest means men can have of correcting their conduct. But my predecessors have not been sparing in this respect. They have all begun and ended, so to speak, by enlarging on this theme: asserting again and again that the study of history is in the truest sense an edu-

cation, and a training for political life; and that the most instructive, or rather the only, method of learning to bear with
dignity the vicissitudes of Fortune is to recall the catastrophes of others. It is evident, therefore, that no one need
think it his duty to repeat what has been said by many, and
said well. Least of all myself, for the surprising nature of
the events which I have undertaken to relate is in itself sufficient to challenge and stimulate the attention of everyone,
old or young, to the study of my work. Can anyone be so in-
different or idle as not to care to know by what means, and
under what kind of polity, almost the whole inhabited world
was conquered and brought under the single dominion of
the Romans, and that too within a period of not quite fifty-
three years? Or who again can be so completely absorbed in
other subjects of contemplation or study as to think any of
them superior in importance to the accurate understanding
of an event for which the past offers no precedent?

2. We shall best show how marvellous and vast our subject is by comparing the most famous empires which preceded and which have been the favourite themes of historians, and measuring them with the superior greatness of
Rome. Those that deserve to be so compared and measured
are the following. The Persians for a certain length of time
were possessed of a great empire and dominion. But every
time they ventured beyond the limits of Asia, they found
not only their empire but their own existence also in danger.
The Lacedaemonians, after contending for supremacy in
Greece for many generations, when they did get it, held it
without dispute for barely twelve years. The Macedonians
obtained dominion in Europe from the lands bordering on
the Adriatic to the Danube—which after all is but a small
fraction of this continent—and, by the destruction of the
Persian Empire, they afterwards added to that the dominion
of Asia. And yet, though they had the credit of having made
themselves masters of a larger number of countries and
states than any people had ever done, they still left the
greater half of the inhabited world in the hands of others.
They never so much as thought of attempting Sicily, Sar-

dinia, or Libya; and as to Europe, to speak the plain truth, they never even knew of the most warlike tribes of the West. The Roman conquest, on the other hand, was not partial. Nearly the whole inhabited world was reduced by them to obedience, and they left behind them an empire not to be paralleled in the past or rivalled in the future. Students will gain from my narrative a clearer view of the whole story, and of the numerous and important advantages which such exact record of events offers.[1]

3. My *History* begins in the 140th Olympiad [220-217 B.C.]. The events from which it starts are these. In Greece, what is called the Social War: the first waged by Philip, son of Demetrius and father of Perseus, in league with the Achaeans against the Aetolians. In Asia, the war for the possession of Coele Syria which Antiochus and Ptolemy Philopator carried on against each other. In Italy, Libya, and their neighbourhood, the conflict between Rome and Carthage, generally called the Hannibalic War. My work thus begins where that of Aratus of Sicyon leaves off. Now up to this time the world's history had been, so to speak, a series of disconnected transactions, as widely separated in their origin and results as in their localities. But from this time forth history becomes a connected whole; the affairs of Italy and Libya are involved with those of Asia and Greece, and the tendency of all is to unity. This is why I have fixed upon this era as the starting point of my work. For it was their victory over the Carthaginians in this war, and their conviction that thereby the most difficult and most essential step towards universal empire had been taken, which encouraged the Romans for the first time to stretch out their hands upon the rest, and to cross with an army into Greece and Asia.

Now, had the states that were rivals for universal empire been familiarly known to us, no reference perhaps to their previous history would have been necessary to show the purpose and the forces with which they approached an undertaking of this nature and magnitude. But the fact is

---

[1] The manuscript is partly illegible in the final three sentences of this passage. The translation suggests the probable sense.

that the majority of the Greeks have no knowledge of the previous constitution, power, or achievements either of Rome or Carthage. I therefore concluded that it was necessary to prefix this and the next book to my *History*. I was anxious that no one, when fairly embarked upon my actual narrative, should feel at a loss, and have to ask what were the designs entertained by the Romans, or the forces and means at their disposal, that they entered upon those undertakings, which did in fact lead to their becoming masters of land and sea everywhere in our part of the world. I wished, on the contrary, that these books of mine, and the prefatory sketch which they contained, might make it clear that the resources they started with justified their original idea, and sufficiently explained their final success in grasping universal empire and dominion.

4. There is this analogy between the plan of my *History* and the marvellous spirit of the age with which I have to deal. Just as Fortune made almost all the affairs of the world incline in one direction, and forced them to converge upon one and the same point, so it is my task as a historian to put before my readers a compendious view of the ways in which Fortune accomplished her purpose. It was this peculiarity which originally challenged my attention, and determined me on undertaking this work. And combined with this was the fact that no writer of our time has undertaken a general history. Had anyone done so my ambition in this direction would have been much diminished. But, in point of fact, I notice that by far the greater number of historians concern themselves with isolated wars and the incidents that accompany them; while as to a general and comprehensive scheme of events, their date, origin, and end, no one as far as I know has undertaken to examine it. I thought it, therefore, distinctly my duty neither to pass by myself, nor allow anyone else to pass by, without full study, a characteristic specimen of the dealings of Fortune at once brilliant and instructive in the highest degree. For fruitful as Fortune is in change, and constantly as she is producing dramas in the life of men, yet never assuredly before this did she work

such a marvel, or act such a drama, as that which we have witnessed. And of this we cannot obtain a comprehensive view from writers of mere episodes.

It would be as absurd to expect to do so as for a man to imagine that he has learned the shape of the whole world, its entire arrangement and order, because he has visited one after the other the most famous cities in it, or perhaps merely examined them in separate pictures. That would be indeed absurd; and it has always seemed to me that men who are persuaded that they get a competent view of universal from episodical history are very like persons who should see the limbs of some body, which had once been living and beautiful, scattered and remote; and should imagine that to be quite as good as actually beholding the activity and beauty of the living creature itself. But if someone could there and then reconstruct the animal once more, in the perfection of its beauty and the charm of its vitality, and could display it to the same people, they would beyond doubt confess that they had been far from conceiving the truth, and had been little better than dreamers. For indeed some idea of a whole may be got from a part, but an accurate knowledge and clear comprehension cannot. Wherefore we must conclude that episodical history contributes exceedingly little to the familiar knowledge and secure grasp of universal history. While it is only by the combination and comparison of the separate parts of the whole—by observing their likeness and their difference—that a man can attain his object, can obtain a view at once clear and complete, and thus secure both the profit and the delight of history.

5. I shall adopt as the starting point of this book the first occasion on which the Romans crossed the sea from Italy. This is just where the *History* of Timaeus left off; and it falls in the 129th Olympiad [264-261 B.C.]. I shall accordingly have to describe what the state of their affairs in Italy was, how long that settlement had lasted, and on what resources they reckoned when they resolved to invade Sicily. For this was the first place outside Italy in which they set foot. The precise cause of their thus crossing I must state without com-

ment; for if I let one cause lead me back to another, my point of departure will always elude my grasp, and I shall never arrive at the view of the subject which I wish to present. As to dates, then, I must fix on some era agreed upon and recognized by all; and as to events, one that is self-evident, even though I may be obliged to go back some short way in point of time, and take a summary review of the intermediate transactions. For if the facts with which one starts are unknown, or even open to controversy, all that comes after will fail of approval and relief. But opinion being once formed on that point, and a general assent obtained, all the succeeding narrative becomes acceptable.

From BOOK II

Aratus of Sicyon and the Achaean League

. . . . . .

37. At the same period, the Achaean League and King Philip, with their allies, were entering upon the war with the Aetolian League, which is called the Social War [220-217 B.C.]. Now this was the point at which I proposed to begin my general history; and as I have brought the account of the affairs of Sicily and Libya, and those which immediately followed, in a continuous narrative, up to the date of the beginning of the Social War and of the second war between the Romans and Carthaginians, generally called the Hannibalic War, it will be proper to leave this branch of my subject for a while, and to take up the history of events in Greece, that I may start upon my full and detailed narrative, after bringing the prefatory sketch of the history of the several countries to the same point of time. For since I have not undertaken, as previous writers have done,

to write the history of particular peoples, such as the Greeks or Persians, but the history of all known parts of the world at once, because there was something in the state of our own times which made such a plan peculiarly feasible—of which I shall speak more at length hereafter—it will be proper, before entering on my main subject, to touch briefly on the state of the most important of the recognized nations and countries of the world.

Of Asia and Egypt I need not speak before the time at which my *History* commences. The previous history of these countries has been written by a number of historians already, and is known to all the world; nor in our days has Fortune wrought any change specially remarkable or unprecedented to them, demanding a reference to their past. But in regard to the Achaean nation, and the royal house of Macedonia, it will be in harmony with my design to go somewhat further back, for the latter has been entirely destroyed, while the Achaeans, as I have stated before, have in our time made extraordinary progress in power and internal unity. For though many statesmen had tried in past times to induce the Peloponnesians to join in a league for the common interests of all, and had always failed, because everyone was working to secure his own power rather than the freedom of the whole, yet in our day this policy has made such progress, and been carried out with such completeness, that not only is there in the Peloponnesus a community such as exists between allies and friends, but an absolute identity of laws, weights, measures, and currency. All the states have the same magistrates, council, and judges. Nor is there any difference between the entire Peloponnesus and a single city, except in the fact that its inhabitants are not included within the same wall; in other respects, both as a whole and in their individual cities, there is a nearly absolute assimilation of institutions.

38. It will be useful to ascertain, to begin with, how it came to pass that the name of the Achaeans became the universal one for all the inhabitants of the Peloponnesus. For

the original bearers of this ancestral name have no superiority over others, either in the size of their territory and cities, or in wealth, or in the prowess of their men. For they are far inferior to the Arcadians and Lacedaemonians in number of inhabitants and extent of territory; nor can these latter nations be said to yield the first place in warlike courage to any Greek people whatever. Whence then comes it that these nations, with the rest of the inhabitants of the Peloponnesus, have been content to adopt the constitution and the name of the Achaeans? To speak of chance in such a matter would not be to offer any adequate solution of the question, and would be mere idle evasion. A cause must be sought; for without a cause nothing, expected or unexpected, can be accomplished. The cause then, in my opinion, was this. Nowhere could be found a more unalloyed and deliberately established system of political equality and freedom of speech, and, in a word, of genuine democracy, than among the Achaeans. This constitution found some of the Peloponnesians ready enough to adopt it of their own accord; many were brought to share in it by persuasion and argument; some, though acting under compulsion at first, were quickly brought to acquiesce in its benefits. For none of the original members had any special privilege reserved for them, but equal rights were given to all comers; the object aimed at was therefore quickly attained by the two most unfailing expedients of equality and humanity. This then must be looked upon as the source and original cause of Peloponnesian unity and consequent well-being.

That this was the original principle on which the Achaeans acted in forming their constitution might be demonstrated by many proofs; but for the present purpose it will be sufficient to allege one or two in confirmation of my assertion.

39. When the Pythagorean clubs in the district of Italy then called Magna Graecia were burnt down, there followed great constitutional disturbances, as was natural on the sudden disappearance of the leading men in each state; and

the Greek cities in that part of Italy became the scene of murder, civil strife, and every kind of disturbance.[1] Deputations were sent from most parts of Greece to endeavour to bring about some settlement of these disorders. But the disturbed states preferred the intervention of the Achaeans above all others, and showed the greatest confidence in them in regard to the measures to be adopted for removing the evils that oppressed them. Nor was this the only occasion on which they displayed this preference. For shortly afterwards there was a general movement among them to adopt the model of the Achaean constitution. The first states to move in the matter were Croton, Sybaris, and Caulonia, who began by erecting a common temple to Zeus Homarios, and a place in which to hold their meetings and common councils. They then adopted the laws and customs of the Achaeans, and determined to conduct their government according to their principles; but, finding themselves hampered by the tyranny of Dionysius of Syracuse, and also by the encroachment of the neighbouring barbarians, they were forced much against their will to abandon them.

Again, later on, when the Lacedaemonians met with their unexpected reverse at Leuctra [371 B.C.], and the Thebans as unexpectedly claimed the hegemony in Greece, a feeling of uncertainty prevailed throughout the country, and especially among the Lacedaemonians and Thebans themselves; because the former refused to allow that they were beaten, the latter felt hardly certain that they had conquered. Then the Achaeans were the people selected by the two parties, out of all Greece, to act as arbitrators on the points in dispute. And this could not have been from any special view of their power, for at that time they were perhaps the weakest state in Greece; it was rather from a conviction of their good faith and high principles, in regard to which there was but one opinion universally entertained.

At that period of their history, however, they possessed

---

[1] The reference is to widespread popular revolts against oligarchy in many cities in Magna Graecia during the fifth century B.C., about which scarcely any information is available.

only the principles; practical steps, and an increase of power, were barred by the fact that they had not yet been able to produce a leader worthy of the principles. Whenever any man had given indications of such ability, he was systematically thrust into the background and hampered, at one time by the Lacedaemonian government, and at another, still more effectually, by that of Macedonia.

40. When at length, however, they did obtain leaders of sufficient ability, their power quickly manifested itself by the accomplishment of that most glorious achievement, the union of the Peloponnesus. The originator of this policy in the first instance was Aratus of Sicyon; its active promotion and consummation was due to Philopoemon of Megalopolis; while Lycortas [father of Polybius] and his party must be looked upon as the authors of the permanence which it enjoyed. The actual achievements of these several statesmen I shall narrate in their proper places; but, while deferring a more detailed account of the other two, I think it will be right briefly to record here, as well as in a future portion of my work, the political measures of Aratus, because he has left a record of them himself in an admirably honest and lucid book of memoirs.[2]

I think the easiest method for myself, and most intelligible to my readers, will be to start from the period of the restoration of the Achaean League after its disintegration into separate states by the Macedonian kings, from which time it has enjoyed an unbroken progress towards the state of completion which now exists, and of which I have already spoken.

41. The period I mean is the 124th Olympiad [284-280 B.C.]. In this occurred the first league of Patrae and Dyme, and the deaths of Ptolemy [I] son of Lagus, Lysimachus, Seleucus, and Ptolemy Ceraunus. In the period before this the state of Achaea was as follows. It was ruled by kings from the time of Tisamenus, son of Orestes, who, being expelled from Sparta on the return of the Heraclids, gained possession of Achaea. The last of this royal line to retain

---

[2] Nothing has survived of this work except for a half-dozen brief quotations by Plutarch.

his power was Ogyges, whose sons so alienated the people by their unconstitutional and tyrannical government that a revolution took place and a democracy was established. After this, down to the reigns of Alexander and Philip, their fortunes were subject to various fluctuations, but they always endeavoured to maintain in their league a democracy, as I have already stated. This league consisted of twelve cities, all of them still surviving, with the exception of Olenus, and of Helice which was engulfed by the sea before the battle of Leuctra. The other ten were Patrae, Dyme, Pharae, Tritaea, Leontium, Aegium, Aegira, Pellene, Bura, and Caryneia. In the period immediately succeeding Alexander [the Great], and before the above-named 124th Olympiad, these cities, chiefly through the instrumentality of the Macedonian kings, became so estranged and ill-disposed to each other, and so divided and opposed in their interests, that some of them had to submit to the presence of foreign garrisons, sent first by Demetrius and Cassander, and afterwards by Antigonus Gonatas, while others even fell under the power of tyrants; for no one set up more of such absolute rulers in the Greek states than this last-named [Macedonian] king.

But about the 124th Olympiad, as I have said, a change of sentiment prevailed among the Achaean cities, and they began again to form a league. This was just at the time of Pyrrhus' invasion of Italy. The first to take this step were the peoples of Dyme, Patrae, Tritaea, and Pharae, and therefore we find no stele recording their adherence to the League. About five years afterwards the people of Aegium expelled their garrison and joined the League, and next the people of Bura put their tyrant to death and did the same. Simultaneously, Caryneia was restored to the League. For Iseas, the then tyrant of Caryneia, when he saw the expulsion of the garrison from Aegium, and the death of the ruler in Bura at the hands of Margus and the Achaeans, and when he saw that he was himself on the point of being attacked on all sides, voluntarily laid down his rule; and, having obtained a guarantee for his personal safety from the Achaeans, formally gave in the adhesion of his city to the League.

42. Why did I go back to these times? First, to show clearly at what epoch the Achaeans entered into the second league, which exists at this day, and which were the first members of the original league to do so; second, that the statement of their principles might rest, not on my word only, but on the evidence of the actual facts. It was in virtue of a sustained policy—by holding out the offer of equality and freedom, and by invariably making war upon and crushing those who, on their own account or with the support of the kings, enslaved their native cities—that they finally accomplished the design which they had deliberately adopted, in some cases by their unaided efforts, and in others by the help of their allies. For in fact whatever was effected in this direction by the help of these allies in after times, must be put down to the principles and policy of the Achaeans themselves. They acted indeed jointly with others in many honourable undertakings, and in none more so than with the Romans; yet in no instance can they be said to have aimed at obtaining from their success any private advantage. In return for the zealous assistance rendered by them to their allies, they demanded in exchange nothing but the freedom of each state and the union of the Peloponnesus. But this will be more clearly seen from the record of their actual proceedings.

43. For the first twenty-five years of the League between the cities I have mentioned, a secretary and two strategi for the whole union were elected by each city in turn. But after this period they determined to appoint one strategus only, and put the entire management of their affairs in his hands. The first to obtain this honor was Margus of Caryneia [in 255 B.C.]. In the fourth year after this man's tenure of office, Aratus of Sicyon, then only twenty years of age, by his energy and courage delivered his city from its tyrant, and, being a passionate admirer of the Achaean principles, caused his city to join the League. Eight years later, Aratus, being elected strategus for the second time, laid a plot to seize the citadel of Corinth, then held by Antigonus; and by his success freed the inhabitants of the Peloponnesus from a source

of serious alarm; and having thus liberated Corinth he caused it to join the League. In his same term of office he got Megara into his hands, and caused it to join also. These events occurred in the year before the decisive defeat of the Carthaginians [in the First Punic War], in consequence of which they evacuated Sicily and consented for the first time to pay tribute to Rome.

Having made this remarkable progress in his design in so short a time, Aratus continued thenceforth in the position of leader of the Achaean nation, and in the consistent direction of his whole policy to one single end, which was to expel the Macedonians from the Peloponnesus, to depose the despots, and to establish in each state the common freedom which their ancestors had enjoyed before them. So long, therefore, as Antigonus Gonatas was alive, he maintained a continual opposition to his interference, as well as to the encroaching spirit of the Aetolians, and in both cases with signal skill and success; although their presumption and contempt for justice had risen to such a pitch, that they had actually made a formal compact with each other for the dissolution of the Achaean League.

44. After the death of Antigonus, however, the Achaeans made terms with the Aetolians, and joined them energetically in the war against Demetrius [who succeeded Antigonus to the Macedonian throne in 239 B.C.]; and, in place of the feelings of estrangement and hostility there arose between them, for the time being, a sentiment of brotherhood and affection. Upon the death of Demetrius, after a reign of only ten years, just about the time of the first invasion of Illyria by the Romans, the Achaeans had a most excellent opportunity of establishing the policy which they had all along maintained. For the tyrants in the Peloponnesus were in despair at the death of Demetrius, who had been their chief supporter and paymaster. And now Aratus was forever impressing upon them that they ought to abdicate, holding out rewards and honours for those of them who consented, and threatening those who refused with still greater vengeance from the Achaeans. There was therefore a gen-

eral movement among them voluntarily to restore their several states to freedom and to join the League. Indeed, Lydiades of Megalopolis, foreseeing with great shrewdness and good sense what was going to happen, had, of his own deliberate choice, already abdicated as tyrant in the lifetime of Demetrius, and adhered to the national league. His example was followed by Aristomachus, tyrant of Argos, Xenon of Hermione, and Cleonymus of Phlius, who all likewise abdicated and joined the democratic league.

45. But the increased power and national advancement which these events brought to the Achaeans excited the envy of the Aetolians, who, besides their natural inclination to unjust and selfish aggrandizement, were inspired with the hope of breaking up the union of Achaean states, as they had before [about 270 B.C.] succeeded in partitioning those of Acarnania with Alexander [II of Epirus], and had planned to do those of Achaea with Antigonus Gonatas. Instigated once more by similar expectations, they had now the assurance to enter into communication and close alliance at once with Antigonus (at that time ruling Macedonia as guardian of the young King Philip), and with Cleomenes, king of Sparta. They saw that Antigonus had undisputed control of Macedonia, while he was an open and avowed enemy of the Achaeans owing to the surprise of the citadel of Corinth; and they supposed that if they could get the Lacedaemonians to join them in their hostility to the League, they would easily subdue it, by selecting a favourable opportunity for their attack, and securing that it should be assaulted on all sides at once.

And they would in all probability have succeeded, but that they had left out the most important element in the calculation, namely, that in Aratus they had to reckon with an opponent to their plans of ability equal to almost any emergency. Accordingly, when they attempted this violent and unjust interference in Achaea, so far from succeeding in any of their devices, they, on the contrary, strengthened Aratus, then head of the League, as well as the League itself. So consummate was the ability with which he foiled their plan and reduced them to impotence. The manner in which this was done will be made clear in what I am about to relate.

46. Aratus saw that the Aetolians were ashamed to declare war openly on the Achaeans, because they could not ignore their recent obligations to them in the war with Demetrius; but they were plotting with the Lacedaemonians, and they showed their jealousy of the Achaeans not only by conniving at the treacherous attack of Cleomenes upon Tegea, Mantinea, and Orchomenus (cities not only in alliance with the Aetolians, but actually members of their League), but by confirming his occupation of those places. In old times they had thought almost any excuse good enough to justify an appeal to arms against those who, after all, had done them no wrong; yet they now allowed themselves to be treated with such treachery, and submitted without remonstrance to the loss of their largest cities, solely with the view of creating in Cleomenes a formidable antagonist to the Achaeans. These facts were not lost upon Aratus and the other leaders of the League, and they resolved that, without taking the initiative in going to war with anyone, they would resist the attempts of the Lacedaemonians. Such was their determination, but immediately afterwards Cleomenes began to build the hostile fort in the territory of Megalopolis, called the Athenaeum, and showed an undisguised and bitter hostility. Aratus and his colleagues accordingly summoned the council of the League, and it was decided to proclaim war openly against Sparta. This was the date [229 or 228 B.C.] and origin of what is called the Cleomenic War.

47. At first the Achaeans were for depending on their own resources for facing the Lacedaemonians. They deemed it more honourable not to look to others for preservation, but to guard their own territory and cities themselves; and at the same time the memory of his former services made them desirous of keeping up their friendship with Ptolemy [III Euergetes], and averse from the appearance of seeking aid elsewhere. But when the war had lasted some time, and Cleomenes had revolutionized the constitution of his coun-

try, and had turned its constitutional monarchy into a tyranny, and, moreover, was conducting the war with extraordinary skill and boldness—seeing clearly what would happen, and fearing the reckless audacity of the Aetolians, Aratus determined that his first duty was to be well beforehand in frustrating their plans. He perceived that Antigonus [Doson] was a man of activity and practical ability, with some pretensions to the character of a man of honour. He however knew perfectly well that kings look on no man as a natural friend or foe, but ever measure friendships and enmities solely by the standard of expediency. He, therefore, conceived the idea of addressing himself to this monarch, and entering into friendly relations with him, taking occasion to point out to him the certain result of his present policy. But to act openly in this matter he thought inexpedient for several reasons. By doing so he would not only incur the opposition of Cleomenes and the Aetolians, but would cause consternation among the Achaeans themselves, because his appeal to their enemies would give the impression that he had abandoned all the hopes he once had in them. This was the very last idea he desired should go abroad, and he therefore determined to conduct this intrigue in secrecy. The result of this was that he was often compelled to speak and act in public in a sense contrary to his true sentiments, that he might conceal his real design by suggesting one of an exactly opposite nature. For which reason there are some particulars which he did not even mention in his own memoirs.

48. It did not escape the observation of Aratus that the people of Megalopolis would be more ready than others to seek the protection of Antigonus and the hopes of safety offered by Macedonia. For their proximity to Sparta exposed them to attack before the other cities, while they were unable to get the help which they ought to have, because the Achaeans were themselves hard pressed and in great difficulties. He also knew that they had special reasons for entertaining feelings of affection towards the royal family of Macedonia, founded on the favours received in the time of Philip, son of Amyntas [338 B.C.]. He therefore imparted

his general design under pledge of secrecy to Nicophanes and Cercidas of Megalopolis, who were family friends of his own and of a character suited to the undertaking, and by their means experienced no difficulty in inducing the people of Megalopolis to send envoys to the League, to urge that an application for help should be made to Antigonus. Nicophanes and Cercidas were themselves selected to go on this mission to the League, and thence, if their view was accepted, to Antigonus. The League consented to allow the Megalopolitans to send the mission; and accordingly Nicophanes lost no time in obtaining an interview with the king. About the interests of his own city he spoke briefly and summarily, confining himself to the most necessary statements; the greater part of his speech was, in accordance with the directions of Aratus, concerned with the general situation.

49. The points suggested by Aratus for the envoy to dwell on were the scope and object of the understanding between the Aetolians and Cleomenes, and the necessity of caution on the part of the Achaeans in the first place, but even more on the part of Antigonus himself: first because the Achaeans plainly could not resist the attack of both, and second because if the Aetolians and Cleomenes conquered them, any man of sense could easily see that they would not be satisfied or stop there. For the encroaching spirit of the Aetolians, far from being content to be confined by the boundaries of the Peloponnesus, would find even those of Greece too narrow for them. Again, the ambition of Cleomenes was at present directed to the supremacy in the Peloponnesus: but, this obtained, he would promptly aim at that of all Greece, in which it would be impossible for him to succeed without first destroying the dominion of Macedonia. They were, therefore, to urge him to consider, with a view to the future, which of the two courses would be more to his own interests—to fight for supremacy in Greece in conjunction with the Achaeans and Boeotians against Cleomenes in the Peloponnesus, or to abandon the most powerful nation, and to stake the Macedonian empire on a battle in Thessaly, against a combined force of Aetolians and Boeo-

tians, with the Achaeans and Lacedaemonians to boot. If the Aetolians, from regard to the good will shown them by the Achaeans in the time of Demetrius, were to pretend to be anxious to keep the peace as they were at present doing, they were to assert that the Achaeans were ready to engage Cleomenes by themselves; and if Fortune declared in their favour they would want no assistance from anyone; but if Fortune went against them, and the Aetolians joined in the attack, they begged him to watch the course of events, that he might not let things go too far, but might aid the Peloponnesians while they were still capable of being saved. He had no need to be anxious about the good faith or gratitude of the Achaeans; when the time for action came, Aratus pledged himself to find guarantees which would be satisfactory to both parties, and similarly would himself indicate the moment at which the aid should be given.

50. These arguments seemed to Antigonus to have been put by Aratus with equal sincerity and ability; and after listening to them he eagerly took the first necessary step by writing a letter to the people of Megalopolis with an offer of assistance, on condition that such a measure should receive the consent of the Achaeans. When Nicophanes and Cercidas returned home and delivered this despatch from the king, reporting at the same time his other expressions of good will and zeal in the cause, the spirits of the people of Megalopolis were greatly elated; and they were all eagerness to attend the meeting of the League, and urge that measures should be taken to secure the alliance of Antigonus, and to put the management of the war in his hands with all despatch. Aratus learned privately from Nicophanes the king's feelings towards the League and towards himself, and was delighted that his plan had not failed, and that he had not found the king completely alienated from himself, as the Aetolians hoped he would be. He regarded it also as eminently favourable to his policy that the people of Megalopolis were so eager to use the Achaean League as the channel of communication with Antigonus. For, as I said above, his first object was if possible to do without this assistance; but if he

were compelled to have recourse to it, he wished that the invitation should not be sent through him personally, but that it should rather come from the Achaeans as a whole. For he feared that, if the king came, and conquered Cleomenes and the Lacedaemonians in the war, and should then adopt any policy hostile to the interests of the national constitution, he would have himself by general consent to bear the blame of the result; while Antigonus would be justified by the injury which had been inflicted on the royal house of Macedonia in the matter of the Acrocorinthus.

Accordingly when Megalopolitan envoys appeared in the League council, and showed the royal despatch, and further declared the general friendly disposition of the king, and added an appeal to the congress to secure the king's alliance without delay; and when also the sense of the meeting was clearly shown to be in favour of taking this course, Aratus rose, and, after setting forth the king's zeal and complimenting the meeting upon their readiness to act in the matter, he proceeded to urge upon them in a long speech that they should try if possible to preserve their cities and territory by their own efforts, for that nothing could be more honourable or more expedient than that; but that, if it turned out that Fortune declared against them in this effort, they might then have recourse to the assistance of their friends, but not until they had tried all their own resources to the uttermost.

51. This speech was received with general applause, and it was decided to take no fresh departure at present, and to endeavour to bring the existing war to a conclusion unaided. But when Ptolemy, despairing of retaining the League's friendship, began to furnish Cleomenes with supplies—which he did with a view of setting him up as a foil to Antigonus, thinking the Lacedaemonians offered him better hopes than the Achaeans of being able to thwart the policy of the Macedonian kings; and when the Achaeans themselves had suffered three defeats—one at Lycaeum in an engagement with Cleomenes whom they had met on a march; and again in a pitched battle at Ladoceia in the territory of Megalopolis, in which Lydiades fell; and a third time decisively at

a place called Hecatombaeum in the territory of Dyme, where their whole forces had been engaged—after these misfortunes no further delay was possible, and they were compelled by the force of circumstances to appeal unanimously to Antigonus. In this crisis Aratus sent his son to Antigonus, and ratified the terms of the subvention. The great difficulty was this: it was believed to be certain that the king would send no assistance except on the condition of the restoration of the Acrocorinthus, and of having the city of Corinth put into his hands as a base of operations in this war; and on the other hand it seemed impossible that the Achaeans should venture to put the Corinthians in the king's power against their own consent. The final determination of the matter was accordingly postponed, that they might investigate the question of the securities to be given to the king.

52. Meanwhile, on the strength of the dismay caused by his successes, Cleomenes was making an unopposed progress through the cities, winning some by persuasion and others by threats. In this way he got possession of Caphyae, Pellene, Pheneus, Argos, Phlius, Cleonae, Epidaurus, Hermione, Troezen, and last of all Corinth, while he personally commanded a siege of Sicyon. But this in reality relieved the Achaeans from a very grave difficulty. For the Corinthians by ordering Aratus, who was commanding, and the Achaeans to evacuate the town, and by sending messages to Cleomenes inviting his presence, gave the Achaeans a ground of action and a reasonable pretext for moving. Aratus was quick to take advantage of this, and, as the Achaeans were in actual possession of the Acrocorinthus, he made his peace with the royal family of Macedonia by offering it to Antigonus, and at the same time gave thus a sufficient guarantee for friendship in the future, and further secured Antigonus a base of operations for the war with Sparta.

Upon learning of this compact between the League and Antigonus, Cleomenes raised the siege of Sicyon and pitched his camp near the Isthmus; and, having thrown up a line of fortification uniting the Acrocorinthus with the mountain called the Ass's Back, began from this time to expect with confidence the empire of the Peloponnese. But Antigonus had made his preparations long in advance, in accordance with the suggestion of Aratus, and was only waiting for the right moment to act. And now the news which he received convinced him that the entrance of Cleomenes into Thessaly, at the head of an army, was only a question of a very few days; he accordingly despatched envoys to Aratus and the League to conclude the terms of the treaty and marched to the Isthmus with his army by way of Euboea. He took this route because the Aetolians, after trying other expedients for preventing Antigonus from bringing this aid, now forbade his marching south of Thermopylae with an army, threatening that, if he did, they would offer armed opposition to his passage. Thus Antigonus and Cleomenes were encamped face to face, the former desirous of effecting an entrance into the Peloponnesus, Cleomenes determined to prevent him.

53. Meanwhile the Achaeans, in spite of their severe disasters, did not abandon their purpose or give up their self-reliance. They gave Aristotle of Argos assistance when he headed a rising against the Cleomenic faction; and, under the command of Timoxenus the general, surprised and seized Argos. And this must be regarded as the chief cause of the improvement which took place in their fortunes, for this reverse checked the ardor of Cleomenes and damped the courage of his soldiers in advance, as was clearly shown by what took place afterwards. For though Cleomenes had already possession of more advantageous posts, and was in the enjoyment of more abundant supplies than Antigonus, and was at the same time inspired with superior courage and ambition, yet, as soon as he was informed that Argos was in the hands of the Achaeans, he at once drew back, abandoned all these advantages, and retreated from the Isthmus with every appearance of precipitation, in terror of being completely surrounded by his enemies. At first he retired upon Argos and for a time made some attempt to regain the town. But the Achaeans offered a gallant resistance, and the Argives themselves were stirred up to do the same by remorse for having admitted him before; and so, having failed

in this attempt also, he marched back to Sparta by way of Mantinea.

54. On his part, Antigonus advanced without any casualty into the Peloponnesus and took over the Acrocorinthus, and, without wasting time there, pushed on in his enterprise and entered Argos. He stayed there only long enough to compliment the Argives on their conduct, and to provide for the security of the city; and then immediately starting again directed his march towards Arcadia; and after ejecting the garrisons from the posts which had been fortified by Cleomenes in the territories of Aegys and Belmina, and putting those strongholds in the hands of the people of Megalopolis, he went to Aegium to attend the meeting of the Achaean League. There he made a statement of his own proceedings and consulted with the meeting as to the measures to be taken in the future. He was appointed commander-in-chief of the allied army, and went into winter quarters at Sicyon and Corinth.

At the approach of spring [223 B.C.] he broke up his camp and got on the march. On the third day he arrived at Tegea, and, being joined there by the Achaean forces, he proceeded to invest the city. The vigor displayed by the Macedonians in conducting the siege, and especially in the digging of mines, soon reduced the Tegeans to despair, and they accordingly surrendered. After taking the proper measures for securing the town, Antigonus proceeded to extend his expedition. He now marched with all speed into Laconia, and, having found Cleomenes in position on the frontier, he was trying to bring him to an engagement, and was harassing him with skirmishing attacks, when news was brought to him by his scouts that the garrison of Orchomenus had started to join Celomenes. He at once broke up his camp, hurried thither, and carried the town by assault. Having done that, he next invested Mantinea and began to besiege it. This town also being soon terrified into surrender by the Macedonians, he started again along the road to Heraea and Telphusa. These towns, too, being secured by the voluntary surrender of their inhabitants, as the winter was by this time approaching, he went again to Aegium to attend the meeting of the League. His Macedonian soldiers he sent away to winter at home, while he himself remained to confer with the Achaeans on the existing state of affairs.

55. But Cleomenes was on the alert. He saw that the Macedonians in the army of Antigonus had been sent home, and that the king and his mercenaries in Aegium were three days' march from Megalopolis; and this latter town he well knew to be difficult to guard, owing to its great extent and the sparseness of its inhabitants; and, moreover, that it was just then being kept with even greater carelessness than usual, owing to Antigonus being in the country; and, what was more important than anything else, he knew that the larger number of its men of military age had fallen at the battles of Lycaeum and Ladoceia. There happened to be residing in Megalopolis some Messenian exiles, by whose help he managed, under cover of night, to get within the walls without being detected. When day broke he had a narrow escape from being ejected, if not from absolute destruction, through the valour of the citizens. This had been his fortune three months before, when he had made his way into the city by the region which is called the Colaeum; but on this occasion, by the superiority of his force, and the seizure in advance of the strongest positions in the town, he succeeded in effecting his purpose. He eventually ejected the inhabitants and took entire possession of the city, which, once in his power, he dismantled in so savage and ruthless a manner as to preclude the least hope that it might ever be restored. The reason of his acting in this manner was, I believe, that Megalopolis and Stymphalus were the only towns in which, during the vicissitudes of that period, he never succeeded in obtaining a single partisan, or inducing a single citizen to turn traitor. For the passion for liberty and loyalty of the Clitorians had been stained by the baseness of one man, Thearces, whom the Clitorians, with some reason, denied to be a native of their city, asserting that he had been foisted in from Orchomenus and was the offspring of one of the foreign garrison there.

56. Since, among those writers who were contemporary with Aratus, Phylarchus is accepted as trustworthy by some, and the opinions of the two authors are opposed in many points and their statements contradictory, and since I follow Aratus in my account of the Cleomenic war, it will be advantageous, or rather necessary, for me to go into the question, and not by any neglect on my part to suffer misstatements in historical writings to enjoy an authority equal to that of truth. The fact is that Phylarchus has, throughout the whole of his history, made statements at random and without discrimination. It is not, however, necessary for me to criticize him on other points on the present occasion, or to call him to strict account concerning them; but such of his statements as relate to the period which I have now in hand, that is the Cleomenic war—these I must thoroughly sift. They will be quite sufficient to enable us to form a judgement on the general spirit and character of his historical writing. It was his object to bring into prominence the cruelty of Antigonus and the Macedonians, as well as that of Aratus and the Achaeans; and he accordingly asserts that, when Mantinea fell into their hands, it was cruelly treated, and that the most ancient and important of all the Arcadian towns was involved in calamities so terrible as to move all Greece to horror and tears. And, being eager to stir the hearts of his readers to pity, and to enlist their sympathies by his story, he talks of women embracing, tearing their hair, and exposing their breasts, and again of the tears and lamentations of men and women led off into captivity along with their children and aged parents. And this he does again and again throughout his whole history, by way of bringing the terrible scene vividly before his readers.

I say nothing of the unworthiness and unmanliness of the course Phylarchus has adopted; let us only inquire what is essential and to the purpose in history. Surely a historian's object should not be to amaze his readers by a series of thrilling anecdotes; nor should he seek after men's probable speeches, nor enumerate the possible consequences of the events under consideration, like a writer of tragedy; but his function is above all to record with fidelity what was actually said or done, however commonplace it may be. For the purposes of history and tragedy are not the same, but widely opposed to each other. In the latter the object is to thrill and delight the audience for the moment by words true to nature, in the former to instruct and convince serious students for all time by genuine words and deeds. In the latter, again, the power of beguiling an audience is the chief excellence, because the object is to create illusion; but in the former the thing of primary importance is truth, because the object is to benefit the learner.

And apart from these considerations, Phylarchus, in most of the catastrophes which he relates, omits to suggest the causes which give rise to them, or the course of events which led up to them; and without knowing these it is impossible to feel the due indignation or pity at anything which occurs. For instance, everybody looks upon it as an outrage that the free should be beaten; still, if a man provokes it by an act of violence, he is considered to have got no more than he deserved, and, where it is done for correction and discipline, those who strike free men are deemed worthy of honour and gratitude. Again, the killing of a citizen is regarded as a most heinous crime, deserving the highest penalty; and yet it is notorious that the man who kills a thief or adulterer is held guiltless, while he who kills a traitor or tyrant in every country receives honours and pre-eminence. And so in everything our final judgement does not depend upon the mere things done, but upon their causes and the views of the actors, according as these differ.

57. Now the people of Mantinea had in the first instance abandoned the League and voluntarily submitted first to the Aetolians and afterwards to Cleomenes. Being therefore, in accordance with this policy, members of the Lacedaemonian community, in the fourth year before the coming of Antigonus their city was forcibly taken possession of by the Achaeans owing to the skilful plotting of Aratus. But on that occasion, so far from being subjected to any severity for their act of treason, it became a matter of general remark how

promptly the feelings of the conquerors and the conquered underwent a revolution. As soon as he had got control of the town, Aratus issued orders to his own men that no one was to lay a finger on anything that did not belong to him; and then, having summoned the Mantineans to a meeting, he bade them be of good cheer and retain their possessions, because, as long as they remained members of the League, their safety was secured. On their part, the Mantineans, surprised at this unlooked-for prospect of safety, immediately experienced a universal reversal of feeling. The very men against whom they had a little while before been engaged in a war, in which they had seen many of their kinsfolk killed, and no small number grievously wounded, they now received into their houses and entertained as their guests, interchanging every imaginable kindness with them. And naturally so. For I believe that there never were men who met with more kindly foes, or came out of a struggle with what seemed the most dreadful disasters more unscathed, than did the Mantineans, owing to the humanity of Aratus and the Achaeans towards them.

58. But they still saw certain dangers ahead from intestine disorders and the hostile designs of the Aetolians and Lacedaemonians; they subsequently, therefore, sent envoys to the League asking for a garrison for their town. The request was granted, and three hundred of the League army were selected by lot to form it. These men on whom the lot fell started for Mantinea; and, abandoning their native cities and their callings in life, remained there to protect the lives and liberties of the citizens. Besides them, the League dispatched two hundred mercenaries, who joined the Achaean guard in protecting the established constitution. But this state of things did not last long: an insurrection broke out in the town, and the Mantineans called in the aid of the Lacedaemonians, delivered the city into their hands, and put to death the garrison sent by the League. It would not be easy to mention a grosser or blacker act of treachery. Even if they resolved to set utterly at nought the gratitude they owed to, and the friendship they had formed with, the League, they

ought at least to have spared these men, and to have let every one of them depart under some terms or another, for this much it is the custom by the law of nations to grant even to foreign enemies. But in order to satisfy Cleomenes and the Lacedaemonians of their fidelity in the policy of the hour, they deliberately, and in violation of the law recognized by all mankind, consummated a crime of the most impious description.

To slaughter and wreak vengeance on the men who had just before taken their city and refrained from doing them the least harm, and who were at that very moment engaged in protecting their lives and liberties—can anything be imagined more detestable? What punishment can be conceived to correspond with its enormity? If one suggests that they would be rightly served by being sold into slavery, with their wives and children, as soon as they were beaten in war, it may be answered that this much is only what, by the laws of warfare, awaits even those who have been guilty of no special act of impiety. They deserved therefore to meet with a punishment even more complete and heavy than they did; so that, even if what Phylarchus mentions did happen to them, there was no reason for the pity of Greece being bestowed upon them; praise and approval rather were due to those who exacted vengeance for their impious crime. But since, as a matter of fact, nothing worse befell the Mantineans than the plunder of their property and the selling of their free population into slavery, this historian, for the mere sake of a sensational story, has told not only a pure lie, but an improbable lie. His wilful ignorance also was so supreme that he was unable to compare with this alleged cruelty of the Achaeans the conduct of the same people in the case of Tegea, which they took by force at the same period, and yet did no injury to its inhabitants. And yet, if the natural cruelty of the perpetrators was the sole cause of the severity to Mantinea, it is to be presumed that Teagea would have been treated in the same way. But if their treatment of Mantinea was an exception to that of every other town, the necessary inference is that the cause of their anger was exceptional also.

59. Again Phylarchus says that Aristomachus the Argive, a man of a most distinguished family, who had been tyrant of Argos, as his fathers had been before him, upon falling into the hands of Antigonus and the League was hurried off to Cenchreae and there racked to death, in an unparalleled instance of injustice and cruelty. But in this matter also our author preserves his peculiar method. He makes up a story about certain cries of this man, when he was on the rack, being heard through the night by the neighbours, some of whom, he says, rushed to the house in their horror, or incredulity, or indignation at the outrage. As for the sensationalism, let it pass; I have said enough on that point. But I must express my opinion that, even if Aristomachus had committed no crime against the Achaeans besides, yet his whole life and his treason to his own country deserved the heaviest possible punishment. And in order, forsooth, to enhance this man's reputation, and move his readers' sympathies for his sufferings, our historian remarks that he had not only been a tyrant himself, but that his fathers had been so before him. It would not be easy to bring a graver or more bitter charge against a man than this, for the mere word "tyrant" involves the idea of everything that is wickedest, and includes every injustice and crime possible to mankind. And if Aristomachus endured the most terrible tortures, as Phylarchus says, he yet would not have been sufficiently punished for the crime of one day, in which, when Aratus had effected an entrance into Argos with the Achaean soldiers —and, after supporting the most severe struggles and dangers for the freedom of its citizens, had eventually been driven out, because the party within who were in league with him had not ventured to stir, for fear of the tyrant— Aristomachus availed himself of the pretext of their complicity with the irruption of the Achaeans to put to the rack and execute eighty of the leading citizens, who were perfectly innocent, in the presence of their relations. I pass by the history of his whole life and the crimes of his ancestors, for that would be too long a story.

60. But this shows that we ought not to be indignant if

a man reaps as he has sown, but rather if he is allowed to end
his days in peace, without experiencing such retribution at
all. Nor ought we to accuse Antigonus or Aratus of crime
if they racked and put to death a tyrant whom they had captured in war, to have killed and wreaked vengeance on
whom, even in time of peace, would have brought praise
and honour to the doers from all right-minded persons.

But when, in addition to these crimes, he was guilty also
of treachery to the League, what shall we say that he deserved? In fact, he abdicated the tyranny of Argos shortly
before [in 229-228 B.C.], finding himself in difficulties owing to the state of affairs brought on by the death of Demetrius. He was, however, protected by the clemency and
generosity of the League, and, much to his own surprise,
was left unmolested. For the Achaean government not only
secured him an amnesty for all crimes committed by him
while despot, but admitted him as a member of the League,
and invested him with the highest office in it—that, namely,
of hegemon and general. All these favours he immediately
forgot as soon as his hopes were a little raised by the Cleomenic war; and at a crisis of the utmost importance he withdrew his native city, as well as his own personal adhesion,
from the League, and attached them to its enemies. For such
an act of treason what he deserved was not to be racked under cover of night at Cenchreae and then put to death, as
Phylarchus says; he ought to have been taken from city to
city in the Peloponnesus, and to have ended his life only after
exemplary torture in each of them. And yet the only severity
that this guilty wretch had to endure was to be drowned in
the sea by order of the officers at Cenchreae.

61. There is another illustration of this writer's manner
to be found in his treatment of the cases of Mantinea and
Megalopolis. The misfortunes of the former he has depicted
with his usual exaggeration and picturesqueness, apparently
from the notion that it is the peculiar function of the historian to select for special mention only such actions as are
conspicuously bad. But about the noble conduct of the
Megalopolitans at that same period he has not said a word,

as though it were the province of history to deal with crimes rather than with instances of just and noble conduct, or as though his readers would be less improved by the record of what is great and worthy of imitation than by that of such deeds as are base and fit only to be avoided. For instance, he has told us clearly enough how Cleomenes took the town, preserved it from damage, and forthwith sent couriers to the Megalopolitans in Messene with a dispatch offering them the safe enjoyment of their country if they would throw in their lot with him; and his object in telling all this is to enhance the magnanimity and moderation of Cleomenes towards his enemies. Nay, he has gone further and told us how the people of Megalopolis would not allow the letter to be read to the end, and were not far from stoning the bearers of it. Thus much he does tell us. But the sequel to this, so appropriate to a historian—the commendation, I mean, and honourable mention of their noble conduct—this he has altogether left out.

And yet he had an opportunity ready to his hand. For if we view with approval the conduct of a people who merely by their declarations and votes support a war in behalf of friends and allies, while to those who go so far as to endure the devastation of their territory and a siege of their town we give not only praise but active gratitude, what must be our estimate of the people of Megalopolis? Must it not be of the most exalted character? First of all, they allowed their territory to be at the mercy of Cleomenes, and then consented to be entirely deprived of their city, rather than be false to the League; and, finally, in spite of an unexpected chance of recovering it, they deliberately preferred the loss of their territory, the tombs of their ancestors, their temples, their homes and property, of everything in fact which men value most, to forfeiting their faith to their allies. No nobler action has ever been or ever will be performed; none to which a historian could better draw his readers' attention. For what could be a higher incentive to good faith, or the maintenance of frank and permanent relations between states? But of all this Phylarchus says not a word, being, as it seems to me, entirely blind to all that is noblest and best suited to be the theme of a historian.

62. He does, however, state in the course of his narrative that from the spoils of Megalopolis six thousand talents fell to the Lacedaemonians, of which two thousand, according to custom, were given to Cleomenes. This shows, to begin with, an astounding ignorance of the ordinary facts as to the resources of Greece—a knowledge which must necessarily be possessed by historians. I am not of course now speaking of the period in which the Peloponnesus had been ruined by the Macedonian kings, and still more completely by a long continuance of intestine struggles, but of our own times, in which it is believed, by the establishment of its unity, to be enjoying the highest prosperity. Still even at this period, if you could collect all the movable property of the whole Peloponnesus (leaving out the value of slaves), it would be impossible to get so large a sum together. That I speak on good grounds and not at random will appear from the following fact. Everyone has read that when the Athenians, in conjunction with the Thebans, entered upon the war with the Lacedaemonians [in 378 B.C.], and dispatched an army of ten thousand men and manned a hundred triremes, they resolved to supply the expenses of the war by the assessment of a property tax, and accordingly had a valuation taken, not only of the whole land of Attica and the houses in it, but of all other property; but yet the value returned fell short of six thousand talents by two hundred and fifty; which will show that what I have just said of the Peloponnesus is not far wide of the mark. But at this period the most exaggerated estimate could scarcely give more than three hundred talents as coming from Megalopolis itself, for it is acknowledged that most of the inhabitants, free and slaves, escaped to Messene. But the strongest confirmation of my words is the case of Mantinea, which, as he himself observes, was second to no Arcadian city in wealth and numbers. Though it was surrendered after a siege, so that no one could escape, and no property could without great difficulty be concealed, yet the value of the whole spoil of the town, including the cap-

tives, amounted at this same period to only three hundred talents.

63. But a more astonishing misstatement remains to be remarked. In the course of his history of this war, Phylarchus asserts that about ten days before the battle an ambassador came from Ptolemy announcing to Cleomenes that the king declined to continue to support him with supplies, and advised him to make terms with Antigonus. And that when this message had been delivered to Cleomenes he made up his mind that he had better put his fortune to the supreme test as soon as possible, before his forces learned about this message, because he could not hope to provide the soldiers' pay from his own resources. But if he had at that very time become the master of six thousand talents, he would have been better supplied than Ptolemy himself. And as for war with Antigonus, if he had become master of only three hundred talents, he would have been able to continue it without any difficulty. But the writer states two inconsistent propositions—that Cleomenes depended wholly on Ptolemy for money, and that he at the same time had become master of that enormous sum. Is this not irrational, and grossly careless besides? I might mention many instances of a similar kind, not only in his account of this period, but throughout his whole work; but I think for my present purpose enough has been said.

From BOOK VI

The Roman Constitution

. . . . . .

2. I am aware that some will be at a loss to account for my interrupting the course of my narrative for the sake of entering upon the following disquisition on the Roman con-

stitution. But I think that I have already in many passages made it fully evident that this particular branch of my work was one of the necessities imposed on me by the nature of my original design, and I pointed this out with special clearness in the preface which explained the scope of my history. I there stated that the feature of my work which was at once the best in itself and the most instructive to the students of it was that it would enable them to know and fully realize in what manner, and under what kind of constitution, it came about that nearly the whole world fell under the power of Rome in somewhat less than fifty-three years, an event certainly without precedent. This being my settled purpose, I could see no more fitting period than the present for making a pause and examining the truth of the remarks about to be made on this constitution. In private life if you wish to satisfy yourself as to the badness or goodness of particular persons, you would not, if you wish to get a genuine test, examine their conduct at a time of uneventful repose, but in the hour of brilliant success or conspicuous reverse. For the true test of a perfect man is the power of bearing with spirit and dignity violent changes of fortune. An examination of a constitution should be conducted in the same way: and therefore, being unable to find in our day a more rapid or signal change than that which has happened to Rome, I reserved my disquisition on its constitution for this place. . . .

3. Of the Greek states, which have again and again risen to greatness and fallen into insignificance, it is not difficult to speak, whether we recount their past history or venture an opinion on their future. For to report what is already known is an easy task, nor is it hard to guess what is to come from our knowledge of what has been. But in regard to the Romans it is neither an easy matter to describe their present state, owing to the complexity of their constitution, nor to speak with confidence of their future, from our inadequate acquaintance with their peculiar institutions in the past, whether affecting their public or their private life. It will require, then, no ordinary attention and study to get a clear

and comprehensive conception of the distinctive features of this constitution.

Now it is undoubtedly the case that most of those who profess to give us authoritative instruction on this subject distinguish three kinds of constitutions, which they designate kingship, aristocracy, democracy. But in my opinion the question might fairly be put to them whether they name these as being the only ones or as the best. In either case I think they are wrong. For it is plain that we must regard as the best constitution that which partakes of all these three elements. And this is no mere assertion, but has been proved by the example of Lycurgus, who was the first to construct a constitution—that of Sparta—on this principle. Nor can we admit that these are the only forms, for we have had before now examples of absolute and tyrannical forms of government, which, while differing as widely as possible from kingship, yet appear to have some points of resemblance to it, on which account all absolute rulers falsely assume and use, as far as they can, the title of king. Again there have been many instances of oligarchical governments having in appearance some analogy to aristocracies, which are, if I may say so, as different from them as it is possible to be. The same also holds good about democracy.

4. I will illustrate the truth of what I say. We cannot hold every absolute government to be a kingship, but only that which is accepted voluntarily, and is directed by an appeal to reason rather than to fear and force. Nor again is every oligarchy to be regarded as an aristocracy; the latter exists only where the power is wielded by the justest and wisest men selected on their merits. Similarly, it is not enough to constitute a democracy that the whole crowd of citizens should have the right to do whatever they wish or propose. But where reverence to the gods, honour for parents, respect to elders, obedience to laws are traditional and habitual, in such communities, if the will of the majority prevail, we may speak of the form of government as a democracy. So then we enumerate six forms of government—the three com-

monly spoken of which I have just mentioned, and three more allied forms: I mean despotism, oligarchy, and mob rule. The first of these arises without artificial aid and in the natural order of events. Next to this, and produced from it by the aid of art and adjustment, comes kingship; which degenerating into the evil form allied to it, by which I mean tyranny, both are destroyed and aristocracy produced. Again the latter being in the course of nature perverted to oligarchy, and the people passionately avenging the unjust acts of their rulers, democracy comes into existence, which in due course by its violence and contempt of law becomes mob rule to close the series. No clearer proof of the truth of what I say could be obtained than by a careful observation of the natural origin, genesis, and decadence of these several forms of government. For it is only by seeing distinctly how each of them is produced that a distinct view can also be obtained of its growth, zenith, and decadence, and the time, circumstance, and place in which each of these may be expected to recur. This method I have assumed to be especially applicable to the Roman constitution, because its origin and growth have from the first followed natural causes.

5. Now the natural laws which regulate the transformation of one form of government into another are perhaps discussed with greater accuracy by Plato and some other philosophers. But their treatment, from its intricacy and exhaustiveness, is within the capacity of only a few. I will therefore endeavour to give a summary of the subject, just so far as I suppose it to fall within the scope of a serious history and the intelligence of ordinary people. For if my exposition appear in any way inadequate, owing to the general terms in which it is expressed, the details contained in what is immediately to follow will simply atone for what is left for the present unsolved.

What is the origin then of a constitution, and whence is it produced? Suppose that from floods, pestilence, failure of crops, or some such causes the race of man is reduced almost to extinction. Such things, we are told, have happened and, it is reasonable to think, will happen again. Suppose accordingly all knowledge of social habits and arts to have been lost. Suppose that from the survivors, as from seeds, the race of man to have again multiplied. In that case I presume they would, like the animals, herd together; for it is but reasonable to suppose that bodily weakness would induce them to seek those of their own kind to herd with. And in that case, too, as with the animals, he who was superior to the rest in strength of body or courage of soul would lead and rule them. For what we see happen in the case of animals that are without the faculty of reason, such as bulls, goats, and cocks—among whom there can be no dispute that the strongest take the lead—that we must regard as in the truest sense the teaching of nature. Originally then it is probable that the condition of life among men was this, herding together like animals and following the strongest and bravest as leaders. The standard of this authority would be physical strength, and the name we should give it would be despotism. But as soon as the idea of family ties and social relation has arisen amongst such agglomerations of men, then is born also the idea of kingship, and then for the first time mankind conceives the notion of goodness and justice and their reverse.

6. The way in which such conceptions originate and come into existence is this. The intercourse of the sexes is an instinct of nature, and the result is the birth of children. Now, if any one of these children who have been brought up, when arrived at maturity, is ungrateful and makes no return to those by whom he was nurtured, but on the contrary presumes to injure them by word and deed, it is plain that he will probably offend and annoy such as are present, and have seen the care and trouble bestowed by the parents on the nurture and bringing up of their children. For seeing that men differ from the other animals in being the only creatures possessed of reasoning powers, it is clear that such a difference of conduct is not likely to escape their observation, but that they will remark it when it occurs, and express their displeasure on the spot, because they will have an eye to the future, and will reason on the likelihood of the same occurring to each of themselves. Again, if a man has been

rescued or helped in an hour of danger, and, instead of showing gratitude to his preserver, seeks to do him harm, it is clearly probable that the rest will be displeased and offended with him when they know it, sympathizing with their neighbour and imagining themselves in his case. Hence arises a notion in every breast of the meaning and theory of duty, which is in fact the beginning and end of justice. Similarly, again, when any one man stands out as the champion of all in a time of danger, and braves with firm courage the onslaught of the most powerful wild beasts, it is probable that such a man would meet with marks of favour and pre-eminence from the common people, while he who acted in a contrary way would fall under their contempt and dislike. From this, once more, it is reasonable to suppose that there would arise in the minds of the multitude a theory of the disgraceful and the honourable and of the difference between them, and that one should be sought and imitated for its advantages, the other shunned. When, therefore, the leading and most powerful man among his people ever encourages such persons in accordance with the popular sentiment, and thereby assumes in the eyes of his subjects the appearance of being the distributor to each man according to his deserts, they no longer obey him and support his rule from fear of violence, but rather from conviction of its utility, however old he may be, rallying round him with one heart and soul, and fighting against all who form designs against his government. In this way he becomes a king instead of a despot by imperceptible degrees, reason having ousted brute courage and bodily strength from their supremacy.

7. This then is the natural process of formation among mankind of the notion of goodness and justice and their opposites; and this is the origin and genesis of genuine kingship, for people do not only keep up the government of such men personally, but for their descendants also for many generations, from the conviction that those who are born from and educated by men of this kind will have principles also like theirs. But if they subsequently become displeased with their descendants, they do not any longer decide their choice

of rulers and kings by their physical strength or brute courage, but by the differences of their intellectual and reasoning faculties, from practical experience of the decisive importance of such a distinction. In old times, then, those who were once thus selected, and obtained this office, grew old in their royal functions, making magnificent strongholds and surrounding them with walls and extending their frontiers, partly for the security of their subjects and partly to provide them with abundance of the necessaries of life; and while engaged in these works they were exempt from all vituperation or jealousy, because they did not make their distinctive dress, food, or drink at all conspicuous, but lived very much like the rest, and joined in the everyday employments of the people. But when their royal power became hereditary in their family, and they found everything necessary for security ready to their hands, as well as more than was necessary for their personal support, then they gave the rein to their appetites, imagining that rulers must needs wear clothes different from those of subjects, have different and elaborate luxuries of the table, and must even seek sensual indulgence, however unlawful the source, without fear of denial. These things having given rise in the one case to jealousy and offence, in the other to outburst of hatred and passionate resentment, the kingship became a tyranny; the first step in disintegration was taken, and plots began to be formed against the government, which did not now proceed from the worst men but from the noblest, most high-minded, and most courageous, because these are the men who can least submit to the tyrannical acts of their rulers.

8. But as soon as the people got leaders, they cooperated with them against the dynasty for the reasons I have mentioned, and then kingship and tyranny were alike entirely abolished, and aristocracy began to grow. For in their immediate gratitude to those who had deposed the despots, the people employed them as leaders, and entrusted their interests to them; who, looking upon this charge at first as a great privilege, made the public advantage their chief concern and conducted all kinds of business, public or private, with dili-

gence and caution. But when the sons of these men received the same position of authority from their fathers—having had no experience of misfortunes, and none at all of civil equality and freedom of speech, but having been bred up from the first under the shadow of their fathers' authority and lofty position—some of them gave themselves up with passion to avarice and unscrupulous love of money, others to drinking and the boundless debaucheries which accompany it, and others to the violation of women or the forcible appropriation of boys; and so they turned an aristocracy into an oligarchy. But it was not long before they roused in the minds of the people the same feelings as before, and their fall therefore was very like the disaster which befell the tyrants.

9. For no sooner has the knowledge of the jealousy and hatred existing in the citizens against them emboldened someone to oppose the government by word or deed than he is sure to find the whole people ready and prepared to take his side. Having then got rid of these rulers by assassination or exile, they do not venture to set up a king again, being still in terror of the injustice to which this led before, nor dare they entrust the common interests again to a few, considering the recent example of their misconduct; and therefore, as the only sound hope left them is that which depends upon themselves, they are driven to take refuge in that, and so change the constitution from an oligarchy to a democracy, and take upon themselves the superintendence and charge of the state. And as long as any survive who have had experience of oligarchical supremacy and domination, they regard their present constitution as a blessing, and hold equality and freedom as of the utmost value. But as soon as a new generation has arisen, and the democracy has descended to their children's children, long association weakens their value for equality and freedom, and some seek to become more powerful than the ordinary citizens, and the most liable to this temptation are the rich. So when they begin to be fond of office, and find themselves unable to obtain it by their own unassisted efforts and their own merits, they

ruin their estates, while enticing and corrupting the common people in every possible way. By which means, in their senseless mania for reputation, when they have made the populace ready and greedy to receive bribes, democracy is destroyed and it is transformed into a government of violence and the strong hand. For the people, habituated to feed at the expense of others, and to have its hopes of a livelihood in the property of its neighbours, as soon as it has got a leader sufficiently ambitious and daring, being excluded by poverty from the sweets of civil honours, produces a reign of mere violence. Then come tumultuous assemblies, massacres, banishments, redivisions of land, until, after losing all trace of civilization, it has once more found a master and a despot.

This is the regular cycle of constitutional revolutions, and the natural order in which constitutions change, are transformed, and return again to their original stage. If a man have a clear grasp of these principles he may perhaps make a mistake as to the dates at which this or that will happen to a particular constitution; but, if he judges without animosity or jealousy, he will rarely be mistaken as to the stage of growth or decay at which it has arrived, or as to the form into which it will change. However, it is in the case of the Roman constitution that this method of inquiry will most fully teach us its formation, its growth, and zenith, as well as the changes awaiting it in the future; for this, if any constitution ever did, owed, as I said just now, its original foundation and growth to natural causes, and to natural causes will owe its decay. My subsequent narrative will be the best illustration of what I say.

10. For the present I will make a brief reference to the legislation of Lycurgus, for such a discussion is not at all alien to my subject. That statesman was fully aware that all those changes which I have enumerated come about by an undeviating law of nature, and he reflected that every form of government that was unmixed, and rested on one species of power, was unstable because it was swiftly perverted into that particular form of evil peculiar to it and inherent in its

nature. For just as rust is the natural dissolvent of iron, wood-worms and grubs to timber, by which they are destroyed without any external injury, but by that which is engendered in themselves; so in each constitution there is naturally engendered a particular vice inseparable from it: in kingship it is absolutism, in aristocracy it is oligarchy, in democracy lawless ferocity and violence; and to these vicious states all these forms of government are, as I have lately shown, inevitably transformed. Lycurgus, I say, saw all this, and accordingly combined together all the excellences and distinctive features of the best constitutions, that no part should become unduly predominant and be perverted into its kindred vice; and that, each power being checked by the others, no one part should turn the scale or decisively outbalance the others; but that, by being accurately adjusted and in exact equilibrium, the whole might remain long steady like a ship sailing close to the wind. The royal power was prevented from growing insolent by fear of the people, which had also assigned to it an adequate share in the constitution. The people in their turn were restrained from a bold contempt of the kings by fear of the Gerusia, the members of which, being selected on grounds of merit, were certain to throw their influence on the side of justice in every question that arose; and thus the party placed at a disadvantage by its conservative tendency was always strengthened and supported by the weight and influence of the Gerusia. The result of this combination has been that the Lacedaemonians retained their freedom for the longest period of any people with which we are acquainted.

Lycurgus, however, established his constitution without the discipline of adversity, because he was able to foresee by the light of reason the course which events naturally take and the source from which they come. But though the Romans have arrived at the same result in framing their commonwealth, they have done so not by means of abstract reasoning, but through many struggles and difficulties, and by continually adopting reforms from knowledge gained in disaster. The result has been a constitution like that of Lycurgus, and the best of any existing in my time. . . .

11. . . . I am fully conscious that to those who have been brought up under the Roman constitution I shall appear to give an inadequate account of it by the omission of certain details. Knowing accurately every portion of it from personal experience, and from having been bred up in its customs and laws from childhood, they will not be struck so much by the accuracy of the description as annoyed by its omissions; nor will they believe that the historian has purposely omitted unimportant distinctions, but will attribute his silence upon the origin of existing institutions or other important facts to ignorance. What is told they depreciate as insignificant or beside the purpose, what is omitted they desiderate as vital to the question, their object being to appear to know more than the writers. But a good critic should judge a writer not by what he leaves unsaid, but from what he says; if he detects misstatements in the latter, he may then feel certain that ignorance accounts for the former; but if what he says is accurate, his omissions ought to be attributed to deliberate judgement and not to ignorance. So much for those whose criticisms are prompted by personal ambition rather than by justice. . . .

As for the Roman constitution, it had the three elements controlling the constitution which I have mentioned before; and their respective share of power in the whole state had been regulated with such a scrupulous regard to equality and equilibrium that no one could say for certain, not even a native, whether the constitution as a whole were an aristocracy or democracy or monarchy. And no wonder, for if we confine our observation to the power of the consuls we should be inclined to regard it as monarchic and kingly; if to that of the Senate, as aristocratic; and if finally one looks at the power possessed by the people it would seem a clear case of a democracy. What the exact powers of these several parts were and still, with slight modifications, are, I will now state.

12. The consuls, before leading out the legions, remain

in Rome and are supreme masters of the administration. All other magistrates, except the tribunes, are under them and take their orders. They introduce foreign ambassadors to the Senate, bring matters requiring deliberation before it, and see to the execution of its decrees. If, again, there are any matters of state which require the authorization of the people, it is their business to see to them, to summon the assemblies, to bring the proposals before them, and to carry out the decrees of the people. In the preparations for war also, and in a word in the entire administration of a campaign, they have all but absolute power. It is competent to them to impose on the allies such levies as they think good, to appoint the military tribunes, to make up the roll for soldiers and select those that are suitable. Besides they have absolute power of inflicting punishment on all who are under their command while on active service; and they have authority to expend as much of the public money as they choose, being accompanied by a quaestor who is entirely at their orders. A survey of these powers alone would in fact justify our describing the constitution as purely monarchic and royal. Nor will it affect the truth of my description if any of the institutions I have described are changed in our time, or in that of our posterity, and the same remarks apply to what follows.

13. The Senate has first of all the control of the treasury, and regulates the receipts and disbursements alike. For the quaestors cannot issue any public money for the various departments of the state without a decree of the Senate, except for the service of the consuls. The Senate controls also what is by far the largest and most important expenditure, that, namely, which is made by the censors every five years for the repair or construction of public buildings; this money cannot be obtained by the censors except by the grant of the Senate. Similarly all crimes committed in Italy requiring a public investigation, such as treason, conspiracy, poisoning, or willful murder, are in the hands of the Senate. Besides, if any individual or state among the Italian allies requires a controversy to be settled, a penalty to be assessed,

help or protection to be afforded—all this is the province of the Senate. Or again, outside Italy, if it is necessary to send an embassy to reconcile warring communities, or to remind them of their duty, or sometimes to impose requisitions upon them, or to receive their submission, or finally to proclaim war against them—this too is the business of the Senate. In like manner the reception to be given to foreign ambassadors in Rome, and the answer to be returned to them, are decided by the Senate. With such business the people have nothing to do. Consequently, if one were staying at Rome when the consuls were not in town, one would imagine the constitution to be a complete aristocracy: and this has been the idea entertained by many Greeks, and by many kings as well, from the fact that nearly all the business they had with Rome was settled by the Senate.

14. After this one would naturally be inclined to ask what part is left for the people in the constitution, when the Senate has these various functions, especially the control of the receipts and expenditures of the exchequer; and when the consuls, again, have absolute power over the details of military preparation and an absolute authority in the field. There is, however, a part left the people, and it is a most important one. For the people is the sole fountain of honour and of punishment, and it is by these two things and these alone that dynasties and constitutions and, in a word, human society are held together; for where the distinction between them is not sharply drawn both in theory and practice, there no undertaking can be properly administered—as indeed we might expect when good and bad are held in exactly the same honour. The people then are the only court to decide matters of lfe and death, and even in cases where the penalty is money, if the sum to be assessed is sufficiently serious, and especially when the accused have held the higher magistracies. And in regard to this arrangement there is one point deserving especial commendation and record. Men who are on trial for their lives at Rome, while sentence is in process of being voted—if even only one of the tribes whose votes are needed to ratify the sentence has not voted—have the

privilege of openly departing and condemning themselves to a voluntary exile. Such men are safe at Naples, Praeneste, or Tibur, and at the other towns with which this arrangement has been duly ratified on oath.

Again, it is the people who bestow offices on the deserving, which are the most honourable rewards of virtue. It has also the absolute power of passing or repealing laws, and, most important of all, it is the people who deliberate on the question of war or peace. And when provisional terms are made for alliance, suspension of hostilities, or treaties, it is the people who ratify them or the reverse. These considerations again would lead one to say that the chief power in the state was the people's, and that the constitution was a democracy.

15. Such, then, is the distribution of power between the several parts of the state. I must now show how these several parts can, when they choose, oppose or support each other.

The consul, then, when he has started on an expedition with the powers I have described, is to all appearance absolute in the administration of the business in hand; still he has need of the support both of people and Senate, and without them is quite unable to bring the matter to a successful conclusion. For it is plain that he must have supplies sent to his legions from time to time, but without a decree of the Senate they can be supplied neither with food nor clothes nor pay, so that all the plans of a commander must be futile if the Senate is resolved either to shrink from danger or hamper his plans. And again, whether a consul shall bring any undertaking to a conclusion or not depends entirely upon the Senate, for it has absolute authority at the end of a year to send another consul to supersede him, or to continue the existing one in his command. Again, even to the successes of the generals the Senate has the power to add distinction and glory, and on the other hand to obscure their merits and lower their credit. For these high achievements are brought in tangible form before the eyes of the citizens by what are called "triumphs." But these triumphs the commanders can not celebrate with proper pomp, or in some cases celebrate at all, unless the Senate concurs and grants the necessary money. As for the people, the consuls are pre-eminently obliged to court their favour, however distant from home may be their field of operations, for it is the people, as I have said before, that ratifies, or refuses to ratify, terms of peace and treaties, but most of all because when laying down their office they have to give an account of their administration before it. Therefore in no case is it safe for the consuls to neglect either the Senate or the good will of the people.

16. As for the Senate, which possesses the immense power I have described, in the first place it is obliged in public affairs to take the multitude into account, and respect the wishes of the people; and it cannot put into execution the penalty for offences against the republic which are punishable with death, unless the people first ratify its decrees. Similarly even in matters which directly affect the senators —for instance, in the case of a law diminishing the Senate's traditional authority, or depriving senators of certain dignities and offices, or even actually cutting down their property —even in such cases the people have the sole power of passing or rejecting the law. But most important of all is the fact that if a single tribune interposes his veto, the Senate not only is unable to pass a decree, but cannot even hold a meeting at all, whether formal or informal. Now, the tribunes are always bound to carry out the decree of the people, and above all things to have regard to their wishes; therefore, for all these reasons the Senate stands in awe of the multitude, and cannot neglect the feelings of the people.

17. In like manner the people on its part is far from being independent of the Senate, and is bound to take its wishes into account both collectively and individually. For contracts, too numerous to count, are given out by the censors in all parts of Italy for the repair or construction of public buildings; there is also the collection of revenue from many rivers, harbours, gardens, mines, and land—everything, in a word, that comes under the control of the Roman government—and in all these the people at large are engaged, so that there is scarcely a man, so to speak, who is not inter-

ested in these contracts and the profits from them. For some purchase the contracts from the censors for themselves, and others go partners with them, while others again go surety for these contractors, or actually pledge their property to the treasury for them. Now over all these transactions the Senate has absolute control. It can grant an extension of time, and in case of unforeseen accident can relieve the contractors from a portion of their obligation, or release them from it altogether if they are absolutely unable to fulfill it. And there are many details in which the Senate can inflict great hardship, or, on the other hand, grant great indulgences to the contractors, for in every case the appeal is to it. But the most important point of all is that the judges are taken from its members in the majority of trials, whether public or private, in which the charges are heavy. Consequently all citizens are much at its mercy and, being alarmed at the uncertainty as to when they may need its aid, are cautious about resisting or actively opposing its will. And for a similar reason men do not rashly resist the wishes of the consuls, because one and all may become subject to their absolute authority on a campaign.

18. The result of this power of the several estates for mutual help or harm is a union sufficiently firm for all emergencies, and a constitution than which it is impossible to find a better. For whenever any danger from without compels them to unite and work together, the strength which is developed by the state is so extraordinary that everything required is unfailingly carried out by the eager rivalry shown by all classes to devote their whole minds to the needs of the hour, and to secure that any determination come to should not fail for want of promptitude; while each individual works, privately and publicly alike, for the accomplishment of the business at hand. Accordingly, the peculiar constitution of the state makes it irresistible, and certain of obtaining whatever it determines to attempt. Nay, even when these external alarms are past, and the people are enjoying their good fortune and the fruits of their victories, and, as usually happens, growing corrupted by flattery and idleness, show a

tendency to violence and arrogance—it is in these circumstances more than ever that the constitution is seen to possess within itself the power of correcting abuses. For when any one of the three classes becomes puffed up, and manifests an inclination to be contentious and unduly encroaching, the mutual interdependence of all the three, and the possibility of the pretensions of any being checked and thwarted by the others, must plainly check this tendency; and so the proper equilibrium is maintained by the impulsiveness of the one part being checked by its fear of the other. . . .

43. Nearly all historians have recorded as constitutions of eminent excellence those of Lacedaemon, Crete, Mantinea, and Carthage. Some have also mentioned those of Athens and Thebes. The former I may allow to pass, but I am convinced that little need be said of the Athenian and Theban constitutions: their growth was abnormal, the period of their zenith brief, and the changes they experienced unusually violent. Their glory was a sudden and fortuitous flash, so to speak; and while they still thought themselves prosperous, and likely to remain so, they found themselves involved in circumstances completely the reverse. The Thebans got their reputation for valour among the Greeks by taking advantage of the senseless policy of the Lacedaemonians and the hatred of the allies towards them, owing to the valour of one, or at most two, men who were wise enough to appreciate the situation. Fortune quickly made it evident that it was not the peculiarity of their constitution but the valour of their leaders which gave the Thebans their success. For the great power of Thebes notoriously took its rise, attained its zenith, and fell to the ground with the lives of Epaminondas and Pelopidas. We must therefore conclude that it was not its constitution but its men that caused the high fortune which it then enjoyed.

44. A somewhat similar remark applies to the Athenians' constitution also. For though it perhaps had more frequent interludes of excellence, yet its highest perfection was attained during the brilliant career of Themistocles, and hav-

ing reached that point it quickly declined, owing to their essential instability. For the Athenian people is always in the position of a ship without a commander. In such a ship, if fear of the waves or the occurrence of a storm induce the crew to be of one mind and to obey the helmsman, they do their duty; but if they recover from this fear, and begin to treat their officers with contempt, and to quarrel with each other because they are no longer all of one mind—one party wishing to continue the voyage, and the other urging the steersman to bring the ship to anchor, some letting out the sheets, and others hauling them in and ordering the sails to be furled—their discord and quarrels make a sorry show to lookers-on; and the position of affairs is full of risk to those on board engaged on the same voyage: the result has often been that, after escaping the dangers of the widest seas and the most violent storms, they wreck their ship in harbour and close to shore. And this is what has often happened to the Athenian state. For, after repelling on various occasions the greatest and most formidable dangers by the valour of the people and their leaders, there have been times when, in periods of secure tranquillity, it has gratuitously and recklessly encountered disaster. Therefore I need say no more about either it or the Theban constitution, in both of which a mob manages everything on its own unfettered impulse— a mob in the one city distinguished for headlong outbursts of fiery temper, in the other trained in long habits of violence and ferocity.

45. Passing to the Cretan polity, there are two points which deserve our consideration. The first is how such writers as Ephorus, Xenophon, Callisthenes, and Plato—who are the most learned of the ancients—could assert that it was like that of Sparta, and secondly how they came to assert that it was at all admirable. I can agree with neither assertion; and I will explain why I say so. And first as to its dissimilarity with the Spartan constitution. The peculiar merit of the latter is said to be its land laws, by which no one possesses more than another, but all citizens have an equal share

in the public land. The next distinctive feature regards the acquisition of money: for as it is utterly discredited among them, the jealous competition which arises from inequality of wealth is entirely removed from the city. A third peculiarity of the Lacedaemonian polity is that, of the officials by whose hands and with whose advice the whole government is conducted, the kings hold an hereditary office, while the members of the Gerusia are elected for life.

46. Among the Cretans the exact reverse of all these arrangements obtains. The laws allow them to possess as much land as they can get with no limitation whatever. Money is so highly valued among them that its possession is thought not only to be necessary but in the highest degree creditable. And in fact greed and avarice are so native to the soil in Crete that they are the only people in the world among whom no stigma attaches to any sort of gain whatever. Again, all their offices are annual and on a democratic footing. I have therefore often felt at a loss to account for these writers speaking of the two constitutions, which are radically different, as though they were closely united and allied. But, besides overlooking these important differences, these writers have gone out of their way to comment at length on the legislation of Lycurgus: "He was the only legislator," they say, "who saw the important points. For, there being two things on which the safety of a commonwealth depends—courage in the face of the enemy and concord at home—by abolishing covetousness he with it removed all motive for civil broil and contest, whence it has been brought about that the Lacedaemonians are the best governed and most united people in Greece." Yet while giving utterance to these sentiments, and though they see that, in contrast to this, the Cretans by their ingrained avarice are engaged in countless public and private seditions, murders, and civil wars, yet they regard these facts as not affecting their contention, but are bold enough to speak of the two constitutions as alike. Ephorus, indeed, putting aside names, employs expressions so precisely the same when discoursing on the two constitutions that, unless

one noticed the proper names, there would be no means whatever of distinguishing which of the two he was describing.

47. In what the difference between them consists I have already stated. I will now address myself to showing that the Cretan constitution deserved neither praise nor imitation.

To my mind, then, there are two things fundamental to every state, in virtue of which its powers and constitution become desirable or objectionable. These are customs and laws. Of these the desirable are those which make men's private lives holy and pure, and the public character of the state civilized and just. The objectionable are those whose effect is the reverse. As, then, when we see good customs and good laws prevailing among certain people, we confidently assume that, in consequence of them, the men and their civil constitution will be good also, so when we see private life full of covetousness, and public policy of injustice, plainly we have reason for asserting their laws, particular customs, and general constitution to be bad. Now, with few exceptions, you could find no habits prevailing in private life more steeped in treachery than those in Crete, and no public policy more inequitable. Holding, then, the Cretan constitution to be neither like the Spartan nor worthy of choice or imitation, I reject it from the comparison which I have instituted.

Nor again would it be fair to introduce the republic of Plato, which is also spoken of in high terms by some philosophers. For just as we refuse admission to the athletic contests of those actors or athletes who have not registered or trained for them, so we ought not admit this Platonic constitution to the contest for the prize of merit unless it can first point to some genuine and practical achievement. Up to this time the notion of bringing it into comparison with the constitutions of Sparta, Rome, and Carthage would be like putting up a statue to compare with living and breathing men. Even if such a statue were faultless in point of art, the comparison of the lifeless with the living would naturally leave an impression of imperfection and incongruity upon the minds of the spectators.

48. I shall therefore omit these, and proceed with my description of the Laconian constitution. Now it seems to me that for securing unity among the citizens, for safeguarding the Laconian territory and preserving the liberty of Sparta inviolate, the legislation and provisions of Lycurgus were so excellent that I am forced to regard his wisdom as something superhuman. For the equality of landed possessions, the simplicity in their food, and the practice of taking it in common, which he established, were well calculated to secure morality in private life and to prevent civil broils in the state, as also their training in the endurance of labours and dangers to make men brave and noble-minded; but when both these virtues, courage and high morality, are combined in one soul or in one state, vice will not readily spring from such a soil, nor will such men easily be overcome by their enemies. By constructing his constitution therefore in this spirit, and of these elements, he secured two blessings to the Spartans—safety for their territory and a lasting freedom for themselves long after he was gone. He appears however to have made no provision whatever, particular or general, for the acquisition of the territory of their neighbours, or for the assertion of their supremacy, or, in a word, for any policy of aggrandizement at all. What he had still to do was to impose such a necessity, or create such a principle among the citizens, that, as he had succeeded in making their individual lives independent and simple, the public character of the state should also become independent and moral. But the actual fact is that, though he made them the most disinterested and sober-minded men in the world as far as their own ways of life and their national institutions were concerned, he left them in regard to the rest of Greece ambitious, eager for supremacy, and encroaching in the highest degree.

49. For in the first place is it not notorious that they were nearly the first Greeks to cast a covetous eye upon the territory of their neighbours, and that accordingly they waged a war of subjugation on the Messenians? In the next place is it not related in all histories that in their dogged obstinacy

they bound themselves with an oath never to desist from the siege of Messene until they had taken it? And lastly it is known to all that in their efforts for supremacy in Greece they submitted to do the bidding of those whom they had once conquered in war. For when the Persians invaded Greece, they conquered them, as champions of the liberty of Greece; yet when the invaders had retired and fled, they betrayed the cities of Greece into their hands by the peace of Antalcidas, for the sake of getting money to secure their supremacy over the Greeks. It was then that the defect in their constitution was rendered apparent. For as long as their ambition was confined to governing their immediate neighbours, or even the Peloponnesians only, they were content with the resources and supplies provided by Laconia itself, having all material of war ready to hand, and being able without much expenditure of time to return home or convey provisions with them. But directly they took in hand to dispatch naval expeditions, or to go on campaigns by land outside the Peloponnesus, it was evident that neither their iron currency nor their use of crops for payment in kind would be able to supply them with what they lacked if they abided by the legislation of Lycurgus; for such undertakings required money universally current, and goods from foreign countries. Thus they were compelled to wait humbly at Persian doors, impose tribute on the islanders, and exact contributions from all the Greeks, knowing that, if they abided by the laws of Lycurgus, it was impossible to advance any claims upon any outside power at all, much less upon the supremacy in Greece.

50. My object, then, in this digression is to make it manifest by actual facts that, for guarding their own country with absolute safety, and for preserving their own freedom, the legislation of Lycurgus was entirely sufficient; and for those who are content with these objects we must concede that there neither exists nor ever has existed a constitution and civil order preferable to that of Sparta. But if anyone is seeking aggrandizement, and believes that to be a leader and ruler and despot of numerous subjects, and to have all look-

ing and turning to him, is a finer thing than that—in this point of view we must acknowledge that the Spartan constitution is deficient, and that of Rome superior and better constituted for obtaining power. And this has been proved by actual facts. For when the Lacedaemonians strove to possess themselves of the supremacy in Greece, it was not long before they brought their own freedom itself into danger. Whereas the Romans, after obtaining supreme power over the Italians themselves, soon brought the whole world under their rule—in which achievement the abundance and availability of their supplies largely contributed to their success.

51. Now the Carthaginian constitution seems to me originally to have been well contrived in these most distinctively important particulars. For they had kings, and the Gerusia had the powers of an aristocracy, and the multitude were supreme in such things as were proper to them; and on the whole the adjustment of its several parts was very like that of Rome and Sparta. But about the period of its entering on the Hannibalic war the political state of Carthage was on the decline, that of Rome improving. For whereas there is in every body, or polity, or action a natural stage of growth, zenith, and decay, and whereas everything in them is at its best at the zenith, the difference between these two constitutions manifested itself at that period. For exactly so far as the strength and prosperity of Carthage preceded that of Rome in point of time, by so much was Carthage then past its prime, while Rome was exactly at its zenith, as far as its political constitution was concerned. In Carthage therefore the influence of the people in the policy of the state had already risen to be supreme, while at Rome the Senate was at the height of its power; and so, as in the one measures were deliberated upon by the many, in the other by the best men, the policy of the Romans in all public undertakings proved the stronger; on which account, though they met with capital disasters, by force of prudent counsels they finally conquered the Carthaginians in the war.

52. If we look however at separate details, for instance at the provisions for carrying on a war, we shall find that

whereas for a naval expedition the Carthaginians are the better trained and prepared—as is only natural with a people with whom it has been hereditary for many generations to practise this craft, and to follow the seaman's trade above all nations in the world—yet, in regard to military service on land, the Romans train themselves to a much higher pitch than the Carthaginians. The former bestow their whole attention upon this department, whereas the Carthaginians wholly neglect their infantry, though they do take some slight interest in the cavalry. The reason for this is that they employ foreign mercenaries, the Romans native and citizen levies. It is in this point that the latter polity is preferable to the former. They have their hopes of freedom ever resting on the courage of mercenary troops, the Romans on the valour of their own citizens and the aid of their allies. The result is that even if the Romans have suffered a defeat at first, they renew the war with undiminished forces, which the Carthaginians cannot do. For, as the Romans are fighting for country and children, it is impossible for them to relax the fury of their struggle; but they persist with obstinate resolution until they have overcome their enemies. What has happened in regard to their navy is an instance in point. In skill the Romans are much behind the Carthaginians, as I have already said; yet the upshot of the whole naval war has been a decided triumph for the Romans, owing to the valour of their men. For although nautical science contributes largely to success in sea fights, still it is the courage of the marines that turns the scale most decisively in favour of victory. The fact is that Italians as a nation are by nature superior to Phoenicians and Libyans in both physical strength and courage, and their habits also do much to inspire the youth with enthusiasm for such exploits. One example will be sufficient of the pains taken by the Roman state to turn out men ready to endure anything to win a reputation in their country for valour.

53. Whenever one of their illustrious men dies, in the course of his funeral the body is carried with every kind of

honour into the Forum to the rostra, as a raised platform
there is called, and sometimes is propped upright on it so
as to be conspicuous, or, more rarely, is laid upon it. Then
with all the people standing round, his son, if he has left
one of full age and he is there, or, failing him, one of his relations, mounts the rostra and delivers a speech concerning
the virtues of the deceased and the successful exploits performed by him in his lifetime. By these means the people
are reminded of what has been done, and made to see it
with their own eyes—not only such as were engaged in the
actual transactions but those also who were not—and their
sympathies are so deeply moved that the loss appears not to
be confined to the actual mourners, but to be a public one
affecting the whole people. After the burial and all the usual
ceremonies have been performed, they place the likeness of
the deceased in the most conspicuous spot in his house, sur-
mounted by a wooden canopy or shrine. This likeness consists of a mask made to represent the deceased with extraordinary fidelity both in shape and complexion. These likenesses they display at public sacrifices adorned with much
care. And when any illustrious member of the family dies,
they carry these masks to the funeral, putting them on men
whom they think as like the originals as possible in height
and bearing. And these substitutes assume clothes according to the rank of the person represented: if he was a consul
or praetor, a toga with purple stripes; if a censor, whole purple; if he had also celebrated a triumph or performed any
exploit of that kind, a toga embroidered with gold. These
representatives also ride themselves in chariots, while the
fasces and axes and all the other customary insignia of the
particular offices lead the way, according to the dignity of
the rank in the state enjoyed by the deceased in his lifetime;
and on arriving at the rostra they all take their seats on ivory
chairs in their order. There could not easily be a more inspiring spectacle than this for a young man of noble ambi-
tions and virtuous aspirations. For can we conceive anyone
to be unmoved at the sight of all the likenesses collected to-

gether of the men who have earned glory, all as it were living and breathing? Or what could be a more glorious spectacle?

54. Besides, the speaker over the body about to be buried, after having finished the panegyric of this particular person, starts upon the others whose representatives are present, beginning with the most ancient, and recounts the successes and achievements of each. By this means the glorious memory of brave men is continually renewed, the fame of those who have performed any noble deed is never allowed to die, and the renown of those who have done good service to their country becomes a matter of common knowledge to the multitude and part of the heritage of posterity. But the chief benefit of the ceremony is that it inspires young men to shrink from no exertion for the general welfare, in the hope of obtaining the glory which awaits the brave. And what I say is confirmed by this fact. Many Romans have volunteered to decide a whole battle by single combat; not a few have deliberately accepted certain death, some in time of war to secure the safety of the rest, some in time of peace to preserve the safety of the commonwealth. There have also been instances of men in office putting their own sons to death, in defiance of every custom and law, because they rated the interests of their country higher than those of natural ties even with their nearest and dearest. There are many stories of this kind, related of many men in Roman history; but one will be enough for our present purpose, and I will give the name as an instance to prove the truth of my words.

55. The story goes that Horatius Cocles, while fighting with two enemies at the head of the bridge over the Tiber, which is the entrance to the city on the north, seeing a large body of men advancing to support his enemies, and fearing that they would force their way into the city, turned round and shouted to those behind him to hasten back to the other side and break down the bridge. They obeyed him, and whilst they were breaking the bridge he remained at his post receiving numerous wounds, and checked the progress

of the enemy, his opponents being panic-stricken, not so much by his strength as by the audacity with which he held his ground. When the bridge had been broken down, the attack of the enemy was stopped; and Cocles then threw himself into the river with his armour on and deliberately sacrificed his life, because he valued the safety of his country and his own future reputation more highly than his present life and the years of existence that remained to him. Such is the enthusiasm and emulation of noble deeds that are engendered among the Romans by their customs.

56. Again, the Roman customs and principles regarding the acquisition of wealth are better than those of the Carthaginians. In the view of the latter nothing is disgraceful that makes for gain; with the former nothing is more disgraceful than to receive bribes and to make profit by improper means. For they regard wealth obtained from unlawful transactions to be as much a subject of reproach as a fair profit from reputable sources is of commendation. A proof of the fact is this. The Carthaginians obtain office by open bribery, but among the Romans the penalty for it is death. With such a radical difference, therefore, between the rewards offered to virtue among the two peoples, it is natural that the ways adopted for obtaining them should be different also.

But the most important difference for the better which the Roman commonwealth appears to me to display is in their religious beliefs. For I conceive that what in other nations is looked upon as a reproach, I mean superstition, is the very thing which keeps the Roman commonwealth together. To such an extraordinary height is this carried among them, both in private and public business, that nothing could exceed it. Many people might think this unaccountable, but in my opinion their object is to use it as a check upon the common people. If it were possible to form a state wholly of philosophers, such a custom would perhaps be unnecessary. But seeing that every multitude is fickle, and full of lawless desires, unreasoning anger, and violent passion, the only resource is to keep them in check by mysterious terrors and scenic effects of this sort. Wherefore, to my mind, the ancients were not acting without purpose or at random when they brought in among the vulgar those opinions about the gods and the belief in the punishments in Hades; much rather do I think that men nowadays are acting rashly and foolishly in rejecting them. This is the reason why, apart from anything else, Greek statesmen, if entrusted with a single talent, though protected by ten checking-clerks, as many seals, and twice as many witnesses, yet cannot be induced to keep faith; whereas among the Romans, in their magistracies and embassies, men have the handling of a great amount of money, and yet from pure respect of their oath keep their faith intact. And again in other nations it is a rare thing to find a man who keeps his hands out of the public purse and is entirely pure in such matters, but among the Romans it is a rare thing to detect a man in the act of committing such a crime. . . .

57. That to all things, then, which exist there is ordained decay and change I think requires no further arguments to show, for the inexorable course of nature is sufficient to convince us of it.

But in all polities we observe two sources of decay existing from natural causes, the one external, the other internal and self-produced. The external admits of no certain or fixed definition, but the internal follows a definite order. What kind of polity, then, comes naturally first, and what second, I have already stated in such a way that those who are capable of taking in the whole drift of my argument can henceforth draw their own conclusions as to the future. For it is quite clear, in my opinion. When a commonwealth, after warding off many great dangers, has arrived at a high pitch of prosperity and undisputed power, it is evident that, by the lengthened continuance of great wealth within it, the manner of life of its citizens will become more extravagant, and that the rivalry for office, and in other spheres of activity, will become fiercer than it ought to be. And as this state of things goes on more and more, the desire of office and the shame of losing reputation, as well as the ostentation and extravagance of living, will prove the beginning of a deterioration. And of this change the people will be credited with being the authors, when they become convinced that they are being cheated by some from avarice, and are puffed up with flattery by others from love of office. For when that comes about, in their passionate resentment and acting under the dictates of anger, they will refuse to obey any longer, or to be content to have equal powers with their leaders, but will demand to have all or far the greatest themselves. And when that comes to pass the constitution will receive a new name, which sounds better than any other in the world, liberty or democracy; but, in fact, it will become the worst of all governments, mob rule.

With this description of the formation, growth, zenith, and present state of the Roman polity, and having discussed also its difference, for better and worse, from other polities, I will now at length bring my essay on it to an end.